PN 1993.5.I88 MAR 1993

KT-211-337

T060923

Filmmaking by the Book

MILLICENT MARCUS

■ ■

Filmmaking by the Book

ITALIAN CINEMA AND LITERARY ADAPTATION

THE JOHNS HOPKINS UNIVERSITY PRESS

BALTIMORE AND LONDON

© 1993 The Johns Hopkins University Press
All rights reserved
Printed in the United States of America on acid-free paper

The Johns Hopkins University Press
2715 North Charles Street
Baltimore, Maryland 21218-4319
The Johns Hopkins Press Ltd., London

Library of Congress Cataloging-in-Publication Data

Marcus, Millicent Joy.
   Filmmaking by the book : Italian cinema and literary adaptation /
Millicent Marcus.
        p.   cm.
   Includes bibliographical references and index.
   ISBN 0-8018-4454-1 (hc).—ISBN 0-8018-4455-X (pbk)
   1. Motion pictures—Italy.   2. Motion pictures and literature—Italy.
3. Film adaptations.   4. Italian literature—Film and video adaptations.   I. Title.
PN1993.5.I88M278   1993
791.43'75'0945—dc20   92-18884

A catalog record for this book
is available from the British Library

To my brothers, Glenn and Warren

Contents

Preface

The epilogue to the Tavianis' film *Kàos*, based on four short stories by Pirandello, presents a dream vision in which the writer is mysteriously summoned back to his native Agrigento by the ghost of his mother. There, in her house by the sea, she recounts an episode from her childhood about flight—physical flight down a sand dune, political flight from Bourbon persecution, imaginative flight from the gravitational pull of this life. Her reminiscence frees Pirandello's creative energies and explains, retroactively, how the stories came to be written that inspired the film we just saw on the screen. In this many-leveled meditation on their art, the Taviani brothers argue that the passage from literary work to film is only one link in an extended chain that includes an imagined pretextual history based on lived experience, memory, and dream.

The Tavianis' example suggests the inadequacy of static, decontextualized comparisons between films and books that inspired them and urges us instead to adopt an approach that is at once dynamic and accommodating, able to account for the impulse that transforms literary into cinematic discourse and for the many factors that determine that transformation. In this study, therefore, I consider the adaptive process as the sum total of a series of encounters: the institutional encounter between literary and film cultures, the semiotic encounter between two very different signifying systems, and the personal encounter between author and filmmaker, sometimes involving an overt oedipal struggle for selfhood.

It is no exaggeration to speak of the meeting between literary and cinematic culture in postwar Italy as an "institutional" one, given the debate about literariness and its suitability to the filmic medium which took place during the 1940s and 1950s, as I will argue in the historical section of my introduction. And the vast semiotic difference between literary texts and audiovisual spectacles gives rise to a body of theoretical considerations—the subject of my second introductory section—that must inform any comparative study of the two media. Yet as important as the institutional and semiotic encounters are to the understanding of the adaptive process, they do not offer exhaustive explanations for the forms that individual cinematic adaptations will take. Since postwar Italian film history is largely auteurist (in reaction to Fascist cinema, which presented itself as an authorless product of a system), I believe that a study of adaptation must concentrate on the filmmakers themselves in their efforts to negotiate the tensions between rival media cultures and signifying systems. I am therefore less interested in formulating an abstract model for literature-film comparisons than in seeing how adaptation works *within* the corpus of an individual filmmaker's production. Thus I have chosen two examples from each of the careers of five exemplary postwar Italian filmmakers to show how adaptation as an artistic exercise differs from one practitioner to another, and how even within the filmography of a given individual, adaptive approaches will vary depending upon the requirements of the particular literary source, the filmmaker's professional agenda at the time of production, and the precise historical context into which the film is born.

My book takes as its subject the adaptational techniques of a group of filmmakers who not only rely on literary sources, but who do so quite self-consciously, and who dramatize that self-consciousness throughout their work. Such filmmakers find it useful, indeed necessary, to define their own authorial task in relation to that of a literary precursor. I will thus include in my study of adaptations the scene or scenes in which the filmmaker acknowledges the literary ancestry of the work and makes that relationship a full-fledged thematic concern, as do the Tavianis in the epilogue to *Kàos* discussed above. Pasolini, to give another example,makes explicit his highly polemical approach to author/auteur relationships in the second episode of his *Decameron*, where a street-corner entertainer who is engaged in an unsuccessful public reading of a Boccaccio story suddenly throws the book aside and announces, "Now I'll tell it in the Neapolitan way," much to the relief and delight of the crowd. It is easy to see in this gesture an iconoclastic Pasolini, reacting not only to this canonical text of the Tuscan high literary tradition, but to what the Italian establishment has made of the *Decameron*—a model of bourgeois decorum, a paragon of linguistic propriety, an epopee of the merchant ideal—in short, a cornerstone of modern elitist education. It is in such umbilical scenes that filmmakers teach us how to read their cinematic rewriting of literary sources. Taking these embedded allegories of adaptation as my own critical point of departure, I then develop their implications for an overall interpretation of the films from which they arise.

The book therefore presents a series of case studies whose sui generis natures require an inductive, pragmatic approach in which the specific problems posed by each adaptation suggest the critical methodology to be applied. Thus Visconti's *La terra trema* (1948) and *The Leopard* (1963) both invite ideological criticism, as it is Resistance history in the former case, and Gramsci in the latter, which mediate the relationship between textual source and filmic adaptation. Vittorio De Sica's *Two Women* (1960), instead, lends itself to feminist analysis, where the first-person narrative of Alberto Moravia's eponymous novel is adapted according to mainstream cinematic conventions that reverse the gendered discourse of the text. De Sica's 1971 adaptation of Giorgio Bassani's *Garden of the Finzi-Continis* is an exercise in medium-specific intertextuality, where the literary gardens of Scriptures, love lyrics, and the Renaissance epic find their filmic equivalents in the escapist paradise of commercial cinematic spectacle. Textual authority becomes a central concern for Pier Paolo Pasolini in adapting *The Gospel According to St. Matthew* (1964), whose scriptural claim to divine truth is incorporated in the subjective camera of the apostle's personal witness. Pasolini's 1971 adaptation of the *Decameron*, instead, is blatantly transgressive, where the medieval paragon of elite linguistic and narrative form is translated into an item of mass media entertainment at its most vernacular. Psychoanalytic and semiotic criticism recommend themselves in the Tavianis' case, where the very novel they adapt in 1977, Gavino Ledda's *Padre padrone*, is a plea for freedom from a patriarchal rule that can be applied to the literary paternity of a film as well as to the authoritarianism of rural Sardinian culture. Liberation is also the theme of *Kàos*, the filmmakers' 1984 adaptation of Luigi Pirandello's short stories, where the writer himself is freed from his prose limitations through the Tavianis' cinema of poetry. The destruction of culturally sanctioned icons reaches its extreme in *Fellini's Casanova* (1974), where the possessive of the title makes explicit the filmmaker's prerogative to personalize and reinvent all his objects of inquiry, thus authorizing what I would call a pseudo-autobiographical critical approach. Fellini's auteurist practices find a powerful defense in Ermanno Cavazzoni's recent novel *Poema dei lunatici* which provides the impetus for the filmmaker's argument against postmodern exhaustion in *La voce della luna* (1989).

This study grows out of my earlier book *Italian Film in the Light of Neorealism*, which involved close readings of several films based on literary models (*The Conformist, Christ Stopped at Eboli,* and *Senso*). But because the focus of that work was historical, the adaptive process could be treated only in a cursory way. The constraints of my previous project convinced me of the need for a separate, systematic study whose very theme would be the relationship of Italian films to their literary sources. Such a study has much to teach us, not only about the filmmaking approaches of preeminent postwar auteurs, but also about how adaptation enables film to reinvent and redefine itself as cultural institution and discursive practice with each literary encounter. What the Tavianis' maternal metaphor for reversion to the literary origins of cinematic inspiration in *Kàos*, or Pasolini's oedipal impulse to destroy his authorial parent in *The Decameron* tell us about adaptation is that this is a highly charged process—one that compels filmmakers to come to terms with their own primal need for self-definition, and critics to account for the consequences.

■ ■

Acknowledgments

I owe my first and most long-standing debt of gratitude to the students of my "Literature into Film" courses; over the years, their own personal investment in viewing films based on literary sources made me aware of the immense scholarly as well as pedagogical appeal of adaptation study. Colleagues, both on campus and off, have also been immensely supportive of the project, offering encouragement while providing hard-nosed criticism when the occasion warranted. Thanks go to Rebecca West, Ben Lawton, Peter Bondanella, and Robert Sklar for their unstinting endorsement of the project from the very beginning. Sympathetic critical readings of parts of the manuscript by Dudley Andrews, Alan Nagel, and members of the U. T. film studies faculty were extremely helpful as I revised.

I also received a great deal of help with the material problems posed by my project. Though the study of cinema has been immeasurably advanced by the accessibility and user-friendliness of videocassettes, it is still crucial for the critic to experience the film as it was meant to be experienced, on the big screen. For this, I am enormously grateful to Stephen Bearden, Texas Union Film Coordinator, who has cheerfully ordered and projected many of the films included in this study. Thanks also to Gianna Landucci and Claudio Rugi of the Mediateca Regionale della Toscana for their courtesy, efficiency, and skill in making available to me the vast resources of their institution.

With the exception of the four photographs from *La voce della luna*, generously provided by Peter Bondanella and Studio Longardi, all of the illustrations come from the Film Stills Archive of the Museum of Modern Art, and Mary Corliss is to be heartily thanked for opening the collection to me at a moment's notice. I would also like to express my gratitude to Patrick and Michael Rodriguez for helping transport material to me in Italy during the copyediting phase of my project.

Grants from the John Simon Guggenheim Memorial Foundation and from the University of Texas University Research Institute enabled me to take a leave of absence from teaching and devote myself fully to researching and writing the bulk of the manuscript. When the time came for publication, Eric Halpern proved to be the most enthusiastic and understanding of editors-in-chief, and Roberta Hughey the most intelligent and conscientious of copy editors.

My final debt of thanks goes to my husband and colleague, Robert Hill, for his unfailing emotional and intellectual support, and for sharing the computer.

■ ■

Introduction: Literature and Film

NEGOTIATING THE TERMS

History

In an article on literary adaptation in the contemporary Italian film industry, Alberto Farassino observes that "even if they have always traveled in the same boat, and have often exchanged favors, writers and filmmakers are used to shoving each other around and often try to push each other overboard. It is an old game: the former disparage the cinema in the name of the purity of literary works; the latter invoke the autonomy of the two languages, even if they don't disdain to exploit the title, the fame, and the narrative substance of the book."[1]

Farassino's observation is triply suggestive for a reading of the Italian history of literary adaptation in film. First, it is couched in figurative language that, though clichéd, replaces the hierarchichal thinking of "fidelity analysis" with the equalizing image of two fretful passengers embarked on the same cultural journey. Second, it suggests that adaptive practice cannot be considered apart from the larger context of literature-film relations, whose most explosive theoretical battles have been fought on the grounds of adaptation. Third, it reveals the profound mutual ambivalence that characterizes the protagonists of film and literary culture, whose insistence on positing some relationship between the two arts, be it one of enmity, emulation, or an uneasy mixture of both, lies at the very root of their impulse to self-definition.

"At this time, the cinema is experiencing one of its periodic phases of great love for the written page," continues Farrasino.[2] In order to understand how precarious this current romance is, and how complex and turbulent a love story precedes it, we must flash back to the origins of the Italian film industry itself and examine its evolving relationship to the written word. But because much fine work has been done on the influence of film on twentieth-century literary aesthetics (the cinemorphic dimension of much contemporary fiction, the genre of the film-novel, to give some of the most obvious examples)[3] and because adaptative practice is a function of how film culture processes literary culture, I approach my study from the latter perspective, though I am aware of the paradox that in adapting cinemorphic texts, film is, in some general sense, borrowing from itself. But my focus is more on the way in which film culture responds to a narrative form that it considers "other," either in its institutional, ideological, or signifying capacity. What complicates film's relationship to such alterity is the fact that *literature* becomes a shifting and unstable term subject to the polemic needs of the moment, making *literariness* for film apologists a term that is always *intéressé*, never to be disengaged from the heuristic value that it can bring to the argument at hand. Thus we see how the nascent film industry, striving for aesthetic legitimacy, equated literature with high culture, prestige, respectability, tradition—in short, with the very condition to which the cinema itself aspired.[4] On the other hand, the neorealist position, as articulated by Zavattini, associated literariness with a retrograde, prewar aesthetics characterized by political detachment, lyrical introversion, decadence, crepuscularism, and worst of all, self-advertising formal virtuosity.[5] As the voice for Italy's newly forged national consciousness, neorealism saw in literariness everything it had repudiated in prewar Fascist culture. Thus *literature* can by no means be considered a fixed term of comparison against which film can measure its institutional and discursive development, but a shifting value whose very vicissitudes reveal a wealth of self-serving strategies.

Farassino's image of the two bickering sea voyagers whose perennial sparring is really an affirmation of their interdependence (how terrible to be alone in that boat!) bears witness to the special bond between literary and film culture which has typified Italian cinema throughout its first nine decades. "Among all the histories of national cinemas," writes Gian Piero Brunetta, "that of the Italian cinema, along the entire arc of its development, is the most bound to the structures, models, and history of universal literature of all times."[6] Lino Micciché acknowledges the importance that literary comparisons have played in the evolution of Italian film theory. "Since the first and most self-conscious theoretical elaborations on the cinema, such a relationship has been intuited, even if not always analyzed, to be one of the most relevant to understanding fully the ontology, and the de-ontology, of the new means of expression."[7] Furthermore, the impulse to appropriate the prestige of authors as scriptwriters and to adapt successful novels to the screen reveals the unusual degree of overlap between the film public and the reading public which distinguishes Italy from its international counterparts.[8]

Given the intimacy of the relations between literary and film culture in Italy, Dudley Andrew's comments on the special light that adaptation can shed on cinema history become particularly relevant to the Italian case. "The choice of the mode of adaptation and of prototypes suggests a great deal about the cinema's sense of its role and aspirations from decade to decade," he argues in a plea for a functional approach to literature-film comparisons.[9] The way in which adaptation operates within the evolving context of Italian film culture as a whole, and within the context of an individual filmmaker's production, provides the organizing principle of my work in this book.

As soon as the early cinema discovered its narrative vocation—a vocation prompted by its very technological condition as a "time-medium" that could juxtapose images in space to simulate their temporal progression—filmmakers turned to literature to fulfill a twofold ideal. By bringing literary culture to the masses, cinema could perform a didactic service while reaping the obvious benefits of an association that would elevate it above the vulgarity of its birth in the penny arcade.[10] Film's indiscriminate plundering of source material, from the classics of world literature to contemporary pulp fiction, made of literature "a great, single text to appropriate without limits for the transcodification of a literary memory and for the production and transmission of a new type of memory with precise purposes of acculturation." This great literary repository lent itself, in a differential way, to two of the three levels that Brunetta identifies in the burgeoning young film industry: the superspectacle, or "costume film," which adapted literary classics or enacted significant historical events and required the greatest expenditure of ideological and semiotic resources; middle-level melodrama, which adapted bourgeois literature, naturalist novels, and pulp fiction; and the comedic style, which derived from vaudeville and the spontaneous manifestations of folk art.[11]

As a cultural institution subject to the dominant ideology and as a powerful instrument of that ideology, film gave expression to Italy's nationalist-imperialist ambitions in the Libyan war (1911–12) by adapting such epics as *El Cid*, *Jerusalem Liberated*, and *The Knights of Rhodes*.[12] Film and literature produced their most momentous prewar collaboration in Giovanni Pastrone's *Cabiria* (1913–14), that important precedent for D. W. Griffith's epic achievements in *Intolerance*. Such was the early film industry's ardor in courting the prestige of literary high culture that it recruited no less a figure than Gabriele D'Annunzio to pen the intertitles to *Cabiria* and to lend his luster to the film's production.[13] Since the advent of narrative cinema coincided with the crisis of the contemporary novel, where the traditional mechanisms of narration were being called into question and formal transparency gave way to a foregrounding of technique, it is not surprising that film should step into the void, becoming the unproblematic storytelling medium that the grand nineteenth-century novel once was, and performing social functions analogous to its literary counterpart in the Ottocento.[14]

World War I signaled a turning point in Italian literature-film relations. The impulse to adapt texts that would support the nationalist-imperialist ideology of prewar Italy gave way to a kind of bourgeois introversion that dictated the screening of D'Annunzian and other contemporary literary models. Recourse to current literary sources allowed the cinema to project "the image of a middle and upper-middle class that celebrates its last rites on the eve of its death, indifferent to the war that surrounds it."[15] The 1920s, properly deemed the "crisis decade" of the Italian film industry in its poverty of inspiration and means, resorted to adaptations of *letteratura garibaldina* as an attempt to rescue Fascist ideology from the brutality of its *squadrista* association.[16] But the industry would have to wait until 1932, when Emilio Cecchi would take over the directorship of the important Cines studio, for literature and film to resume any collaboration of cultural consequence. Cecchi not only worked to recruit as screenwriters some of the country's most celebrated men of letters, including Moravia, Soldati, Levi, Alvaro, Zavattini, and Pirandello himself, but he also launched film criticism as a serious discipline that would monitor the industry and imbue it with a sense of critical accountability.[17]

It was the cultural adventure of neorealism that brought literature-film relations to the forefront by making literariness itself the battleground on which the new movement was to define its identity. But here the critic must proceed with the utmost semantic caution in identifying the multiple rhetorical uses to which the term *literature* is put. What makes the neorealist case even more complex is today's tendency to revisit neorealism and to rewrite its story. Rethinking the place of literature in neorealism is thus part of a larger contemporary revisionist project—that of discounting the polemical stance of the neorealists themselves by pointing out the nontransparency of the medium, its artistic self-consciousness, and its crypto-continuities with previous and subsequent cinematic culture. Thus the critic is faced with a double unraveling operation: first to trace the protean shifts in the notion of literariness within the theoretical pronouncements of neorealists themselves, and then to account for today's critical revisionism, which casts an ever more deconstructive eye on the manifest content of 1940s and early 1950s cinematic thought.

Neorealism's antiliterary bias finds its most militant formulation in Cesare Zavattini's essay "Alcune idee sul cinema," written in 1952 as a retrospective justification for the aesthetics of his own great neorealist collaborations with Vittorio De Sica in *Shoeshine* (1946), *Bicycle Thief* (1948), and *Umberto D* (1951). It is in this treatise that Zavattini articulates his "poetics of immediacy," in which story is seen as an obstacle to the direct rendering of human experience. To resort to story—above all a *derived* story—is to reveal the moral cowardice of an industry wedded to spectacle, to evasion, to fear of the brute force of social suffering. "The most important characteristic and the most important innovation of neorealism, it seems to me, therefore, is that of being aware that the necessity of a 'story' is none other than an unconscious way of masking our human defeat and that the imagination, as it was thus exercized, did nothing other than superimpose *dead schemes on living social facts* [emphasis mine]." [18] Later in the same essay, Zavattini argues against narrative closure, against facile solutions that mask the real intransigence of the social plights explored by realist cinema. What Zavattini rejects in the notion of story is plottedness, contrivance, the false imposition of dramatic structure on social problems that defy the formal requirements of beginning, middle, and end—in short, he rejects the attempt to contain and domesticate social experience by means of literary mediations. But later on in Zavattini's own essay, he undercuts such antiliterary militancy by admitting the need for narrative fictions. Cinema must "tell reality as if it were a story" (14), he concedes, in an acknowledgement that the public's "hunger for story" is every bit as strong, if not stronger, than its "hunger for reality," and that any recounting, no matter how understated and antispectacular, is nonetheless narrative. "*Paisan, Open City, Shoeshine, Bicycle Thief, La terra trema,* all contain some things of an absolute significance which reflect the concept that everything can be recounted, but always in a certain metaphorical sense, because there is still an invented story, not the documentarist spirit. In certain films, such as *Umberto D,* the analytic fact is much more evident but always in a traditional presentation. We have not yet reached the center of neorealism" (9–10). The implication is that the center of neorealism, where film would reach a pure state of storylessness, is unattainable in actual practice—that it remains an ideal to which neorealist poetics aspires without ever hoping to arrive, much like the asymptote approaching the line that will serve as its tangent only at a point in infinity.[19] The same pattern of taking a firm antiliterary stand and then tempering it recurs in his pronouncements about the screenwriter who, he says, should be eliminated along with all other "technical professional apparatus" (16). He later qualifies this stance (which would effectively put him out of business), by arguing against the division of labor that would separate screenwriting from the drafting of the subject and the shooting of the film. With the screenwriter isolated, the story would be conceived as an end in itself, obedient to its own formal requirements and indifferent to the sociopolitical impulse of the subject matter or the documentarist impulse of the filmmaking process. What emerges from Zavattini's pattern of asserting a hard-line antiliterary position and then partially retracting it is not the desirability of storyless cinema as much as a rearrangement of priorities in such a way that social reality would no longer provide the raw materials for plot; instead, plot would serve the didactic needs of social reality.

The antiliterary bias of neorealism, as articulated by Zavattini and as seconded by such critics as Carlo Bo and Luigi Chiarini, can be interpreted as a reaction against a prewar cinema culture characterized by two kinds of literariness: the highly plotted, evasive, commercial sort that Zavattini explicitly condemned, and the aesthetically refined, formally dazzling experiments of the so-called calligraphic school, whose choice of literary models (Fogazzaro in the case of Soldati, Pushkin in the case of Castellani, De Marchi in the case of Lattuada) would not offend Fascist censors and whose technical innovations would not take film into "dangerous" new areas of epistemological inquiry. The calligraphers' use of adaptation thus provided a model of how literature served Fascist ends in indirect and therefore more insidious ways than did the unabashed filming of such obvious nationalist-imperialist vehicles as *Scipione l'africano* (Carmine Gallone, 1937). According to Carlo Lizzani, calligraphic filmmaking syphoned off the energies of young artists whose talents could have been tapped for the burgeoning realist cause. "Here is the danger," Lizzani writes, "that this formalist cinema, this cinema of attention to literary reality and not to the reality of the country would become hegemonic and would gather around itself a movement of interests of young filmmakers just like us."[20]

Despite such an inducement to reject all literary models and despite the received wisdom (institutionalized by Zavattini) that neorealism's poetics of immediacy precluded literariness *tout court*, the young group of critics and filmmakers who gravitated around the journal

Cinema and who, in 1941, laid the theoretical groundwork for the protoneorealist achievement of Visconti's *Ossessione*, made Verga their patron saint and verismo their cultural point of departure."We saw as more worthy of attention an approach to reality through, yes, literature," claims Lizzani, "but through *a type* of literature like that of Verga that seemed to us to draw nearer to the realities kept hidden for more than twenty years by the regime."[21] This paradoxical admission of the need for recourse to literary models in order to capture reality on film anticipates the truth that semiotics is urging upon us today: that there is no such thing as "innocent," precodified reality, and as such it is better to make a free and conscious choice of codifying systems than to leave that choice to the invisible artificers of ideology. With Verga, the *Cinema* group was simply replacing one set of mediations with another, more congenial to their own ideological purposes.

But Verga's inspirational value did not go uncontested, and the controversy surrounding his elevation to the status of poetic forefather of the new film movement was to contain, in miniature, all of the theoretical issues that the debate on adaptation would later raise. The war was waged on the pages of *Cinema* beginning with the seminal article by Giuseppe De Santis and Mario Alicata entitled "Verità e poesia: Verga e il cinema italiano." Arguing that the best cinema has always taken its inspiration, both technically and thematically, from literature, De Santis and Alicata ask why it is that Italian film has usually turned to inferior textual sources, with such lamentable results as those produced by the D'Annunzian rhetoric of *Cabiria* and the "risotts with truffles of Antonio Fogazzaro." Why not follow the French lead in turning to the realist tradition of the nineteenth century for inspiration in forging "a revolutionary art inspired by a humanity that suffers and hopes?" In Italy, it is Verga who offers such a model. "To those of us who believe in art, especially as a creator of truth, the Homeric and legendary Sicily of *I Malavoglia*, of *Mastro don Gesualdo*, of 'L'amante di Gramigna,' of 'Jeli il pastore,' seems to us at the same time to offer the most solid, human, miraculously virgin and true environment that could inspire the fantasy of a cinema that seeks things and facts in a time and space of reality, to rescue itself from the facile suggestions of a mortified bourgeois taste."[22]

De Santis and Alicata's plea is met by the standard repertory of objections raised against literary intrusions by all the advocates of cinematic purity. It is Fausto Montesanti who gives voice to these arguments in his rebuttal article in *Cinema* entitled "Della ispirazione cinematografica." Where his opponents claim that literary interchange produces the best in cinema, Montesanti retorts that film has always remained subservient to literature and that adaptation makes explicit its inferior status as a repository of recycled stories, of poetic hand-me-downs already discovered and elaborated in another medium. If the cinema is to find its own vocation, according to Montesanti, it must do so without recourse to preestablished, prefabricated truths. "We will dare to hope, instead, that truth and poetry could be born from the spiritual labor of poets who, without any debt toward preexistent forms of art, would succeed in mirroring themselves in the new language. We would wish that the persons and things born uniquely from films as a function of the new means of expression and not translated from preceding expressions be conceived cinematographically and that should there be literary reminiscences (inevitable in certain cases), it would be up to the critics to discover them, not the artists to seek them out."[23]

Montesanti's response is interesting not only for what it adds to the theoretical debate on neorealism but also for its antipication of the kinds of issues that semiologists and narratologists will consider several decades later. In his argument for the autonomy of cinematic discourse—and in this he locates himself in the venerable tradition of Vachel Lindsay and Sergei Eisenstein—Montesanti posits that meaning cannot be transferred from one medium to another, that signification is generated by, and bound to, the specific material conditions of the discourse, that narrativity is inseparable from its concrete artistic expression, or to use Émile Benveniste's terms, that story and discourse defy analytical separation. But Montesanti undercuts his claim for the purity of film language when he tries to appropriate for his argument those undeniably cinematic films that are literary adaptations. "Even in the extremely rare cases in which the impulse is offered by a novel (*Varieté*, by Felix Hollander, *Blue Angel*, by Heinrich Mann) the subjects no longer have anything in common with the literary precedents, which they completely transcend."[24] Here, Montesanti wants to have it both ways, acknowledging the excellence of certain adaptations while vindicating the autonomy of cinematic discourse by insisting on the *looseness* of the adaptations and the films' supercession of their literary sources. What emerges is a continuum of literature-film relations ranging from faithful adaptations, to free adaptations that rise above the limits of their textual origins, to entirely original cinematic creations. The arbitrariness of this system is obvious, given Montesanti's moralizing bias toward cinematic autonomy: if he likes an adaptation, it will fall to the morally "right" end of the spectrum with the only criterion of placement being that of personal taste.

In their polemic response ("Ancora di Verga e del cinema italiano," also published in *Cinema*), De Santis and Alicata take Monetesanti to task not only for his arbitrariness but also for his denial of what they consider to be the central achievement of the modern aesthetic consciousness: "the recognition of the unity of the arts." By insisting on a system of rigid categorization by genres, Montesanti confuses "the autonomy of the expressive means with the autonomy of poetry" and thus denies film the benefits of its association with a grand narrative tradition that exists before its expression in any one concrete artistic medium. In the face of Montesanti's attack, De Santis and Alicata posit a two-pronged defense. Given that the mediocre, lower-middle-class character of Italian film is indissolubly bound to literary influences of a banal and trivial sort, why not replace those influences with a model of the culture's best narrative tradition, as exemplified by verismo? Second, they hasten to posit the critical distinction between story and discourse which allows them to place the Verghian model on the more abstract level of translinguistic narrativity that will in no way dictate the specific terms of its concrete artistic manifestation. "We did not intend to attribute the specification of a given literary genre, but rather to indicate with that name [Verga's] a particular rhythm of fantasy, a given use of the categories of space and time, that is not only of literature, nor particularly of the novel . . . but can be usefully applied to define the needs and the results of a given painting style . . . and therefore especially of the cinema, in which a similar narrative element, with only a few exceptions, is always present and essential." [25]

Alberto Asor Rosa suggests that the example of grand nineteenth century narrative was what enabled neorealism to get beyond the *piccoli realismi* of the prewar years. [26] The underlying issue was not to accept or refuse literary intrusions but to discriminate between "good" literature and "bad," between salubrious models that will inspire the exploration of the medium in politically progressive and morally responsible ways, and models that encourage the inertia and indifference of the prewar "risottos with truffles" and the other bland confections served up by the calligraphers or their less accomplished colleagues working within the confines of the Fascist cinema.

Today's revisionist critics who seek to temper the polemical extremes of Zavattini's pronouncements on neorealist aesthetics can therefore find much to support their arguments in the De Santis–Alicata position, and in such admissions as those by Carlo Lizzani, one of the movement's practitioners and historians, who vouches for the eclectic literary experiences that contributed to neorealist thought. Among the neorealists were partisans of virtually every available poetic and narrative tradition, including "crepuscularists and Verghians,

Proustians and surrealists, Marxists and idealists. Enthusiasts of Belli and Porta, of Ungaretti, Cardarelli, or Montale, followers of Hemingway, of Alain Fournier, or of Kafka. This is our hinterland, these were our readings."[27] As one of the prime movers of cinematic neorealism, Luchino Visconti makes a powerful claim for the importance of the literary impulse in the formation of a new cinematic consciousness. "A recent debate on the relationships between literature and film has found me spontaneously on the side of those who have faith in the richness and validity, for the cinema, of a literary inspiration," writes Visconti in "Tradizione e invenzione"(1941). Dismissing the Montesanti argument for a cinematic purity that precludes literary interventions, Visconti aligns himself with De Santis and Alicata in their plea for a return to the grand models of nineteenth-century narrative as a way of overcoming the poverty and banality of the prewar cinematic imagination. "In such a situation, it becomes natural, for anyone who believes sincerely in the cinema, to turn his eyes with nostalgia on the great narrative constructions of the classics of the European novel and to consider them the source of perhaps the truest inspiration today."[28]

The literature-film battle flares up again in 1954 in conditions somewhat reminiscent of those that led to their crucial theoretical encounter almost a decade and a half earlier on the pages of *Cinema*. When the coherence of the neorealist vision had given way to the fragmentation and mannerism of 1950s *realismo rosa*, a return to nineteenth-century narrative models promised the same kind of corrective that it had offered to 1940s theorists, eager to transcend the *piccoli realismi* of the prewar years. Visconti's controversial new film, *Senso* (1954), rekindled the debate, and because Zavattini's manifesto of neorealism had concentrated on antiliterary values, literariness became the basis for the film's theoretical defense. For Guido Aristarco, editor of the influential postwar journal *Cinema nuovo*, Visconti's *Senso* signaled a progressive step in the evolution of Italian cinema toward the critical realism of Georg Lukács. A spirited debate erupted on the pages of *Cinema nuovo* between Zavattini and Luigi Chiarini, on the one hand, who attacked the film for its spectacular, operatic style, its use of glamorous movie stars, its retreat into history, and its recourse to a literary model (the eponymous novella by Camillo Boito) and Aristarco, who articulated a theory of critical realism which justified Visconti's departures from neorealist orthodoxy in suggestively literary terms.[29] Aristarco set up a series of binary oppositions between Zavattinian neorealism, on the one hand, and Viscontian realism, on the other. While the former limits itself to passive observation, surface description, and chronicle, the latter involves active participation, narration, and history. Zavattini's antiliterary bias did not stop Aristarco from finding a nineteenth-century analogue to his poetics of immediacy in the naturalism of Zola, whereas Visconti's grand realist design met its counterpart in the novelistic example of Balzac.

It should come as no surprise that literariness in the 1954 debate would prove once more to have the semantic pliancy that has lent it to a variety of polemical uses. For Zavattini and Chiarini, it connotes contrivance, escapism, spectacle—a profoundly amoral abdication of neorealist imperatives to unmediated social reportage. For Aristarco, instead, literariness is invested with the positive morality of Georg Lukács's critical realism, which celebrates the kind of inquiries into the dynamics of the historical process that only the novel can achieve, when endowed with "typical" characters who embody the salient conflicts of their era and who are informed by the "necessary anachronism" or a heightened awareness of the material forces that condition their lives.[30] Literature and film undertake a two-tiered collaboration in the 1960s. On the one hand, routine film "translations" of successful contemporary novels appear in significant numbers, featuring what Lizzani calls the "explosion of the *personaggio*," and including the works of Carlo Cassola, Vasco Pratolini, Giorgio Bassani, and Alberto Moravia.[31] On the other hand, developments in France inspire a progressive rethinking of adaptive practices. The phenomenon of the *École du regard* convinces such writers as Alain Robbe-Grillet and Pier Paolo Pasolini that cinema and literature are equipped in equal measure to embody the aesthetic achievements of the avant-garde.[32] For Pasolini, film and literature are parallel and equivalent manifestations of a narrative idea that preexists its expression in concrete artistic form, so that when *Teorema*'s release as a film coincided with its publication as a novel, such simultaneity served to deny any notion of a hierarchy of forms. The novel could neither be given logical priority as a literary source nor be endowed with logical posteriority as a novelization of the film.[33]

Developments in France also dictated another trend in Italian literature-film relations. The cult of originality, of cinematic purism, and of signature filmmaking that accompanied the *nouvelle vague* with its *politique des auteurs* naturally conspired to discourage adaptation.[34] The return to adaptation in the 1970s, therefore, indicated a normalization, after the *"furori"* of 1968, and a reflection of the quest for personal, private themes both by "professional aesthetes" and by the "ex-prophets" of the movie camera whose disappointments in the revolution manqué would explain the introversion and nostalgia of the contemporary cinematic imagination.[35] If literariness for the 1970s came to mean the cinema's backlash against the authorial and political excesses of the preceding decade, it nonetheless did not amount to a total withdrawal from the *impegno civile* and the moral debates that have typified postwar realist film production, since this was the decade that saw the adaptations of the great novelistic revisitations of Fascism, war, and Resistance, including Vittorini's *Uomini e no,* Levi's *Cristo si è fermato ad Eboli,* Silone's *Fontamara,* Viganò's *L'Agnese va a morire,* and Moravia's *Il conformista.* But literariness for the 1980s was reduced to questions of commodity and craftsmanship, as the appetite for the "well-narrated" film and as the marketing of the filmable novel reveals.[36] The existence of such agencies as the Milanese Grandi & Vitali, which makes matches between film producers and eligible novels, the race to purchase movie rights, the creation of new professions (literary consultants in production companies, novelist-screenwriters) suggest that industrial needs are now the overriding factor in the literature-film collaboration.[37] The complacency of the marriage has both positive and negative implications for the cinema, suggesting on the one hand that the medium has reached such artistic respectability that neither film nor literature feels threatened by adaptive encounters and that film need no longer bridle at literary reminders of its relative youth and mass appeal. On the other hand, the passionate theorizing and the opportunities for self-definition and self-discovery sparked by the periodic clashes between literary and film cultures are sadly absent from today's theoretical arena. As if eager not to rock the boat, when filmmakers avail themselves of literary inspiration they do so with a prudence, almost a deference, that precludes the kinds of outrageous, transgressive gestures that could regalvanize the debate and stretch the limits of cinematic inventiveness. Though adaptation is seen not as a flight from authorial self-assertion but rather as a challenge to appropriate another's voice and make it one's own, the choice of literary precursors is notoriously pallid and anemic.[38] For example, a dead writer is preferable to a living one who may take umbrage at the filmmaker's poetic liberties, as Bassani so vociferously did with respect to De Sica's *Garden of the Finzi-Continis,* or more recently, as Marco Lodoli did in the face of Giuseppe Bertolucci's *Strana la vita.* The dead writers of choice may be famous, but rarely are they sacred monuments, and if they are, the preference is for shorter texts (such as Arthur Schnitzler's novella "Dr. Grasler, Spa Physician," adapted by Roberto Faenza, or Tolstoy's novella "Father Sergio," filmed by the Taviani brothers) because they lack the intrusive interpretive baggage of the better known works from the literary canon. Even Fellini, whose adaptive boldness has led him in the past to take on the giants—Poe, Petronius, and Casanova—now turns to the newcomer Cavazzoni (*Poema dei lunatici*), although he assures us that this text has provided only a minimal point of departure in the idea of its two central characters. Such defensiveness reveals a residual need to assert the autonomy of the medium in the face of extracinematic encroachments.

If we can see in Farassino's image of the two bickering sea voyagers a progressive decline in the fervor of their argument, this may be attributable to a number of causes. For one, the cultural sea itself is becalmed, lulled into the torpor of apparent peace, surface prosperity, the quelling of post-1968 extremism, the return to the private domain—in short, the Reaganization of contemporary social consciousness. For another, film technique has made enormous strides since World War II, reaching heights of *film écriture* that have earned the medium the cultural status and artistic respectability it long sought in its periodic attempts to appropriate literary prestige and then to spurn it in search of its own independent vocation.[39] A third factor is the elaboration of analytic tools that acknowledge and explain the autonomy of cinematic discourse and that make possible a methodologically sound comparison between literary and filmic narration. I refer here to the psychoanalytic, semiotic, feminist, and ideological approaches to the production and consumption of cinematic works. With the advent of methodologies that do not borrow from linguistic models (with their built in proliterary bias), adaptation can be rescued from the tyranny of fidelity analysis, with its arbitrariness, emotionalism, and barely disguised morality, and subjected instead to the scrutiny of critics who honor the cinema's claim to expressive self-sufficiency. And this is the subject of the next section.

Theory

STORY AND DISCOURSE

Criticized for his audacity in abandoning theatrical conventions and experimenting with the syntactic possibilities of montage, Griffith said to the executives of the Biograph Company, "Well, doesn't Dickens write that way?" "Yes," they replied, "but that's Dickens; that's novel writing; that's different." "Oh, not so much," said Griffith. "These are picture stories; not so different."[40] Seven decades later, the French theorist Jean Mitry was to insist that "the means of expression *in being different* would express different things—not the same things in different ways."[41] These diametrically opposed positions, implicitly or explicitly stated, lie at the root of many theoretical pronouncements about adaptation. In its most recent version, the debate hinges on the separability of story and discourse, of narrative (or diegesis, *récit*), and its concrete artistic medium of expression. According to Paul Ricoeur, Roland Barthes, and A. J. Greimas in France, Angelo Moscariello and Gianfranco Bettetini in Italy, and Seymour Chatman on this side of the Atlantic, there exists a universal, nonspecific code of narrativity which transcends its embodiment in any one particular signifying system. Such narrativity is both "distinct from the linguistic level" and "logically anterior to it, whatever the language system chosen for its manifestation may be."[42] Those who oppose the story/discourse distinction, including Jean Mitry, and Gérard Genette in France, Luigi Chiarini, Emilio Garroni, and Galvano della Volpe in Italy, insist that meaning is indivisibly bound to the concrete material terms of its realization in art and that it is absurd to posit a significance separable from, and equally available to, a plurality of discursive systems. According to such critics, adaptation per se is impossible. For them, it is more proper to speak of inspiration or "resymbolization"—the attempt to recreate, in another medium, the aesthetic experience of the textual source.[43]

Given the polemic force of the arguments for and against the story/ discourse distinction, and given the obvious difficulty of reconciling what seem to be mutually exclusive theoretical stands, I would propose a solution that will preserve and exploit the heuristic power of each of them, while deferring judgment as to the truth of their pronouncements. By accepting the principle of undecidability, we can entertain both theories as working hypotheses capable of generating useful operating models without diluting the power of either polemic position. I would suggest that the separability of story and discourse is a useful, indeed a necessary, assumption for the adapter, who must posit the existence of a narrativity that lends itself to cinematic as well as literary form. The distinction is not tenable, I would argue, for the public reception of the two media, whose psychological and sociological consequences are so intimately bound to their medium-specific languages that to distinguish between them becomes an exercise in academic frivolity. In what follows, I explore the implications of the story/discourse debate for approaches to the production and consumption of films based on literary sources.

The filmmaker who would adapt a novel faces a series of practical decisions: how to condense a text of several hundred pages to a ninety-minute format; how to visualize its characters and settings; how to organize literary space and time by cinematically appropriate means; how to externalize inner states of mind and to dramatize, through dialogue and actions, the complexities of human relationships; how to orchestrate the narration in the rhythm of tensions and pauses necessary to maintain viewer engagement; how to order the sequence of events in a way that motivates their linkage, either by psychological or material causality; and how to give an overall structure to the narrative by respecting or polemically rejecting the need for exposition, climax, and denouement. To summarize, the adapter must forge a strategy for converting a diegetic text (one that narrates or tells) into a mimetic text (one that represents or shows). Such practical decision making will gain logic and coherence only after a double interpretive act, predicated on the story/discourse distinction, has been carried out. The good adapter, aware of the unique properties of literary and cinematic form, must first infer from the textual source a preliterary idea—one that stands prior to its written expression. In other words, adapters must operate according to the fiction (and it is *only* a fiction) that they are reversing the author's creative process. Having arrived at this preliterary idea by induction, the adapter must then deduce its cinematically appropriate form, according to Pudovkin's notion of the "plastic material" that bodies forth the abstractions and sentiments of the precursor text.[44] The separability of story and discourse enables us to construct a geometric paradigm for adaptation where discourse provides the base of an isosceles triangle, bounded by the book and the film at either end, and story provides the point of intersection of the two equal sides. Successful adaptation precludes direct movement along the base of the triangle and requires instead a process of decomposition and recomposition in a new discursive form, as the Tavianis will say, of *Padre padrone*, or of a cinematic return to a prototext that preexists its literary formalization, as Lino Miccich. will say of Visconti's *La terra trema*.[45] Perhaps the best way to express the bilateral symmetry of this paradigm is to argue that the cinematic adaptation of a book is itself *écriture*, (a writing) conceived as process, as the dynamic materialization of a prior idea.[46]

The separability of story and discourse undermines some of the most commonplace arguments against adaptation—that films derived from novels lack originality, that they encourage imaginative laziness, and that they discredit the autonomy of the medium. Such criticism presupposes the direct movement from book to film without the intervening movements of induction and deduction which produce an appropriate cinematic "re-writing." It is this triangular itinerary that rescues adapters from the banal exercise of literal-minded illustration by leading them to an awareness of the unique signifying properties of each medium and by inviting them to find specifically cinematic solutions to the narrative challenges posed by the text. Far from an incentive to laziness, adaptation thus conceived becomes an important motive for experimentation in the cinema, forcing the newer medium to revise and expand its technical repertory, much as Griffith did in the encounter with Dickens which resulted in his discovery of parallel montage.[47]

Those critics who agree that literature and film share a common narrative vocation on an abstract level of analysis but who insist on the unique signifying properties of each medium are wary of subverting that uniqueness by falling back on linguistic terminology (with its built-in proliterary bias) to talk about cinematic discourse. "With a disconcerting nonchalance," writes Moscariello," one speaks about metaphor, metonomy, synechdoche, and so forth *à propos* this or that film. Having freed itself from the ancient debt to painting, the cinema seems destined to revert to that of literature." Moscariello's answer to what he later calls "the demon of analogy" is to fashion a new vocabulary, or rhetoric, of film tropes, using the notion of semantic equivalence to discover the terms of cinematic expressivity. When true semantic equivalences are found, the cinematic adaptation will become a self-sufficient "re-writing" of the original—it will stand as a new work, on the level of signifiers, that points to the prior narrative idea as its signified.[48]

But this model for adaptive practice is not without its theoretical drawbacks. While heuristically valuable as a reenactment of the adapter's modus operandi, its critical applications do not always rise above the level of sophisticated fidelity analysis. If the most avid proponents of faithfulness expect a literal-minded transcription of the novel in film, more advanced thinkers, like biblical allegorists, distinguish between the letter and the spirit of the original and, in an enlightened recognition of the unique discursive requirements of the two media, ask only that the adaptation be faithful to the spirit of its precursor text. Such criticism, however, amounts to nothing more than a glorified exercise in personal taste, for the spirit of the text is an ad hoc interpretive construct that serves to justify the critic's own subjective standards in judging an adaptation as acceptable or not. The question "Faithful to what?" gains further complexity in the arguments of John Ellis, who claims that the inferred spirit of the source text is really a *memory* of that text, subject to all the velleities and idiosyncracies to which personal reminiscence is prone: the life circumstances of the reader at the time of the reading, the intervening events that will attenuate the memory and tinge it with new associations, and so on. Ellis further argues that the textual spirit is a function of cultural as well as personal memory, and that the canonization of a literary work will greatly influence the kinds of expectations we bring to its adaptation. Given the status of the inferred spirit as a product of personal and cultural subjectivity, it is astonishing that any adaptation can ever meet the kind of viewer expectations so generated. Ellis concludes, therefore, that adaptation can only succeed when it manages to *efface* those memories by creating a new one so powerful as to convince us that it coincides with our own.[49] The danger, then, of the story/discourse distinction is that it can legitimize the kind of fidelity criticism that separates letter from spirit and insists on the adaptation's faithfulness to the second. But when corrected by Ellis's demystifying operation, the triangular model regains its heuristic value as a description of an ideal adaptive strategy.

As a generative model designed to explain the production of films based on literary sources, the separability of story and discourse reveals its considerable speculative possibilities. But the consumption of such films requires a very different set of working hypotheses. For the consumers of literary and filmic discourse, meaning cannot be separated from the concrete vehicle of its artistic expression, where the respective signifiers of literature and film "act in a different way on the consciousness. Their perception is different, and just as the mental organization of them is different, they do not open up the same conceptual horizons."[50] Added to the most obvious perceptual dissimilarity between a medium that makes the significant visible and one that makes the visible significant[51] is the difference between the deferred synthesis of literature (our reading affords a linear, progressive sense of the whole) and the immediate synthesis of cinema (we see all that is in a frame simultaneously).[52] This has considerable relevance to our mental construction of literary characters, whose visualizations are never complete and who remain open to further reimaging upon each narrative encounter. The open-endedness of literary characterization (physical as well as psychological) which follows from the deferred synthesis of the reading process makes of characters vague phantasmata whose mystique lies in their very resistance to descriptive closure. "The reader of *Tom Jones*," writes Wolfgang Iser, "is able to visualize the hero virtually for himself, and so his imagination senses the vast number of possibilities; the moment these possibilities are narrowed down to one complete and immutable picture, the imagination is put out of action, and we feel we have somehow been cheated."[53] It is film's immediate synthesis that preempts the reader's imagination and occasions the kind of anger so often met by disappointed viewers of adaptation.

But perhaps the strongest argument for the inseparability of story and discourse and the consequent irreconcilability of responses to cinematic and literary narration is to be found in the psychoanalytic approach of many contemporary filmologists. According to Christian Metz, film simulates an oneiric state in which the viewer experiences a diminished wakefulness by producing what he calls a "paradoxical hallucination"—"hallucination" because the subject confuses levels of reality, "paradoxical" because it is not endogenous but caused by external stimuli.[54] As a result, film images have a doubly powerful effect on the viewer's psyche. Because they originate in the material world, Metz explains, these stimuli move along the "progressive path" from sense organs to perceptual centers in the brain to be stored as mnemonic traces in the preconscious or unconscious, depending on the degree of threat they pose to conscious thought (114). In normal waking states, the psychic energy released by external stimuli will be dissipated in action: in movement toward an object of desire or in avoidance of a source of psychic or physical unpleasure. The diminished wakefulness of the film state, however, where purposive action is replaced by inertia, causes such energy to be channeled along the "regressive path" that creates from unconscious and preconscious impulses the illusion of perceptual images (hallucinations or dreams). Thus, film perception receives double reinforcement, both from without and within, as external stimuli travelling along the progressive path are met by the mind's own spontaneous image-making activity (117–18).

In addition to the processes of identification and projection which explain the medium's oneiric powers, Edgar Morin includes those of integration (the way we complete the meaning of a shot with our own knowledge and experience) and exchange (the way the cinema system integrates the viewer in the flow of the film and the flow of the film in the psychic flow of the viewer). For these reasons, Morin argues that film is far more permeable to the subjectivity of the viewer than the novel is to its reader's psychodynamics, explaining why "the image penetrates much more directly into the consciousness of the viewer than does the word," according to Carl Dreyer's formulation.[55]

The differences between literary and cinematic signification derive not only from the variant perceptual factors but also from their disparate status as institutions. To read a book and to see a movie, though they might treat the same story, are two very distinct activities with vastly different sociocultural implications. Reading, no matter how elevated or degraded its textual object may be, is a participation in literary culture, a personal affirmation of an ongoing written tradition taught by our schools, perpetuated by our libraries and publishing houses, and watched over by the arbiters of taste. Film going is a collective ritual and an assent to the seductions of mass culture (even in the case of the art-house film, which confirms mass culture in the very vehemence of its rejection), a consumerist venture whose food concessions and movie-inspired commodities put spectators' appetites at the forefront of the cinema situation. Added to this are the concrete experiential differences between reading and film viewing (at least in the prevideo age)—the former a solitary act entirely controlled by the reader, the latter a mass event controlled by the technology of the medium. The vast differences in their material and institutional circumstances thus keep literary and cinematic experiences aesthetic worlds apart.

BROADENING THE PERSPECTIVE

As useful as the story/discourse approach is for generating models that explain how adaptations are produced and consumed, it does limit the scope of our inquiry in one important respect. Adaptation criticism has always had as a dramatic subtext the adversary relationship between literature and film, a dualism that is reinforced by both upholders and detractors of the story/discourse distinction. Those who argue that meaning is inseparable from its concrete artistic medium establish the opposition between the two art forms on obvious "technical-formal" grounds.[56] For upholders of the story/discourse distinction, the assumed antagonism between the two media is what prompts the quest for narrative affinities at a higher level of abstraction. Semiotics avoids this dualistic impasse by reframing the relationship in a way that allows for the continuities and interpenetrations of the two arts on the discursive level. For example, cinematic signs, like literary ones, must be read.[57] The cinema is no longer seen as the place where the natural world can speak to us in all its prelinguistic innocence, as Bazin, Kracauer, Zavattini, and even Pasolini have argued. Bazin's notion of cinema as the apotheosis of the real, Kracauer's celebration of the medium as "the redemption of physical reality," Zavattini's hymn to an art that revealed the truth in the quotidian, Pasolini's theory of the cinema as "the written language of reality"—all these presuppose that the profilmic world has a phenomenological integrity that is directly available to the screen.[58] But Maria Corti's objection to Zavattini's poetics of immediacy can apply to every argument for profilmic innocence: "the things that speak by themselves" can all too easily become "things made to speak from above."[59] What subverts Bazin's "cosmophany," and what makes the world's apparently innocent speech the inevitable conduit of ideology, is the fact that all perception is mediated by codes that organize and filter our cognitive input.[60] Far from the triumph of the natural world over the world of signs, as Bazin saw it, film invites semiotics' most consequential operation—that of exposing the cultural in what purports to be the natural by demystifying the ideological process that makes of "nature" or "the real" yet one more human contrivance.[61]

If the profilmic world is anything but the "unstylized reality" that Panofsky saw as the filmmaker's raw material, how much more mediated and codified will be the finished film, even when it pretends to Zavattinian and Bazinian objectivity?[62] It follows that the processing of film images is by no means automatic, but the result of perceptual skills acquired and refined over a lifetime of experience in the world, in movie theaters, and now, before the video screen. Though film lacks the double articulation of written-spoken languages, the image is nonetheless a two-dimensional, mechanically reproduced sign, not identifiable with its three-dimensional, ontologically unique referent in the profilmic world.[63] Added to the interpretive work of primary recognition of the image—an admittedly easy task given the high degree of motivation of the cinematic sign—are the perceptual codes that come into play, including those of camera angle, color, physiognomy, and body language, as well as the interpretation of film's editorial conventions.[64] On the level of images, shots, shot interrelations, and editorial devices, film signification is inseparable from the unique context of each work. Eco aptly observes that Antonioni's *Blow-Up* is a meditation on the unintelligibility of images outside their narrative context.[65] Similarly, a dissolve can mean a flash-forward, flashback, a change to a parallel plot, or simply a step forward to the next chronological development in the narrative, depending upon the literal circumstances of its occurrence.[66]

If montage lies at the core of film's expressivity, as Eisenstein would argue and as Metz's attempt to develop a film syntax reaffirms, then semiotics' failure to codify this technique implies the impossibility of any effort to formulate general laws of cinematic signification. "The syntagmatic principles of connecting shots are not encoded at all," remarks Mast, "as the connection of subjects, predicates, and objects in a sentence. Understanding a connection between shots is more properly analogous to understanding a poetic trope than to understanding a sentence—relating the specific device to the contextual grid of the specific work rather than to a pre-existing code."[67] Because each film gives rise to its own syntactic laws and constitutes therefore a sui generis system of signification, then a semiotics of the cinema must abandon the universalizing ambitions of Metz's *grande syntagmatique du cinéma*, for example, and confine itself to case-by-case investigations. This humbling of its holistic aspirations, however, is not meant to belittle what semiotics can otherwise bring to comparative study of literature and film, such as the insight that the two systems are each complexes of interlocking codes, some of which are unique to their respective media, some of which are nonspecific cultural codes, and some of which are shared by the two.[68] As Cohen put it, "What makes possible, then, a study of the relationship between two separate sign systems, like novel and film, is the fact that the same codes may reappear in more than one system."[69] Narrativity, of course, is the most obvious of such shared codes, and it is this that prompts Mathieu-Colas to posit his "restrained narratology," which cuts transversally across both literary and cinematic texts, rather than Barthes's translinguistic universal, which subsumes all concrete storytelling discourses.[70] By insisting that narrativity is just one of the many codes that constitute cinematic signification, semiotics suggests that traditional critical approaches, especially fidelity analyses, err in privileging the literary source as the key to the film's signifying strategy. "Thus the danger of fidelity criticism," according to Christopher Orr, "is that it impoverishes the film's intertextuality either by ignoring the other codes that make the filmic text intelligible, or by making those codes subservient to the code of a single precursor text. The ultimate effect of this critical process is the disavowal of the text as a multidimensional space in which a variety of writings, none of them original, blend and clash."[71]

Orr's argument not only vindicates film's intertextuality but also calls into question two of the underlying moral assumptions on which traditional fidelity analysis is based: the imperatives to originality and to purity of discursive means. André Lefevre's essay on translated literature offers perhaps the best rebuttal to attacks on film adaptations as "unoriginal." Lefevre coins the term *refraction* to talk about the way a text is reworked to suit the needs of a particular public. Refractions can thus include Biblical stories retold for an audience of children, Classic Comics, *Reader's Digest* condensations, anthologized masterworks, Monarch notes and study guides, opera libretti, as well as foreign language translations. Lefevre argues against the absolutist thinking that posits a textual source as a supreme authority to be strictly followed in any translation process and suggests instead that all texts are refractions—that "the poetics of a literature is its central refracted text: at the time of its formulation it implicitly or explicitly reflects the dominant practice of the time."[72] Lefevre's comments serve to relativize the argument about translation and, by extension, about adaptation, justifying the kinds of accommodations that refractors must make to the evolving ideological and aesthetic demands of the publics whom they address.

Advocates of cinematic originality also reverence the purity of cinematic means. In so doing, they defy not only the postmodernist bent of contemporary criticism but also the wisdom of connoisseurs throughout film history who have celebrated the medium as the synthetic art par excellence, as that amalgam of literature, music, dance, and painting which enabled the seventh art to subsume all others.[73] It was this very "plurisensibility" that led Marinetti to consider film the perfect medium for futurist aspirations to a totalizing aesthetics for the modern age.[74]

Yet film's discursive heterogeneity should not add fuel to the proliterary bias of fidelity critics who see the adaptation as an inferior version, in a macaronic tongue, of a formally pure source. The novel is itself a mixed form whose mongrel status has often made it suspect among the apostles of generic homogeneity in literature. As an eclectic genre whose popular origins gave rise to the etymology of the term in most Romance languages (*roman, romance, romanzo*—literature in the vernacular), the novel, like the cinema, is a porous, highly refractable form that resists the kind of normative, canonizing gestures that fidelity critics make when setting it on a pedestal to which no cinematic illustration could ever aspire.[75]

The sharing of codes indigenous to each medium as well as nonspecific cultural and ideological codes common to all the arts, and the challenging of cherished assumptions about originality and discursive purity, make it necessary to renegotiate the terms of the debate on adaptation in light of the new findings in semiotics and postmodernism. Literature and film cease to be fixed monolithic entities locked in eternal combat like the personified abstractions of a Psychomachia and reveal themselves instead to be fluid constellations of codes, subject to many of the same intertextual influences and ideological constraints. Thus the history of literature-film relations becomes one of continuities and interpenetrations in which the nineteenth-century novel is read as moving toward the condition of cinema, and cinema, in turn, is seen as fulfilling its literary legacy.[76] Disciplinary boundaries are further undermined by the discovery of an exquisitely literary moment *within* the filmmaking process. "The concrete element in the relationship between cinema and literature is the screenplay," wrote Pasolini in the famous essay "La sceneggiatura come 'struttura' che vuol essere altra struttura."[77] It is because of its patently literary affinities that partisans of cinematic purity such as Luigi Chiarini so often opposed the very existence of a screenplay, preferring informal notes that would provide only the loosest of guidelines for procedures on set.[78]

The technique of screenwriting involves four distinct phases marked by three transitions, the last of which transforms an essentially literary document into a blueprint for its audiovisual realization: (1) subject—the story idea in its most succinct form, (2) story line—the list of narrated events, (3) treatment—the elaboration of the story idea in prose form, and (4) screenplay—dialogue, camera movements, descriptions of gestures and sets. "The treatment is the phase of cinematographic writing that most closely approaches the literary genre of the novel," states Massimo Moscati in his *Manuale di sceneggiatura*. "If he wishes, the writer may insert, in the treatment, states of mind and behaviors of characters in an objectivization that is proper to the novelist and not to the scriptwriter who, on the contrary, must visualize a state of mind, not describe it."[79] The suggestion is not so much that the treatment provides a kind of catharsis for the writer's novelistic impulses, allowing him or her to discharge them in order to undertake the task of pure cinematic writing, but instead that the literary condition gives the story its imaginative life, making the treatment a kind of agar dish where the narrative idea can receive stimulation and nourishment. This literary inspiration must eventuate in a screenplay that, unlike a novel, is not an end in itself but looks ahead to its fulfillment in another medium.[80] It is a functional text, like a user's guide or a recipe, whose nature is therefore provisional and utilitarian, yet also aesthetic in that it aims toward ulterior realization in another art form (as opposed to a washing machine or a soufflé).

Because the screenplay inhabits a never-never land between literature and technical writing, it has a tendency to escape public notice, along with its author, whose anonymity has become the subject of recent critical and professional regret.[81] Pasolini attributes screenwriting's peculiar status to its double semiotic itinerary—that of standard fictional signification, and that of allusion to another art work yet to be realized.[82] The screenplay is thus a text that makes *process* its reason for being,[83] and scriptwriters must operate on the premise that they should strive "to express what in the final product can no longer be expressed by writing."[84] In less paradoxical terms, this means that screenwriting must achieve a certain expressive economy and virtuality whereby the visualization process is built into the text itself, so that "what is described by the action implicitly requires the kind of shot that the scriptwriter visualized in the writing."[85] Thus the film script recapitulates the modus operandi we have been attributing to adaptive practice, with the difference that screenwriting *motivates* the processes of induction (of preliterary idea) and deduction (of appropriate cinematic means) that the adapter had to work so hard to achieve.[86] "The screenplay reveals therefore a volume of generative strategies that are hidden in the final product," writes Abruzzese, in explaining how scripts give explicit formulation to their own dynamics of change.[87]

Adaptation writ large is thus the basis of all filmmaking, whether seen from the perspective of the screenwriter who presides over the passage from a literary to an audiovisual conception, or from the perspective of Lefevre's "refractors" who make of all art works a priori accommodations to the needs of specific publics, or from the perspective of semioticians who insist that human creativity is never a direct, spontaneous response to "nature or "inner vision" but always adapts a preconceived idea, thanks to the mediations of perceptual, aesthetic, and sociocultural codes. Construed in its broadest sense, then, adaptation ceases to be the battleground for authors versus auteurs, rival signifying systems, or opposed cultural institutions and becomes, instead, the site for the enactment of art's quintessential transformatory operations.

In thinking about adaptation, I have found it useful to set up a critical straw man to justify the need for a revisionist approach. That straw man has been fidelity analysis, with its unexamined assumptions about the relative cultural status of literature and film, its imperative to slavish illustration, and its intolerance for interpretive freedom. Recent critical methods have rescued adaptation study from the reductiveness of fidelity analysis by providing vocabularies devoid of any built-in preference for one medium over another. We should be wary, however, of replacing fidelity analysis with a single theory that would be equally reductive in its orthodoxy. Given the heterogeneous and sometimes contradictory nature of the models offered by semiotics, feminism, psychoanalysis, and ideological criticism, I recommend an approach that uses them selectively as working hypotheses, without embracing any one as a totalizing theoretical explanation. "It will no longer do to let theorists settle things with a priori arguments," concludes Andrew. "We need to study the films themselves as acts of discourse. We need to be sensitive to that discourse and to the forces that motivate it."[88] And since all films that take their inspiration from literature represent sui generis solutions to the problems of adaptation, let us conduct our inquiry on the only level where our conclusions can speak with authority—on the concrete level of cinematic practice with each adaptive encounter.

1 · Visconti's *La terra trema*

THE TYPOLOGY OF ADAPTATION

In no case is the irrelevance of fidelity criticism more evident than in Luchino Visconti's *La terra trema* (1948), where the impulse to adapt Giovanni Verga's novel *I Malavoglia* came at a relatively advanced stage in the film's elaboration.[1] Visconti's original idea, to film a trilogy on the proletarian struggle in contemporary Sicily, had nothing to do with adaptation, and it was only later, when he decided to limit himself to one of the projected three episodes, that he found it necessary to turn to Verga's text to give flesh and bones to his inspiration. Therefore we can pose none of the questions that fidelity criticism normally asks of adaptation: Is the film faithful to the letter and/or the spirit of the original? Does it follow the novel's aesthetic and ideological dictates in morally responsible ways? Is it an interpretation that serves to promote and enrich our reading of the book without effacing it in the public mind? Visconti's adaptive procedure reverses the direction of such questioning and asks instead how the novel may contribute to the elaboration of the film in progress. I do not mean this in a strictly technical way, as if the writer, speaking through his novel, were to function as a kind of script doctor, rushed in at the last minute to save an ailing screenplay before putting it into production. I mean that as Visconti's conception changed and he realized the need for greater depth and complexity in character development, setting, and story line, he was naturally drawn to a model of grand, novelistic proportions. Yet Visconti's debt to Verga goes beyond characterization, setting, and plot to the ideological contradiction at the core of verismo itself. Before exploring the buried affinities that make *La terra trema* a deeply engaged critical rereading of *I Malavoglia*, let us consider how Verga was appropriated by 1940s culture of the Left and how this played a part in the film's imaginative prehistory.

What emerges from a study of this writer's cultural function during and after the war is a peculiar doubleness. As the rallying point for cinematic dissidence in the early 1940s, Verga stood as an alternative, a counterforce, to the official culture of the times—a position suited to his own rejection of Manzonian Catholic paternalism and his elevation of Sicily's underclasses to the highest level of literary dignity.[2] But Verga's apotheosis in dissident film culture of the early 1940s owes nothing to the progressive, historicizing logic we would expect of Marxist critics fighting for a new, engagé art. "Giovanni Verga has not only created a great work of poetry," wrote Mario Alicata and Giuseppe De Santis in 1941, "but he has created a country, a time, a society: to those of us who believe in art, especially as a creator of truth, the Homeric and legendary Sicily of *I Malavoglia* and *Mastro don Gesualdo*, of 'L'amante di Gramigna' and 'Jeli il pastore,' seems to us to offer at the same time the most solid and human, most miraculously virgin and true environment that can possibly inspire a cinema that sees things and facts in a time and space of reality."[3] Though the allusion to a society represented in all its historic and geographic specificity makes this a realist plea, the Sicily that De Santis and Alicata find in Verga is also "Homeric and legendary,"—a place without concrete temporal and spatial coordinates. This concept of an ahistorical, transcendent landscape that stands as an allegory of eternal human truths precludes any realist analysis of the material causes that may lend themselves to corrective social action. Far from construing Sicily as a concrete product of specific historical determinants, De Santis and Alicata see it as the sum total of a series of literary mediations: Sicily equals their reading of Verga's reading of Homer, suggesting an infinite regress of intertextual borrowings that establish the island setting as a kind of poetic trope or rhetorical figure with an imaginative life of its own.

Visconti's participation in this literary relay is obvious from his own comments on Sicily after a visit there in 1941. "To me, a Lombard reader, accustomed by traditional conditioning to the limpid rigor of the Manzonian fantasy, the primitive and gigantic world of the fishermen of Aci Trezza and of the shepherds of Marineo always seemed to me elevated in an imaginative and violent tone of epic: to my Lombard eyes, happy even with the sky of my land that is 'so beautiful when it is beautiful,' Verga's Sicily really seemed the island of Ulysses, an island of adventures and fervid passions, situated immobile and proud against the breakers of the Ionian Sea."[4]

For Visconti, as for De Santis and Alicata, Sicily stands in polar opposition to something else, be it the decadent, bourgeois world of Fascist culture in the second case, or the filmmaker's personal and aesthetic formation in the first. Visconti makes explicit the series of
regional and literary stereotypes which gives rise to his Sicilian perspective: North versus South, Manzoni versus Verga, changeability (as
dramatized by the weather) versus stasis, intellectual clarity (Manzoni's limpid rigor) versus turbid passions, modernity versus prehistory,
human drama versus epic heroism, and so on. Sicily thus exists as a
photographic positive, generated in dialectical opposition to a known
universe whose famililarity, intelligibility, and in De Santis' and Alicata's case, banality, prompts the quest for a world of mythic alternatives. That this is an imaginary alternative, with no grounding in concrete historical reality, is evident in Visconti's admission that his
attraction to Verga is an aesthetic one. "The power and the suggestiveness of the Verghian novel appear to hinge on its intimate musical
rhythm, and therefore the key to a cinematographic realization of *I
Malavoglia* is perhaps entirely here, that is in trying to feel again and
to gather the magic of that rhythm . . . that gives the religious and fatal tone of ancient tragedy to that humble occurrence of everyday
life" (31).

It is significant that of all the Muses operative in the novel, Visconti
singles out the one whose art is least intellectual, closest to mute feeling, in keeping with the filmmaker's own lifelong penchant for melodrama in its original etymological sense. If it is musical treatment that
will elevate the story from the level of "peasant chronicle" to that of
ancient tragedy, we realize how far we are from a critical realist perspective whose means would be rigorously intellectual, and whose
end would be the cinematic equivalent of the historical novel, as Lukács defines it. In the conclusion to his remarks on Verga, Visconti
makes explicit the link between musicality and the ahistoricism of his
Sicilian revery. "I want immediately to announce that if one day I will
have the fortune and the strength to realize the film I dreamed of on *I
Malavoglia*, the most valid justification for my attempt will certainly
be the illusion that touched my spirit in a distant hour, giving me
the conviction that for all the viewers, as for myself, the sound alone
of those names—Padron 'Ntoni Malavoglia, Bastianazzo, la Longa,
Sant'Agata, la Provvidenza—and of those places—Aci Trezza, Capo
dei Mulini, il Rotolo, la Sciara—will serve to open a fabulous and
magical scenario where words and gestures will have the religious relief of things essential to our human fellow feeling" (31). For Visconti,
the music of the names gives them an evocative force similar to the
taste of Proust's madeleine, though they transcend the strictly per-

sonal and secular power of Proustian involuntary memory in their collective religious appeal. These exotic names, derived from a dialect
with ancient Greek and Arabic roots, exert a mantra's effect on Visconti's Lombard ears, for they have the power to conjure up lost worlds
(or newly found ones) of the imagination.

But much transpired between 1941 and 1948 to radicalize Visconti's
approach. Clandestine anti-Fascist activity during the Nazi occupation, consequent imprisonment, and eventual enrollment in the Communist party were to impel him to recast his art in politically progressive terms. "Then came the war," he wrote, "with the war the
Resistance, and with the Resistance the discovery, for an intellectual
of my formation, of all the Italian problems as problems of *social structure* beyond those of *cultural, spiritual, and moral orientation.* The differences, the contradictions, the conflicts between North and South began to impassion me beyond the fascination exerted on me, as a
northerner, by the 'mystery' of the South and of the islands."[5] Furthermore, the neorealist movement in film, which had found in Visconti a progenitor (his 1942 *Ossessione* was hailed as a prototype), had
lost the urgency and vigor of its historical birth in the Resistance and
was in need of the kind of revival that *La terra trema* promised to provide. "The causes of *La terra trema*," Visconti explained, "came also,
basically, from this perplexity that increased in me day by day, seeing
the movement going off course, losing its prestige. Whence at a certain
moment came the need to return to the true origins, to pure truth,
without any trickery. . . . At the time of *La terra trema* I remember that
my professional conscience said to me: you must do that, you must
arrive at the extreme limit of the procedure, you must make no concessions. You must instead demonstrate that this is the right path and
that the others are by now erroneous. . . . With *La terra trema* it seems
to me that I really achieved realism."[6]

Though spoken in 1963, with the hindsight of Cesare Zavattini's
theoretical formulation of neorealism in 1952, Visconti's pronouncements on his realist aspirations in *La terra trema* invite comparison with
Verga's own manifesto in the introduction to the short story "L'amante
di Gramigna." Visconti's allusion to a procedure to be taken to its extreme limit recalls the claims to methodological rigor that would make
of verismo "a science of the human heart" by putting the reader "face
to face with the naked and clean fact . . . that modern analysis tries
to follow with scientific scruple."[7] Dedramatization is the necessary
consequence of Verga's quest for perfect objectivity and rational detachment. "We gladly sacrifice the effect of the catastrophe to the logical, necessary development of passions and events toward the catas-

trophe rendered less unexpected, less dramatic perhaps but no less fatal" (168). It is in its authorial implications that Verga's theorizing has most relevance to Visconti's working methods. When the novel has reached its perfect realization, Verga continues, "the hand of the artist will remain absolutely invisible . . . the work of art will seem to be done by itself . . . like a natural fact, without preserving any point of contact with its author, any stain of its sin of origin" (168–69). Indeed, Visconti's own announced strategy for achieving realism is to strive for maximum authenticity of means and to minimize authorial intervention. He shot on location, with no preestablished screenplay, in order to insure the spontaneity of his response to the reality he found in Aci Trezza, using nonprofessional actors who invented the dialogue after Visconti explained to them the dramatic situation they were to portray.[8] Visconti's fanatic adherence to realist procedural demands, however, had the paradoxical effect of sabotaging the film's realism by requiring expedients of a formalist sort. By insisting that the actors speak their own authentic language, a regional dialect so idiosyncratic and localized that not even other Sicilians could decipher it, Visconti would have condemned his film to utter unintelligibility had he not had recourse to voice-over narration. This intrusive, anticinematic device serves to frame and contain the film, distancing us from its documentary immediacy and announcing an authorial presence that paternalistically manipulates the representation from above and presumes to interpret it for us.[9] Another obvious antirealist implication of Visconti's modus operandi is that the absence of a screenplay, while increasing spontaneity, gives absolute power to the auteur, who must subject the entire production to his own unifying sensibility. But the most clamorous antirealist implication is obviously the recourse to a literary model for what was to have been a documentary on the plight of the Sicilian proletariat.

According to the original plan, *La terra trema* was to have included three interweaving stories: one about fishermen, one about miners, and one about peasants, all of whom would revolt against the injustice of their exploitation at the hands of their economic oppressors.[10] The first story, which was eventually the only one to be filmed and whose subtitle, "Episodio di mare," remains in the finished version as a relic of the initial idea, tells of one family's attempt to circumvent the unfairness of the wholesalers by going into business for themselves at the urging of the eldest son, Antonio. In the second episode, a group of unemployed miners, led by a certain Cataldo, resolves to pool its resources and set up a cooperative in an abandoned sulfur mine. The protagonist of the third episode is Saracino, who leads his fellow peasants in a movement to occupy the vast uncultivated lands of the *lati-fondisti*, in defiance of Mafia intimidation. Using the technique of parallel montage, Visconti planned to structure the film according to the "reciprocal rhythmical and conceptual affinities" of the three episodes, which would "mix and complete each other in turn in a crescendo that, starting with the first disordered and dispersed nucleus of a family of fishermen, moves to the problem in a mine and then on land, amplifying it to the point of making it assume the grandeur of the chorus."[11] The film privileges the notion of class solidarity, which spells the difference between defeat and success—Antonio's initiative fails because it is limited to the confines of the family unit, while Cataldo and Saracino prevail because they are supported by the collectivity. In the film's concluding sequence, victorious peasants charge onto the land on horses whose thunderous hoofbeats make the earth tremble and give the film its name.

Within a month of his arrival in Sicily, Visconti knew that the interlacing of episodes would not work, and he abandoned that synthetic structure for one in which the three discrete stories would succeed each other in turn. But the idea of a trilogy itself was discarded when Visconti realized that the fishermen's plight alone required the grandeur and complexity of treatment that in literature only the novel could achieve. Thus, at the expense of his original ideological program, which was to prove, through examples, the superiority of class action over individual revolt, Visconti chose to expand the "episodio di mare" into a full-fledged cinematic treatment.[12] It was at this point that he turned to *I Malavoglia* to provide the novelistic expanse required by the newly reframed project.

Perhaps the best barometer of the ideological change that Visconti himself underwent between 1941 and 1948 is his recharacterization of Verga's 'Ntoni Malavoglia. The rather diffuse, ineffectual attempts to rebel against the status quo which led the novel's 'Ntoni to seek refuge in physiçal escape, drunkenness, debauchery, criminality, and finally the forced exile of imprisonment are channeled into political and economic activism on the part of the film's 'Ntoni.[13] *La terra trema* is, in fact, the chronicle of an individual's *prise de conscience,* and as such, it may be seen as an autobiographical reference to Visconti's own political awakening in the light of Resistance history. Visconti's 'Ntoni is thus the New Man so touted by the Resistance in its promise to remake Italy according to its own progressive ideals.[14] Since a conversion experience seems to intervene between Visconti's 1941 encounter with Sicily and his 1948 adaptation of *I Malavoglia,* it would be no exaggeration to set *La terra trema* in a kind of typological relationship to Verga's work, as it fulfills the meaning of the novel in light of the revealed truth of the anti-Fascist struggle. The transformation of 'Ntoni Mala- voglia into 'Ntoni Valastro thus bears witness to a revelation whose decisiveness divides all history into a before and after and that de- mands that any post-Resistance rereading of an earlier text make ex- plicit the new perspective from which it looks back. Since Visconti could count on the presence of the novel in the minds of his viewers, he can consciously play off his New Testament *Terra trema* against Verga's *I Malavoglia*, making the relationship less one of adaptation than of typological fulfillment of an earlier textual promise.[15]

If this were all there was to Visconti's adaptive strategy, however, *La terra trema* would be a mere thesis film, reduced to illustrating its ideo- logical awakening at the expense of the earlier, "benighted" text. But Visconti avoids such arrogant reductivism by keeping Verga alive in his film in ways that heighten the tension between old and new orders and prevent *La terra trema* from lapsing into dogma. In the conflict between the film's ideological program and its much maligned aes- theticism, Visconti dramatizes the tension between old and new and thus responds to a contradiction in Verga himself which Marxist critics have been quick to point out.

Writing in the 1870s and 1880s, Verga could not help reflecting the ideological turmoil of a largely agrarian society moving rapidly toward industrialization.[16] In his rejection of the gospel of progress preached by the apostles of the industrial revolution, Verga turns to an image of primitive, subsistence society for the values that he finds so grievously lacking in contemporary urban, industrial life (23ff.). This polemical need explains why the writer chooses so closed, ahistorical, and fos- silized a world when Sicily itself, its countryside as well as its cities, was undergoing explosive social changes as a result of the uprisings of 1848 (73). Since the Risorgimento, even the customs of the proletariat had evolved, and a class consciousness was emerging as a result of contact with the North and compulsory military service (73–74). But Verga's ideology required a hermetically sealed world, impervious to external historical forces, obedient to its own inexorable laws of na- ture, fatality, and the necessity of human suffering (71). In the nostal- gic evocation of this elemental world where the passions are simple and their unfolding follows their own inner logic, Verga's fiction re- sembles a pastoral—not that of shepherd-poets piping their love songs among meadows and rills, but the subsistence pastoral of domestic moderation, where desire is commensurate with need, and need can be met by the fruits of hard labor. At the center of the subsistence pastoral is the patriarchal family that dedicates its energies to work, religion, frugality, cooperation, obedience, and a self-effacing commitment to the common good.

Thus Verga's answer to the unease felt by so many European writers in the wake of the industrial revolution—an unease that they expressed in ways as diverse as G. K. Chesterton's medievalism, Tolstoy's conservative anarchism, or Leftist rejections—is the subsistence pastoral, populated by Vico's natural man and tinged with backward-looking romanticism.[17] But Verga's respect for Aci Trezza folkways is by no means unalloyed. The village is teeming with malicious gossips (la Zuppida), intriguers (Don Silvestro, Piedipapera), shrews (la Vespa), weaklings (Don Franco, Turi Zuppido), and hypocrites (Zio Crocifisso), whose features are drawn with such caricatural excess that, if it were not for the Malavoglia's central tragedy, the novel would be pure social satire.[18] No solidarity is shown the Malavoglias, whose misfortunes are greeted with scorn or avoidance. Except for Alfio Mosca, the only good characters outside the family are women—orphans or widows—and thus doubly victims. In its density of interrelationships, its richness and variety of character types, its rigid power hierarchy, its deeply personal yet profoundly uncharitable human dynamics, the village is therefore a paradigm of *in malo* social organization. What further qualifies Verga's celebration of Aci Trezza is the fact that Padron 'Ntoni, the personification of patriarchal, rural values, is the one who precipates the family's decline. It is he who embarks on the speculative adventure that will lead the Malavoglias to ruin, and as if he sensed how transgressive his actions are, he justifies his decision with the proverbial language that bespeaks the conservative wisdom of the status quo. Using the technique of free indirect discourse, Verga tells us that Padron 'Ntoni invests in the lupins "per menar avanti la barca" ("to move the boat ahead"),[19] echoing the metaphoric association of the boat with the Malavoglias' fortunes that had typified several earlier proverbs about family governance: "Per menare il remo bisogna che le cinque dita s'aiutino l'un l'altro" ("To row the oar the five fingers must help one another") (55), "Senza pilota barca non cammina" ("Without a pilot the ship won't run") (56). It is not so much that Padron 'Ntoni sins by defying the standard code of plebeian decorum but that the code itself is flawed, as embodied by the elder Malavoglia.

Thus Verga's ideology is deeply conflictual, both in the macroscopic tension between capitalist, industrialized, progressive urban culture and its preindustrial, rural, patriarchal antithesis, and in the microscopic divisions that rend the village and the family from within. No ideal is unequivocally celebrated in *I Malavoglia*, whose subsistence pastoral falls victim not only to social and natural hostility but also to its own inner frailty. The only consolation for Verga is the literary pleasure of a reverie predicated on distance and on the impossibility of its historical realization, making the novel a wish-fulfillment fantasy whose awareness of its own limits is built into the fantasy itself. In many ways *I Malavoglia* is the story of the destruction of a pastoral ideal—an ideal that we can only know and experience as absence, as loss, as what our life is not. Aci Trezza is thus a place in the mental geography of the city dweller whose memories, daydreams, and discontents have conspired to produce an earthly paradise both cherished and blamed for its very impossibility.

Visconti was by no means indifferent to the problematics of Verga's Aci Trezza. The conflict that ravages Verga's representation from within is externalized and historicized by Visconti, who makes Padron 'Ntoni's flawed expression of pastoral ideals in *I Malavoglia* into a conscious positive political choice by 'Ntoni Valastro. Thus when Verga's patriarchal protagonist violates his own conservative dictates by financial speculation and sets the family on its dizzying course to ruin, he reveals the inexorable human yearning for improvement which will threaten any social equilibrium. But when Visconti's younger 'Ntoni makes a similar choice for *benessere*, he does so after engaging in the kind of reasoned economic analysis that could lead to a new Utopia, this time of a Marxist sort.[20] The Verghian tension between a longed-for pastoral order and the awareness of its loss finds its equivalent in the temporal dialectic of *La terra trema*, where the primitive circular time of the villagers' daily routine gives way to the progressive, historical time of 'Ntoni's political awakening.

A subsistence economy is a cyclical one, moving from a yesterday of work to a today of consumption in order to fuel the bodies that must embark on a tomorrow of more work, and so on. "A sip of wine, some bread, sardines," says the voice-over, "they were earned with yesterday's labor to have the strength to return to the sea tonight [the Valastros are nocturnal fishermen] to earn sardines, wine, and bread for tomorrow."[21] It is this subsistence cycle, where all earnings are consumed and nothing remains to invest in a future, that 'Ntoni strives to transcend in a linear movement toward prosperity. The decision to engage in economic speculation, to risk and invest, to mortgage the present in the name of a hypothetical tomorrow is couched in the language of linearity. "And the Valastros go to Catania to mortgage their house, the only asset they have, to be able to conquer the hope of a better future." What keeps the other villagers from following suit, and from forming the collectivity that would guarantee the success of

'Ntoni's venture in Marxist terms, is a certain failure of the imagination which prevents them from entertaining a constructive fantasy of the unknown. "But no one else follows them because everything is frightening to the poor and one does not think that things can change, and the worst is always to come." In *La terra trema*, the opposite of poverty is not wealth, but imagination—the ability to conjure up the mental image of an alternative and to project it onto a possible future. The visionary nature of 'Ntoni's economics and his failure to inspire a kindred resolve in his peers suggests that power in Aci Trezza is less material than ideological, according to Althusser's famous definition of ideology as "the representation of the individual's imagined relationship to the real conditions of his existence."[22] 'Ntoni is able to wrest control of that representation only once, in the wharfside revolt, as we shall see. But it is Raimondo who stages in the flamboyant scene of the boat christening the definitive spectacle of the "imagined relationships" that constitute village ideology. This ceremony comes upon the heels of the Valastros' final defeat when they are evicted from their ancestral home under the cover of night. Raimondo's apotheosis follows both logically and chronologically from this misfortune as he christens the new fleet that will consolidate his economic dominance of the town.

The scene begins with a pan of the new boats in a hyperbolic disclosure of Raimondo's increasing wealth. Visconti next cuts to a reverse shot of the crowd which convinces us of Raimondo's popular support. From this perspective, we see the small, white-clad priest weave slowly in and out of the boats as he bestows his benediction upon them. Now Visconti cuts to a low-angle shot that monumentalizes Raimondo as he towers over the crowd astride his boat in exactly the same position that Lorenzo had occupied vis-à-vis the fishermen when bargaining to their disadvantage in an earlier scene. Images of the aged baroness who is stuffing her mouth with sweets, followed by a cut back to Raimondo as the white-clad priest slowly makes his way across the screen, reveal the authorities whose interests are being served by this pageantry. Church and decaying aristocracy have an obvious stake in maintaining the status quo and thus throw their full institutional weight behind the boss's attempts at economic and political containment. In his toast to Aci Trezza, where "you're all good workers, except for a few who're sick in the head and want to do for themselves" (93), Raimondo identifies the health of the body politic with his own class interests and sophistically generalizes those interests to the masses by arguing for the trickle-down theory—that his prosperity means more work and prosperity for all. In the scene's penultimate

shot, the prow of a new boat is foregrounded against the figures of
Nedda and Lorenzo, whose engagement signals yet one more defeat
for 'Ntoni and one more Darwinist proof that sexual rewards come to
the dominant. When a young girl hands Raimondo a tray of rice in the
final shot, and the boss throws it over the heads of the crowd, he is
consecrating the illusory marriage of his economic interests with the
common good. The celebration is not only a marriage, however, but
also a birth, as the christening of the boats gives them the prestige of
new lives being initiated into the community, establishing the village
as a family with an organic integrity and an implied power structure
that enhances Raimondo's campaign for hegemony. In this rite of
dominance masquerading as a promotion of the public welfare, Raimondo shows himself to be a skilled ideologist in the Althusserian
sense, impresario of the spectacle that "naturalizes" the injustice of
popular oppression at the hands of the capitalist bosses.

Though Visconti transforms Verga's critique of the subsistence
pastoral into a Marxist analysis of the system, he nonetheless remains sensitive to the novelist's nostalgia and longing for the world
whose inner frailty has doomed it to extinction. Visconti's own much-
maligned aestheticism can be seen as a way of inscribing Verga's elegiac perspective into the film and thus can be justified as an important
component of his adaptive strategy.[23] If *La terra trema* is read typologi-
cally as a fulfillment of *I Malavoglia* in light of the Marxist dispensation,
then the presence of Verghian elements in the film will be necessary
to maintain its ongoing typological tension. I am thinking here especially of the visually sublime, though critically controversial, scene of
the Valastro women who await their men on the storm-lashed beach,
or *sciara*, of Aci Trezza.[24] Visconti lingers on these images for longer
than the narrative itself would require, using seven different camera
positions in a short space of time to give visual interest and grandeur
to such static figures of despair.

The scene opens with a medium shot of the women in silhouette
wearing black shawls whose fringes blow about in the wind like the
wings of primeval birds. In the next five shots, the camera draws progressively nearer to the women, but never so close as to violate their
privacy, and always films them from a low angle that maintains their
moral dominance of the frame. A final long shot, taken from behind
and above the women against the raging surf, works less to diminish
their figures than to ennoble them in their visual association with so
awesome and powerful a setting. The effect of the camera work and
the mise-en-scène is to abstract the women from their concrete historical circumstances and to project them into a mythic sphere of timeless,

universal truths.[25] In moments such as these, Visconti recalls the Homeric associations of his 1941 encounter with Verga when the novel's mystique played a large part in the filmmaker's early inspiration.

The film's sound track constitutes another recall to Visconti's earlier encounter with *I Malavoglia*, whose "power and suggestiveness," he wrote in 1941, "appear all to hinge on its intimate musical rhythm."[26] Though nondiegetic music is used sparingly throughout the film, its sound track is intensely musical, from the frequent tolling of the church bells, to the crooning of the happy 'Ntoni or Nicola's co-worker Jano, to the miscellaneous shouts of the nocturnal fishermen and the wharfside negotiators, to Zio Nunzio's flute rendition of Bellini's "Ah, non credea mirarti," to the constant background noise of the sea.[27] Critics have also noted, somewhat cynically, that Visconti's insistence on having his characters speak in dialect serves less his realist interests than his overriding aestheticism—that the musicality, not the authenticity, of the language is what recommended it to the filmmaker's "Lombard ears."[28] The very lyricism of this sound track thus offers another medium-specific equivalent to the sweeping nostalgia of Verga's narrative perspective.

Visconti's inordinate attention to the figures of the Valastro women as they wait on the *sciara* makes of them what I would call superdiegetic or supernarrative images whose function exceeds their literal purpose in the story. Such imagery is common in *La terra trema*, and it occurs in moments of intense aesthetic self-consciousness, either to define Visconti's relationship to cinematic models, or to comment on his own authorial presence in ways that amount to a signatory code in Christian Metz's semiotics. The superdiegetic images of the women on the rocks, for example, allude to Flaherty's *Man of Aran* (1934) where Maggie and her son await their men on the storm-battered shore.[29] But the Flaherty allusion also serves to differentiate Visconti's style from his predecessor's, whose turbulent camera matched the turbulence of the scene it records with its short takes, its complicitous, jerky movement, its staccato intercutting between shots of white-water violence and shots of Maggie's agitated response. Where Flaherty's camera was an active participant in the drama, identifying with Maggie's anxiety, Visconti's style maintains its Olympian calm, observing the natural spectacle and its human victims with contemplative detachment, not unlike Verga's narrator in *I Malavoglia*.

Superdiegetic images also suggest the presence of another important model for *La terra trema* in Sergei Eisenstein, whose works Visconti had seen and admired during his Parisian sojourn in the 1930s.[30] Eisenstein's work abounds in supernarrative images that derive logically from his famed montage technique, where close-ups, intercutting, and conflictive juxtapositions form the basis of the filmmaker's dialectical approach to meaning. Eisenstein's typical procedure is to single out a detail from the mise-en-scène which will come to bear considerable symbolic weight by dint of strategic returns in close up throughout a scene or sequence. The meaning of *Potemkin* (1925), for example, can be said to reside in the series of superdiegetic images that combine on a figurative level to form an allegory of class struggle. Thus the maggots on the meat that is the sailors' ration, plus the eyeglasses of the doctor who proclaims its edibility, plus the cross of the priest who charges that dissent is heresy amount to a call to revolution whose answer is seen in the clenched fists of the on-shore population. The most famous and bravura example of superdiegetic imagery is, of course, the baby carriage whose agonizing fall down the Odessa steps absorbs all the meanings of helplessness and innocence that could possibly attach to this scene of gratuitous carnage.

Not surprisingly, superdiegetic imagery of an Eisensteinian sort occurs in *La terra trema* in one of the three scenes edited according to the Soviet filmmaker's montage techniques.[31] This is the scene of the fishermen's rebellion against the bosses whose refusal to deal fairly has riled 'Ntoni into a frenzy of defiance. Given the failure of his ploy to replace the elderly with young men to negotiate with the wholesalers, 'Ntoni has no choice but to disrupt the unacceptable commercial proceedings and precipitate a general revolt. The action begins with a medium shot of Lorenzo as he voices the litany of low prices that has thrown 'Ntoni into such a rage. "Four hundred twenty-five lire" he chants with such infuriating insistence that 'Ntoni cannot refrain from grabbing his lapels and ordering him to stop selling. When Lorenzo resists, 'Ntoni runs back down the quay to the scales, which he seizes and displays to his co-insurgents. This gesture of demonstration is of the utmost importance, for it reveals the performative aspect of 'Ntoni's rebellion. By seizing the scales and showing them to his comrades, 'Ntoni signals both that the men are to follow his revolutionary lead and that he has appropriated the power to make meaning. The scales are both the wholesalers' instrument of economic exploitation and the traditional symbol of distributive justice. But like the cross in *Potemkin* whose original meaning had been perverted by the priestly apologist for the regime, Lorenzo's scales deny their iconography in their service to fraud. When 'Ntoni seizes the scales and uses them as his call to arms, he counteracts the wholesalers' betrayal of justice and reinvents the original iconography by consecrating their symbolism to the fishermen's cause. Like Eisenstein's clenched fists, the scales transcend their concrete diegetic purpose to proclaim their universality.

Foregrounded by two lines of listeners who converge at the point where 'Ntoni holds the scales aloft, this image self-proliferates, inspiring any number of similar seizures. A cut to brawling fishermen and wholesalers on shore shows that 'Ntoni's rhetorical gesture has worked. When 'Ntoni returns on-screen shouting, "What are we waiting for? Look what I'm going to do with these devil's scales! I'm throwing them into the sea"(23), his symbolic reclamation of the scales is complete. The scene ends with a low-angle shot of another scale tosser, whose exact replication of 'Ntoni's gesture reaffirms its rhetorical force.

Just as the rebellion is an interlude in the otherwise quiet and resigned civic life of Aci Trezza, so is the film technique and the imagery of the scene an exception to Visconti's standard operating procedure. In general, Visconti rejects Eisenstein's constructive montage for one that privileges the mise-en-scène, letting the eye wander freely throughout a space that is splendidly three-dimensional, thanks to deep-focus technology and the filmmaker's talent for organizing all visual planes in meaningful ways.[32] It is in his respect for the time-space continuum and the organic integrity of the profilmic world of Aci Trezza that Visconti provides the cinematic equivalents of literary verismo. The thickness of Verga's descriptive technique, its density, and its narrative layerings find their analogues in such justly famous episodes as the morning ablutions of the newly returned fishermen.[33]

Other instances of deep-focus photography include glimpses of activity in neighboring houses and lots: women weave, construction workers build, children play. Life is being lived on all visual planes, Visconti is telling us, just as Verga insists on the abundance and thickness of chronicle at Aci Trezza. Perhaps the most complex use of deep-focus photography, and its most eloquent support for Verga's communitarian ideal, is the scene of 'Ntoni's triumphant exchange with his neighbors upon his return from Catania. The scene opens with an over-the-shoulder shot from the viewpoint of the neighbor Giovannina, who looks on with amusement as 'Ntoni addresses his love lyrics to her. "A happy man sings! Good for you!" (41). "Yes," he answers, "I'm happy, for I won't kill myself anymore working for other people, I'll work for myself now!" As the camera moves slowly left, it keeps 'Ntoni in focus in the lower right, while managing to include the distant figure of Blondie, shouting her comments from a balcony high in the top central portion of the frame. Next to 'Ntoni in the foreground is a profusion of leaves—a reference perhaps to the medlar tree that is the Malavoglias' trademark (theirs is the *casa del nespolo*). A reverse shot, this time from Blondie's perspective, locates 'Ntoni in deep focus far below, amid the stones, leaves, and roof tiles of the courtyard and its residential surrounds. The camera pans right to the next balcony, then cuts to 'Ntoni's low-angle view of Vicenza high above him, whose comment makes explicit the link between the solidarity theme and Visconti's mise-en-scène. "'Ntoni, neighbors are like roof tiles! They're always pouring water on each other!" The camera next traces a downward arc, shooting from behind 'Ntoni's back as he lies down to take his ease and gives a self-satisfied laugh. In deep focus, we see yet another neighbor—this time from a window in the opposite tower. It is Nunzio, whose comments are musical as he pipes 'Ntoni's theme song, "My Treacherous Love," on the flute. By now the camera has nearly completed a 360-degree rotation during which it has discovered a series of choral respondents to 'Ntoni's state. A less plastic filmmaker would have made Verga's chorus into a flat, theatrical device, serving a purely decorative purpose. But by placing the Valastros' neighbors at various depths throughout the visual field, Visconti's staging provides spatial analogues to Verga's multilayered chorality.

Deep-focus photography also serves to convey by visual means what the novel tells us about the Malavoglias' attachment to the house by the medlar tree. When 'Ntoni announces his plan to mortgage the house, the positioning of Mara, their mother, and their brother Maccherone along the axis that leads from the outer courtyard to a series of inner rooms reveals the organic continuity between this family and the domestic space that they are about to lose. Visconti's love of portraiture finds thematic justification in the way he frames characters in windows with lengthy, static shots that link their images indissolubly to the surrounding architectural structure. Mara is frequently thus framed. Her relationship with Nicola is introduced by a window shot of her watering a pot of basil—the floral signal to would-be suitors that an eligible young woman resides within. For Nicola, who is appropriately a builder of houses, Mara's identification with her homestead and its implied prosperity place her above him in the social hierarchy. In a second instance of such framing, Mara and Lucia pose at the window to watch the forced sale of the anchovies—a transaction that eventually leads to the forfeit of their house through bankruptcy.

A more complex instance of portraiture involves the family photograph whose fixed image of the Valastros at their prime provides a grim measure of the family's steady decline. Four times during the course of the film, Visconti calls our attention to the portrait as a way of marking the stages of the Valastro's descent, beginning with the introductory cleaning of its surface by Lucia, who is thus moved to comment on the prenarrative death of their father, Bastianazzo. When Cola chooses to embark on a life of crime, his farewell to the photo is

Mara, Lucia, and Vanni watch from the house, whose apparent solidity belies their tentative hold on it.

Cola bids farewell to the family portrait as he leaves to embark on a life outside the law.

an acknowledgement as much of his moral as of his geographic straying from family tradition. In the wake of her seduction by Don Salvatore and her subsequent quarrel with Mara, Lucia's leave-taking is far less ceremonious, though Visconti is careful to film her as she passes before the family photo on the way out the door that she will never again reenter. In its final appearance, the family photo says imagistically what Verga devotes an entire subplot to expressing in the romance and marriage of Alessi and Nunziata: the restoration of the Valastro/Malavoglia fortunes. When Mara hangs the photo next to the Sacred Heart on the rent-house walls as 'Ntoni and his brothers set out for work, the suggestion is that the Valastros will survive and will rededicate themselves to the values and traditions embodied by the idealized family image. But a close-up of the photo subverts this facile reading, which would effectively deny the entire Marxist thrust of the film and imply that 'Ntoni's consciousness-raising was aberrant, reversible, and false. Upon careful examination, the photograph reveals its tacky artifice—the family poses before a painted backdrop of Mt.

Etna which is framed by painted drapery to give the illusion of a picture window. To add to its unreality, 'Ntoni is dressed in his naval uniform, connecting this photo to another one whose illusory power is enough to whet Cola's appetite for escape. In the aftermath of his conversation with the black marketeer, as he mulls over his decision to leave, Cola rifles through 'Ntoni's storage chest to find tokens of his brother's military service on the continent. The uniform, the photo of 'Ntoni in a debonnaire pose amidst the fake finery of the studio, and postcards of some city's tourist attractions all spark Cola's desire for flight.

So self-conscious a director as Visconti, aware as he was of forging a new path in neorealism, could not use still photography in his film without charging it with metacinematic significance. The photograph, in many ways, stands as a foil for Visconti's filmmaking—as an idealized image frozen in time, it is at variance with the fluid and deteriorating conditions of Valastro life. As such, still photography projects an illusory image whose glamor and inaccessibility can seduce the spectator into dangerous reveries of the most escapist sort, or into a desire to return to an imagined golden age of familial bliss. Because it is a kinetic medium, cinema can challenge the fixed ideal of the frozen photographic image by subjecting it to the rigors of time, history, and change, thus exposing its illusionism and its perilous glamor. In this way, still photography provides Visconti with an occasion to define, by opposition, his critical-realist contribution to Italian cinema.

The photograph joins another favorite Viscontian motif, the mirror, to define the complex interplay of illusionism and narcissistic projection in Cola's feelings for his brother. Setting 'Ntoni's photoportrait in the lower left-hand corner of the mirror frame, Cola comments, "I don't believe that in the rest of the world the people are as bad as they are in Trezza! And I'm fed up with living here!" (73). As he utters this escapist wish, Cola's juxtaposition of 'Ntoni's glamorous photographic image with his own reflection only heightens his imitative desires. But 'Ntoni's response, and the camera's perspective, give the lie to such illusionism. "Don't say that!" 'Ntoni objects. "Because we were born in Trezza and we have to die in Trezza! Even if we have to suffer for it!" (74). Shooting into the mirror, the camera now captures 'Ntoni's reflection alongside the romanticized photograph of himself in uniform. In the comparison between the portrait, which stands for a magically remote time and place, and the mirror image of the present 'Ntoni, Visconti implies a journey and a return. But in Cola's mind, there is only a journey. "You can talk that way, 'Ntoni, because you know the world. You've been to Taranto . . . Bari . . . even La Spezia!

The fishing port of Aci Trezza is bounded by the Faraglioni, the legendary rocks thrown by Polyphemus to block Ulysses' escape from the harbor.

There's a lot of world outside this village. A man could make his fortune!" (74). At this point, the camera shifts position and shoots from behind 'Ntoni's shoulder to capture Cola's reflection in the mirror as he imaginatively merges his identity with that of the sailor in the photograph. "Cola!" 'Ntoni replies. " The sea's salty all over the world. As soon as we're outside our rocks [the Faraglioni] the current can destroy us!" (74)

'Ntoni's reference to the Faraglioni is the verbal counterpart of what we have been seeing throughout the film—images of the huge, jagged rocks in the harbor of Aci Trezza which mark the boundaries of the safe world and which figure most prominently in the scene of the Valastros' lone embarcation on their first day of financial independence. The juxtaposition of 'Ntoni's bowed-down sail next to the jagged outline of one of the Faraglioni suggests how the family has transgressed the boundary between acceptable and unacceptable commercial practices. It is because he is in debt and must recoup his investment that

'Ntoni is forced to fish farther out where the catch is better but the risks far greater. Significantly, the first use of nondiegetic music, a sad romantic strain, occurs in this scene.

The mythology of the Faraglioni is invoked ironically at the film's end in the title of the business that will employ 'Ntoni at such terrible personal cost. Raimondo's firm is called "Cyclops Company— Transportation and Sale of Fish," recalling Polyphemus's disastrous hospitality to Ulysses and his hurling of the rocks into the harbor to impede the hero's escape. His rudeness and his obstruction of 'Ntoni's adventurism make Raimondo a modern-day Polyphemus who reverses the direction of the Homeric myth by defeating the new Ulysses. In this profoundly ironic allusion to the cyclops, Visconti is revisiting his own 1941 encounter with "the island of Ulysses," now seen from the vast ideological distance of the postwar years. In the light of the Marxist dispensation there can be no individual heroics, no solo epic conquests, only class actions that must doggedly pit themselves against the entrenched interests of the system. Verga too saw the futility of individual revolt, but he was without the ideological tools, or the necessary temperament, to transform that social discontent into class consciousness. In *La terra trema*, Visconti rewrites Homer and Verga according to Marx, making 'Ntoni Valastro the typological fulfillment of an ancient warrior and a defeated Risorgimento fisherman whose restless energy finds its appropriate expression in his protagonist's political awakening.

2 · Visconti's *Leopard*

THE POLITICS OF ADAPTATION

"My film is not and could not be a transcription into images of the novel," Visconti said of *The Leopard*.[1] "Even while maintaining a great fidelity to the novel which has inspired it . . . a film must have its own expressive originality. And not only from the visual side."[2] In this important manifesto of his film's autonomy from the eponymous work by Giuseppe Tomasi di Lampedusa, Visconti indicates two lines of inquiry for scholars of adaptation. His insistence on "expressive originality" suggests that *The Leopard* will be no literal-minded illustration of the book, but that it will honor the story/discourse distinction by separating out elements peculiar to the literary form from elements that instead will lend themselves to autonomous cinematic expression. And when he claims that his originality comes "not only from the visual side" he is asserting an autonomy that exceeds Galvano della Volpe's "technical formal" comparison of the two arts.[3] For Visconti's film, released in 1963, is also a highly politicized interpretation of the novel, whose appearance in 1958 generated considerable public controversy. "I became impassioned by the critical polemics on the content of the novel, to the point of wanting to be able to intervene and state my thinking. Perhaps this is the reason that pushed me to accept the offer to make the film."[4] Thus Visconti's *Leopard* is a polemic response to the debate surrounding the novel, a *prise de position* in the heated political atmosphere of early 1960s Italian critical thought.[5] What makes Visconti's cinematic defense of the novel so unassailable, as we shall see, is his use of Marxist cultural heroes—Gramsci and Lukács—against *The Leopard*'s detractors within the Left. In the following pages, Visconti's self-proclaimed originality will thus be studied as a two-fold phenomenon: as a medium-appropriate response to Lampedusa's literary discourse, and as a critical intervention in the debate surrounding the novel's release.[6]

Visconti remains remarkably faithful to Lampedusa's plot line but wisely chooses to omit the novel's pathetic flashforwards to 1888 and 1910, concentrating on the years between 1860 and 1862 when Fabrizio enters his prime, only to make the pact with history that will bring about the demise of his family fortunes. The decision to focus on those pivotal two years not only allows the film stylistic and dramatic unity but gives full expression to the contradiction at the heart of Visconti's aesthetics. This Marxist aristocrat, whose sentiments and tastes are all on the side of life *before* the revolution, is nonetheless a passionate advocate of the need for social change, for a radical overhaul of the old order.[7] "I can understand his nostalgia," Visconti said of the prince, "but his world had to go and that is what I want to show in the film."[8] By ending his *Leopard* with the Pantaleone ball, rather than with the prince's death in a squalid Palermo hotel room or with the daughters' self-mummification among worthless relics of a religious or family past, Visconti avoids the retroactive judgment that such scenes impose upon the aristocratic universe of 1862 and indulges his sympathy for what "had to go." This editorial decision also focuses our attention on the final *political* developments of the story—Garibaldi's defeat at Aspromonte, which gives rise to Visconti's most momentous addition to the novel in the inclusion of the news that the rebel prisoners will be shot at dawn. Significantly, the last we see of Tancredi, Angelica, and Calogero is in a carriage leaving the ball, happy at the sound of the firing squad that puts an end to any "subversive" threat to the new regime. "It's just what was needed for Sicily," yawns Calogero. "Now we can relax." As a fellow traveler in Calogero's carriage, Tancredi is implicated in his father-in-law's reactionary stance, while Fabrizio's moral revulsion is expressed in his return home by another path, on foot.[9] Tancredi's opportunistic preference for his father-in-law over his uncle (and adoptive father) in political matters had already surfaced in the ball scene, where the young man had applauded Pallavicino, whom Fabrizio had found insufferable.[10] "He says some things that are very, very sensible," Tancredi remarks of the colonel's justification for executing the rebel prisoners. "It's true, the new regime needs order, legality, laws. Above all, any anarchic attempt must be suffocated. No more adventures and disorder. Even if that implies harsh and often painful measures, like the execution of those fanatics who defected to join Garibaldi. They are deserters!"[11] It is Concetta, Fabrizio's daughter and rival of Angelica for Tancredi's affections, who gives words to the young man's apostasy. "Once you wouldn't have spoken this way!" Thus the final judgment on the aristocratic splendor of the ball is not Lampedusa's relegation of it to the trash heaps of history in 1910, but the inner moral corruption that leads a Tancredi to jump on the revolutionary bandwagon in 1860 and then happily to consign the band to the firing squad in 1862.

Other departures from Lampedusa's narrative scheme include the omission of Padre Pirrone's visit to San Cono where he resolves a family feud involving sexual passion and property in a degraded rerun of the Tancredi-Angelica betrothal, and the addition of two sequences, one of which was sadly eliminated from the film's final cut. This deleted scene, published in the shooting script, includes Calogero's denial of peasant suffrage on the grounds that only property owners may vote.[12] The other added sequence (happily included in the film's final cut) is the celebrated Battle of Palermo, including the scenes of Tancredi's wounding and the lynching of local functionaries who had collaborated with Bourbon rule. In the virulence of popular outrage against the old order, and the military daring expressed in the rebel campaign, Visconti gives life to the revolutionary impulse whose existence in the novel is reduced to verbal reportage. Though the dramatis personae of *The Leopard* offer no equivalent to Count Roberto Ussoni of *Senso*, whose selfless commitment to the Risorgimento ideal redeemed the possibility of aristocratic allegiance to the revolution, such commitment is implicit in the Battle of Palermo sequence. By including Tancredi in that event, Visconti sets him up as the functional equivalent of Ussoni—a device that only heightens our disappointment in his subsequent moral decline.

The addition and subtraction of scenes thus amounts to a deliberate politicizing strategy on Visconti's part. "I don't think that I've added anything to the ideas of Lampedusa; I have only enlarged on some themes which interested him less and are just hinted at in the novel, although hinted at with great clarity. . . . Tancredi was the kind of man who always swims with the tide, betting on a certainty."[13] For Visconti, Tancredi represents the phenomenon of *trasformismo*—the neutralization and appropriation of revolutionary movements to serve the interests of the ruling elite. According to Visconti, *trasformismo* typifies all post-Risorgimento history, culminating in the postwar betrayal of Resistance ideals.[14] It is this emphasis on *trasformismo*, with its implicit critique of the contemporary Italian political scene, so grimly compromised by the coalition of the Christian Democrats with the neofascist Movimento Sociale Italiano under Tambroni, that makes

Visconti's film an answer to the novel's detractors on the Left. Through recourse to Gramsci and Lukács, Visconti counters the charges leveled against the text by Mario Alicata, Guido Aristarco, Pier Paolo Pasolini, and Elio Vittorini who argue that the novel is a refined literary exercise, lacking any positive prescription for social change to remedy the defects it so rightly perceives in Risorgimento history. Though Alicata sees in chapter 1 the premise for a great historical novel, "it degenerates into a mechanical repetition of the same psychological situation" and, like a broken record, fixates on the theme of the Risorgimento as a trick played on those who naively entertain the hope of progressive social change.[15] Vittorini, who originally turned down the manuscript when Lampedusa submitted it for publication in Einaudi's "I gettoni" series (Bassani later accepted it for Feltrinelli), found *The Leopard* objectionable in its very vision of literature. Novels, according to Vittorini, must "renew our relationship with history and re-establish one with nature," and they must "provoke the reader to accept or reject what they represent."[16] For Aristarco, who had aggressively defended *Senso* against its neorealist critics, *The Leopard* abdicated its claim to *engagement* in its lack of a Ussoni figure to exemplify political activism of a noble and disinterested sort.[17]

Visconti's politicizing strategy invites us to see how Lampedusa's text authorizes the Gramscian and Lukácsian terms of the cinematic adaptation. In light of the film, we are asked to read back into the novel the critique of *trasformismo* that fulfills Gramsci's prescription for a revisionist history of the Risorgimento: "that, in Italy, there take place an intellectual and moral reform bound to the criticism of the Risorgimento as 'royal conquest' and not 'popular movement.'"[18] I can imagine no better demonstration of this thesis than Tancredi's actions, which he immediately ascribes to monarchist motives in defending his rebel partisanship to his skeptical uncle. "A Falconeri should be with us, for the King," Fabrizio insists. "For the King, yes, of course. But which King?" Tancredi answers, revealing that his anti-Bourbon activism is hardly antimonarchist.[19] By exposing the young man's rebel activity as a temporary expedient that facilitates, by momentarily masking, his true royalist allegiance, Lampedusa restores the term *revolution* to its etymological roots. Fabrizio is, after all, an astronomer by avocation, and for him, revolution describes the circular movement of heavenly bodies, not the tumultuous overthrow of earthly regimes.[20] Tancredi's political identity traces a similar circular path, from monarchist through revolutionary, to return to the point where he began. Though Savoy replaces Bourbon, Victor Emmanuel replaces Francesco, and constitutional monarchy replaces its feudal counterpart, the chromatic return to royal blue reveals the true relation of identity between Tancredi's political before and after. Thus the Tancredi plot constitutes the perfect fictional enactment of Gramsci's critique of the Risorgimento as "conquista regia e non movimento popolare," as a failed or betrayed revolution.

Another way in which the novel fulfills the Gramscian appeal for rethinking the Risorgimento is in its challenge to the notion of national unity on which all Italian historiography is based. Official histories presuppose that Italy was always an organic whole whose unity was suppressed by a series of foreign dominations until its popular liberation in 1870.[21] Such a fiction conceals the reality of imperialist conquest by the House of Savoy, which cleverly managed to identify its own dynastic interests with those of the mythic totality. Thus Lampedusa devotes both a sentimental and a political subplot to its demolition in the advent of the two northern guests to Donnafugata. Though Concetta's refusal of Cavriaghi's suit is less a commentary on the count's personal unacceptability than on her undying love for Tancredi, such a preference for her own kind (they share not only a fatherland but the blood tie of sibling parents) suggests the provincialism that makes of Italy so many self-sufficient regional units. Cavriaghi's failed courtship thus becomes a sentimental allegory for the failure of Italian unity as a political program—a judgment playfully expressed in the culinary antagonism between north and south. "She's Sicilian to the marrow," Tancredi explains to Cavriaghi. "She's never left here; she might never feel at home in a place where one has to arrange a week ahead for a plate of macaroni!" (192). A similar culinary incompatibility disconcerts Chevalley, whose sojourn in Sicily has been marred by "the oil in the cooking" that has "upset his insides" (195) for a month.

Chevalley's part in demolishing the myth of Italian unity goes beyond gastronomy, however, to the fictional basis of national parliamentary rule. Thus, in his opening remarks to the prince, Chevalley makes a slip that reveals the true coercive nature of Italian unification. "After the happy annexation, I mean, after the glorious union of Sicily and the Kingdom of Sardinia [the Savoys' home base], the Turin government intends to nominate a number of illustrious Sicilians as Senators of the Kingdom" (201). Fabrizio declines the invitation in a beautiful and moving reply that amounts to a defense of Sicilian integrity against the onslaughts of imperialist history.

Do you really think, Chevalley, that you are the first who has hoped to canalize Sicily into the flow of universal history? I wonder how many Moslem imams, how many of King Roger's knights, how many Swabian scribes, how many Angevin barons, how many Jurists of the Most Catholic King have conceived the same fine folly, and how many Spanish viceroys too, how many of Charles III's reforming functionaries! And who knows now what happened to them all! Sicily wanted to sleep, in spite of their invocations; for why should she listen to them if she herself is rich, if she's wise, if she's civilized, if she's honest, if she's admired and envied by all, if in a word, she is perfect? (212–13)

Like a neurasthenic who resorts to sleep to escape from an intolerable reality, Sicily has rebelled against an agonizing history of subjugation by denying history, by stepping outside time and sinking into "voluptuous immobility" (206). To accept the parliamentary title, and the implied advent of a new foreign conquest, would signify a retrospective assent to an entire history of colonial submission—a history of which the Risorgimento would simply constitute the latest chapter. The paratactic structure of Fabrizio's litany of invaders, with the unnecessary repetition of "how many" before each name, reduces the list to the kind of sameness that all externally imposed regimes have for their unwilling subjects. As the next name on the list of foreign conquerers, the Piedmontese will assume the same undifferentiated coercive status, joining the ranks of Moslem imams, Spanish viceroys, and Angevin barons in their indifference to the true interests of their subjects.

A fundamental interpretive error underlies much leftist criticism of the novel: the assumption that Fabrizio's *immobilismo* is presented as normative, as the only legitimate relationship to obtain between an enlightened individual and an intransigent historical course.[22] Instead, Fabrizio's abdication is a polemic response, proper to his own social and cultural formation, a specific result of a series of specific determinants, not a universal blueprint for human conduct. Lampedusa portrays Fabrizio as both detached and socially conditioned. As such, he is the vehicle of a judgment that he cannot act upon but that can nonetheless furnish the basis for a Gramscian criticism of the contemporary status quo. As an exposé of *trasformismo* and of the fiction of national unity, *The Leopard* can help us challenge the founding premise of present-day Italian statecraft in its idealized Risorgimento birth. "If writing history means making history in the present," Gramsci remarked, "a great book of history is one which in the present helps the forces in the process of developing become aware of themselves and therefore more concretely active and effectual."[23]

Much has been written about the *smallness* of *The Leopard*, whose restriction to a single center of consciousness and to the few external events that impinge upon it disqualifies the book from the ranks of the historical novel.[24] According to Lukács, however, such smallness is appropriate to the genre, whose purpose is to make us "re-experience the social and human motives which led men to think, feel, and act just as they did in historical reality. . . . In order to bring out these social and human motives of behavior, the outwardly insignificant events, the smaller (from without) relationships, are better suited than the great monumental dramas of world history."[25] Nor is the prince living out his personal drama in a historical vacuum or in times devoid of interest, but in a context of convulsive political and social change to which the protagonist responds with what Lukács calls the "necessary anachronism," or an awareness of historical relations that is much clearer than that available to the men and women of the time.[26] Such is the superiority of Fabrizio's vantage point that he seems to witness history from the perspective of the ending, *sub specie mortis*.[27] This allows Lampedusa to endow him in 1862 with the antiquarian hindsight that his daughters will live out so pathetically in 1910.[28] It also allows Visconti to endow the film with a political double focus that sees in the *trasformismo* of Risorgimento radicalism its twentieth-century counterpart in the postwar neutralization of Resistance ideals.[29]

The work of the historical novelist, according to Lukács, is to penetrate facts "in order to elicit their inner connections and then to find a story and characters which can express this inner connection better than what is immediately discoverable."[30] In Tancredi's courtship of Angelica and their ensuing marriage, Lampedusa has constructed a felicitous narrative vehicle for the coalescence of class interests that came to rule the newly formed state. Angelica's sexual and financial attraction for Tancredi reveals the promise of new vitality and economic means that led the aristocracy to find sustenance in the recently enriched bourgeoisie.[31] Indeed Angelica's wealth typifed the way in which the agrarian middle class preyed upon the feudal estates they so often administered in the absence of their landlords, creating the paradoxical symbiosis between an enfeebled aristocracy and its bourgeois usurpers.[32]

By populating his story with those who *live* history, rather than with those who *make* it, Lampedusa is honoring Lukács's preference for "maintaining" over "world-historical" individuals, for protagonists who are "typical" in that they embody the salient contradictions of their age, rather than for the generals and kings who manipulate events from above.[33] Visconti heightens our awareness of the split between maintaining and world historical figures in his editing technique, which brackets the story with two historical events: the landing at Marsala in May 1860 and the battle of Aspromonte in late August 1862. Garibaldi is the protagonist of this offstage historical drama, which begins with his military apotheosis and ends with his humiliating defeat by royalist forces, marking the death of the Risorgimento's revolutionary dream. Never seen in the novel or the film, Garibaldi is still an important presence—the offstage hero whose tragic fall enables Tancredi to rise in the company of his unscrupulous future father-in-law. By keeping Garibaldi out of sight, Lampedusa and Visconti preserve his aura, allowing him to remain the larger-than-life figure that is revealed to us only through echoes: the apocalyptic ravings of Fabrizio's brother-in-law Màlvica, who invests Garibaldi with the power to extinguish aristocratic rule, and the self-congratulatory declamations of Pallavicino, who boasts that he "saved" the general from his disreputable following.

Visconti had said that his film would be an intervention in the debate on Lampedusa's novel, a defense of the text against its detractors on the Left who deplored its lack of progressive *engagement*. By underscoring the political themes of *The Leopard*, Visconti has made explicit the ways in which the book fulfills both Gramsci's call for a critical rethinking of the Risorgimento and Lukács's prescription for the historical novel. By elevating the Garibaldi story to the level of heroic counterplot, by adding the Battle of Palermo sequence with its lynching of Bourbon collaborators, by alluding to the execution of royalist deserters to the rebel cause, and by making Tancredi's endorsement of that execution the film's final political reference, Visconti places the birth and death of the revolutionary process at the film's ideological core. But this is far from the defeatism with which Lampedusa's novel was charged. Indeed, the intensity of Visconti's disappointment is a measure of his faith in the ability of history to incarnate a political idea. Such a faith implies, as its corollary, confidence that the material world can be a receptor of the ideal, embodying it as Aristotelian nature can embody the very form of its perfection. It is this materialist optimism that explains Visconti's film style in *The Leopard*, which is far more naturalistic than in *La terra trema*, for example. Though the novel offered numerous occasions for the kind of superdiegetic imagery that abounded in *La terra trema*—the family coat of arms, the morning star, the dead soldier all immediately come to mind—Visconti steadfastly refuses to violate the naturalistic flow of images by singling them out for close-ups and returning to them in a cumulative build-up of figurative meanings. His rigorous commitment to naturalism, the sensuous texture of his imagery, and the lushness of Nino Rota's sound track all amount to a faith in the expressive possibilities of embodied discourse. It is no coincidence that so many critics have commented upon the physicality of Visconti's cinema, on his ability to body forth so meditative a novel that Geoffrey Nowell-Smith calls it "a long interior monologue by the Prince."[34] Though Burt Lancaster was imposed upon an unwilling Visconti by Twentieth-Century Fox (his first two choices were Marlon Brando and Sir Laurence Olivier), the plasticity of this former trapeze artist's acting style well suits the film's need to externalize the inner workings of the princely consciousness.[35] The maniacal attention to physical accuracy that has inspired such epithets as "the Tolstoy of interior decorating" in his dedication to the "philology of the set, the pedantry of detail," is yet one more proof of Visconti's faith in the eloquence of the material world.[36] For Visconti, as for Kracauer, the choice to speak through film signifies "the redemption of physical reality."

Wide-angle shooting and cinemascope projection, Visconti's answer to Hollywood competition, gives full play to this faith in the expressive possibilities of the material.[37] Two scenes immediately suggest how mise-en-scène speaks competently of inner states of being. "I belong to an unfortunate generation, swung between the old world and the new, and I find myself ill at ease in both" (209), Fabrizio had said to Chevalley. This existential discomfort is enacted in the ball scene, in Fabrizio's isolation and detachment from all the frenetic proceedings. But no moment is more telling than the one following Fabrizio's hallucination about the devolution of young girls into monkeys through inbreeding. Foregrounded against a crowded room shot in soft focus, a technique unusual for a director enamored of depth photography—Fabrizio is truly "out of it," excluded from the three dimensionality of social spaces. Only as Calogero walks by and enters the room does the focus sharpen—an optical expression of his acceptance in the aristocratic world that sees class compromise as its key to survival.

Since dance is the metaphor *per eccellenza* of social order in its imposition of collective rules and rhythms on the movements of consenting individuals, it is no accident that in the film's original version, the ball scene should last one hour and comprise one-third of *The Leopard*'s entire footage.[38] As in the novel, the ball is microcosmic: it stands not only for the self-enclosed universe of nineteenth-century Sicilian aristocracy but also for a ceremonial reenactment of the entire plot of *The Leopard*, which Visconti said all boils down to the history of a marriage contract.[39] The ball thus constitutes "a forceful means of expression, an enlargment, by use of hyperbole . . . those [pages] summarize the action, are the microcosm, so to speak, of all the conflicts, of all the

values, of all the perspectives of the novel."⁴⁰ The filmic medium is
ideally suited to the expression of social harmony through the kinetic
metaphor of dance, as Hollywood musicals have amply shown, and as
Visconti's many imitators both in Italy and the United States have enthusiastically reaffirmed.⁴¹ Visconti's considerable gifts as operatic and
theatrical choreographer stand him in good stead for the task, as does
the discovery of the unpublished Verdi waltz which makes the film a
musical event as well as a cinematic one. Dance itself retells the story
of the marriage contract, in all its social and moral ramifications, from
acceptance to compromise to inner corruption and decay. Angelica's
effortless and knowing participation in the mazurkas and waltzes of
the day signals her absorption into this society whose very existence
is predicated on such collective rites of self-glorification. What her social absorption implies for the aristocracy—its progressive coarsening
and vulgarization—is made clear by Calogero's sporadic comments
from the sidelines. "Nice place you've got here, Princess. . . . You can't
build houses like this anymore, with today's gold prices. . . . What
beautiful candelabras—how much land are they worth?" Such comments reveal the governing bias of the bourgeoisie in its insistence on
the exchange value of all things, and its refusal to see worth as its own
end, as aesthetically, spiritually, or sentimentally self-justifiable.

When Fabrizio leads Angelica in a waltz that commands center stage
as the others give way to the stellar couple, he is performing an important ceremony of generational and sociological succession. Fabrizio
is hereby conferring his blessing on the marriage, handing down the
mantle of familial power and prestige to Tancredi and Angelica, and
sanctioning this merging of the classes. For a moment, the intoxication
of the dance revives the illusion of immortality that had led Fabrizio to
endorse the marriage—the illusion that he and his class would continue to live as a result of this revitalizing sacrament of unity. "For a
second, that night, death seemed to him once more 'something that
happens to others' " (264). When Visconti's camera pans the faces of
the onlookers, their expressions tell us, in visual shorthand, of psychological agendas thwarted or abetted by this engagement. In a close-up
of Tancredi, Visconti reveals the young man's sexual rivalry with his
uncle. A medium shot of Calogero blowing a kiss to Angelica locates
him among the candelabra whose exchange value he so lovingly contemplates, just as the exchange value of his daughter is being realized
on the dance floor. Two group reaction shots are striking in their symmetrical composition and their isolation of female Salina disappointment amid the general gaiety of the scene. In one such shot, Stella
stands to the right of two beaming dowagers—her face alone bespeaks

The prince leads Angelica in a waltz that signals the passage of power from one generation, and one social class, to the next.

the bitterness of an emotionally starved marital life, brought home to her by her husband's gallant attentions to Tancredi's future bride. Perhaps running through her mind is her version of the "flames for a year, ashes for thirty" description of marriage that Fabrizio had offered to Father Pirrone when approached on behalf of Concetta. In a second reaction shot, Concetta mirrors her mother's expression of chagrin. What Stella mourns in her own marriage gone stale has been denied Concetta a priori: she will never experience the flame that produces such an enduring quantity of ashes. To Concetta's right is Francesco-Paolo, jolly despite the displacement of all Fabrizio's male children by their glamorous cousin.

Choreography becomes political in the line dance toward the end of the ball. No sooner has Tancredi uttered his reactionary rationale for supporting the execution of the rebels than the couple is beset by dancers who swoop into the room, encircle them, and include them in their progress. As the dancers snake throughout the rooms, insinuating themselves among the older revelers still seated at supper, their movement includes all of aristocratic Sicily in the celebration of political and class compromise. Significantly left beind is Concetta, who had labeled Tancredi's apostasy for what it was, refusing herself to make the kind of moral accommodation required to survive.

Perhaps the greatest difficulty in adapting *The Leopard* is the novel's confinement, for the most part, to a single consciousness—one that moves with astonishing ease from cosmic speculations to the minutiae of coffee stains, from reminiscence to prophecy, and from self-pity to enlightened self-mockery within the space of a single paragraph. A lesser filmmaker would be daunted by so formidable an adaptive challenge, but Visconti manages to find a series of cinematic equivalences to the fluid shifts in princely consciousness which the novel's language so deftly explores. I will take as my point of departure Gregory Lucente's superb analysis of Fabrizio's vacillation throughout the novel between disinterested historical insight and *méconnaissance*, between clearheadedness and willed self-mystification. Since his nephew is always the object of princely blindness ("Tancredi could never do wrong in his uncle's eyes" [32]) and is the source of the political strategy that will hoodwink Fabrizio into believing that the old order will survive intact ("if we want things to stay as they are, things will have to change" [40]), we would expect Visconti's cinematic technique for rendering the prince's *méconnaissance* to surface in the film's initial encounter between uncle and nephew.

Following the novel's own prescriptions, Tancredi first appears on-screen reflected in Fabrizio's mirror. "Good morning, *zione* [literally, 'big uncle']!" "Tancredi, what were you up to last night?" The camera stays trained on the mirror as Tancredi responds in a way that doubly reinforces his status as princely self-projection. "What was I up to? Nothing, *zione*. I was with some friends. A holy night. Not like certain acquaintances of mine who were having fun . . . in Palermo." By alluding to Fabrizio's womanizing, Tancredi pays tribute to the virility that would allow a middle-aged man to believe himself still young, while linking his uncle's sexual infractions with his own political ones. "Boys will be boys," Tancredi is essentially telling Fabrizio in anticipation of the strategy that will keep them forever boyish in a rejuvenated social order. The camera finally leaves the mirror and shoots Tancredi head-on as he reports, "I saw you with these eyes, at the place of the roadblock at Villa Airoldi while you were speaking with the sergeant. Nice things at your age! And in the company of a reverend. Libertine ruins!" For this last exclamation, the camera cuts back to Fabrizio, who blots his newly shaved chin with a show of remorse that only barely conceals his true pleasure at this testimony to his masculine prowess. "After all, you're right," he responds. Now the prince moves toward a full-length mirror and sheds his dressing gown to reveal a formal white shirt that awaits the ritual tying of the cravat. "Why are you dressed this way?" he asks Tancredi, whose inappropriate mountaineer's attire so sharply contrasts with the aristocratic finery Fabrizio is putting on. Turning toward Tancredi Fabrizio continues, "Are you going to a masquerade in the morning?" The camera cuts to the young man in close-up, grown suddenly serious. "I'm leaving, *zione*. In an hour. I came to say goodbye." A cut back to Fabrizio reveals an expression of considerable alarm. "You're leaving? Where are you going? What happened? A duel?" The prince's unthinking adherence to the old order, where the only kind of trouble that a young man could incur would involve questions of personal honor, gives Tancredi a rhetorical ploy for justifying political expedience. "A big duel, uncle. A duel with the King." By speaking of Garibaldi's campaign in terms of feudal honor, Tancredi is thus able to "recuperate" the revolution for his own class interests.

The mise-en-scène gives visual expression to Tancredi's double-dealing by positioning another mirror to the right of the young man, reflecting the side and back of his head as he presents a three-quarter facial view to the camera. This lateral mirror, which we can see but Fabrizio cannot, suggests that Tancredi's duplicity is not only toward the revolutionary cause that he joins only to exploit, but to the uncle who stands to be hoodwinked by Tancredi's seeming commitment to the status quo. "You're crazy, my son. To go and join up with that lot. They're all mafiosi and swindlers. A Falconeri must be with us, for the King." With this reply, Fabrizio turns to his own reflection in the full-length mirror, thus linking the family name, Falconeri, and the ideal of monarchy with his own self-image as aristocracy incarnate. Tancredi responds, "For the King, sure, but for which King? Even you've said it, *zione*. If only King Ferdinand were alive. But Franceschiello, God forbid, isn't up to the task." As Tancredi utters these lines, he rises and walks toward a painting of a family tree whose significance will be revealed in his next quip: "So you want the Republic of Don Peppino Mazzini?" At this point, Fabrizio enters the frame and turns back toward the camera to catch his reflection in the shaving mirror positioned just to the camera's left. Tancredi continues, "Believe me, *zione*, if we aren't there too, they'll foist a republic on us. If we want everything to stay as it is, everything must change. Have I explained myself?" Now the intricate relationship between mirrored images, familial hopes, and political opportunism begins to take shape. The small reflection of Tancredi in his uncle's looking glass functioned as narcissistic self-projection, flattering Fabrizio's sense of virility and preparing him for the idea that Tancredi is indeed operating in the interests of class survival. Thus the image in the full-length mirror, incarnating an aristocratic ideal, will be maintained intact by Tancredi's political maneuverings, as will the family fortunes represented in the genealogical tree on the back wall. However, these fond chimeras of the princely consciousness are called into question by the third mirror, whose lateral image of Tancredi is accessible to us but not to Fabrizio, suggesting the existence of other, more ignoble Tancredis whose personal agendas elude, and even mock, his uncle's understanding.

As vehicles of *méconnaissance*—of idealized self-images pointing toward familial survival—mirrors and paintings abound in the film. When Tancredi brings a Tuscan general to the palace to admire the ceiling frescoes, it is the willed spectatorship on the part of a revolutionary officer which signals the family's free passage into the future. It is significant that Visconti uses a subjective camera to film the frescoes, imitating the general's own admiring gaze at this celebration of aristocratic splendor. As the general looks up, the camera cuts to the baroque pantheon of the ceiling frescoes. "At the center is the lightning-bearing Jupiter," Fabrizio explains. The camera moves with considerable dispatch through the ranks of Juno, Mars, Venus, and Mercury. To remind us that this is indeed a subjective gaze, the camera then moves behind a candelabra partially to obstruct the view. A cut back to the general as the source of this perspective is followed by a return shot of the ceiling. "On the other side," continues Fabrizio, "Thetys with all her entourage and Dryads, Apollo surrounded by clouds, and all together they exalt the glory of the House of Salina."

The delusion that Tancredi's marriage to Angelica will guarantee familial survival is ingeniously expressed through portraiture in two scenes surrounding the engagement. When Fabrizio first announces Tancredi's wish to the hysterical Stella, Visconti films the prince against a bedroom wall decorated with miniatures. One painting is of a young woman—too small to reveal any resemblance to Stella. But when Fabrizio throws a huge shadow over the portrait as he snuffs out the candle and verbally browbeats his "Stelluccia" into accepting the fact of Tancredi's social apostasy, the visual parallels to the psychology of their relationship are clear. But the social continuity implicit in portraiture—the concept that the familial ideals of the past will live on, producing new young aristocratic subjects to sit for such portraits in the future—gives the lie to Fabrizio's hopes. For this marriage of Tancredi to Angelica will not promote familial survival but will hasten the Salinas' demise in its failure to produce heirs and its deterioration of the standards of dignity and taste to which Fabrizio's behavior had always aspired.

Paintings abound in the "toad-swallowing" episode when Fabrizio must break the news of Tancredi's marital intentions to a slimy and gloating Calogero. The five paintings, which represent the prince's demesnes at Salina, Querceta, Ragattisi, Argivocale, and Donnafugata, reveal at once the historic grandeur of the family's feudal status and its present usurpation by the likes of Calogero himself. The squalid reality of this engagement is that it brings together "pedigree in search of property" with "property in search of pedigree"—a truth that Visconti reinforces visually by cutting to the painting of once-glorious Donnafugata as Calogero triumphantly inventories the wealthy fiefdoms of Settesoli and Gibildolce which will constitute the landed part of Angelica's dowry. "Lands of the highest quality," Calogero announces as we see the back of his head to the left of the painting of Donnafugata. Turning toward the camera, the father of the bride adds boastfully, "Five hundred acres of vineyards and olivegroves at Gibildolce." As the camera nears Calogero's expression of beaming self-satisfaction we too are forced to swallow this toad, causing us to share Fabrizio's humiliation. The camera next zooms in on the painting and focuses on the shield with the leopard rampant, to the aural accompaniment of Calogero's snicker. In this audiovisual juxtaposition, Visconti offers his own commentary on the delusion that this marriage will stop the downward spiral of Salina fortunes. The scene ends with Calogero's announcement of his own family's nobility, to be conferred as soon as the paperwork is done. Far from the joyous reception that the soon-to-be Barone del Biscotto had envisioned, this news is met with signs of indifference. Fabrizio and Father Pirrone exit in baronial midsentence, as Visconti pans to the portraits of Salina ancestors who, if alive, would feel nothing but contempt for this marriage.

Portraiture receives its definitive gloss in the interview with Chevalley, where Fabrizio stands against a painting of one ancestor or sits with his guest before the fireplace topped by four such portraits, after talking of Sicily's desire for sleep, for oblivion, for "voluptuous immobility." By freezing time, the portraits bear witness to this willed atemporality, this exile from a history that passes over the island only to plunder and exploit it from above. In their withdrawal from the world historical order, the Salinas create their own self-enclosed family universe, expressed by the "constellation of family miniatures" (200)

that greet any visitor to this inner sanctum and that has "in the center
of the constellation, acting as a kind of polestar," (201) the portrait of
Fabrizio himself.

Where paintings offer the illusory promise of familial permanence
throughout the film, their dilapidated state in the abandoned rooms of
the palace's upper stories reveals that they are subject to the same
processes of physical decay that blight the bodies they seek to immor-
talize. As Tancredi and Angelica wander through this labyrinthine
space, they pass images of forgotten ancestors whose portraits have
been ravaged by insects and beasts. In the scenes where the lovers
meander in search of each other, vainly calling out their partners'
names in a suggestion of the ultimate failure of their courtship to produce a true union of separate selves, Angelica stops before a painting,
"The Siege of Antioch." Not by coincidence, the hero of this battle was
the historic Tancredi, crusader and prince of Antioch, who was instru-
mental in ousting the Turks from the city in 1098. Visconti's camera
lingers on a medium shot of Angelica as spectator of this painting,
whose subject matter she probably could not identify but whose momentary blockage of her quest for the modern Tancredi invites us to
speculate on its meaning for their love. If Angelica is looking for the
kind of Tancredi that such a painting would provide, then she too is a
victim of *méconnaissance*, of heroic expectations doomed to disappoint
her. Like the prince who sees in Tancredi an idealized self-image and
savior of the familial future, Angelica sees him as her knight in shining
armor, prepared to redeem his lady from the indignity of her own
familial past.

It is in the ball scene that this pattern of idealized self-reflection in
paintings and mirrors reaches its culmination and its denouement. As
Fabrizio contemplates the excellent reproduction of Jean Baptiste
Greuze's "Death of the Just Man" displayed in Don Diego's study, his
intent spectatorship gives retroactive meaning to all the previous examples of portraiture and reveals their ultimate referent to be not the
familial continuity promised by Tancredi's marriage to Angelica, but
the extinction of the class ideal that Fabrizio terminally embodies. In
other words, the deluded narcissism that led Fabrizio to see in his
nephew an idealized self-image and the savior of his class carries
within it the same fatality to which all narcissisms necessarily lead.
The "Death of the Just Man" simply makes explicit the hidden referent
of all such earlier mirrorings and portraits whose intimations of immortality, through the agency of Tancredi, now reveal their fraudu-
lence. With this final instance of self-mirroring, the prince sees the
earlier mirrors for what they are, breaks their mystifying spell over

Tancredi and Angelica join the prince as he contemplates the Greuze painting in Don Diego's study.

him, and accepts the demise of the self and of the world that dies in his wake. "He began looking at a picture opposite him, a good copy of Greuze's 'Death of the Just Man,'" Lampedusa tells us.

> Immediately afterward he asked himself if his own death would be like that; probably it would, apart from the sheets being less impeccable (he knew that the sheets of those in their death agony are always dirty with spittle, discharges, marks of medicine), and it was to be hoped that Concetta, Carolina, and his other womenfolk would be more decently clad. But the same, more or less. (260–61)

The shift from ekphrasis to personal prophecy makes this less a moment of art appreciation than of self-mirroring, where Fabrizio projects himself into the painting and reads it as a forecast of his own death, whose blend of *eros* and *thanatos* will indeed be realized in the figure of Venus, wearing a "brown travelling dress and wide bustle," appearing "modest, but ready to be possessed" (292) as she leads him "to her own region of perennial certitude" (273).

Because the film version cannot make us privy to Fabrizio's interior monologue without externalizing it in dialogue, Tancredi and Angelica must intervene earlier in the scene to provide the excuse for the prince to verbalize his funereal thoughts. The first part of the scene, in which Fabrizio contemplates the painting in mute solitude, is thus given retroactive justification by the dialogue of the second part, which explains the aptness of Visconti's directorial choices. As the scene opens, Fabrizio enters Don Diego's study alone and in a state of some physical distress—the somatization of his dire forebodings. He drinks from a decanter, sits on a couch, mops his brow, looks up, shakes his head, and looks up again before the camera cuts to the painting above the mantle which has so captured his attention and seems to objectify his inner state. The camera is trained on the painting only briefly, but long enough for us to see its bright, neon pinks, greens, and whites against a black background, and to note its off-center composition that gives more importance to the buxom daughters and the bewildered dog than to the dying man consigned to a secondary recess of the pictorial plane.[42] Visconti then cuts back to the prince, who gets out his glasses to facilitate his inspection of the work. Photographed from behind the prince, the next shot includes his head and the painting within the same frame, where the flattening of planes creates a great deal of spatial ambiguity. There are candelabra surrounding the painting, but they seem to overlap the pictorial space in a way that calls into question their status as images—are they painted or profilmic?—and challenges any absolute determination we might make as to the boundary between the two art works, Greuze's and Visconti's. I can think of no better cinematic expression of the protagonist's imaginative entrance into the painting than this spatial ambiguity, which is resolved in the film's next shot, taken laterally, with Fabrizio's face in three-quarter view and the candelabra projecting from the painterly surface into the viewer's space. When Fabrizio takes out a cigar and lights it with the flame of a candle, the casualness of the gesture suggests the ease with which he contemplates the spectacle of his own death, which "calmed him as much as that of the others disturbed him" (261).

At this point, Fabrizio turns away and puffs great clouds of white smoke into the darkness, when the dance music in the adjacent ballroom stops and the young couple makes its entrance into the study. Now all that was implicit in Fabrizio's spectatorship will be made the matter of a dramatic exchange between the prince and the fiancés, whose youthful indifference to their mortality gives the encounter a poignance that it lacks in the novel's interior monologue. The camera cuts to a dorsal view of the prince surrounded by Tancredi and Angelica, but the center of the composition remains the painting on the opposite wall which draws all lines of vision to it. "Are you courting death?" asks Tancredi in a formulation that makes explicit the novel's constant twinning of sensuality and death motifs. As if triggered by Tancredi's witticism, Fabrizio directs his courtliness toward Angelica, kissing her hand and complimenting her on her beauty. Seated once more, with the camera on him alone, the prince wonders aloud if his death scene will resemble that of the Just Man. When Fabrizio arises and approaches the painting once more, then turns to his listeners and reminds them to repair the family tomb at the Capuchins, a series of reaction shots alternating between Tancredi and Angelica sets up a complex system of spectatorship. As Fabrizio watches the painting and embraces its meaning for his own demise, so Tancredi and Angelica watch him in this vicarious act of dying. But even as Greuze's mourners are more exhibitionistic than grief stricken, more attuned to their own sexual allure than to the agony of their parent, so are Tancredi and Angelica too sexually self-involved to experience another's pain. In this infinite regress of subject-object relations, where objects are dying and subjects within the same artistic plane are oblivious to the moribund's plight, it is only *across* the arts that true imaginative linkage can be experienced. Thus this relay of identifications between subjects in one medium for objects in another implicates us in its logic, positioning us in the continuum of empathy that extends from the Just Man through Fabrizio to the filmgoing audience, and shunning the false histrionics that only mask the solipsism of the internal publics within the painterly and filmic planes.

Adding yet another complication to Fabrizio's spectatorship is the authorial component of the painting, which gives the Just Man's demise a class referent. Jean Baptiste Greuze (1725–1805) was a genre painter whose popularity and material fortune suffered great damage as a result of the French Revolution. Painted by a victim of violent social change, "Death of the Just Man" can easily be read as class death by a spectator himself contemplating the end of an era. In the relay of image makers—Greuze, Lampedusa, Visconti—the film offers a succession of aristocratic authors each contemplating the death throes of his class in an anterior artistic embodiment.

Since Visconti's film omits the novel's postscriptive chapters 7 and 8, including "The Death of a Prince," it must build that death into the ball scene through a series of imagistic anticipations. The Greuze encounter goes far toward discharging the film's debt to Lampedusa's seventh chapter, but not quite far enough. The pattern of enchantment introduced by Tancredi in the earlier shaving-mirror scene, where the collaborationist strategy ("if we want things to stay as they are, things will have to change") deluded Fabrizio into thinking that his nephew held the key to familial survival, requires a symmetrical mirror at the end to disenchant the prince. Where Lampedusa reserved the revelation of Fabrizio's disappointment until his death in 1888, with the final acknowledgement that "the last of the Salinas was really he himself, this gaunt giant now dying on a hotel balcony" (285–86), Visconti dramatizes that awareness in a mirror scene at the ball which matches and undoes the narcissistic projection underlying Fabrizio's avuncular love for Tancredi. The line dance that signals the absorption of Tancredi and Angelica into aristocratic society has just ended when the camera cuts to a lavatory where the prince contemplates his image in a looking glass. Now there is no youthful Tancredian image smiling back at him from the depths of the mirror in fond promise of immortality for himself and his class. There is only an aged, broken visage, whose solitary tear bespeaks Narcissus's own grief that the beloved image is his own. This, of course, is Visconti's anticipation of Lampedusa's mirror scene in chapter 7, where Fabrizio, near death, regards his reflection and finds there "a Leopard in very bad trim" (283). There is no music in the lavatory scene, but as the prince closes his eyes to shut out the spectacle of his ravaged face, the strains of the Verdi waltz, wafting in from the ballroom orchestra, begin once more. The camera cuts to a lateral shot from the left, revealing a side mirror that reflects the prince's back, reminding us of a similarly positioned side mirror in the scene of Tancredi's introduction. It had been this mirror that had called into question the integrity of Tancredi's idealized image as the narcissistic projection of his uncle and as the family's savior from historical ruin. Now the camera follows Fabrizio's approach to an adjacent room full of brimming urinals—the fitting objective correlative for Fabrizio's own intimation of personal waste and class demise.

Retroactively, then, the entire film becomes the portrait of a dying class whose death mask is perhaps most forcefully represented in the celebrated scene of the Mass at the cathedral of Donnafugata, which dramatizes Fabrizio's insights on the comparative longevity of aristocracy and church. The subject had been broached earlier, in the observatory with Padre Pirrone, when Fabrizio had explained that "Holy Church has been granted an explicit promise of immortality; we, as a social class have not. Any palliative which may give us another hundred years of life is like eternity to us" (53). This insight is confirmed cinematographically during Mass when the camera pans from the baroque high relief of God in the top of the apse to rest on the aristocrats ensconced in their pews below. Formal and chromatic techniques

Attending services at the cathedral of Donnafugata, the newly arrived Fabrizio and Stella strike funerary poses that foretell the demise of their class.

speak eloquently of comparative institutional longevity. Though frozen in plaster, the baroque God is all movement and effectuality—he strikes a dynamic pose that promises the immediate translation of his will into action, his authority into deeds that will inestimably alter the course of human events. Such decorative reminders of divine potency only heighten our awareness of how rigid and immobile our protagonists are, and how passive their demeanor. Chromatically, the vibrant reds of the altar boys' robes accentuate the anemia of the dust-covered Salinas, who are reduced to so many funerary statues of themselves by their stillness, exhaustion, and pallor.[43]

This sculptural group portrait, which stands as a kind of collective death mask for the family and for its social class, reveals the way in which Visconti will use portraiture throughout *The Leopard* to define his own ambivalent relationship to the subject matter. In *La terra trema*, the Valastro family portrait had served as a foil for his own neorealist filmmaking, which aspired to challenge the illusionism and glamor of the idealized photographic image. In *The Leopard*, the family portrait is put to more complicated moral and metacinematic uses, expressing the profound contradiction at the core of Visconti's style. Sentimentally and aesthetically implicated in Fabrizio's world but ideologically committed to its demise, Visconti's backward-looking perspective lets him have it both ways. He can revel in the aristocratic art of life while condemning it by portraying its historically necessary end, making the family portrait the perfect expression of such terminal refinement. The static quality of Visconti's film style, characterized by long takes, and indulgent lingerings on flower arrangements and sitting-room decor, can be explained as the filmmaker's compliance with Fabrizio's will to stop time, to freeze-frame this world on the verge of extinction.[44] Some occult awareness of their coming plight seems to motivate the family members to arrange themselves spontaneously into group portraits throughout the film, as if posing for the nostalgic eye of the future. In the flashback that explains how a Tuscan general of Garibaldi's army granted the Salinas permission to go on vacation during the military upheavals of 1860, Visconti's camera positions itself behind the officer's back as he gazes upon the family prettily arranged for his visual delectation. What marks this as an important moment stylistically is that Tancredi turns around and speaks directly to us, calling attention to the camera and violating the prohibition against looking straight into it. "The general has said 'your excellency'—it's his first infraction of Garibaldi's orders."

By finding ways to materialize the workings of the princely consciousness, Visconti has doubly fulfilled his aspiration to "expressive originality . . . not only from the visual side" in adapting *The Leopard*. In his intricate use of mirrors and paintings to trace Fabrizio's course from *méconnaissance* to dispassionate historical insight, the filmmaker has achieved a medium-appropriate rewriting of Lampedusa's novel, and one that constitutes a polemical response to the ideological controversy surrounding the book's release. By emphasizing the theme of the betrayed revolution, Visconti reads back into the novel the Gramscian critique of Risorgimento history so necessary for any contemporary program of progressive social change. If the Garibaldis and Ussonis of history are its revolutionary leopards and lions, while the Tancredis and Calogeros are its jackals and hyenas, then Visconti's film should be seen less as a document of this zoological Fall than as a plea for a new breed—one whose critical intelligence and personal commitment will help realize the dream of Gramscian rebirth.

3 · De Sica's *Two Women*

REALIGNING THE GAZE

In adapting Moravia's *Two Women* (*La ciociara*), Vittorio De Sica and his scriptwriter Cesare Zavattini were able both to relive the days of their great collaborations in *Shoeshine, Bicycle Thief, Miracle in Milan,* and *Umberto D* and to address the momentous change that the Italian film industry had undergone since neorealism.[1] While the antiwar argument of the film and the severity of its black-and-white, on-location photography enabled De Sica to exploit the rich memories of his neorealist triumphs, his casting of Sophia Loren as the lead and his edulcoration of the novel's ideology allowed him to accommodate the industrial requirements of a cinema threatened by Hollywood competiton and eager to please the newly prosperous public of "Il Boom," Italy's postwar "economic miracle."[2]

To begin with, De Sica's recourse to a Moravia novel makes his film part of a sweeping industrial trend. Since 1954 Moravia has been plundered by the cinema, whose thirst for adaptable novels was matched by what Vito Attolini calls the "cinematografizzazione" of Italian narrative since World War II: "In writers like Moravia, filmic language, understood in its attributes of clarity, concreteness, and verisimilitude, shapes not only the prose but the construction of the story, its structural principles: at this point, the transition to the screen becomes almost natural."[3] It should come as no surprise, therefore, that Moravia has had more intimate associations with the cinema—as scriptwriter, as consultant, and as film critic for some of Italy's most influential periodicals.

Despite the highly cinemorphic nature of Moravia's narrative, however, its screen adaptation poses a series of formidable obstacles. The distinction between the diegetic vocation of literature (it narrates or tells its story) and the mimetic vocation of film (it represents or shows) is aggravated in Moravia's case by his insistence on the genre of the first-person *romanzo-saggio* (essay-novel) as the only medium adequate to the radical subjectivity of human experience. Moravia reveals the logic of his generic preference in a telling comparison between literature and film: "The reader who can find at the cinema all the immediate and dramatic representation which he needs, always asks more of a novel: that it also be an essay, or a reflected, mediated, indirect representation."[4] In Cesira, the first-person narrator of *La ciociara*, Moravia has given us a speaker whose constant references to her own story-telling function make explicit the didactic purpose of the *romanzo-saggio*. So often does Cesira write, "I reported this . . . to give an idea of how . . . " that it becomes a kind of verbal trademark whose frequency alerts us to its strategic, metanarrative uses. Cesira's compulsive need to justify her digressions, to state the rationale of her narrative ordering, is not only in keeping with her insecurity as a semiliterate urbanized peasant needing to prove her authority to an educated reading public, it is also Moravia's way of explicitly relating each episode to the novel's overall ideological structure, or what he calls its "thematic skeleton around which the meat of the narration takes form."[5] Of course, Cesira is not always a reliable narrator, and her own exegesis is not consistently adequate to Moravia's meaning, yet the author cannot help but applaud her quest for intelligibility because this manifests the didactic impulse behind the *romanzo-saggio*.

When Cesira addresses "those who are likely to read these reminiscences," she establishes herself as a writer of memoirs engaged in the solitary act of transcribing her reminiscences for a hypothetical readership of the future.[6] Yet the many other references to her narrative function throughout the novel characterize this as an oral performance, not a literary one. Such devices as "since I am on the subject" (134), "as I have said" (213), "You should have seen that German!"(245), and "The subject [lack of sanitation] is not a very pleasant one"(142) conjure up an immediate audience of listeners whose need for continuity and sense of propriety Cesira is only too eager to oblige.[7]

This attention to story-telling technique has important implications for the journey of consciousness that Cesira undergoes as a result of her experiences during the Nazi occupation of Rome and southern Italy.[8] As the unenlightened Cesira of the opening pages whose early marriage to a Roman shopkeeper had rescued her from the abject poverty of her peasant childhood, she had sung the joys of the material prosperity that had blessed her married life, despite her widowhood before the war. The first part of the memoir is accordingly full of inventories, of lists of items in her dowry, of catalogues of household bric-a-brac, of menus, and of food stocks, lovingly enumerated in a celebration of material plenitude. Such listing requires only a paratactic linkage of ideas in which all things are reduced to a kind of ontological sameness in Cesira's acquisitive monomania. But contact with Michele changes all that.[9] The paratactic habits of a mind filled with inventories, catalogues, and lists gives way to the syntactic process of philosophizing, of ordering ideas in a hierarchy of importance which gives structure and logic to the chaos of human events. It is significant that the final inventory that Cesira rehearses is subordinated to a higher didactic purpose. "I remember the list, and I give it here so as to show what people's lives were like in the autumn of 1943" (104). The catalogue that follows, of flour, low-grade beans, chick peas, vetch, lentils, oranges, lard, sausage, and dried fruit, represents the subsistence inventory on which Cesira and Rosetta must depend to survive the winter. As such, it retrospectively gives the lie to all the earlier inventories of food and luxury items whose promise of infinite plenitude is so rudely discredited by historical circumstance. It takes history, and Michele, to disabuse Cesira of the paratactic mentality of those who live from inventory to inventory. The lists disappear altogether from Cesira's prose as she seeks a meaning that finds its justification in ideas and ideals, not in the catalogues of goods that have so betrayed her in times of privation.

Moravia's emphasis on the textuality of Cesira's narration implies a time frame and an epistemology that are typical of confessional literature. There are two Cesiras in the novel—the benighted, self-absorbed widow who experiences the events of the story as they unfold in time, and the memorialist who tells the story from the perspective of the ending. At the start of the novel, Moravia places a temporal and cognitive gulf between Cesira-protagonist and Cesira-narrator, but as the story progresses, their identities gradually converge until they fuse at the end with the climactic revelation of Michele's posthumous teaching. "But sorrow had saved us at the last moment, and so in a way the passage about Lazarus held good for us too, since at last, thanks to sorrow, we had emerged from the war which had enclosed us in its tomb of indifference and wickedness, and had started to walk again along the path of our own life, which was, maybe, a poor thing full of obscurities and errors but nevertheless the only life that we ought to live, as no doubt Michele would have told us if he had been with us"

(339). After the symbolic death by rape, and Rosetta's consequent fall into promiscuity, Cesira is resurrected as the writer of this memoir, witness to the salvific effects of Michele's humanitarian example.

The cognitive abyss that separates Cesira-narrator from Cesira-protagonist finds three-fold expression in the novel. Through verbal foreshadowing, imagistic ill omens, and hindsight, the narrator claims her epistemological superiority over her characters. And though we do not learn of her daughter's rape until it actually occurs, we have been recruited into the narrator's superior perspective by constant flashforwards to the time when all will ultimately be known.[10] This puts us in a strange cognitive double bind where we are implicated in the protagonist's ignorance yet participate in the narrator's condescension toward her unenlightened prior self. The most overt instances of self-patronizing involve the technique of hindsight and include some variant on the *non sapevo ancora* (I didn't yet know) formula to hint at a future doom that will discredit whatever complacency the protagonist can manage in the present. Thus Cesira "did not yet know" (75) how much her money would diminish in value, though she posits all her survival hopes in its dwindling powers. Likewise, "not knowing we should have to live there for a long time" (87) she cleans the squalid room that was to be the site of a brief sojourn, a belated Ferragosto. Similarly, events would soon contradict the refugees' delight in the news of the liberation. "Poor things, they did not know that this English advance would in itself bring us fresh troubles" (235). And when Cesira and Rosetta are riding the crest of their personal good fortune, "I did not know yet how little, in reality, we were to be envied" (280). These dire prognostications are soon confirmed in the rape and in Rosetta's surrender to promiscuity—events that recall a series of verbal and imagistic foreshadowings. Rape, or the murderous destruction of young girls, recurs throughout the novel: in a neighbor's insistence that English parachutists will attack Rosetta but will spare Cesira as too old, in the account of a veteran of the Libyan campaign who boasts that young girls were vaginally impaled on bayonets and then discarded in a heap, and in the fear that a German soldier might massacre Rosetta in retaliation for the killing of his own daughter.

Such forebodings find poetic reinforcement in an intricate web of animal metaphors whose emphasis on sheep and goats elevates Rosetta's ordeal to the level of sacrificial rite. By likening her daughter to a sheep, Cesira associates her with the network of animal imagery to follow: "She did not at all resemble me physically: she had a face rather like a little sheep, with big eyes that had in them a soft, almost melting expression, a delicate nose drooping slightly downward over her mouth, and a beautiful, full-lipped mouth that jutted out a little over a curved-back chin. Her hair, too, reminded one of lamb's wool" (14). Rosetta's emblematic status as Every-Italian emerges in the train scene, where her compatriots are crowded into third-class corridors and compartments, "like beasts being taken to the slaughter" (35). As Jan Kozma-Southall argues in her thorough analysis of the novel's animal imagery, Moravia conflates caprine and ovine allusions so that when a goat is graphically butchered, and Rosetta objects that "after all, I'm made of flesh too and the flesh I'm made of isn't so very different from the flesh of that she-goat" (148), we are reminded of her earlier lamb-like attributes and are invited to see both as a premonition of sacrifice.[11] Rosetta's candidacy for the slaughter is explicitly formulated in the prelude to the rape itself, when Cesira leads her ever compliant daughter to the scene of the impending atrocity "just like a lamb being led to the slaughter, not knowing what is happening and licking the hand that guides it toward the knife" (276).

But the slaughterhouse of the novel is also a church, a setting that makes for intense dramatic irony while opening up larger patterns of interpretive significance. Nor is this just any church—it is the church of Cesira's hometown and the final destination of their journey into a safe, mythic familial past. That mother and daughter should be violated in such a setting makes their assault a triple transgression: of their persons, of the promise of ecclesiastical sanctuary, and of the dream of a return to primal innocence. But situational irony does not exhaust the meaning of this setting, which confers upon Rosetta's victimization the sublimity of sacrifice.[12] As the scapegoat of the events, or as the sacrificial lamb, Rosetta expiates the sins of others. Her suffering serves as penance for those who are vicariously cleansed and pardoned through her ordeal. The most obvious beneficiary of Rosetta's expiation is, of course, her mother, whose sexual infraction with Giovanni before their flight from Rome stood as the original sin that exiled Cesira from the Eden of home and hearth. Yet far more is at stake than vicarious penance for a sexual peccadillo—an interpretation that would trivialize and personalize the historical scope of Rosetta's suffering. To reduce the atrocity to such petty moral bookkeeping would be to engage in the kind of novelized history that attributes the Allied failure at Anzio to a broken engagement or Mussolini's fall to his affair with Clara Petacci, as the protagonists in the novel are wont to do. But Rosetta's significance exceeds the personal in her identification with all those Italians on the train who are "like beasts being taken to the slaughter."[13] As such she takes her place in a long tradition of feminized national personifications, ranging from the warrior goddesses of Columbia, Athena, and Lady Liberty to the harlot of Dante's lament in *Purgatory* 6.76–78: "Oh, servile Italy, inn of pain / Ship without pilot in a great storm. / Not a woman of the province, but of a brothel." Dante's reading of Italian history as a fall from rustic innocence forms the subtext of Lina Wertmuller's *Love and Anarchy,* where fascism's violation of the body politic makes all Italy a bordello, ready to service the needs of its ruling clientele.[14] In the novel, Cesira makes explicit this tendency toward feminizing personifications of the Italian plight. As she and Michele scour the town of Fondi for food supplies, they come upon a madwoman named Lena who offers them her breast milk in the absence of provisions. "That bare breast that she offered to all and sundry, on the high road, seemed the clearest possible symbol of the situation in which we Italians found ourselves in that winter of 1944: bereft of everything, like the beasts that have nothing except the milk they give to their young" (197). Like so much of Cesira's editorializing, however, this interpretation just misses the point. What Lena allegorizes is not the lack of food, but the shameless exhibition of her body and the profligate squandering of what that body can offer. It is the focus on the female body as spectacle and as commodity that makes Lena's example so important, both as a foreshadowing of what will happen to Rosetta's body, and as an index of its metaphoric function throughout the text. If the rape dramatizes the way in which the history recorded in the novel impinges on the lives of its protagonists, then Rosetta's body becomes the quintessential historical text, a tablet on which public events imprint themselves in all their violence and invasiveness.[15] That the rape is an inscription is symbolically expressed when the blood writing of Rosetta's "slaughtered virginity" (289) is exposed to a jeep passing by. Crazed by shock and grief, Cesira parades the crime before the eyes of two French officers, lifting up Rosetta's skirts to reveal the traces of her daughter's ravishment. "I saw at once that the blood had started flowing again and her thighs were all bloodstained, and there was a trickle of blood right down to her knee, of red, living blood that shone in the sunlight" (292).

It is crucial that this rape is also a defloration. Not only does Rosetta's "slaughtered virginity" heighten the horror of the act, it also dramatizes the irreversibility of the history that inscribes itself on her body. For Cesira's governing illusion throughout *La ciociara* has been that the events of the occupation and liberation are reversible—that the evacuation from Rome will be momentary and that mother and daughter will return to find themselves and their world unchanged. Cesira's conviction that they will emerge from the war unscathed finds its expression in her faith that Rosetta's personal life cycle will proceed undisturbed, that the war will just be an annoying parenthesis in an otherwise smooth transition into adulthood. "My blessed child, once this bad moment is past, everything will be all right, you'll see it will. . . . The war will come to an end, we shall have plenty of everything again, and you'll get married and be with your husband, and then, you'll be happy" (21). Thus Rosetta's routine progress toward marriage serves as proof of their immunity to historical devastation. On the very eve of the rape, Cesira has her most intense wish-fulfillment fantasy of postwar return to normalcy in an imagined vignette of Rosetta as a young wife and mother, nursing her new baby at the dinner table surrounded by husband and mother. Not surprisingly, this fantasy centers on Rosetta's body, on the act of unbuttoning her blouse and offering the breast as the madwoman Lena had done in a revelation of the personifying function of female corporeality. What this elaborate fantasy reveals retrospectively is that all of Cesira's dreams for a return to the prewar status quo have been predicated on Rosetta's body—on the return of that body intact to Rome where it could be lawfully possessed and impregnated by a husband who would squire her into a future of familial bliss. The stabilizing function of Rosetta's virginity—its proof that nothing irreversible has happened—emerges in the aftermath of Cesira's tryst with Giovanni. "She at least would be what I myself now no longer was" (21), Cesira consoles herself, making Rosetta's chastity a relic of her own prefallen state. At one point Cesira in fact makes defloration the sign of historical irreversibility when she philosophizes that "no one who has stolen or killed, even in war, can ever hope to go back, afterward, to what he was before—in my opinion, anyhow. It would be . . . as though a woman who was still a virgin allowed her virginity to be broken under the illusion that she could go back to being a virgin again later, by some extraordinary kind of miracle that has never been known to happen" (217–18). Far more than a moral or religious issue, then, Rosetta's virginity becomes a bulwark against history—Cesira's proof that private lives transcend public events.

Given its importance in her psychic economy, no wonder Cesira makes her daughter's body the focus of such inordinate visual interest, provoking the sly smiles of critics who see in the maternal gaze a barely disguised vehicle for male authorial lust. And they are right, for Cesira's is a transvestite gaze, as we realize when she marvels at Michele's indifference to the spectacle of Rosetta's nudity. "I have always thought that any man who *was* a man, on seeing my Rosetta, standing naked, rubbing the hollow of her back with a cloth and at

each stroke making her splendid, firm, high breasts tremble slightly—
such a man, I say, ought at least to be disturbed at the sight and to go
red or pale, according to his temperament" (139). It is clear, in such
passages as these, that Moravia has not entirely succeeded in subli-
mating his own prurient interest in the subject matter, where Cesira's
invocation of an imagined male voyeur constitutes a reversal of his
own authorial attempt to see through female eyes. To her regret,
Cesira will learn what happens when Michele's indifferent gaze becomes Clorindo's lascivious one as she observes Rosetta's body in the
aftermath of a night with her lover, dressed in Frederick of Hollywood
finery. "This garterbelt changed her completely, her body no longer
looked the same. Before, it had been a healthy young body, strong and
clean, the body of the innocent girl that she was; now, with this garterbelt, so very tight and so very black, it had something provocative and
vicious about it: the thighs looked too white, the hair too blond, the
buttocks too exuberant, the belly thrust too far forward. It was not the
body of Rosetta who had been my daughter; it was the body of Rosetta
who made love with Clorindo" (311). When Cesira had conjured up a
sexually interested Michele, Rosetta's body had been the incarnation
of health, hygiene, and solidity. Now, through the imagined lubricious
gaze of Clorindo, Rosetta has lost the proportion and consistency of
the classic nude—she is all excess and paradox, dressed but not
dressed, revealingly concealed, offered and withheld—already expert
in the double game of the coquette. Thus by appropriating the male
gaze, Cesira can view Rosetta through Michele's and Clorindo's eyes
in ways that measure the degree of her daughter's degradation as a
result of historical circumstance. Despite the sexual ambiguities of
Cesira's fetishistic interest in her daughter, Moravia's argument is inestimably enhanced by this pretext for focusing on the body that will
so tragically experience the meaning of history's blood writing.[16]

Rosetta's virginity is not the only antihistorical element in Cesira's
psychology. If her daughter's maidenhood is proof against history, so
too is nature, whose idealization in the world of the novel takes the
classic form of the city-country debate. "All the things that make life
difficult in Rome don't exist in the country," Cesira reassures Rosetta.
"We shall be comfortable and we'll sleep well and above all, we'll have
plenty to eat. You'll see: they've got pigs, they've got flour, they've got
fruit, they've got wine, we shall live like kings" (20). As the photographic positive of which the war-torn city is the negative, the country
is the imagined remedy to all urban ills, from material privation to
psychic insecurity. Significantly, the threat of war finds its most con-

crete embodiment in Cesira's and Rosetta's fear of rape by English para-troopers—a fear that is specifically alleviated by the prospect of urban flight. "But oh Mum, is it true that the parachutists do things like that to women?" asks Rosetta. "No, it's not true," answers her mother, "and in any case, we're leaving tomorrow and going to the country and nothing will happen there, so don't worry" (27). The idealized countryside benefits not only from its opposition to a lived urban re-ality but also from its association with a Rousseauesque nature that restores humankind to its most authentic, primordial self. For Cesira, whose own past is rural, the flight into nature is thus a double return, to civilization's origins and to her own. "I had been a peasant (*conta-dina*) before I had been a city dweller (*cittadina*)" (41). It is significant that Cesira finds in the *contadina* her truer self, and that in distin-guishing the refugees from the permanent peasant inhabitants of Sant'Eufemia, Cesira naturally identifies with the latter, though her recent socioeconomic history should ally her with the other urban evacuees.

Illusions die hard, and when Cesira finds the people of the lowlands "false, dishonest, dirty and treacherous"(70) she simply shifts her ideal into nature's more remote recesses, convinced that only in the moun-tains can authentic humanity be found. As if to fulfill her dreams of Edenic innocence and plenty, Cesira's arrival at Sant'Eufemia coincides with a sumptuous anniversary feast by Filippo Festa, Michele's father, making the mountain retreat a type of prelapsarian garden that spon-taneously offers its fruits for the gratification of all natural appetites.

Just as Rosetta's intact body stood for immunity to history's on-slaughts, so is this rural haven associated with women's nature, with wifehood and motherhood that life, unobstructed by historical contin-gency, promised Cesira's daughter. Nature's power to renew and re-vitalize is seen as a maternal gift—as the breast that nourishes its progeny in its offering of undisturbed sleep, unadulterated foods, and pure, elemental sensations. The three allusions to breastfeeding in the novel reveal how war disrupts the natural order allegorized by such maternal nurturing. Between Cesira's fond memories of suckling her infant daughter and the fantasy of Rosetta herself as a nursing mother comes the deranged figure of Lena, wandering about a war-torn land-scape offering her breast to all passersby. It should come as no surprise that when Cesira confronts her own self-deception, she projects her anger onto a personified Mother Nature as the daughter disappointed by maternal insufficiency. "This was indeed the real country," muses Cesira, "my own beloved countryside in which I had been born and brought up, and to which I had returned, in the perplexities of famine and war, as one turns to a very ancient mother, . . . and the country had betrayed me" (328).

■ ■ ■

The function of Rosetta's body in *La ciociara* and the alignment of gazes which fetishizes that body in a historically appropriate way pose grave problems for the adaptation of the novel into anything but a radically subversive, alternative cinema. By directing a scopophiliac gaze on her own daughter, Cesira is doing within the novel what viewers of mainstream cinema do to women in general, according to Laura Mulvey's pioneering study on visual pleasure and the narrative film.[17] Mulvey's argument that spectators experience a narcissistic identification with male protagonists whose objectifying gaze at the women within the film becomes normative for the audience's own optic has important implications for the adaptation of a novel whose historical discourse is predicated on a female's fetishizing view of her daughter. Nor is it unthinkable that Moravia's alignment of gazes could be achieved in a cinematic adaptation—this is not one of the built-in impossibilities of adaptation from the one medium to the other. The transposition of a diegetic text where the *telling* is accomplished through a first-person subjectivity whose discourse is wedded to a peculiar way of looking does not preclude its *showing* in a mimetic text whose subject also becomes an object of the public gaze. The fact that we necessarily see Cesira in the film does not make it impossible for us also to see through her eyes. But such an adaptation would have to be willing to challenge gendered ways of looking which are typical of mainstream cinema, and thus to forego the visual pleasures of narcissistic identification and scopophilia which that cinema so expertly provides.

De Sica and Zavattini are indeed qualified to undertake so radical a visual realignment, for *Bicycle Thief* had revealed in them powerful critics of mainstream viewing codes. It is no accident that the protagonist of *Bicycle Thief*, Antonio Ricci, should be robbed as he is putting up a poster for the film *Gilda*, whose star, Rita Hayworth, epitomized the female imagistic source of Hollywood's visual pleasures. As a distraction that blinds Antonio to his plight, the image of Rita Hayworth is shown to be at variance with lived reality—a dangerous substitute that seduces us into a passive state of inattention. By associating this image with Antonio's misadventure, De Sica and Zavattini announce their departure from mainstream cinema and from the relay of gazes which makes possible its seductions. Nor are we permitted the narcissistic identification with Antonio which would make of a him a conventional Hollywood hero, the agent of the gaze and forger of meanings that the female image would then bear. Such an alignment is derailed by the presence of Antonio's son Bruno in the film, whose idealizing gaze at his father is discredited by subsequent events. If our temptation to identify with Antonio is reinforced by Bruno's filial adoration, that alignment becomes subject to unbearable strain and final collapse under the weight of Antonio's increasing incompetence and despair. What makes explicit the dynamic of the gaze is the technique of visual cuing by which Bruno had looked up to Antonio for behavioral directives throughout the film. By the end of *Bicycle Thief*, however, when Antonio has abdicated all parental authority in his capitulation to crime, the kind of message that Bruno sends in his filial glances is solicitousness for a fellow human being, and no longer the unquestioning deference of a son.[18]

Thus, in disrupting our narcissistic identification with the male agent of the gaze, and in challenging our scopophiliac look at the female object, *Bicycle Thief* subverts the double source of visual pleasure provided by mainstream cinema. Such hyperawareness of conventional film optics and such an aversion to them make De Sica and Zavattini the ideal adapters of a novel whose alignment of gazes is both iconoclastic and central to its historical discourse. It is therefore surprising that the filmmakers missed this opportunity to advance their earlier quarrel with mainstream visual alignments.

And not so surprising, given the conditions that the film's financier, Carlo Ponti, imposed on the production: that his wife be cast as Cesira, and that the rushes be viewed daily to safeguard her *diva*'s image.[19] To vitiate yet further Moravia's discourse on the body of Rosetta as historical text, the presentation of Loren's glamor required an axiomatic insistence on her youth, thus requiring a prepubescent daughter to replace the voluptuous eighteen-year-old of the novel. Though the rape of a twelve-year-old increases the melodramatic horror of the crime, it weakens the force of Cesira's pride in the chastity of so ripe and nubile a daughter. In the novel, such pride is the mainstay of Cesira's antihistoricism, making Rosetta's defloration invasive proof of history's irreversible course. And though such a criticism might sound suspiciously like fidelity analysis, I would argue that *Two Women* is disappointing in purely *cinematic* terms—setting aside its relationship to its textual source—given the film's bondage to mainstream visual alignments that De Sica himself had challenged in his less commercial endeavors.

Though the English title, *Two Women*, is felicitous in its reference to Rosetta's sudden and brutal coming of age, De Sica's shift of emphasis from filial to maternal body would be better served by the title *One Woman and an Appendage*. Whether our attention is on Cesira as mother or as fetishized love object, her physical primacy on-screen is assured by Loren's star presence.[20] Nor are these comments meant to detract from the power of her maternal performance, whose affective verisimilitude and visual iconography well dramatize the novel's theme of failed parental solicitude. As the patron saint of *La ciociara*, the Madonna presides over a chain of maternal protection that extends from her throne in the heavenly court through Mother Nature to Cesira and, by extrapolation, to Rosetta and the fantasized *pupo* of the narrator's daydream.[21] All this is ironically inverted in the rape scene, watched over by an off-kilter painting of the Madonna and Child, set in the church of Cesira's motherland. It is this ineffective Mariology that lends *Two Women* its governing image in the pietà that brackets the film as Cesira cradles Rosetta in the opening scene and at the end when they grieve together for the death of Michele.[22] Both images are set in similarly centered compositions, and the final pietà is strikingly filmed with a dolly shot that passes through a strange, sideways keyhole to frame the two women in an irregular cameo composition. Gestures of maternal solicitude throughout the film recall the iconography of the opening and anticipate its closing scene: Cesira will bathe, groom, and lift Rosetta in various scenes and prepare a makeshift bed for her before the rape, while poignantly combing her hair in its traumatic aftermath.

But Loren's body invites something far different from the range of gazes that the mother's image normally inspires: primary narcissism in the pre-oedipal child, desexualized distance in the post-oedipal male, identification in the woman or girl. Loren's body is eroticized in *Two Women* by a series of male gazes strategically positioned throughout the film to establish the terms of our spectatorship.

The most important gaze-setting sequence is the one immediately following Cesira's enactment of the pietà, and it introduces the second term of the film's Madonna-whore polarization. Cesira has just gone to request the help of Giovanni in watching over the house and store during her absence from Rome. Despite the squalid setting of their embrace amidst the mountains of coal in Giovanni's fuel dispensary, the cinematography, the star presences of Loren and Raf Vallone, and the alignment of gazes mark this as no neorealist representation of working-class lust. When Giovanni slowly and methodically closes off every light source in this subterranean cave of love, he is setting up a play of chiaroscuro effects to glamorize Loren's frightened yet knowing eyes.[23] Earlier in the scene, his casual, amused expression had sud-

denly given way to a hungry look that had accompanied the declaration "You can ask me anything."[24] Coyly refusing to acknowledge the
erotic impulse behind such generosity, Cesira replies, "I know, you've
always been a real friend of my husband." "If it were for *that* scoun-
drel, I wouldn't even lift a finger," Giovanni replies, immediately disa-
vowing any selfless motivations. When Cesira leaps to her feet in anger, she is met again with the hungry look and the command to sit
down, which she unhesitatingly obeys. Such an exchange suggests
one of two possible psychodynamics—that Cesira's protestations are a
seductive game whose bluff is called, or that she is sincere in her resistance but that Giovanni's gaze implies a set of subject-object relations
that she is powerless to defy. Whichever of the two explanations ob-
tains, the gaze becomes a self-fulfilling prophecy, transforming her
into its ideal recipient, whether by coercion or by disclosure of her own
secret longings.

Predictably, her yielding to this libidinal self prompts the emergence
of its polar opposite in the now-tarnished image of the Madonna.
Rosetta becomes the projection of her guilty conscience when Cesira
invokes her daughter as a measure of her shame. "Never let my
daughter know," Cesira implores Giovanni. "For me, it's as if this
never happened." Toward the end of the film, Michele's more innocu-
ous advances occasion a similar recourse to Rosetta as personified
superego. "If Rosetta saw us, we'd make a nice picture," Cesira tells
Michele as they disentangle from the embrace that a German air raid
has made possible in their joint quest for shelter. The invocation of
Rosetta in moments of sexual guilt serves a two-fold purpose—it reveals Cesira's oscillation between the extremes of seductress and pro-
tectress, and it suggests a cause-and-effect linkage between her own
erotic license and the physical defilement of her daughter. Such a connection is made explicit when Michele equates flight from Rome with
moral flight from the self. "Isn't there some safe place in the world?"
Cesira asks him when the mountains are illuminated by Allied flares
to spy out enemy troop movements. "No, and it's right that there
isn't," Michele answers with obvious personal, moral overtones.
When Cesira boasts that "there are no sins on my conscience. Well,
there's one from the other day. But it's not a sin for which I should
die," she gives her sexual peccadillo moral center stage in the great
drama of expiation to follow. In the film's final scene, as she quotes
Michele's line "You can't escape yourself," the entire tragedy of rape
and murder is reduced to the level of personal punishment for Cesira's
moral lapse. What Moravia had intended as a cosmic commentary on
the way in which history is written on the body becomes a private

morality tale that punishes Cesira for the very desires she arouses. It is significant that Moravia's Cesira is spared rape by the assailant who knocks her unconscious, while De Sica's Cesira suffers the same sexual fate as her daughter. Such treatment enables her to be punished in kind for the arousal she excites, while permitting her a state of disarray that exposes her physical assets to great voyeuristic advantage and enhances her erotic allure.

The memory of Giovanni's normative gaze is kept alive in the film through Michele, whose sexual jealousy mounts with every mention of his rival until it explodes in the disastrous scene of the scriptural recitation. The Michele subplot could be entitled "The Conversion of a Gaze," for it traces the movement from asceticism to a head-over-heels infatuation. What draws our attention to Michele's optics is, of course, his glasses, trademark of the intellectual, whose eyes are re-served for the viewing of disembodied truths. Reversing the Holly-wood cliché of the spinster ugly duckling turned eroticized swan when she takes off her glasses and lets down her hair, Michele removes his spectacles before kissing Cesira.[25] This suggests that it is *she* who has been doing the seducing all along, as an earlier scene strongly hints. When Michele had issued his manifesto of political ideals, he had been met with incomprehension and sexy poses on the part of his listener. The exchange took place during a walk in the mountains—an appro-priate setting for the enunciation of Michele's Rousseauesque faith in natural man, and when Cesira took umbrage at his reference to her as a peasant, he explained, "Today it's a compliment. Today the true bar-barians are city dwellers. With peasants you can begin again after the war. They're the ones who can build something new." "You'll never change peasants or cheat them," answers Cesira, impervious to Michele's meaning. Though both Cesira and Michele are talking about nature, they do so in ways that reveal the ideological abyss separating their views. For Michele, nature is the ideal end to which all things aspire, reachable through education and historical progress. Michele's ideology is thus dynamic and process oriented, predicated on the per-fectability of the human condition within the historical order.[26] For Cesira, instead, nature is *human* nature, a fixed entity that transcends history and reduces humankind to the eternal Darwinian struggle for material dominance. "I don't trust anyone," she declares. Because her belief system precludes disinterested love, she interprets Michele's concern for her as carnal in origin and obligingly stretches out in the grass for his visual delectation. Given her retrograde assumptions about human nature, she cynically becomes the object of the only look that she imagines herself worthy of—the voyeuristic leer whose expec-

Cesira assumes the cheesecake pose reminiscent of the Rita Hayworth poster in
Bicycle Thief.

tation invites its bestowal. For this indeed becomes Michele's own gaze
in due time. It is a sad commentary that Cesira's cheesecake pose is so
reminiscent of the Rita Hayworth poster in *Bicycle Thief* and of the system of gazes which De Sica had so vehemently rejected in forging the
new optical alignments of neorealism.

Even the women in the film appropriate the male way of looking.
Concetta's glance is a mercenary one as she sizes up Cesira and Rosetta
for the profit they can bring her on the Fascist flesh market. Such a
consumerist mentality allows her the following vicarious male appreciation of their beauty: "What pretty creatures, how my sons' eyes are
popping out!" Not surprisingly, Concetta is willing to benefit politically from their feminine appeal by playing the pimp and consigning
the two women to militia headquarters where work in the kitchen
would not substitute for services of another sort. Most flagrant, however, is Rosetta's own appropriation of the male gaze. "Michele loves
you," Rosetta observes. "He's right. You're so beautiful!" Far from the
critical function that Bruno's gaze at his father had performed in *Bicycle
Thief,* Rosetta's merely confirms the conventional view of Cesira's

beauty and makes of her daughter an accomplice in the universal conspiracy to fetishize this body.

Nor are such glances directed singly at Cesira—when a trainload of soldiers and evacuees turn their sights on her voluptuous figure, they dramatize, within the film, Sophia Loren's spectacular function for the collective viewing public. A comparative study of the novel and film will reveal the way in which this early scene sets the terms for Loren's status as visual icon throughout the remaining footage. The most obvious adaptive change is De Sica's addition of an internal public within this scene. In the novel's corresponding passage, mother and daughter are ominously alone when they get off the train. Their very solitude is portentous, revealing Cesira's ineptitude as guide and anticipating the final isolation that will make them such easy prey for their attackers. Forced to proceed on foot and at a loss as to how to carry their luggage, Cesira produces two *cercine* or cloth rings and teaches Rosetta how to balance her suitcase on her head, in the manner of peasant women of the Ciociaria. This procedure, described at some length, functions as a kind of initiation rite into peasant culture, so that in their very locomotion to the motherland, they are, in a sense, already there. Rosetta's instinctive ability to carry the suitcase like *una ciociara* proves to Cesira her daughter's peasant birthright. "She was born in Rome but, after all, she's a *ciociara* girl too: blood will always tell" (41).

This important rite of return, with its occult proof of racial identity and its ominous solitude, becomes in the film a pretext for folkloristic indulgence and spectator positioning. In the film the novel's deserted railroad car is packed full of young Nazi soldiers who help the women unload their suitcases and prompt Cesira's observation that "those Germans aren't so bad." Indeed, her attempt to get information out of them ("When will this war end?") is met with such good-natured charades and onomatopoeia that the Germans seem more like actors in a comic opera than like the melodramatic embodiments of evil they will become as they lead Michele to his death. In the train scene, these innocent young recruits seem as much victims as the Italian evacuees who are also passengers on the same historical journey. Against this background of jollity and fellow feeling, Cesira and Rosetta hoist their suitcases onto their heads in an overt folkloristic performance whose appreciation by the German soldiers is signaled by a burst of wild applause. Far from the private pilgrimage into a mythic, rural past, this *ciociara* walk becomes a public spectacle whose ogling German audience serves as a model for the film's viewers who are thus doubly positioned: as tourists and voyeurs in this land of statuesque earth goddesses. What's more, the performative aspect of the rite has im-

Cesira teaches Rosetta the *ciociara* walk while a trainload of admiring male passengers looks on.

portant metacinematic applications. As Cesira plays the part of *la cio-ciara*, abandoning her city ways for the rustic habits of her peasant past, we are made aware of another level of performance—Loren is playing Cesira, shedding her movie-star sophistication for the plebeian simplicity of her own biographical past.

If this scene establishes the mainstream visual alignments of the film in accordance with the industry's requirements imposed by Ponti in casting his wife as Cesira, another scene implicitly challenges those requirements by stating, in veiled terms, De Sica's resistance to them. This is the scene of Michele's scriptural reading to the residents of Sant'Eufemia, and here De Sica acknowledges and criticizes the industrial dictates to which he is bound. In Michele's obstructed relationship to the Gospel, De Sica allegorizes his own obstructed relationship to Moravia's text, making the forces that block the character's recitation indicative of the external pressures that preclude an ideologically responsible adaptation. As Michele tries to read the story of Lazarus to the assembled listeners, he is plagued by interruptions: a hungry child demands bread, the mailman arrives with news of Anzio, Cesira reads a passage from Giovanni's letter. "You're all dead—worse than Lazarus," Michele fulminates. "Flour, fear of thieves, hidden inventories—not even Christ could resurrect you!" Though Michele's tirade identifies one of the vices that keeps his listeners from entertaining higher truths—their materialism—another obstruction emerges from the mailman's annals of war. "The Anzio landing went badly because of a woman," he announces, revealing the popular need to reduce all historical causality to personal passions. The limited attention span of his listeners, their material obsession and their mania for sentimentalizing explanations reveal why the Gospel's lessons are lost on them. On a metacinematic level, such considerations explain the industrial logic behind De Sica's adaptive strategy. In casting Sophia Loren as the lead, Ponti insists that the filmmaker indulge the public's need for visual spectacle, for glamor, and for the primacy of passion in the conduct of human affairs. Significantly, no sooner does De Sica denounce such pandering through Michele's invective against his listeners' inattention than he backs down by having Michele confess his infatuation for Cesira in the next scene. "I too am dead," he admits. "I'm not honest with you. I love you." This amorous confession all but undoes Michele's denunciation in the Lazarus scene, where death had meant spiritual death—the moral bankruptcy of life lived from inventory to inventory. In this subsequent scene, Michele revises his interpretation to mean sentimental death and in so doing entirely vitiates the power of his antimaterialist crusade—proof of his capitulation to the emotions and of the film's surrender to compromise with the industry.[27]

This is not to argue that the discourse of *Two Women* is totally inadequate to its story's expressive needs. Where Cesira's presence does not exhaust the semiotic resources of the mise-en-scène, the film is able to give felicitous embodiment to the story's psychological and dramatic power. Through the techniques of deep-focus and cinemascope photography, De Sica has found admirable visual expression for Cesira's ideal of nature as the alternative to a war-ravaged historical order.[28] These effects are especially pronounced in the scene of Cesira's arrival at Sant'Eufemia, where an aerial establishing shot maps out the vast idyllic reaches of this natural haven, while Filippo's banquet suggests its Edenic abundance. Cinemascope makes of the chicory-gathering scene a painterly tableau, as deep-focus photography suggests the three-dimensional vastness of the landscape in which the Fascist diehards, Scimmiozzo and the party secretary, wish to lose themselves in humiliation on the day of Mussolini's fall. When the story's dramatic intensity reaches such levels that it usurps Loren's star claims on our attention, De Sica can give free reign to his cinematic inventiveness and offer us scenes that reveal the medium at its most powerful. The episode of Michele's seizure by retreating German soldiers is a case in point. Since De Sica closely follows the novel in this scene, it will be instructive to read the textual passage with the filmmaker's technical equivalents in mind.

The albino leader of a small group of desperate and famished German soldiers has ordered Michele to serve as their guide through the Ciociaria. When Michele's father insists that he take his son's place on the mission, the albino responds:

> "You're too old. Your son will come, it's his duty," and brushing Filippo unceremoniously with the barrel of his pistol, he went over to Michele and signed to him, again with the pistol, to precede him. "Come along," he said. Someone shouted, "Michele, make a bolt for it." You should have seen that German! Exhausted as he was, he turned like lightning in the direction from which the shout had come and fired. The bullet was lost among the stones of the terrace, but the German had succeeded in intimidating the peasants and evacuees and preventing them from doing anything to help Michele. . . . Filippo gave a kind of roar and made as if to rush after them. . . . Finally Filippo recovered himself and taking his wife around the shoulders and helping her along said to her, "He'll come back all right. . . . There's no doubt he'll come back. . . . He'll show them the way and then he'll come back. (245–46)

With the economy necessary to all cinematic adaptations, De Sica condenses a scene that is spread over the course of three text pages into one minute of screen time, much to the benefit of its dramatic effect. Music, whose sparing use throughout the film heightens its impact, begins ominously as the albino tells Michele that it is his duty to accompany his men down the mountain. The sense of threat mounts as the camera appropriates Michele's point of view on the approaching albino, whose menacing presence therefore includes us in its sphere of victims. A cut positions us above the shoulder level of the advancing German soldiers so that we do not share their gaze (such an identification would violate an emotional taboo), but we nonetheless see what they see at a higher angle: Michele striding backwards, screen right, his hands up in total helplessness as he reassures the onlookers with verbal false cheer. The camera maintains its high-angle view but

A retreating German soldier orders Michele at gunpoint to guide his men down the mountain. (This publicity still was taken from a lower angle than the shot in the film.)

now cuts to a position to the right of the onlookers, between them and the soldiers who are offscreen to the extreme right, dollying alongside the group as it follows Michele's progress. De Sica wisely chooses to place Filippo's dialogue at this earlier point in the scene, making his marital reassurances and paternal anguish a prelude to the climactic pistol shot. "He'll come back—don't worry," Filippo consoles his wife. No sooner is his husbandly duty discharged, however, than he gives in to his parental panic. "Michele!" he cries hysterically in a juxtaposition that would be comic were it not for the dead seriousness and psychological verisimilitude of his vacillating emotions. A cut gives us an eye-level view of the retreating soldiers and their guide, while we hear Cesira's voice on the sound track calling out, "Michele, escape!" Though the novel refuses to identify this voice, the film's attribution of it to Cesira heightens our dramatic involvement by making the protagonist its endangered source. We see the soldiers turn around and then cut to what they see, but again ours is a higher-angle view, which

both avoids our need to share their point of view and dwarfs the onlookers who are so diminished by their helplessness to act and resist.
At this point, the gunshot rings out. Cross-cutting between the soldiers who have resumed their journey and the onlookers photographed in high angle leaves us with a final synthetic impression—the
image of Michele's back as he leaves the stage forever, against the
sound track of his mother's sobs.

De Sica's cinematic expressivity is nowhere more evident than in the
rape scene itself, where the narrative requires a transfer of emphasis
from Cesira's spectacular body to Rosetta's newly violated one.[29] Such
a forfeit of Cesira's monopolistic hold on the viewers' somatic attention
frees De Sica to explore the enormous cinematic possibilities of this
climactic scene. A comparison with Moravia's text will suggest the aptness of De Sica's technical equivalents.

> In that moment I heard a faint sound of footsteps and voices from
> the entrance, I turned, and like a lightning bolt, I saw standing at
> the door something white that immediately disappeared. . . .
> Seized by a sudden anxiety I got up and said to Rosetta: "let's get
> out of here . . . it's better that we leave." At that moment I heard a
> faint sound of footsteps and voices from the direction of the door.
> I turned around and caught a glimpse like a flash of lightning of
> something white which appeared in the doorway and immedi-
> ately disappeared again. . . . Seized with a sudden uneasiness I
> got up and said to Rosetta: "let's go away . . . we'd better go." She
> rose at once, crossing herself. I helped her to put the box [of
> canned goods given by British army command] on her head, put
> the other on my own head, and then we walked to the door. I
> started to push open the door which was now closed, and found
> myself face to face with one of those same soldiers, who looked
> like a Turk, dark and pock-marked, with a red hood pulled down
> over his black, brilliant eyes and his body wrapped in a dark cape
> over the white robe. He placed a hand on my chest and pushed
> me back inside, saying something that I did not understand, and
> I saw that behind him there were others, but I could not see how
> many because he seized me by the arm and was pulling me into
> the church, while the others came rushing in after us. (287)[30]

The rest of the passage, up to Cesira's awakening from her swoon,
details the struggle with her assailant, who eventually knocks her
unconscious.

De Sica makes a series of dramatically successful modifications to
the passage. The setting lacks the off-kilter Madonna and Child paint-

ing of Moravia's description, but it shows a blank, ruined wall where the painting should have hung, and it adds the wreckage of a recent bombardment: a hole in the church roof and a huge crater left in the floor. Such signs of devastation (and violent penetration into a privileged space) serve first as ominous foreshadowings and later as objective correlatives for the women's ordeal. Furthermore, unlike Moravia's characters, De Sica's Cesira and Rosetta are lying down for naps when the Moroccans enter, thus heightening their vulnerability to assault. Threatening music begins on the sound track as a large human shadow, surrounded by a shaft of light, appears on the floor before the pew on which Cesira is resting. The light shaft then widens to accommodate a second shadowy figure, clearly carrying a bayonette, who makes a beckoning gesture to his unseen comrades at the door. A close-up shows Cesira's uneasy expression as she rises to fetch Rosetta. The camera cuts to a remarkably eerie mise-en-scène of Rosetta asleep in her pew, while a smiling figure of a turbaned Moroccan stands beside a column and then glides noiselessly behind it. After Cesira rouses Rosetta and suggests their escape, a camera positioned high above the altar shows a horde of soldiers rushing from the door. A desperate chase scene ensues as the camera follows Cesira from the central nave to a lateral one where she kneels down and the soldiers leap over her like so many frenzied rodents. These acrobatics prompt demonic laughter from more soldiers watching at the doorway. Cesira momentarily holds them at bay by threatening to hurl a rock, but the chase soon resumes. What we hear on the sound track throughout this sequence is the name Rosetta shouted at the top of Cesira's lungs. Compared to Moravia's scene, which is far more static in that Cesira is immediately overpowered, the film uses its medium-specific genius for action to great dramatic advantage. The frantic chase builds the energy level of the scene to the breaking point, expressing both the intensity of the women's resistance and the ferocity of the attackers' resolve.

Once felled, Cesira and her point of view are rendered by four cameras, one showing her face in close-up from the assailant's perspective, a second reversing that shot, a third positioned at the side, shooting at Cesira through the legs of one of the bystanders, and a fourth reversing that shot, showing Cesira's view of her daughter as framed by the same soldier's legs. A cut to Rosetta shows her yelling "Mamma" from the perspective of an immediate onlooker whose view is momentarily blocked by the head of the rapist as he mounts her. Upon penetration, the camera zooms to Rosetta's shocked face, whose split lip and staring eyes register the horror of what has just happened. This image then

Cesira tries to comfort Rosetta after the rape in the abandoned church of Vallecorsa.

dissolves, and that of Cesira's inanimate body emerges in its place. Thus the camera makes us privy to the violation that the novel's Cesira missed in her unconsciousness.

The scene is remarkable in many ways, not least of which is its defiance of cinematic convention. The church's space has no continuity—it is a confusing agglomerate of spaces whose relation to each other is unclear, thus including us in the protagonist's disorientation. Also, the subjective camera from the Moroccan attackers' point of view forces us into an unholy alliance of gazes that only increases the transgressive quality of the scene.

The novel continues:

> I remained lying there for some time, almost incapable of moving, then I tried to rise and at once I felt a sharp stabbing pain in the back of my neck. I forced myself to get to my feet and looked round. At first I saw nothing except the floor of the church littered with the tins of food which tumbled out of the two boxes at the

moment when we were assaulted; then I raised my eyes and saw
Rosetta. Either they had dragged her or she had fled to just before
the altar, and she was lying, flat on her back, her clothes pulled
up over her head, naked from the waist down to the feet. Her legs
remained open, just as they had left them and you could see her
belly, white as marble, and the fair, curly hair like the head of a
little goat, and on the inside part of her thighs and on the hair was
blood. (289)

For obvious reasons of propriety, the film omits so clinical a revelation of Rosetta's "slaughtered virginity." That the novel's Cesira lingers
voyeuristically on this sight should come as no surprise, given her
fetishizing relationship to Rosetta's body all along, and given its importance in Moravia's historical discourse. This is history's blood writing at its most graphic; this is atrocious proof that no human life is
above historical contingency. And though it might strike us as gratuitous for a grieving and traumatized mother to engage in metaphoric
thinking at this moment in the action, Cesira's simile of the *capretto*
serves a crucial symbolic function, completing the cycle of animal imagery that pervades the novel and confirming Rosetta's identity as the
scapegoat—the sacrificial victim of humankind's collective guilt.

Though De Sica cannot fetishize Rosetta's body and therefore cannot
appropriate Moravia's discourse on historical inexorability, he does
find a powerful imagistic way of linking this rape to history. When the
film's Cesira awakens from her swoon, her first dizzy glance is at the
hole in the roof of the church which we see through her eyes. From
there, the subjective camera swings down with lightning speed to the
spectacle of Rosetta's inanimate body, bathed in the light that the hole
in the roof lets in. This is a hideously ironic epiphany, making the shaft
of light like a divine dispensation that illuminates the body strategically placed before the altar. Later in the sequence, when the camera
returns to its former position high in the apse, we see the women
standing on either side of the huge crater dug by the bomb that had
pierced the roof. Though the film fetishizes the wrong body and thus
foregoes Moravia's historic discourse, it manages to endow the rape
with an allegorical significance that exceeds its literal confines. The
scene's double rite of profanation—of the village church and of Rosetta's maidenhead—universalizes and sacralizes the ordeal in a powerful
filmic refiguration of history's own blood writing.

4 · De Sica's *Garden of the Finzi-Continis*

AN ESCAPIST PARADISE LOST

At the center of Giorgio Bassani's novel (1962) and Vittorio De Sica's film (1970) is a garden, a natural, physical space so replete with poetic, theological, art historical, and philosophical significance that it rightly dominates the titles of both works.[1] The garden, called the Barchetta del Duca, is, "to be more precise, the vast park that surrounded the Finzi-Contini house before the war, and spread over almost twenty-five acres to the foot of the Mura degli Angeli on one side, and as far as the Barriera of Porta San Benedetto on the other."[2] But Bassani's decision not to call his book *The Park of the Finzi-Continis* or even simply *The Finzi-Continis* reflects as much the intertextual wealth invoked by the garden as its greater euphony. By virtue of this title, then, the book insists upon its relationship to an entire history of textual gardens, from Eden through the love gardens of medieval romance to the enchanted gardens of the Renaissance epics written in the Este court of the novel's Ferrarese setting. This history suggests, too, a variety of literary ancestries for Micòl Finzi-Contini, the tutelary spirit of the novel's garden, in the Beatrices and Mateldas of Dante's earthly paradise, in the Laura of Petrarch's *locus amoenus*, as well as in the Alcinas and Armidas of Ferrara's own Ariosto and Tasso. Finally, the garden constitutes a psychological metaphor for the Finzi-Continis' passivity and withdrawal in the face of Fascist anti-Semitism—a response that invites fruitful comparison with Freud's category of neurotic denial.

Nor is De Sica's a literal-minded transcription of this central textual

Micòl takes Giorgio on a tour of the garden's botanical wonders.

image, whose Edenic and romantic associations are adapted in cinematically appropriate ways. Thus his *Garden of the Finzi-Continis* plumbs film history to find medium-specific analogues for the paradise lost and the enchantresses of Bassani's textual garden, while ultimately rejecting mainstream cinematic convention by disrupting its traditional alignment of gazes. If Bassani's garden is also an exposé of the state of mind that shuts out history and abdicates any moral responsibility for its progress, De Sica's film refuses to be a garden by renouncing any easy withdrawal into the cinematic consolations that typified his postneorealist years. Thus in adapting this novel to the screen, De Sica had to accommodate not only the material differences between the two media but the ideological demands of his own postneorealist agenda. Before exploring this complex process of transformation, however, let us consider the poetic image on which so much of Bassani's historical vision is based.

It should come as no surprise that the archetypal garden of the Judeo-Christian tradition lends its iconography to the Barchetto del Duca, whose first Edenic attribute is its remoteness and its consequent difficulty of access.[3] Enclosed by high walls, the Barchetto del Duca is a veritable *hortus conclusus* that only admits the protagonist into its inner reaches after nine years of waiting—a delay simulated by the textual distances that the reader must traverse before finally entering the garden in part 2, chapter 3. Edenic, too, is the garden's prodigious botanical wealth and variety, which make it an arboreal microcosm in its "lindens, elms, beeches, poplars, planes, horse chestnuts, pines, firs, larches, cedars of Lebanon, cypresses, oaks, ilexes, and even palms and eucalyptuses" (11), so that the five-hundred-year-old plane tree offers a Finzi-Continian equivalent to the Tree of Life, and Micòl's fund of arcane information, both vegetal and human, makes her the honorary custodian of the garden's numerous Trees of Knowledge.[4] As prelapsarian Eden was a place of absolute leisure whose soil gave spontaneously of its abundance and precluded the necessity of work, the Barchetto del Duca is a locus of pleasure and beauty, free of utilitarian concerns. In Italian, the distinction between *giardino* (ornamental garden) and *orto* (vegetable garden) emphasizes its Edenic leisure, as does the topographical centrality of the tennis court, itself a miniature *hortus conclusus* in its fenced-off cultivation of recreational pursuits. Eden's timelessness, its blissful repose in the luxuriance of eternal spring, finds its Finzi-Continian equivalent in the *estate di San Martino*, or Indian summer, which blesses that series of tennis-playing afternoons. "We were really very lucky with the season. For ten or twelve days the perfect weather lasted, held in that kind of magical suspension, of sweetly glassy and luminous immobility peculiar to certain autumns of ours" (56).

The garden mentality is thus, by necessity, ahistoric. It acknowledges neither time, nor change, nor the encroachments that history may make on its privileged domain. Accordingly, it stands as a metaphor for the Finzi-Continis' passivity in the face of the anti-Semitic threat. In psychological terms, such behavior is a function of neurotic denial—the procedure "whereby the individual refuses to recognize the existence of a painful anxiety-provoking external reality or internal demand."[5] Like the garden wall that excludes unwelcome influences, neurotic denial screens out all threats to the individual's psychic equilibrium. As a collective psyche, the Finzi-Continis practice a common art of denial, ignoring all signs of Alberto's increasing debilitation, Micòl's transgressive sexuality, and the ever-tightening noose of racial persecution. The quintessence of Finzi-Continian denial is the plan to improve the family tennis court—a project that originates in response to filial complaints, but that comes to assume thaumaturgic proportions in its promise of an Edenic future dedicated to eternal play, presided over by a healthy Alberto and an untainted Micòl. The film uses a powerful visual metaphor to reveal how dysfunctional this defense mechanism is—how denial invites the very death it seeks to obliterate. As Ermanno watches over the tennis court improvements, the mise-en-scène bears a striking resemblance to a fresh grave site with mounds of dirt piled high on each side, as if awaiting the arrival of the dead.

Though the Finzi-Continis' withdrawal from external reality represents the most extreme form of historical denial, their refusal to resist the course of Jewish persecution is typical of most of their coreligionists whose obliviousness to impending doom took the form of early and massive collaboration with the Fascist regime. Convinced that their liberation from the ghetto during the Risorgimento campaign of the 1860s had been an invitation to full citizenship in the newly formed Italian state, Jews had enthusiastically participated in the civic life of their fatherland. Thus, when the Infornata del Decennale of 1933 opened up Fascist party membership to the population at large, Jewish enrollments were high, reaching the ninetieth percentile in such cities as Ferrara. And though the 10 percent of noncompliants included the Finzi-Continis, such resistance represented as much the family's aristocratic distaste for all partisan politics as its rejection of Fascism per se.

Because of their previous Fascist allegiances, most of the Jews in the novel must practice more subtle and complex forms of denial. Freudians associate this defense mechanism with *splitting*, the "simultaneous experience within the ego of two contradictory responses to reality, acceptance and denial, without the ego needing to produce a compromise between the two or repress the one or the other."[6] Examples of such splitting abound in the story, where characters both accept their persecution and deny its virulence by citing a series of mitigating circumstances. One of the novel's most accomplished splitters is the protagonist's father, who manages to find ingenious ways to convince himself that the racial laws, onerous as they are on paper, do not substantially alter the quality of Jewish life as lived in Ferrara. The ban on obituary notices in the press has not been burdensome because no one of consequence has died in the month since the edict was handed down—only two old women in the rest home on Via Vittoria, and of these, only one was a real Ferrarese. Nor has the ban on phone listings been enforced, as the old directory has yet to be replaced with a purged one, while Jewish employment of Gentile domestic help continues despite its official prohibition, and Jews have been allowed to maintain their membership in the various business and sports clubs to which they belong. Of course, the very cataloguing of leniencies proves the existence and the potential ferocity of the list of prohibitions it seeks to disprove. Like all parodies, the protagonist's father's exercise in denial becomes a backhanded affirmation of the very truth against which he rebels.

Adriana Trentini and Bruno Lattes engage in variant forms of splitting in their response to anti-Semitism at the Eleanora d'Este Tennis Club. On the verge of winning a tournament, the couple is interrupted in midset and the contest postponed until the next day—a stalling device that would allow time for Bruno's letter of expulsion to arrive by registered mail and thus avoid the embarrassment of a Jewish victory. Adriana, herself Gentile and unscathed by the mass expulsions, is incensed less about the principle of discrimination than its style. "Did they have something against Bruno? If so, they could easily have forbidden his entering the tournament. . . . But once the tournament had begun, or rather, almost ended, moreover, with his winning, by a hair, one of the competitions, they should never have behaved the way they had. Four to two! What a lousy trick! A lousy thing like that was worthy of savages, not of well brought-up, civilized people!" (53). For Adriana, mixing politics and sports is "bad taste"(53)—she is far more concerned with etiquette than with ethics and is indifferent to the human consequences of her partner's expulsion from the club.

Bruno's indignation is similarly misplaced. Refusing to address the overarching issue of social injustice, Bruno projects his anger onto the person of one Gino Cariani, secretary of GUF (Gioventù Universitaria Fascista), whose sycophantic desire to please the local leadership and thus further his own political ambitions dictates such anti-Semitic zeal. Bruno's response to discrimination is to give it a name and a face, to reduce it to the level of personalities, rather than to acknowledge it as an example of the larger, more universal and terrifying operations of Nazi-Fascist inhumanity. To contain this experience by limiting it to the malevolence of a single, inconsequential young man is to engage in the kind of splitting that both accepts and sanitizes an intolerable reality.

A more subtle form of denial typifies the narrator's account of his expulsion from the municipal library. Narrated in one of those interminable afternoons spent in Alberto's study, the episode is exploited for polemic purposes that have nothing to do with the real issue of racist persecution. Since Alberto's suite has become a stage for a political struggle between the protagonist and Malnate, nothing said in that forum is exempt from partisan appropriation. The narrator's particular axe to grind is Malnate's Marxist faith in the masses, and he

tells this story not to attack the Fascist leadership responsible for pro-
mulgating racist policy but to revile the plebeian Poledrelli, the janitor
who orders the protagonist to leave the premises. All the victim's bile
is reserved for evidence of Poledrelli's vulgarity: his inability to speak
in anything but dialect, his immoderate consumption of *pastasciutta*
and consequent obesity, his pompous delight in one-upping a social
superior. Like Bruno, the narrator is reductive in his outrage, personifying the abstract phenomenon of social injustice in one despicable
antagonist, himself devoid of power, whose ancillary attributes become the misplaced object of the victim's rage. "However, he, Malnate, should be very careful . . . not to be taken in by the false appearance of good nature on that broad, plebeian face. Inside that chest,
thick as an armoire, there was housed a heart this tiny: rich in folk
humors, all right, but not at all to be trusted!" (113).

In a politicizing move typical of De Sica's adaptive technique, as we
shall see later on, the film reverses the protagonist's splitting operation
by shifting his anger from Poledrelli, the plebeian instrument of the
anti-Semitic order, to its authoritarian source. Unlike the novel's narrator, the film's protagonist (called Giorgio) does not submissively
leave the premises but demands to see the director, Dr. Ballola. As the
film cuts from the library reading room to the director's office, the
sound track reports Ballola's answer to Giorgio's unvoiced *why*. We
hear Ballola well before we see him, so that his feeble explanation,
"I'm sorry, dear boy. I'm sorry but it's not up to me,"[7] seems to come
out of nowhere, in keeping with his disavowal of all personal responsibility for his Fascist compliance. But De Sica's camera sabotages Ballola's attempt to deny his complicity by panning left and revealing the
corporeal source of the disembodied voice of his disclaimer. "Directives are directives," he explains in a formulation whose tautological
equivalence of subject and predicate makes authority a self-sufficient,
self-reflexive syllogism needing no recourse to external principles of
justification. "If it were up to me . . ." "If it were up to you?" Giorgio
chimes in, and though his face remains off screen, we can well imagine
its look of cynical impatience. "Personally," Ballola continues, "I'd be
delighted for a talented young man like you, also for the old friendship
between me and your father . . . [you are] our hope for national literature," but he does not complete the thought, appropriately enough for
a man who is absolutely unprepared to act on his own personal recog-
nizance. Ballola also cannot complete the sentence because he has inadvertently slandered the Fascist cause by implicitly opposing it to a
series of unimpeachable ideals: the acknowledgment of artistic genius,
the sanctity of old friendships, the future of Italian letters. At this

point, the camera pans back to Giorgio so that the viewers share Ballola's discomfort in having to face the concrete object of Fascist racial policy.

In an attempt to divert the protagonist from his outrage and shame, Ballola abruptly shifts rhetorical gears. "By the way, how are we progressing with the poetry? Are you still writing?" Here the personal pronouns are strategic. In the editorial "we," Ballola presumes to reincorporate Giorgio's literary accomplishments into the national cultural arena from which he has just been banished by Fascist decree. In fact, the very next verb reaffirms Fascist hegemonic control in its insistence that the "tu" and "Lei" of second person informal and formal usage, respectively, be replaced by the uniform "voi," according to the Reform of Custom Act of 1938. In the question "Scrivete, scrivete sempre?" (Are you still writing?), the Fascist verbal form used by Ballola excludes the protagonist from the national literary patrimony to which he is supposedly being recruited. At this juncture, the contradictions in Ballola's rhetorical performance reach such a pitch of absurdity that they risk rupturing the fictions of civilized exchange. As he breaks off the interview, the director is placed in the paradoxical position of pleading with his victim: "Be patient, but I . . . ," and here Giorgio completes the predictable excuse. "I know, you have a family. All Italy has a family." In his insistence on using the non-Fascist form of address ("Lei") and in his contemptuous rephrasing of the Fascist slogan "Patria e famiglia," Giorgio commits a double, if futile, gesture of resistance. Where Mussolini's propagandists would make the state into a kind of superfamily whose organic unity and ties of loyalty would find their best analogue in blood kinship, the Ballola interview implies the most cynical of continuities between public and private spheres: that obedience to the one can best be achieved through threats to the other.

If the garden condition is one of exclusivity, of being closed off spatially by walls and temporally by exemption from historical change, then the novel's first gardens are the cemeteries that punctuate the prologue and the opening pages of part 1. Once established as important examples of the garden theme, cemeteries recur throughout the text—in Micòl's translation of the beautiful sepulchral poem by Emily Dickinson, in Ermanno's funerary cult of the Italian Jewish past, and in the tennis court excavations that promise a future foreclosed by illness and deportation. It is the narrator's visit to the Etruscan necropolis of Cevetri in 1957 which inspires the novel's writing—a commemorative impulse whose built-in a priori revelation that the Finzi-Continis have suffered tragic, premature deaths endows the text with a double

epistemology that locates us both inside and outside time.[8] By sharing
the protagonist's mystified perspective and the narrator's ex post facto
omniscience, we are granted a two-fold perspective that informs our
judgments of all Micòl's actions, even her most callow and calculating
ones, in the light of the death that awaits her. Bassani's novel comes to
fulfill a specific funerary function by the end of the prologue, which
concludes with a rhetorical question that makes this act of writing an
exercise in classical *pietas*.[9] "Whereas for Micòl, the second born child,
the daughter, and for her father, Professor Ermanno, and her mother,
Signora Olga, and Signora Regina, Signora Olga's ancient, paralytic
mother, all deported to Germany in the autumn of '43, who could say
if they found any sort of burial at all?" (7).

What Holocaust history denied the Finzi-Continis will be provided
by this writing, which will give burial to the dead so that they may
speak the mortal truths that funerary literature pronounces, from Fos-
colo to Carducci to Emily Dickinson (through Micòl's translation). In
contrast to the architectural monstrosity of the Finzi-Continis' mausoleum, this novel will provide appropriate Etruscan burial in its dignity,
its delicacy, and its plenitude of life. The Etruscan analogy is significant not only for the temporal distance that it interposes between the
narrator and the object of his own commemoration but also for suggesting a certain theory of death which characterizes the narrator's
own memorialist aspirations.[10] "We entered the most important tomb,
the one that had belonged to the noble Matuta family: a low under-
ground room that contains about twenty funeral beds set inside many
niches in the tufa walls, and heavily decorated with polychrome stucco
figures of the dear, trusted objects of everyday life: hoes, ropes, hatch-
ets, scissors, spades, knives, bows, arrows, even hunting dogs and
marsh fowl" (5–6). The spectacle of the intact Etruscan family whose
second life is seen as continuous with the first, accommodating the
"dear trusted objects" of its days on earth—such a spectacle presents
the greatest possible contrast to the fate of the Finzi-Continis, dispersed, dispossessed, and dismembered by Holocaust history. Indeed
the objects that the Matuta take with them in death are full of contrastive significance for the Finzi-Continis. Fiercely functional and assertive, these objects affirm the family's will to domesticate a hostile environment and to shape the world in its own image in opposition to
the garden mentality, which passively awaits history's verdict. So positive and life-affirming an approach to burial provides a model for Bassani's commemorative project. Etruscan self-assertion will counteract
the very *forma mentis* that invited Finzi-Continian doom. Thus Bassani
will proceed by giving his subjects burial in the fullest Etruscan rega-

lia—a goal facilitated by the family's own enthusiasm for the creation of exquisite, personalized domestic spaces.

It is the literariness of this novelized epitaph of the Finzi-Continis that prompted so much leftist criticism of the novel as an abdication of the postwar imperative to politically committed art.[11] But I would argue that Bassani's literary strategy, and particularly his intertextual characterization of Micòl, is what propels us into history, forcing us to take into account the concrete material circumstances of a death that so violently distinguishes her from her sisters in the lyric, romantic, and epic tradition of Italian letters. Indeed, her role as muse, whose inspirational function is predicated on inaccessibility, as Marilyn Schneider so compellingly claims, places Micòl in a long literary tradition of women who had to die to inspire conversions (and the impulse to write about them) in their poet-lovers.[12] But *donne angelicate* invariably die natural deaths, expiring quietly of disease or childbirth in ways that do not shatter our calm. Micòl, instead, dies the most unnatural death imaginable, a fact which Bassani relegates to the extranarrative apparatus of the prologue and epilogue because it has no place in a story about a stilnovist lady who inspires a conversion and a memorialist writing. "My story with Micòl Finzi-Contini ends here," the narrator concludes, because such a fiction, by dint of its literary pedigree, cannot accommodate a death whose unnaturalness would derail the poet's journey toward personal, lyric fulfillment. But this is precisely Bassani's point in juxtaposing two such discordant genres as the novel of sentimental education and that of Holocaust chronicle. It is this juxtaposition that propels us into history and keeps us there throughout the course of the entire narration.[13]

There is a second literary tradition that informs the novel and provides an equally powerful push toward historical consciousness, though it offers sharply contrastive analogues to the figure of Micòl. Indeed no "garden" novel so self-consciously set in Ferrara could fail to acknowledge the enchanted gardens of the *Orlando furioso* and the *Gerusalemme liberata*, whose Alcina and Armida each serve to divert their warrior-lovers from military pursuits. Though devoid of the moralizing Renaissance judgment of these false gardens, which exploit their Edenic exemplar by manipulating the gap between appearance and essence, Bassani's text nonetheless recognizes the mortal danger they pose as temptations to withdraw from history and embrace their invitation to oblivion.[14] Micòl, like Alcina or Armida, entices the narrator into the garden of historical forgetfulness where, like the crusading knight, he sheds his armor and ignores the inevitable signs of impending doom. Bewitched by this enchantress, the narrator is lulled

into the same ahistorical stupor that keeps the Finzi-Continis from taking the necessary steps to stave off Apocalypse, or at least to escape it.
Significantly, the moment of disenchantment, when the spell is broken
and the protagonist is freed from bondage to his erotic obsession, coincides with his return to historic consciousness. As the narrator's sexual curiosity leads him toward the Hütte where he is sure that Micòl
and Malnate are trysting, his summons to the watchdog, Jor, meets an
unexpected response.

> But then, as if in reply, a faint sound, heartsick, almost human,
> suddenly arrived from very far away, through the night air. I rec-
> ognized it at once: it was the old, beloved voice of the clock in the
> square, striking the hours and the quarter hours. What was it say-
> ing? It was saying that, once again, it had grown very late, that it
> was foolish and wicked, on my part, to continue torturing my
> father in this way, who, surely, also that night, concerned because
> I hadn't come home, was unable to fall asleep: and that finally it
> was time for me to resign myself. Truly. Forever. (197)

What breaks the protagonist's spell is the call of time, and the fact that
it issues from the piazza clock makes this an intensely public voice, the
collective voice of the *vivere civile* which he had so long ago ceased to
hear in his romantic monomania. The weakness of this voice, and the
distance it must traverse, is a measure of just how far the protagonist
has withdrawn from the public sphere, but the fact that the sound is
old and dear makes its summons a return and a recuperation of lost
values. This disenchantment is a freedom not only from erotic obsession but also from its attendent self-absorption, so that now the narrator is able to participate in another's suffering and to take responsibility for its alleviation. It is his father's voice, then, which calls him
back to the world of public accountability in the name of the history
that threatens the garden from without.

But the protagonist is not the only character to suffer a disenchantment that banishes him from an illusory paradise, for the father who
calls him back to the public sphere must himself undergo a painful
reckoning. "In life," his father tells him,

> if one wants to seriously understand how the world works, he
> *must* die, at least once. And, since this is the rule, better to die
> young, when you still have so much time ahead of you to pull
> yourself together and resuscitate. . . . To understand, when you're
> old, is bad, much worse. What's to be done then? There's no time
> left to start over again from the beginning, and our generation has
> made so many mistakes! (190–91)

In this confession, the father explicitly compares his political disappointments with his son's romantic ones. Blind Fascist allegiance and adolescent infatuation are both gardens that benumb the critical intelligence and paralyze the will to act, so that only the death of the deceived self can insure survival. Critics who fault the novel's withdrawal into sentimental trivialities, or who argue for the irrelevance of the love plot to the persecution chronicle, fail to see the convergence of political and romantic themes in this climactic father-son encounter that reveals, retrospectively, how the romantic narrative has functioned allegorically for the Jewish "garden" mentality all along, signifying the historical obliviousness that had allowed the Jews to suspend their disbelief in Fascist betrayal.[15] It is significant that Bassani's protagonist makes his nocturnal garden visit *after* reconciling with his father, as if his parent's admission of political disenchantment were necessary to the protagonist's act of self-emancipation. The fact that the Micòl-Malnate tryst is the protagonist's *self-generated* fantasy reveals the protagonist's psychological readiness to experience the liberating effects of the primal scene in the Hütte.

De Sica's film has been faulted for its explicit rendering of the sexual epiphany that the novel's protagonist fantasizes but never verifies. Such explicitness has been seen as a surrender to the medium's voyeuristic appeal and as an excuse for gratuitous erotic display. But I would argue that the scene is eminently justifiable as a cinematic expression of the novel's enchantment-disenchantment theme, done in a medium-appropriate language that brilliantly approximates Bassani's intertextual technique. De Sica's strategy is to find cinematic equivalents of the Armidas and Alcinas of Renaissance literary history, and he does so in the femmes fatales of the prewar film industry, the enchantresses and seductresses of the silver screen who epitomize the narcotic, diversionary power of Hollywood cinema. Several critics have compared Dominique Sanda's performance in *The Garden of the Finzi-Continis* to that of the young Greta Garbo, and I think that Joseph von Sternberg's fetishized treatment of Marlene Dietrich is also a model for Micòl's representation.[16] Dietrich's influence is especially powerful in the primal scene, whose rhetoric of disenchantment warrants close visual analysis.

It is night when Giorgio climbs the garden wall in a final desperate attempt to reach Micòl. As he passes all the familiar landmarks—the tennis court, the *magna domus*, the Hütte—Giorgio finds them transformed by the night into ominous signs of the spectacle that awaits him. The light issuing from Micòl's bedroom window is just such a sign—it directs his gaze to the Hütte where Jor's custodial presence acts on him with the force of revelation. De Sica's camera zooms in on the dog and cuts back to Giorgio's somber expression as the music stops and is replaced by the portentous sound of hooting owls. After Giorgio runs to the Hütte, we see him from within, shot through the grating on the window, whose constrictive framing and protective bars provide a perfect visual metaphor for his psychic enslavement to obsession. A cut shows us what Giorgio himself has just seen: Micòl in eery chiaroscuro, her illuminated face tilted upward in revery, her lower body enveloped in shadow. After another cut to Giorgio, the camera returns to Micòl as her sight line converges with his, signaling her awareness of his presence. At this point Micòl throws off her covering, and the camera pans to Malnate's face, asleep in profile, softly illuminated. Heightening Micòl's drama of self-disclosure, she turns on the light, exhibiting the cold, clinical beauty of her naked torso. But the cruelty of this exhibition is not unalloyed—by shooting Micòl through the same window bars that had figured in Giorgio's erotic entrapment, De Sica's camera denies her the status of free agent. Herself incapable of intimacy—victim of elaborate psychic defenses or of a tragic foreknowledge that precludes sentimental attachments—she will be consigned to a series of future incarcerations: deportation centers, cattle cars, and finally, Dachau or Buchenwald. Thus the climactic close-up of Micòl, framed by window bars that anticipate her doom, is a powerful representational paradox. On the one hand, she is the archetypal femme fatale, the diva who visits destruction upon others but herself remains unscathed, while on the other hand, she is history's quintessential victim, the innocent object of Nazi genocidal rage.

But the demystification of the diva is not the only unmasking that occurs in this scene. Though it is Micòl who is literally unmasked in her nudity, it is she who unmasks Giorgio by switching on the light, throwing off her covering, and returning his gaze, making explicit her status as visual spectacle, and his as voyeur. By shattering his illusion of invisibility and reversing the subject-object relationship, Micòl breaks the spell of narcissistic projection on which Giorgio's erotic fantasy is built. The return gaze, along with the sight of a nudity that preempts the need for imaginative speculation, forces Giorgio to accept that Micòl is indeed *other*, a separate subject able to make him, in turn, into its object of consciousness.[17] In her cold, stony beauty, Micòl is the Medusa who depetrifies her lover by breaking the trance of her sensual appeal even as that appeal is most fully displayed. Her return gaze also has important implications for Micòl's relationship to conventional feminine portrayals in film. If visual pleasure in mainstream cinema derives from viewer identification with an active male agent who in turn directs a fetishizing look on the passive female object of desire, then any interruption of such alignments will challenge our complacency and call into question the traditional systems of representation on which our spectatorship is based.[18] It is significant that Micòl reverses the conventional alignment of gazes at the moment when she is most diva, when her representation comes closest to the image of the fetishized Hollywood star. With her return gaze, Micòl renounces her membership in the sisterhood of cinematic sirens and its attendant narrative invulnerability. "There is always a certain excessiveness, a difficulty associated with women who appropriate the gaze, who insist on looking," writes Mary Ann Doane. "Woman as subject of the gaze is clearly an impossible sign," and as a result, such a woman either takes off her glasses or gets punished.[19] The second, tragically, is Micòl's fate—a fate whose foreknowledge may be precisely what compels her to disenchant Giorgio, to banish him from her false paradise and liberate his energies to act in self-defense.

De Sica's iconoclasm in the primal scene is also a moral *prise de position*. Like the novel, which reveals the dangers hidden in the garden mentality, De Sica's film will not be a garden—it will refuse the easy escapist pleasures so expertly provided by the "cinema of consolation" (including his own postneorealist production). Indeed, the temptation to make a "garden" film is there in the lush musical score composed by the director's son, Manuel, in the visual appreciation of the Finzi-Continis' botanical wealth, in the elegiac treatment of 1930s-style dress, decor, and taste captured by the sepia tones of the photography and the recurrence of such pop music as "Sentimental over You," and in the poignant spectacle of a youth for which there will be no old age.[20] The film could easily wallow in sentimentality, nostalgia, and a self-pity that identifies with the victims and abdicates any responsibility for their historic plight.[21] But the film renounces its own temptation to escapism and pleasurable withdrawal by insisting on the cinema's realist vocation—not in any literal, documentarist sense but in the moral imperative, enshrined by neorealism, to historical accountability.[22] Film's mission, according to the neorealists, is not only passively to record reality but actively to forge it by enlightening and arousing the public to undertake corrective social action. In filmic revisitations of Fascism and war, the realist purpose is twofold: to reveal the hidden continuities between present and past in order to counteract any tendency to disown Fascist history, and to instill a sense of personal responsibility that precludes the kind of moral abdication required for authoritarian control. In an interview with Charles Thomas Samuels, De Sica acknowledged the moralist impulse that drew him

to Bassani's novel and explicitly contrasted his film to the previous
"consolatory" productions for which he is now seeking absolution.
"After the disaster of *Sunflower* [a Carlo Ponti enterprise starring Loren
and Mastroianni] I wanted to make a true De Sica film, made just as I
wanted it. I accepted this subject because I intimately feel the Jewish
problem. I myself feel shame because we all are guilty of the death of
millions of Jews . . . I wanted, out of conscience, to make this film,
and I am glad I made it."[23]

When Giorgio says to his father early in the film, "We stood by si-
lently when it wasn't happening to us," his indictment of public tolerance for persecution explains De Sica's own return to a cinema of
moral accountability. Given this ethical impulse to make *The Garden of
the Finzi-Continis* it should come as no surprise that De Sica would shift
Bassani's emphasis from inside to outside the garden, where the Holocaust chronicle takes place. This change in emphasis has important
consequences for the comparative structuring of novel and film, for it
requires that the circular movement of the text be replaced by the film's
linearity, thus riveting our attention on the *what* of history, on its relationship of cause and effect, and on its sequential unfolding of Holocaust logic. The novel, instead, inscribes its end in its beginning so
that our curiosity about plot is replaced by an interest in the process
by which *then* becomes *now*, by which persons and events become
commemorative texts. For example, the passage at the opening of
part 1, chapter 6, arrests the narrative flow in order to foreground the
novelist's act of imaginative reevocation. "How many years have gone
by since that far-off afternoon in June? More than thirty. Nevertheless,
if I close my eyes, Micòl Finzi-Contini is still leaning over the wall of
her garden looking at me, and speaking to me" (33). Such a stop-action
technique serves to call our attention to the process of writing itself
and to the back-and-forth movement of consciousness which produces
the first-person narration.

Bassani's repudiation of the film is well known, and one of his quar-
rels with it concerns De Sica's failure to honor the novel's twofold temporality. As the collaborator on an earlier version of the screenplay that
was radically modified, to Bassani's great chagrin, the novelist had included a series of black-and-white flashforwards of the roundup of
Ferrarese Jews following the Nazi takeover of September 8, 1943.[24]
Such a technique would have served to remind the viewers of the narrator's ex post facto perspective, while it would have obviated the need
to include such obvious didactic devices as the little Nazi flag on the
basket of the newsboy's bicycle in the scene of Giorgio's fleeting encounter with Bruno Lattes. But, with the exception of the film's flash-

backs to 1929, De Sica chooses to respect the time-space continuum of the realists' code and to focus our attention on the *what* of Holocaust history, rather than on the *how* of its representation. In the two scenes where De Sica makes explicit his cinematic self-consciousness, the net effect is less to dramatize the artistic process than to emphasize its historical-moral accountability. Appropriately, the two scenes are set in a movie house, and each insists on the relevance of what is occurring on-screen to what is transpiring in the streets. In the first such metacinematic episode, Giorgio and Malnate witness a newsreel of burning wreckage along with footage of Hitler and Goebbels haranguing the German masses, followed by clips of Mussolini's attempts to imitate his Nazi exemplars. Unable to restrain his contempt, Giorgio erupts in a string of invective that provokes his viewing neighbors' irritation. "Dirty Jew," they retaliate, and when a scuffle breaks out, Malnate intervenes to remove Giorgio from the fray. A second scene in the same movie house has far more sinister consequences. Now, the wartime chronicle depicted in the newsreel has as its off-screen counterpart the handcuffing and arrest of Bruno Lattes on the theater floor.

Because De Sica critiques the garden mentality from without, whereas Bassani does so from within, the film must meet its obligations to history by fully representing the events that Bassani merely adumbrates in the prologue and epilogue. Thus, Alberto's death and funeral are dramatized, as are the signs that foretell disaster: the concentration camp reports at the pensione in Grenoble, Mussolini's declaration of war, the roundup of Lattes, the ceremonial eviction of the Finzi-Continis, and their final wait for deportation.[25] It is in this scene that De Sica announces his definitive departure from the cinematic "garden" of consolation by literally opening out his film to universal history. He does so by photographing Micòl and her sobbing grandmother against the background of a map of the world in the classroom where they are being held for detention. The grandmother's weeping expresses the family members' collective grief at a paradise forever lost, and their entrance into a global order whose worst iniquities will be visited upon them. The figure of Micòl in this scene is of surpassing importance to an interpretation of De Sica's "antigarden" strategy in adapting Bassani's text. Her unclothed diva image in the Hütte, where a profusion of soft, blond curls had framed a face of exceeding glamor, has given way to a chastened figure of grief and sobriety in the black-clad, severely coiffed Micòl of successive scenes: those of Alberto's death and funeral and of her farewell to the house on the eve of deportation. It is as if Micòl's disenchantment of Giorgio in the Hütte had

The world map in the schoolroom where Micòl and her grandmother await
deportation marks the Finzi-Continis' definitive exile from Eden.

occasioned her own imagistic transformation, and now the fetishized
siren becomes the *mater addolorata* who cradles her grandmother, in-
fantilized by old age and grief, in the pietà pose reminiscent of Cesira's
in the concluding shots of *Two Women*. So radical a change of feminine
iconography cannot help but have metacinematic implications for a
film that rejects the "garden" of conventional visual pleasure for a rigorous confrontation with Holocaust chronicle.

The film's last flashback occurs in this schoolroom setting—it is
Micòl's childhood memory of completing and submitting her final
exam as a private student and skipping off in the relief of its aftermath. Through this memory of social privilege and academic success, Micòl reexperiences the essence of the garden condition—perfect
childhood innocence and bliss preserved intact within the sanctuary
of memory—just as she is most violently torn away from its protective
confines. In this juxtaposition between garden oblivion and present
historical consciousness, between the Finzi-Continis' private Eden and

this schoolroom map of the world, lies the difference between what De Sica's film could have been and what it is. In that comparison, the filmmaker was able to revisit and subsume an entire cinematic career, dedicated alternately to crowd-pleasing exercises in entertainment and to uncompromising explorations of social injustice. "I am happy that I made it," De Sica told Samuels of *The Garden of the Finzi-Continis*, "because it brought me back to my old noble intentions." [26]

It is in his adaptation of the novel's two seders, or Passover suppers, that De Sica gives powerful voice to his "old noble intentions." The narrator's seder is described with direct reference to the genocide that awaits most of the guests at this celebration. "It was not a happy supper," the protagonist tells us of his own family's holiday observance.

> Though set with great care, indeed, for this very reason, the table in the breakfast room had taken on an appearance quite similar to the one it presented on the evenings of Kippur, when it was prepared only for Them, for the family dead, whose bones lay there, in the cemetery, down at the end of Via Montebello, and yet They were quite present here, in spirit and in effigy. Here, in their places, we were seated, the living. But our number reduced, compared to the past, and no longer happy, laughing, vociferous, but sad and pensive like the dead. . . . I look at uncles and cousins, most of whom, a few years later, would be swallowed up by German crematory ovens: they didn't imagine, no surely not, that they would end in that way, but all the same, already, that evening, even if they seemed so insignificant to me, their poor faces surmounted by their little bourgeois hats or framed by their bourgeois permanents, even if I knew how dull-witted they were, how incapable of evaluating the real significance of the present or of reading into the future, they seemed to me already surrounded by the same aura of mysterious, statuary fatality that surrounds them now, in my memory. (124–25) [27]

De Sica's scene begins on a far more festive note, but when this jollity gives way to collective paranoia, the change provides a sinister commentary on the Nazi-Fascist threat. Unlike the sad little breakfast room where the narrator's supper takes place, De Sica's brilliantly lit dining room has a table covered in white, surrounded by guests singing a traditional postseder song. The scene opens with a dolly shot whose movements in either direction around the festive table keep the space as animated as is its company. When the camera finally pivots to reveal Giorgio to the right, a telephone's ring interrupts the song and beckons him to a booth in the adjoining room. Intercut with close-ups of Giorgio's frustrated and repeated *prontos* are shots of the guests whose chanting subsides with each increasingly menacing ring. After the second prank call, Giorgio returns to the table to learn that his uncle has also been the victim of such harassments. When the third call comes, the singing stops entirely as father, uncle, and Giorgio all turn their heads in alarm. A cut returns us to the now familiar booth where Giorgio's angry *pronto* modulates into a relieved and delighted "oooehi, Alberto!" A collective sigh of relief issues from the guests, who enthusiastically return to their song, which happens to be a musical rendition of a counting game used to teach children Old Testament lore through numbers. The juxtaposition of scriptural numerology with the increasing tally of harassing phone calls is not without a bitter appropriateness. As Andrea Gurwitt insightfully observes, the novel's direct confrontation with impending Nazi horror in this scene finds its filmic counterpart in these menacing phone calls, which serve as powerful dramatic devices for introducing the public threat into the privacy of the home.[28]

The scene of the Finzi-Contini seder is one of far greater formality than that of Giorgio's family, with a burnished wood table stripped of its white cloth, crowned by a crystal chalice. Prophecy, thus visualized, becomes the scene's central dramatic motif. Whereas in Giorgio's house the guests remained anonymous, here the camera plays the part of the gracious host, introducing us to the celebrants individually by slowly panning each one in close-up as he or she greets the new arrival.[29] After a polite interrogation of Giorgio, the company turns its attention to the chalice, whose beauty, luminosity, and centrality to the mise-en-scène suggest important analogies to Micòl herself. Like Micòl, it hails from Venice, and like her (dazzlingly blond and dressed in white), the chalice is the only other radiant element in this shadowy setting. Surrounded by a ring of cards that depend upon it for meaning, the chalice suggests Micòl's own solar centrality to the family system that orbits around her. As Alberto summarizes the chalice's oracular performance for Giorgio, the camera constantly cuts to Micòl, though she remains wordless throughout this segment. When Alberto predicts that the war will end with the total victory of the forces for good, a cut to Micòl's face coincides with the sound track's *concludere* before the camera returns to her brother and then zooms to the chalice.

The scene ends with a visual statement of Giorgio's insubstantial place in the Finzi-Continis' universe as the final shot reveals his face reflected in the polished wood of the table, suspended like a pale moon inside the ring of cards surrounding the goblet. For Giorgio will indeed be spared the ordeal of redemptive sacrifice that awaits the

Finzi-Continis. In the play of light and shadows and the imagistic link-age of Micòl with the prophetic theme of the film, De Sica establishes her as the Pascal lamb, the sacrificial victim of World War II history. The darkness is the racist policy whose shadows have already cast themselves in this room in the report of academic discrimination that Micòl suffered in Venice, and in Ermanno's exhortation to Giorgio to hurry and complete his degree before it's too late. From an ex post facto perspective, Micòl's radiance in that darkness is both poignant and auspicious—poignant in its transience, auspicious in its anticipa-tion of "the total victory of the forces of good." It is this faith in the exemplary power of human suffering to elevate mass consciousness that underlies neorealist filmmaking and attracts De Sica to the novel as a way of returning to his earlier "noble intentions." Micòl's sacri-fice thus serves a double salvific purpose, redeeming history as the arena for human salvation and enabling De Sica to reclaim his neoreal-ist past.

For Bassani, there is no atonement for the Fall in the historic order. Paradise can only be regained through art, which alone can restore the primal unity left behind in Eden. Where De Sica's film bears witness to the history whose future course can be entrusted to an enlightened and progressive mass public, Bassani's novel can only be a monument, a purely imaginative reevocation of lost opportunities and lost lives. It is Micòl's language, with its disparity between meaning and expres-sion, which prompts the protagonist's concluding meditations on the limits of his own commemorative act. "And as these, I know, were only words, the usual, deceitful and desperate words that only a true kiss would have prevented her from uttering: let them, and only them, seal here what little the heart has been able to remember" (197) (the Italian *ricordare* also means "to record"). In the contrast between the novel's ending, which focuses self-reflexively on the artistic process of commemoration, and De Sica's final shot of the empty garden, whose lifeless confines conjure up Auschwitz, lies the key to the film's adap-tive strategy. This is De Sica's cinematic equivalent of Bassani's com-posite garden-cemetery image, for the film's farewell montage of the Barchetto del Duca includes a shot of the front gate closed with lock and chain and ends with footage of the unkempt tennis court sur-rounded by a fence resembling the barbed wire of the *lager*. In the unsubtitled Italian version of the film, phantasmatic images of Micòl and Alberto playing tennis are superimposed on the court in an eery conflation of past and future—a special effect that the English-language distributors chose to delete from their prints. This entire se-quence in both versions has as its musical accompaniment the Kaddish, or Jewish lament for the dead, with recognizable references to Micòl, Auschwitz, and Treblinka incorporated into the Hebrew lyrics. Thus Bassani's delicate alignment of funerary and garden imagery is turned into a wrenching historical indictment by use of such specifically cinematic devices as montage and sound-image juxtaposition. It has been De Sica's task to transform Bassani's gorgeous Etruscan monument to Micòl into a plea for moral accountability, and he has done so by removing her epitaph from its literary garden and by rewriting it in a medium whose neorealist past is revitalized by the encounter. Like Giorgio, who rejects the garden in the end, De Sica finally refuses the Eden of cinematic escapism by opening his film out to history and forcing us to accept the consequences.

5 · Pasolini's *Gospel According to St. Matthew*

THE GAZE OF FAITH

Adaptation study meets perhaps its most formidable challenge in Pasolini's *Gospel According to St. Matthew*,[1] where all the standard difficulties of transforming a written narrative into an audiovisual spectacle are immeasurably complicated by the sanctity of the textual source, which asks of its readers an unqualified assent to its historical and spiritual authority.[2] Unlike a film on the life of Christ based on an original screenplay, which need not worry about its relationship to a divinely ordained narrative voice (*The Greatest Story Ever Told* builds human authorship into its very title), Pasolini's reliance on Matthew means that he must confront the Evangelist's claim to speak directly for God. As the first Gospel, and as the one most intent upon proving Christ's fulfillment of the messianic promise, Matthew's writing is so replete with Old Testament prophecies that his voice aligns itself with them, appropriating the absolute authority of their divine source in accordance with Christ's own charge to his Apostles when he sent them forth: "For it is not ye that speak, but the Spirit of your Father which speaketh in you" (Matt. 10:19–20). A faithful adaptation of Scriptures, therefore, requires a cinematic equivalent to this narrative voice that presents itself as God's writing, as a direct expression of divine will at work in human events. And Pasolini is emphatic about his fidelity to Matthew. "My idea is this," he wrote to Lucio S. Caruso of the Pro Civitate Christiana, the Christian educational association that was to sponsor his film:

To follow the Gospel According to St. Matthew point by point, without making a script or adaptation of it. To translate it faithfully into images, following its story without omissions or additions. The dialogue too should be strictly that of St. Matthew, without even a single explanatory or connecting sentence, because no image or inserted word could ever attain the poetic heights of the text. It is this poetic elevation that so anxiously inspires me. And it is a work of poetry that I want to make. Not a religious work in the current sense of the term, nor a work in some way ideological. To put it very simply and frankly, I don't believe that Christ is the son of God."[3]

The contradiction here is blatant, and it resides at the heart of Pasolini's adaptive strategy: how can he presume to make a faithful adaptation of Matthew's text while rejecting the central tenet of the Christian faith to which it bears witness? How can an atheistic adaptation of the Gospel find an acceptable equivalent for the narrative voice that insists upon its continuity with the Holy Word? Without a visual architecture that gives expression to Matthew's providential perspective, how can a verbatim transcription of his Gospel be anything but an arid exercise in parody, or a condescending study of primitive folk belief? That the film transcends its own contradictory premises to become an aesthetically powerful and theologically satisfying adaptation we have ample proof in the acclaim it won from all critical sectors, so that after its screening at the Venice Film Festival in September 1964 Enzo Siciliano could call it "a success that gained applause from opposed ideological and political camps. Only the fascists remained isolated."[4]

Such a response, coming from both the Left and the Catholic establishment, tells us that Pasolini manages to pull off an atheistic retelling of the Christ story without yielding to the twin temptations built into his project: those of a hypocritical assumption of Christian sympathies in the interests of poetic coherence, or of a scientific analysis of the Christ phenomenon in dialectical-materialist terms.[5] How Pasolini manages to evade this twofold trap is a question that the filmmaker has addressed repeatedly in interviews and in his own writings, with intriguing, provocative, and not always convincing results. It will be my task in the following pages to scrutinize Pasolini's self-explanatory remarks and to posit my own theory for reconciling the director's professed atheism with the deeply satisfying religiosity of his film.

With striking and perhaps deliberate appropriateness, Pasolini's commentary organizes itself on four interpretive levels, following the fourfold scheme of the Biblical hermeneutic tradition. Though his atheist's reading requires a radical realignment of the Patristics' historical, moral, typological, and anagogical senses, it is nonetheless significant that Pasolini, like the Biblical exegetes, insists on the verticality of his *Gospel's* meaning. Auerbach's observations that the episodic, disjointed nature of Scriptural narrative itself forces us to seek unity not in the horizontal progression of events but in their vertical connection to an overarching idea could well apply to Pasolini's filmic sequences, whose lack of transitions, withholding of expository data, and rejection of cause-and-effect logic force us outside the story line to extra-narrative principles of order. Pasolini's willful refusal to articulate the relationship of the part to the narrative whole provides the perverse structuring concept of his *Decameron,* while interdisciplinary terms are announced in the title of *Teorema,* whose plot progression is governed by the geometry of familial relationships with a mysterious outsider.[6]

That Pasolini privileges the paradigmatic layering of meanings over the syntagmatic movement of plot is made explicit in his important theoretical manifesto, "The Cinema of Poetry," where he argues that all films have their origin in the pregrammatical brute world of primal images taken directly from nature, memory, or dreams, and that conventional narrative structure (belonging to the cinema of prose) is an artificial imposition that masks the true power of film language.[7] In the name of his cinema of poetry, then, Pasolini constantly disrupts the horizontal narrative flow of film images so that the movement along what Jakobson calls the metaphoric axis takes precedence over its metonymic progression.[8] This insistence on the vertical proliferation of meanings not only aligns Pasolini with the Biblical allegorists themselves but also explains one of the literary attractions of Matthew's text for him, with its "barbaric-practical functionality . . . [its] abolition of chronological time, its elliptical leaps of the story with the internal 'disproportions' of the didascalic stases (the stupendous, interminable Sermon on the Mount)."[9] It is these very flaws (in a conventional narrative sense), that draw Pasolini to Matthew, whose ellipses, aporia, and disjunctions accord well with the filmmaker's own aversion to the conventional narrative structure of "prose cinema." In fact, one of Pasolini's editorial strategies in paring down Matthew to fit a 140-minute film format is to remove the meager psychological motivations that the Evangelist offers in his own text, so that the scriptural explanation for Herodias's animus against John the Baptist, who railed against her marriage to her brother-in-law, is absent in the film, making her request for his decapitation that much more gratuitous and unexpected. Similarly, scriptural motivations are deleted from such scenes as Christ's walking on the water, where Pasolini seems to prefer the arbitrary and the mysterious to the motivated prodigy of Jesus' act to save his storm-threatened disciples. By disposing of motivational links and of all transitional cause-and-effect, temporal, or spatial locators that maintain the narrative flow, Pasolini exaggerates a tendency already present in Scriptures toward narrative disjunction in accordance with his preference for a vertical, paradigmatic cinema of poetry.

The impulse to verticality, to supraliteral understandings, is also evident in Pasolini's polemical relationship to neorealist style, which is at once appropriated and subverted in strategic ways. Thus Pasolini invokes the historical and geographical concreteness of neorealism, its pretense to documentary authenticity, only to deny such a materialist reading in an assertion of his story's supercession of material limits.[10] This complex strategy begins with Pasolini's choice of location. Having visited Israel and found it too modern and its inhabitants either too industrial or too heathen for his purposes, Pasolini chose to set his Gospel in Southern Italy, filming the Jerusalem scenes in the cave-city called the Sassi di Matera, the Bethelehem scenes in the smaller cave-town of Barile, the Capernaum scenes in Crotone and Massafra, the desert scenes in Calabria and on the slopes of Etna, and the rich, indoor and courtyard scenes in the Norman castles of Apulia and Basilicata.[11] Pasolini's decision to use such settings, rather than to reconstruct antiquities in Israel (or Cinecittà) bespeaks the neorealists' commitment to use "what's there," to film what landscapes and townscapes have to offer without technical intervention. "I knew I would remake the Gospel by analogy," Pasolini told Oswald Stack. "Southern Italy enabled me to make the transition from the ancient to the modern world without having to reconstruct it either archaeologically or philologically."[12] Yet such a decision reflects an ahistorical bias that runs strongly counter to the committed ideals of much neorealist filmmaking. When Pasolini claims that his *Gospel* will not be a "work of reconstruction but of substitution—of the Hebrew world of 2,000 years ago with the world of Southern Italy, with an archaic, pastoral, pre-industrial life that has relevant pre-historic characteristics," we realize that this is yet another expression of Pasolini's romantic primitivism—the poetics that embues all his films from *Accattone* through *The Trilogy of Life*, in addition to his *borgata* novels and his dialect poetry.[13] Not only does the primitive Gospel setting provide a perfect vehicle for Pasolini's celebration of Third-World, rural, pre-industrial, subproletarian society, so too does Matthew's Christ, who is far more dissident and anarchic than his counterparts in Mark, Luke, or John. If Pasolini's romantic primitivism can be seen as the idealized inversion of everything he deplores in contemporary urban,

bourgeois, rationalist industrial society, then Matthew's Christ becomes the romantic primitivist *per eccellenza.* "Nothing seems to me
more contrary to the modern world than that figure . . . [who] should
have, at the end, the same violence of resistance [as Matthew's], something that radically contradicts life as it is configuring itself around
modern man."[14]

Thus, by setting his film in a locale that is Palestine *only by analogy,*
and by populating it with the subproletariat of his romantic imagin-
ings, Pasolini dehistoricizes the neorealist tradition whose look he so
consciously cultivates in the unreconstructed outdoor sets and the
antispectacular style of its presentation. A similar ambivalent use of
neorealistic technique can be found in Pasolini's casting and directing
of actors, whose socioeconomic provenance is usually appropriate to
the roles they play, but whose performances are always willfully antinaturalistic. Not surprisingly, the entire cast is composed of nonprofessionals, from the crowds recruited from the local populace, to
the disciples (Peter is played by a Roman Jewish ragpicker, Judas by
a Communist truck driver, Matthew, whose higher educational level
qualifies him to write down the story, by a music critic and photogra-
pher, Herod II by a writer, and so forth), to Mary herself, played by
Pasolini's own mother in the later scenes.[15] Despite their natural affinities for their parts and their innocence of acting technique, Pasolini
insists that they deliver their lines with a wooden self-consciousness
in a trancelike monotone that defies neorealist verisimilitude. A similar doubleness characterizes Pasolini's costumes, whose primitiveness
and understatement make their wearers seem like organic extensions
of the primeval landscapes they inhabit, until the camera alights upon
the bizarre, tall hats of the Palestinian ruling class, inspired by the
paintings of Piero della Francesca.[16] This extravagant sartorial detail,
bespeaking a taste aesthetic worlds away from ancient Palestine, disrupts the stylistic unity of the film and destroys the impression of
documentary authenticity associated with the neorealist look. It soon
becomes clear that Pasolini invokes neorealism only as a measure of
his own distance from it: he may be filming real towns and natural
settings, but they are not Palestinian; he may be representing Matthew's cast of characters, but they are still creatures of the filmmaker's
own romantic primitivism; his actors may be nonprofessionals, but
they are nonetheless acting; his costumes may be understated, but
they are also aesthetically mediated.

Nor has this self-subverting use of neorealism been a mere polemical
exercise—it serves a definite function within the film of pushing us
beyond the level of the literal, material story line. It is in fact the insis-

tence on aesthetic mediations, on the origin of his style in the visual arts, which leads us to the next level of Pasolinian allegory, for his film is very much about the history of Gospel representations in art. "I did not want to reconstruct the life of Christ as it really was," Pasolini told Stack. "I wanted to do the story of Christ plus 2,000 years of Christian translation, because it is the 2,000 years of Christian history which has mythicized this biography, which would otherwise be almost insignificant biography as such. My film is the life of Christ plus 2,000 years of storytelling about the life of Christ. That was my intention."[17]

If this statement of artistic purpose seems overly ambitious in its pretense to account for two millenia of Christian representations, Pasolini does narrow down his scope somewhat later to focus on the graphic arts. "At least for an Italian like me, painting has had an enormous importance in these 2,000 years, indeed it is the major element in the Christological tradition."[18] As a student at the University of Bologna who studied with the celebrated art historian Roberto Longhi, Pasolini had considerable personal cause to attribute his vision of Christ to painterly models. The filmmaker's account of his initial inspiration for making the *Gospel* is highly revealing of his stylistic mediations. He tells how a reading of Gospels triggered "a double series of figurative worlds often linked with each other: the physiological one, brutally alive, of the Biblical time that appeared to me in the trips to India or on the Arabic coasts of Africa, and the one reconstructed from the figurative culture of the Italian Renaissance, from Masaccio to the black mannerists."[19] In fact, attentive readings of Pasolini's and of various critics' commentaries on his film begin to read like museum catalogues or art history indexes with their accumulation of visual sources for the film's iconography, including Romanesque sculpture, Byzantine mosaics, Duccio, Giotto, Masaccio, Piero della Francesca, Mantegna, Pollaioulo, the *officina ferrarese, mannieristi neri,* El Greco, and Rouault. Given the heterogeneity of eras, styles, and media, the critic confronted with such a list would expect the resultant work of art to be a disjointed miscellany of influences, an inchoate mass of disparate and discordant elements arbitrarily combined to form what Pasolini himself calls a "stylistic magma."[20] What emerges instead is a marvelously wrought palimpsest, containing layer upon layer of cultural and artistic testimonies to the power of the Christ story to inspire its representations in art. Pasolini's *Gospel* thus finds its architectural equivalent in Rome's San Clemente, where a baroque exterior covers a Byzantine internal structure, which itself is built upon crypts of Mithraic and paleo-Christian cultic worship, or in the cathedral of Syracuse on the island of Ortygia, where an eighteenth-century facade covers an early Christian church built over a temple to Athena.

In filming this palimpsest of art historical references, Pasolini is in-
dulging his penchant for pastiche or, as he prefers to call it, contamination. When the filmmaker announced in 1964 that "the sign under
which I work is contamination," he was referring not only to a generalized love of antithesis, of heterodox elements that clash and conflict
to animate his art, but also specifically to the "linguistic pluralism" that
he so admired in the style of Carlo Emilio Gadda.[21] In describing the
"magma of techniques" that he used in his *Gospel*, this notion of contamination comes to mean the refusal of any conventional matching of
form and content, the emphatic denial of any culturally sanctioned
ideal of stylistic decorum.[22] In *Accattone* (1961), the scandalous relationship between subject matter and style had already been established,
but to keep that scandal alive, Pasolini had to rethink his camera technique in the *Gospel*. In the earlier film, Pasolini had achieved contamination by treating his subproletarian characters and settings with
"sacral, hieratic, religious" dignity, using a great deal of frontality,
flattening the perspective, slowing the pace, and accompanying the
images with elevated musical commentary.[23] Thus the brawl between
Accattone and his brother-in-law amidst a crowd of *borgata* onlookers
is ennobled by Pasolini's visual lingering on the spectacle, his centered, balanced cinematography, and his musical choice of the Bach
Mass in B Minor, which gives the action a quasi-liturgical solemnity.
But when Pasolini began making *The Gospel*, he experienced an acute
crisis of confidence when he realized that "a hieratic Christ was not a
Christ"—that to film the Gospel using his sacral approach was like
"taking coals to Newcastle," and that his commitment to stylistic contamination would require a radically different shooting technique.[24] "I
turned everything upside-down, I used the strangest lenses, I put together some close-ups, one shot with twenty-five, and one shot with
a hundred, I used the zoom on the entire lens, like those used for bike
races—I used them for representing the Apostles behind Christ."[25]
Thus if subproletarian skirmishes in the *borgate* are to be filmed with
liturgical dignity in the name of Pasolinian contamination, it should
come as no surprise that the Passion be filmed like a sports event.

Nowhere in the film is this scandalous relationship between style
and content more evident than in the adoration of the Magi, whose
most flamboyant art historical manifestations are International Gothic,
with its profusion of oriental exotica in the camels, monkeys, and gold
leaf over molded gesso of Gentile da Fabriano or Lorenzo Monaco. In
contaminating this scene by rejecting its traditional extravagance of
representation, Pasolini is, paradoxically, returning to the true notion
of Biblical sublime, whose source is the simplicity and purity of *sermo
umilis* itself.

In a deliberately antispectacular version of International Gothic adoration scenes, Mary (at left) looks on as the three kings pay reverence to her child.

> When they had heard the King, they departed, and lo the star which they saw in the East, went before them, till it came and stood over where the young child was. And when they came into the house, they saw the young child with Mary his mother, and fell down, and worshipped him: and when they had opened their treasures, they presented unto him gifts, gold, and frankincense and myrrh. (Matt. 2:11)

Pasolini's strategy is to simplify even the Scriptural account, omitting the grandiloquent device of the star and setting the action outdoors on the slope whose contours determine so much of the blocking of this scene. Taking place in broad daylight in a space filled with the sights and sounds of children playing, the episode begins as one of the many realistic genre scenes that Pasolini describes throughout his screenplay. A long shot reveals the figures of the three kings weaving down the slope, accompanied by a flock of boisterous children whose playful sounds soon give way to the voice of Odetta singing "Motherless Child" in the film's first example of musical contamination. A cut to a medium shot of Joseph and Mary with the infant in her arms reveals the humility of the sacred family in this high-angle perspective that locates the spectator above them in space, and in the absence of any of the customary iconographic props (manger, midwives) which would associate them with the protagonists of the lush art historical adorations. All conspires here to emphasize the paradox that such lofty luminaries would kneel before the infant child of such humble parents. Indeed, it is Mary who first pays obeisance to the kings, for her instinctive response is to rise in their presence. Much of the opening of the scene is devoted to the kings' slow progress down the slope, in a complex serpentine movement from right to left, then left to right and back in a possible topographical allusion to Benozzo Gozzoli's *Procession of the Magi* in the chapel of the Palazzo Medici-Riccardi in Florence, whose gorgeous cavalcade curves along a road that recedes into the background according to the laws of one-point perspective.[26]

If Pasolini's zig-zag blocking alludes to this art historical tradition, its effect is also to emphasize the precipitousness of this slope and the movement of *descent* that brings the kings to the humble object of their worship. In an unexpected and tremendously moving interpolation, Pasolini then has Mary hand the infant over to the oldest of the kings, whose awkward handling of the child is both touching and realistic in a man obviously unaccustomed to caring for newborns. Cuts to close-ups of Joseph and of a smiling Mary maintain the mystery and privacy of their emotions: for Joseph, this worship could be confirmation of the angel's announcement that Mary's pregnancy was divinely generated or simply another element in a bewildering series of events that exceed his understanding; while for Mary, this could be vindication of her honor or simply hyperbolic reinforcement of her own joy and awe in mothering. Other reaction shots are riveted on children's faces, until the black-clad king nods that the gifts be brought forth. A long shot follows the progress of three boys who weave their way down the slope bearing the royal offerings, but Pasolini's camera refuses to alight on the gifts, zooming in instead to the face of one of the young porters, kneeling before the child in rapt adoration. On this image of worshipful and radiant youth, Pasolini fades out the scene, whose wordlessness and stirring musical accompaniment had only added to the sense that a sacred rite had been performed.

As the stylistically and thematically incongruous matching of visual imagery with the sound track of Odetta's "Motherless Child" suggests, music features prominently in Pasolini's strategy of contamination.[27] This eclectic and surprising sound track mixes the highbrow with the popular, European with Third World, baroque and classical with modern, and secular with spiritual. Incongruities reminiscent of the metaphysical poets' "violent yokings" abound in the film, such as the jazz lament accompanying the agonizing progress of a cripple toward Christ, who cures him on the Sabbath despite the censorious witness of the Pharisees, or the Hebrew dirge that provides the background for the magis' approach to Jerusalem.

If Pasolinian contamination in its narrowest sense means a scandalous relationship of style to content, then the Salome episode constitutes one of the film's most blatant scandals. Where modern representations of the scene aspire to express the corruption and perverse eroticism of its subject matter in the decadence of Aubrey Beardsley's or Gustave Moreau's Salomes, for example, or the dripping sensuality of the dancer in the Italian silent film *Erodiade* (1912), Pasolini opts for the simplicity and grace of a Filippo Lippi nymphet. So conditioned are we to thinking of Salome as a voluptuous siren, vamping around a banquet room to an audience of leering admirers, that when Pasolini's delicate and chaste young woman begins her dance, we find ourselves wondering, Can this be Salome? To disarm us yet farther, Pasolini introduces Salome on-screen as a child, absorbed in some solitary game with a marble, and though a cut to John the Baptist languishing in prison should alert us to her identity, the sinister effect of the juxtaposition is subordinated to the seeming innocence of her portrayal. A close-up of Salome's marble game that leads to a shot of her smiling mother only reinforces the impression of child's play, which is followed by images of a tightening maternal bond: Herodias dresses her daughter, smiles, turns solemn, and plants a more-than-affectionate kiss on the girl's lips. This sudden seriousness of expression and this fleeting caress are telling us that what we have just witnessed is no routine mother-daughter interlude, but the sealing of a pact—whose terms will be fulfilled by the ensuing performance.

Pasolini rigorously rejects any temptation to baroque decadence in the sound track as well as in his visuals, choosing a Renaissance flute solo rather than some lush orchestral accompaniment or some musical attempt at orientalism. The Renaissance purity of the music is matched by the classical balance of the dance's mise-en-scène, where a central arch organizes the background space and a U-shaped table, flanked by black-clad courtiers, is crowned by the white-robed Herod wearing an Andrea del Castagno hat. The camera follows Salome in close-up as she dances holding a sprig of white flowers, her body completely gowned and her shoulders chastely enveloped in the white veil that would become such a tease in conventional representations of the scene. Intermittent cuts to Herod's heavy-lidded eyes reveal as much

aesthetic pleasure as lechery, along with the cuts to the sober and re-
spectful courtiers. At the end of the dance, in a moment of supreme
delicacy, Salome bows and then runs back to her mother whom she
embraces before both turn to read Herod's expression. In the first
words of the entire sequence, the monarch proclaims, "I'm well
pleased with your dancing. Ask of me what you will and I shall grant
it." Now Salome raises her head from Herodias's shoulder as mother
and daughter meet each other's eyes in mutual confirmation of their
pact. Salome turns to her stepfather and utters her first and only
words of the episode: "Have brought to me here, on a dish, the head
of John the Baptist." Significantly, her voice is too deep for so lithe and
young a girl, suggesting that it is Salome's mother who speaks through
her, as if by some sort of genetic ventriloquism. A reaction shot of
Herod finds him as shocked as the restrained style of the episode will
allow. "It is granted," he concedes.

The murderous epiphany forces us to reinterpret, in retrospect, the
scene's visual codes, so that the initial cut to John in prison becomes a
motivated juxtaposition, the intense maternal kiss seals a partnership
in crime, and the slim adolescent girl becomes merely a pared-down
version of the fleshly Herodias, whose identically coiffed hair, similar
damask gown, almond eyes, and only slightly more dimpled chin
make her a flashforward of what her daughter will eventually become.
From the perspective of the scene's end, we realize that Salome's body
is a deceptive sign, a false signifier of youthful innocence whose real
function was to serve as the instrument of a worldly woman's desire
for revenge. In Pasolini's refusal of conventional representations of Salome, the young girl's sadistic complicity with her mother strikes us
with a brute force that no sleazy portrayal could ever achieve, for it
manages to include us in Herod's own deception at the hands of this
sinister couple.

Pasolini's figurative strategy is nowhere more evident than in the
iconography of Christ himself, whose physical conformity to the filmmaker's ideal was so difficult to achieve that it took him a year to find
the proper facial match. The filmmaker's casting of Enrique Irazoqui
had, of course, art historical logic—the young man "had the same
handsome and proud face, human and detached, of the Christs
painted by El Greco. Severe, even hard in certain expressions."[28] "I
didn't want a Christ with soft features, with a sweet gaze, as in Renaissance iconography," Pasolini told Luigi Cardone. "I wanted a
Christ whose face also expressed strength, decision, a face like that of
the Christs of medieval painters. A face, in short, that corresponded
to the arid and rocky landscapes in which his preaching takes place."[29]

"I wanted a Christ whose face . . . corresponded to the arid and rocky landscapes in which his preaching takes place."

By choosing this dark, stern, bearded Jesus, Pasolini has adopted the Byzantine image of the *pantocrator*, or judging Christ, and has vehemently rejected the other iconography available to him in the fair-haired, clean-shaven Good Shepherd of the classical tradition, ancestor of the idealized Aryan representations of the God-man in today's media culture. In so doing, the filmmaker denies us the sense of familiarity and predictability that makes us numb to the force of the Gospels, for if conventional representational codes tame and domesticate the figure of Christ so that we can no longer hear the ferocity of his message, Pasolini makes that message fresh again by recasting its spokesman in unfamiliar and unsettling ways.

It should be emphasized here that Pasolini is not dispensing with contemporary representational codes in the name of something new—he is being iconoclastic in the name of something very old, and he is thereby exposing the conventional figurations of Christ for what they are: debased and mongrel versions of earlier, inspired responses to the generative power of the Gospels in art. This means rejecting the entire cinematic genre dedicated to representing the Bible on film: the religious superspectacle, from the silents (*Ben Hur, Quo Vadis*), through Cecil B. De Mille's biblical productions (*The Ten Commandments, King of Kings, The Sign of the Cross*), to their 1950s and 1960s remakes. With its material extravagance, operatic overstatement, enormity of scale, and star-studded casts, the genre substitutes grandiosity for grandeur in its quest for a style adequate to its narrative content. After all, the greatest story ever told requires the greatest expenditure of technical means for the telling. Once the early industry seized upon biblical subject matter as a pretext for spectacle, and once the Hollywood studio system put its imprimatur on the genre, religious filmmaking became an exercise in ever-escalating opulence, a challenge to exceed in lavishness all previous productions, and thus to up the ante for all future competitors.

If Pasolini is beholden to any earlier makers of religous films, however, it is to the Rossellini of *Francesco giullare di Dio*, the Carl Dreyer of *The Passion of Joan of Arc*, the Robert Bresson of *Diary of a Country Priest*, or the Luis Buñuel of *Viridiana*, and if any competition occurs, it is over stylistic simplicity and austerity of means, the very opposite of the Hollywood relationship to generic precedent. Thus where European critics seemed less stupefied by Pasolini's antispectacular approach, perhaps because they were aware of such alternatives for religious film production, many American critics made this the basis of their reviews, and one saw in Pasolini's stylistic choice a deliberate polemic intent, an overt attack on the Hollywood genre of biblical extravaganzas.[30]

Pasolini's strategy of defamiliarization is not limited to visual style, however. His Christ is also emotionally strange and difficult, a figure whose visionary monomania makes him demanding and unnerving. "One can't love this saint burning with fire for his own mission," comments Sandro Petraglia.[31] This Jesus is designed to disturb and disorient us, and when Pasolini does include footage of familiar, pietistic scenes (the miracles), it is only to intensify the contrast with his other, more abrasive and alienating image of Christ. "The jump from these kind of holy picture scenes to the passionate violence of his politics and his preaching is so great that the Christ figure in the film is bound to produce a strong sense of unease in the audience," Pasolini told Stack.[32] This is why the filmmaker forgoes the Christs of John, Luke, and Mark for Matthew's Christ, whose "implacability, absolute rigor, the lack of any concession, the always-being-present-to-himself in an obsessive, obsessing manner, with a rigor that borders on madness," qualifies him so well for Pasolini's defamiliarizing operation.[33] Indeed, Matthew's Christ is unfamiliar in the etymological sense of the word when he literally disowns his natural family in a scene that serves to deny us any sentimental identification with this unbending spiritual master. A comparison of the biblical passage with the filmic episode reveals how Pasolini's Christ negotiates the rival claims of his two families: the apostolic one of his own creation, and the biological one which created him.

> While he yet talked to the people, behold, his mother and his brethren stood without, desiring to speak with him. Then one said unto him, Behold, thy mother and thy brethren stand without, desiring to speak with thee. But he answered and said unto him that told him, Who is my mother? and who are my brethren? And he stretched forth his hand toward his disciples, and said, Behold my mother and my brethren! For whosoever shall do the will of my Father which is in heaven, the same is my brother, and sister, and mother. Matt. 12:46–50.

In adapting this biblical passage, Pasolini uses techniques of rhetorical amplification and theatrical mise-en-scène to stage Christ's repudiation of his biological kin. The filmmaker complicates Matthew's adverb of place by verticalizing the scriptural "without" of Mary's positioning, and the "forth" of Christ's gesture to his disciples. Pasolini thus blocks the scene along a vertical axis that then modulates into a diagonal, becoming horizontal only once, for a fleeting and transgressive moment. Christ is preaching from a battlement of the city wall, and Pasolini's lateral view of this complex stone edifice, like an architect's cross-section of gothic structural design, gives great visual excitement and movement to this otherwise static scene. In its asymmetry and its diagonal staircase, which leads the eye from bottom left to top right to find the preacher perched, small and dark, atop the uppermost battlement, crowning a double series of inlaid Romanesque vaults, the composition places Christ in turbulent isolation and creates two orders of listeners—the disciples arrayed along the staircase, and the unseen crowd amassed far below, offscreen to the right. Though the biblical passage does not specify who bears tidings of Mary's arrival, Pasolini's camera makes John and James the messengers in an important anticipation of Christ's own preference for his apostolic family over his biological one. A dolly shot follows their progress up the diagonal staircase, when a cut to the long shot that locates Christ in this elaborate architecture reminds us of his isolation on high.[34] The only horizontal movement in the scene occurs now—as John and James reach the top of the staircase to the battlement and approach Christ from behind, a slightly low-angle close-up from the disciples' perspective shows a stern Christ turning toward them, followed by a match shot close-up, from a slightly elevated angle, of John, who announces, "Thy mother and thy brethern are without, waiting to speak to thee." Though the scriptural passage provides Christ's immediate answer, Pasolini's protagonist does not even deign to respond but turns back to the crowd and continues to preach. And where the Gospel's reticence suggests that Mary remains without, that Christ does not lay eyes on her in this scene, Pasolini stages an elaborate exchange of glances between mother and son, foreshadowing the *Stabat Mater* episode of his film's Passion. To reinforce our sense that mother and son inhabit separate moral spheres, Pasolini opposes Christ's asymmetrical, uneasy mise-en-scène to the centered, balanced composition of Mary's descent of a staircase, where she beholds her son in close-up from behind. Though this view of the aloof preacher is far too close to be a match shot of Mary's perspective, it is more cogent than a realistically positioned long shot because it presents Christ as physically near, and yet agonizingly inaccessible.

At this point, Pasolini doubles the scriptural announcement of Mary's arrival by having James repeat John's earlier notification. "Thy mother is here, she's with thy brethren." Only now does Christ turn. The reaction shot of Mary, too close to be from Christ's perspective, nonetheless conveys a pleading look that she expects her son to acknowledge. What he sees is an image of maternal supplication so genuine and pitiful that he can ignore it only by violating all laws of psychological verisimilitude. When the camera returns to Christ, the scriptural questions, Who is my mother? And who are my brethren? only confirm what the play of gazes has already revealed, and Mary's downcast eyes signal her acceptance of maternal defeat. Where the biblical Christ stretched out his hand to indicate the apostolic referents of his command, "Behold my mother and my brethren," Pasolini's camera performs the same gesture by cutting from Jesus to John to James to the other disciples gathered on the diagonal stairs. The scene ends with the image of Mary looking up at her son with a reverence that asserts his spiritual authority and denies her any privileged status within the larger family of his followers.

The film's Christ is not only an emotionally unsettling figure, he is also extremely unsettling in a political way, and this brings us to the third level of Pasolini's biblical allegory. That *The Gospel According to St. Matthew* is a profoundly political statement does not automatically place it in the Marxist camp, however, for the film is less a materialist inquiry into the concrete historical condition of Roman-occupied Judea than a study of politics construed in its broadest sense as the use and abuse of institutionalized power.[35] Pasolini's political supertext is announced immediately in the film's dedication to "the dear, familiar shade of Pope John XXIII" and in the director's own insistence that his *Gospel* is inconceivable outside the context of the Second Vatican Council, with its aspiration to opening a dialogue with the Left.[36] Such a position has opened him up to leftist charges of betrayal, and to having exploited the dialogue to his own advantage—charges to which Pasolini responds with pride, "I have contributed to the dialogue . . . I have helped to produce it, and I think I was right to do so."[37] That this is indeed a "dialogue" film, interested in relating the Ur-text of the Christian faith to the twentieth-century struggle against Nazi-Fascist oppression, is evident in the contemporary references of several key images and scenes. Thus the iconography of the holy family's flight into Egypt is modeled on photographs of Spanish refugees fleeing the Civil War across the Pyrenees, the massacre of the innocents recalls both the Holocaust and the murder of Slavic babies by Fascist soldiers who threw them into the air to their deaths, while the costumes of the Roman military and Herod's soldiers evoke those of the Italian police and of Mussolini's *squadristi*, respectively.[38] Though such references may be indecipherable to the general public, they do explain some of the film's anomalies (my students laughed uncomprehendingly at the unrealistic tossing of babies in the massacre scene), and Pasolini insists that such contemporary allusions were a necessity, a propulsive force in his inspiration to make *The Gospel*. "I absolutely needed a moment of current events, that perhaps in the film doesn't ever emerge because not everyone is aware of it, but I needed this in shooting it."[39] In the Pharisees and Sadducees, Pasolini saw a metaphor for the dominion of the contemporary ruling class, and in the Roman soldiers' taunting of Christ the accused, he saw a typical example of colonialist cruelty and indifference to the native population.[40]

Of course, Pasolini's political agenda is best enhanced by making the Sermon on the Mount the centerpiece of his film. In order to give this "stupendous, interminable sermon," as Pasolini calls it, visual interest, the filmmaker privileges it by removing the discourse from any natural, physical context and rearranging its order for greater thematic coherence.[41] Throughout this long sequence, Christ is shot in varying degrees of close-up, in three-quarter view from a slight low angle, sometimes bareheaded, sometimes shawled in black or white, with a variety of light intensities and climatic conditions. There is never a reaction shot and no visual allusion to the mountain setting, just a succession of alternating backgrounds staged in a studio (unlike the rest of the film, which was made on location) and whose effect it is to abstract these pronouncements from any specific worldly or dramatic context.[42] Thus, while deeply political, the new law that emerges from this sermon is also ahistorical—a generic denunciation of social injustice, a universal attempt to speak for the underclass that has always remained outside of history. It is the highly politicized Christ of the Sermon on the Mount, then, who takes precedence over the other possible Christs that Pasolini could have chosen to represent, and it is his power to arouse the masses into a revolutionary fervor, dramatized in the ever-increasing numbers of followers and his increasingly abrasive confrontations with the Palestinian old guard, that points the way to crucifixion.[43]

Nor is the political theme of the film devoid of autobiographical relevance for a Pasolini himself alienated and pilloried, at one time or another, by all sectors of the Italian establishment. Critics have noted the high degree of personal investment that went into this production, from the moment that Pasolini experienced his lightning-bolt inspiration to make *The Gospel* to the filmmaker's extraordinary degree of concentration on set, and this intensity has been attributed to autobiographical causes.[44] Personal identification with the Gospel story explains both Pasolini's casting of his mother as Mary and of his friends as disciples (Simon is played by the writer Enzo Siciliano, Mary of Bethany by the authoress Natalia Ginzburg, Joseph by her brother, and John by Ginzburg's nephew, and so on) and his temptation to see Christ as the embodiment of his own keenly felt "otherness," his often articulated opposition to contemporary social norms, his uncompromising and passionate commitment to his own prophetic calling.[45] But Enzo Siciliano's comment that Pasolini was "fired by an inscrutable need for expiation" suggests a far deeper affinity between the film-maker and his protagonist in their shared vocation for martyrdom.[46] Pasolini was to formulate this insight in the essay "Il cinema impopolare"(1970), in which he equates artistic freedom with the transgression of societal dictates toward self-preservation.[47] It is the artist's task to flaunt such social norms through a self-sacrificial exhibitionism— the individual must take up a position on the firing line and invite a spectacular death that will free the public from bondage to society's conservational norms. Though Pasolini never mentions Christ in this essay, the cultural paragon of self-sacrifice could not have been far from his mind, and surely this obsession with an exemplary death, a *"morte spettacolare,"* is what underlies the film's insistence on Christ's frequent references to martyrdom at the behest of social authority.

Christ's political dissidence is also rife with anticlerical implications for the modern church, whose institutionalized power structure exhibits uncomfortable similarities to the Jewish religious establishment of Old Testament times.[48] Pasolini's iconography of hats in fact suggests the contemporary relevance of Christ's anticlericism when the film-maker has one of the Pharisees wear a bishop's mitre. In his opposition to modern-day church hierarchy, Pasolini aligns himself with the progressive Catholicism of the 1960s, whose worker-priest movement and whose countercultural thrust found justification in paleo-Christian political and social marginality. Nor is such anticlericism contradicted by the film's dedication to Pope John XXIII, whose social thought was consonant with that of Matthew's revolutionary Christ.

The way in which *The Gospel* gives voice to Pasolini's panreligious impulse, rather than to a specifically sectarian religiosity, brings us to our fourth and final level of interpretation. Pasolini's decision to make a paleo-Christian film rigorously respecting the Gospel, and not a life of Christ based on an original screenplay, enables the filmmaker to celebrate the moment when the Christian faith was still fluid and uncodified, and when the nascent cult compellingly expressed the universal human desire for transcendence. Such panreligiosity is evident throughout Pasolini's art, in his anthropological explorations of primitive cultures embued with a sacrality and a cosmic wonder that he finds so lacking in today's rationalist world (*Medea, Oedipus Rex*), in his survey of the medieval fabulist tradition where superstition and unproblematic religious faith provide so dazzling a wealth of storytelling possibilities (*Decameron, Canterbury Tales, Arabian Nights*), in *Teorema* and in the plays *Orgia* and *Affabulazione* where primitive religiosity finds its way into a modern setting. That Pasolini's anthropological interest is a function of his own visceral religiosity is made clear in numerous examples of self-interpretation.

> Nothing I've ever done has been more fitted to me myself than *The Gospel* for reasons that I talked about before—my tendency always to see something sacred and mythic and epic in every-thing, even the most humdrum, simple and banal objects and events. So in this sense *The Gospel* was just right for me, even though I don't believe in the divinity of Christ, because my vision of the world is religious—it's a mutilated religion because it hasn't got any of the characteristics of religion, but it is a religious vision of the world. So making *The Gospel* was to reach the maximum of the mythic and the epic.[49]

This, however, does not suffice to explain how a militant atheist can manage to film a satisfying life of Christ. There remains the central problem that Jesus himself poses to his followers at Capernaum: "He who is not with me is against me." It is not enough to argue, as one critic does, that Pasolini admires Christ without adoring him, or to use the filmmaker's own artful dodge, that Christ is divine in a metaphoric sense because he has acheived the maximum of human possibilities within the natural order.[50] To accept this explanation is to be "against me" and to make a film whose perspective essentially contradicts the messianic significance of Christ's ministry. Pasolini's success in resolv-ing this contradiction is evident in the film's overwhelmingly positive Catholic reception. Were the film to remain fixated on the clash be-tween its atheistic perspective and its apostolic content, such review-ers as J. Robert Nelson of *Christian Century* would hardly be moved to observe that "doubtless he had no evangelistic intent; indeed, he con-siders himself a communist. But what he has achieved is not only a work of art, it is a cogent and authentic commendation of Jesus Christ." Nor would Moira Walsh of the Catholic periodical *America* argue that "despite its extreme unpretentiousness, its incompleteness, its deliberate lack of ethnic and topographical authenticity (or perhaps because of them), [the film] does succeed in confronting us with the reality of Christ's life and teaching, not in the comfortable context of the no-longer-relevant past, but as a direct and ever-renewing chal-lenge to every age." Nor would the OCIC, the international Catholic cinema office, have honored the film with the following citation: "The author, who is said not to share our faith, has given proof in his choice of texts and scenes of respect and delicacy. He has made a fine film, a Christian film that produces a profound impression."[51]

The key to this atheist filmmaker's success in telling the story of Christ without hypocrisy, condescension, or the kind of "metaphysical anxieties" that blight a film like Scorsese's *Last Temptation of Christ* lies in Pasolini's recourse to the Gospel text as the basis of his screenplay.[52] "I naturally wanted to hold myself absolutely faithful to Matthew for aesthetic reasons," Pasolini told *Filmcritica*, "because it seemed to me the most just, also historically, because I didn't want to make a life of Christ, neither did I feel the desire to do it, because I didn't have ideas that were theologically or socially precise on what I would have done, I didn't want to compose the Gospels and reconstruct a life of Christ with dialogues added, etc., I wanted truly to do it with Matthew and I remained faithful to the idea."[53] The key phrase here is "I didn't want to make a life of Christ," for any ex nihilo telling would have involved questions of narrative authority, which would have caught Pasolini between the unacceptable alternatives of bad faith or Marxist demystification. Instead, his decision "to do it with Matthew" means that his film will be a representation of the believer's gaze, but that it will achieve that mimesis without hypocrisy by showing the source of the gaze in Matthew's own subjectivity. The film thus tells the story of the genesis of the believer's gaze, and it does so through the play of two looks—the third-person limited perspective of Matthew, filmed with a hand-held camera using cinéma vérité methods, and a second, omniscient, divinely ordained perspective, filmed with Pasolini's sacralizing technique, which is how Matthew represents his own gaze within the scriptural account.[54] Thus, it is the Evangelist who authorizes the film's omniscient perspective, making this an omniscience *from within*, a textually justified appropriation, and one that constantly reveals its human source in Matthew's apostolic witness. "I, a nonbeliever, was telling the story through the eyes of a believer," Pasolini explained to Oswald Stack.[55] This was "Christ as Matthew saw him."[56]

Pasolini's preference for Matthew over John, Luke, and Mark may also be traced to the need to play off the two cinematic gazes, for this evangelical voice offers the firmest grounds for the establishment both of the film's human and of its divine perspectives on the Christ event. As the Gospel most intent upon proving that Jesus fulfills the Old Testament messianic promise, Matthew has the highest incidence of prophetic quotations of all the Evangelists—sixty, to Mark's twenty-three and Luke's twenty-five, where ten are presented as Matthew's own personal reflections.[57] Pasolini's understanding of Matthew's divine spokesmanship is revealed in his use of the same actor to dub the voice-overs expressing: (1) God's words (e.g., "This is my beloved son in whom I am well pleased"); (2) Old Testament prophecies (e.g., "Behold a virgin will conceive and will bear a son, and they will call him Emmanuele, that means God with us"); and (3) the Evangelist's own textual exposition (e.g., the genealogy of the House of David). Visually, this divine perspective is rendered throughout the film in a series of aerial establishing shots, unusual in Pasolini, including the important overhead introduction to the baptismal scene which explicitly aligns the camera with the voice of God uttering his paternal delight, and the overhead shot of Christ's entrance into Jerusalem, whose elevation is too great to represent the perspective of the children in the trees so frequently depicted in medieval frescoes and predellas. Pasolini's recurrent pans of the lunar Lucanian countryside, which in their altitude and sweep exceed the visual possibilities of any human witnesses to the events, suggest both the filmmaker's almost fetishistic love for this landscape and his cinematic mimesis of the divine perspective on it.

Matthew's Gospel is also ideally suited to the establishment of the human, in situ gaze in its focus on the apostolic community—a focus that may escape us in reading the text, where the disciples function as mere accessories to Christ's ministry or as instruments for the realization of the divine plan, but that Pasolini emphasizes in scene after scene of the group wandering through the Lucanian countryside.[58] Such an emphasis is not unusual in Pasolini, whose interest in male bonding, and whose insistence that Utopia resides in the possibility of an egalitarian community of men, underlies his characterization of the *ragazzi di vita* of his Roman novels, as well as his depiction of the subproletarian youth of *Accattone* and the artist's workshop of his *Decameron* frame tale. In the many scenes of the group wandering through a landscape so stark and hostile that the Master and his disciples seem to be the only inhabitants of an alien planet, Pasolini reminds us of Christ's initial apostolic charge and the third-person limited perspective introduced into the film at that moment. Soon after the first four Apostles, Peter, Andrew, James, and John, are recruited, a jump cut takes us to the time when all twelve are assembled to learn of their mission. Pasolini has Christ call the apostolic roll at this point, cutting to the men's faces in close-up as the names are recited. By matching our visual introduction to each disciple with Christ's naming of him, Pasolini makes such naming a double christening—a calling into being at once cinematic and spiritual, an initiation into both a new life in Christ, and a life on-screen.

Here Pasolini uses the free indirect subjective camera that he discussed at such length in his "Cinema of Poetry" as the filmic mimesis of the *stile indirect libre* or *erlebe Rede* of prose fiction, where the narra-

Christ stands against the Galilean skyline with Andrew (center) and Peter (right).

tive approximates in third person the direct words or thoughts of a character.[59] This stylistic "removal of quotation marks" occurs in film when the camera imitates the subjective viewpoint of a character through its visual technique, as Antonioni does when he makes Giuliana's neurosis in *Red Desert* an alibi for his own highly abstract cinematic vision.[60] Once Christ has called his disciples into being, they in turn can look at him and bestow upon him the gaze that will ultimately represent itself, in Holy Writ, as the omniscient gaze of the divine mind. But Pasolini reveals that originary gaze to be an emphatically human one, expressed in the hand-held camera that follows Christ along with the disciples down the slopes of city streets, around corners, and through narrow alleys as he dispenses his apostolic advice, in a truncated version of Matthew, chapter 10, verses 5–42. By reserving the final close-up of the speaker's face for the line, "Think not that I am come to send peace on earth: I come not to send peace but a sword," Pasolini privileges this formulation of Christ's militancy.[61] It is significant, too, that Pasolini chooses to omit the scriptural conclusion to this sermon, with its emphasis on the positive value of apostolic reception ("He that receiveth you receiveth me"), insisting instead on the disruptiveness of his ministry ("For I am come to see a man at variance against his father").

The free indirect subjective of this early scene is exasperated to the point of violence in the two trials near the film's end, shot in a cinéma vérité style that Pasolini terms "almost Godardian" in its intrusive-ness.[62] By locating the center of consciousness in Peter, Pasolini is translating the biblical indication, "But Peter followed him afar off unto the high priest's palace, and went in, and sat with the servants, to see the end" (Matt. 26:58). The merging of the camera's perspective with Peter's is announced in the approach to Caiaphas's court, as the Apostle joins the crowd up the stairs, proceeds down the hallway in close range, and is framed frontally in close-up before a match cut of the trial setting shows that all will be seen through these particular eyes. Such a limited and remote perspective, so surprising in a film that otherwise abounds in close-ups, is agonizing in all the information that it withholds from the spectator. This is deliberately poor report-age, newsreel footage shot with an eyewitness authenticity that bor-ders on the amateur. With the exception of one medium shot of Jesus, whose black-mantled figure reveals nothing about him, the scene is filmed in long shot, and what we see is further obstructed by a little pavilion stationed in the midst of the tribunal. The camera movements themselves are frustratingly ineffective in clarifying our viewpoint as Pasolini pans right and left, only to replace one series of obstructive heads with another. Christ literally disappears behind a viewer's head when the death sentence is pronounced, and finally, when he is sub-jected to crowd harassment, the camera returns to an extreme close-up of Peter's eyes, revealing that the true focus of this scene has not been the sacrificial victim, but the psychology of the witness who is soon to deny his master according to plan.

For the trial before Pontius Pilate, Pasolini uses the same cinéma vérité techniques, but now they are exasperated to the point of hys-teria, with jerky camera movements, quick cuts, and a cacophonous sound track all expressing the crisis atmosphere of the scene. The ac-tion here, and on the road to Golgotha, is presented through the eyes of John, the youngest of the disciples, whose adolescent emotionalism allows Pasolini to unleash all the affective power of his subjective cam-era so that we become fully involved witnesses to the events. Unlike Caiaphas's trial, set outdoors in a spacious, sunlit courtyard, this scene takes place indoors, in a darker, more congested space whose back wall is laden with a low, Roman arch and whose center is occupied by a large round well. The jury is seated along the circumference and, like Peter's perspective in the earlier trial, John's is frustratingly limited, so that pans right and left never succeed in freeing his viewpoint from obstructions. During the most rhetorically charged moments of Pilate's oration, when the defendant's objections or public protest might have changed the course of events, Pasolini cuts to extreme close-ups of John's eyes registering the agony of his paralysis to act: when Pilate asks, "Hearest thou not how many things they witness against thee?" looking for any excuse to exonerate the accused; when he proclaims, "Today is the Passover, and as every Passover, I want to free a prisoner, whichever one you want. Whom do you want me to free, Barabbas or Jesus called Christ?" hoping to find crowd support for his own sense of justice; and when he asks in vain, "What shall I do then with Jesus which is called Christ?" after the crowd requests Barabbas's release.

John's long-shot perspective and the blockage of heads denies us vital information: we never see Barabbas, and though we are able to discern the pitcher and hear Pilate's declaration, "I am innocent of the blood of this just man. You see to it," we never see him washing his hands. As Christ is brought forward by military escort but never enters our line of vision for the heads that obstruct our view, our confusion is only increased by a series of disorienting frames—a brief long shot of a group emerging rear right from a vaulted tunnel, a shot of John changing position to get a better view, and a shot of a vaulted tunnel (the same one as earlier?) arrayed with eating or idling soldiers, awaiting the arrival of Christ from the rear left.

This frenzied, highly emotional subjective camera prevails throughout the final episodes of the Passion, culminating in the *Stabat Mater* sequence of anguished maternal close-ups alternating with low-angle shots of Christ's face in pain. The film only returns to its accustomed calm in the postmortem scenes, where the subjective camera relinquishes its hold on our attention and the omniscient perspective reasserts itself, as Resurrection events come to fulfill Christ's messianic promise. In only one final instance does the subjective camera recur, and that is in the ecstatic scene of the rush to see the risen Christ, accompanied by the jubilant strains of the Missa Luba. Here a tracking shot in close range at eye level with the runners enables the camera to be an active participant in the crowd, whose joy translates into vigorous physical movement. But the subjective camera is no mere dramatic device at this point in the Gospel narrative—it is theologically appropriate in its mimesis of the human witness to the revelation that authorizes the divine perspective of its "other" gaze.

In the interaction of the two gazes, and the story of the genesis of the first from the second, Pasolini's film gives true cinematic expression to the meaning of his title. Though English language distributors insisted upon adding the titular "Saint," the Italian reads simply *Il*

Vangelo secondo Matteo, suggesting the interplay of two perspectives, the very human one of its scribe, and the divine one of salvation history, whose pivotal moment he records. There is indeed a conversion of a gaze within this film, but it is Matthew's, not Pasolini's, and by building that story into his *Gospel,* the filmmaker avoids making a hypocritical or demystifying life of Christ. When the film ends with Christ's own parting words to his Apostles, "And lo, I am with you always, even unto the end of the world," there is a way in which Pasolini's filmic renewal of the Gospel story helps verify that promise.

■ ■

6 · Pasolini's *Decameron*

WRITING WITH BODIES

Where *The Gospel According to St. Matthew* precipitated a stylistic crisis
in Pasolini's filmmaking and forced him to revolutionize the technique
that had served him so well in *Accattone, Mamma Roma,* and *La ricotta,*
The Decameron signaled a radical thematic and ideological shift in his
approach to his art.[1] As the first film of the *Trilogy of Life*—a triptych
that was to include *The Canterbury Tales* (1972) and *The Arabian Nights*
(1973)—*The Decameron* marked a move away from overt ideological
filmmaking, with its cultivation of elite audiences, its renunciation of
mainstream representational codes, and its fixation on the difficulty of
communication, toward a more easily consumable cinema that reveled
in its popular appeal.[2] It is no accident that *The Decameron* became one
of the highest grossing films of 1971, and that it inspired an entire
subgenre of sequels: *Decameroticus, Decameron proibitissimo, Le calde
notti di Giovanni Boccaccio, Decameron nero, Quando le donne si chiamavano
Madonne, Il meglio del Decameron e degli scrittori erotici del '500, Boccame-
ron: una cavalla tutta nuda,* and the ingeniously entitled *Racconti proibiti
di niente vestiti.*[3] Thus the film industry as well as the viewing public
joined Pasolini in the celebration of the physical world, in the gaiety
and "the sheer joy of telling and recounting" that freedom from overt
ideological imperatives conferred on his art.[4] "Up to the time of the
Trilogy my filmmaking motivations were ideological," Pasolini told Oswald Stack and Rosamund Lomax. "Now they're ontological. When
you're young, you have a greater need of ideology in order to live. But
when you grow older, life becomes more restricted and sufficient unto
itself. This *Trilogy* constitutes a declaration of love to life."[5] But else-

where, Pasolini attributes his withdrawal from ideological filmmaking to darker causes. The gaiety of the *Trilogy*, "the great desire to laugh is born from the definitive setting aside of 'hope.' I'm devoid, practically and ideologically, of every hope," he told Sergio Arecco. History has not fulfilled the Marxist-Hegelian promise that thesis and antithesis will eventuate in the longed-for synthesis of social justice. "My dialectic is no longer ternary, but binary. There are only oppositions, irreconcilable: no *sole del futuro*, no better world."[6]

This withdrawal into a mythic past and the loss of faith in historical progress do not by any means imply a rejection of the contestatory role of art, however. If there are only irreconcilable oppositions, then the artist must bear witness to them, occupying the firing line of public debate, playing the dissident role of Matthew's Jesus or the Old Testament prophet who constantly reminds us of unpleasant truths. Pasolini chooses to represent the past not to escape social relevance but to engage the present in polemical comparison. "I prefer to move in the past now because I believe the past to be the only force that can contest the present," Pasolini told Gideon Bachmann.[7] Here, as elsewhere in his art, sexuality provides the weapon for Pasolini's frontal attack on the contemporary status quo. Far from an entertaining romp in the medieval hay, the eroticism of the *Trilogy* is strategic—it stands as an alternative to the compromised and fallen expressivity of the technological world. With the "unreality of the subculture of the mass media and therefore of mass communication, the last bulwark of reality appeared to be 'innocent' bodies in the archaic, dark, vital violence of their sex organs," Pasolini wrote in the "Abiura dalla *Trilogia della vita.*"[8] The untrammeled physicality of the *Trilogy*, its insistent creatural realism, means that each character "communicates with his own body, his own sanguine humors, his own material made color, mud, shattered teeth, sex, sweat," as Sandro Petraglia so aptly put it.[9]

Pasolini's recourse to the past and to the great erotic storytelling tradition from England to the Middle East is thus recourse to the naked human body as an irreducible medium of communication, to a semiosis of corporeality unobstructed by the civilizing veils of clothing and libidinal repression that culture has imposed upon it. Free to indulge their appetites, exposed in all their imperfections and innocence, the nude bodies of men and women in the *Trilogy* constitute a primal language, a prelapsarian physiological expressivity. But there is another side to Pasolini's vitalism. *The Decameron* is pervaded by a sense of death—for every naked reveler there is a corpse swathed in burial shrouds being carted along in a casket or carried aloft on a plank.[10] Tingoccio's exuberant fornication with his *comare* (mother of his godchild) is seen to be terminal—the jump cut from his postcoital return home to his postmortem funerary journey suggests a cause-and-effect linkage, John Donne's candle burning at both ends.

The dark side of Pasolini's vitalism and the insistence that this past contest the present make his film anything but the easily consumable product that its commercial success and its numerous cinematic off-spring would suggest. Pasolini's corporeal semiotics, his technique of "writing with bodies," has the effect of defamiliarizing the Middle Ages, just as his antispectacular approach to the Christ story defami-liarized *The Gospel According to St. Matthew*. By removing the gowns and doublets and armor that clothe the nudity of medieval characters and by omitting the tapestries and the warm blazing hearths that mask the physical discomfort of their domestic life, Pasolini denies us the cozy complacency of conventional representations in storybooks and film.[11] Living in dark, mold-encrusted rooms, fighting dental problems unsuccessfully, coping with outdoor plumbing, Pasolini's characters in their corporeal expressivity convince us of the physical hardship of medieval life and increase the experiential distance between our reality and theirs.

But Pasolini's most consequential defamiliarizing operation is cul-tural, for the filmmaker is reacting not just to his textual source but to what Italian civilization has made of it in the intervening six centuries: a mainstay of the canon, a *Galateo* of polite behavior, a model of lin-guistic decorum. It is to this last that Pasolini directs his most obvious criticism, for the *questione della lingua* so importantly arbitrated by the Tuscan *trecentisti* receives a very un-Tuscan solution in Pasolini's film. By translating Boccaccio's normative latinizing prose into Neapolitan street talk, Pasolini is challenging the Tuscan-centricity of the Italian language and thereby criticizing Tuscany's dominance over the entire culture since the time of Boccaccio. In his essay "Nuove questioni lin-guistiche," Pasolini credits this linguistic autocracy with the imposi-tion of a pseudonational language on the whole country in defiance of its plurilinguistic, regional, dialectal nature.[12] By replacing Boccaccio's exemplary Tuscan prose with Neapolitan dialect, the filmmaker is figu-ratively restoring to the common folk control of linguistic usage—a gesture whose political implications accord with Pasolini's overall popularizing intent. Accordingly, early in the film he makes explicit this linguistic strategy in the interval between the tales of Andreuccio and Masetto, when an old man gives a public reading of the *Decame-ron*, specifically the second story of the ninth day. The teller quotes Boccaccio's first sentence directly from the text, then interjects one phrase of some interest to our argument. Quoting Boccaccio he reads,

An old man (bottom right) discards the *Decameron* text and proceeds to tell a Boccaccio tale in Neapolitan dialect, while Ser Ciappelletto (top center) works the crowd.

"Saper dunque dovete in Lombardia" ("You must know, therefore, in Lombardy"); then he improvises, "Dove ce stanno quelli che parlano toscano" ("Where those who speak Tuscan live"); and then he finishes Boccaccio's sentence. Impatient with the reading, the teller tosses the book aside and continues, "Signori miei, mo' ve spiego alla napole-tana" (Gentlemen, now I'll explain it Neapolitan style).[13] The telling in dialect is clearly more successful than the reading in Tuscan, but here Pasolini carries his linguistic critique a step further. As the speaker develops the lively tale of the abbess who mistakes her lover's britches for a wimple, the attentive audience becomes prey to a pickpocket whom we later recognize as Ser Ciappelletto. The story telling has put the listeners off guard, making them as inattentive as the poorly dressed abbess in the tale. Pasolini here seems to be attacking verbal narration as itself distracting, at variance with empirical experience and therefore to be replaced with the semiotics of bodies, the "corpo-real writing" that will lead our attention back to the only reality that can be authentically lived.

This episode exemplifies what I would call an "allegory of adapta-tion" or an "umbilical scene" in which the film reveals the traces of its derivation from the parent text and discloses its interpretive strategy. The street-corner storyteller is a figure for Pasolini himself who trans-forms the elitist, literary source into an accessible item of popular en-tertainment. "Mo' ve spiego alla napoletana" could serve as the film's epigraph in its revelation of Pasolini's intent to restore the popular origins of Boccaccio's own storytelling art by reversing the medieval writer's refinement and elevation of his narrative raw materials. Thus where Boccaccio homogenized and gentrified his culturally disparate sources, which ranged from gossip, practical jokes, proverbs, folk leg-end, fabliaux, chronicle, exempla, and romance to hagiography, Paso-lini returns to the popular roots of Decameronian inspiration and re-stores that legacy to the mass culture from which it derived.[14]

The filmmaker is at his most antiliterary in his very first complete episode—the tale of Andreuccio (2.5)—where the only character in the entire film to speak Boccaccio's language, full of grammatical in-versions, hypotaxis, gerunds, and so forth, is the Sicilian prostitute, Fiodaliso. It is the very style of her telling that convinces Andreuccio of its unassailable truth. Pasolini accentuates the treacherous elegance of her tale within a tale by implicitly comparing it to a parallel, though differently styled, internal narration—that of Andreuccio as he re-counts his adventures to the two robbers who have found him by ol-factory clues. The protagonist's style is the diametrical opposite of Fiodaliso's, for his is paratactic, devoid of causal links, ordered by no device more complex than chronology. Andreuccio's naive discourse proves nearly as fatal to him as Fiodaliso's had been, for he thereby inadvertently reveals to the thieves how easily he can be duped. Not a whit too soon, Andreuccio learns his lesson and discovers how to read other speakers' verbal cues, as his had been read by his predators. When the thieving sacristan assures his accomplices that "i morti non mangiano gli uomini" ("the dead don't eat men") (26), Andreuccio correctly decodes this verbal message to his own belated advantage. In fact, many of the stories that Pasolini chooses to include in his film are about the instability and duplicity of language. Thus Caterina is able to invoke the nightingale to escape her overprotective parents and enjoy the embraces of her beloved (5.4), and through the language of incantation Don Gianni succeeds in making a cuckold of Pietro while not quite succeeding in making a horse of Gemmata (9.10). Most importantly, Ser Ciappelletto's false confession reveals the extremes to which linguistic falsification, and listener gullibility, can lead.

In this attack on verbal discourse as unstable and deceptive, Pasolini rejects Boccaccio and at the same time endorses his innermost significance. As author of the literary text, Boccaccio is indeed a self-conscious manipulator of dangerous and misleading verbal discourse. But he is also his own harshest critic, continually exposing the verbal ruses and deceptions of his characters, and hence of himself as the supreme manipulator of words. By introducing the volume with the tale of Ser Ciappelletto, the arch-storyteller who creates a fictional self and is canonized for it, Boccaccio issues a warning to his readers about the untrustworthiness of literary discourse, his own in particular. Thus, Pasolini's critique of Boccaccio's literariness coincides with the medieval writer's own frank appraisal of his poetic vocation. Where Boccaccio challenges literary discourse *from within*, using language in playful and self-sabotaging ways that call its truthfulness into question, Pasolini replaces literary discourse with corporeal writing, denuding the book of its refined integument, de-euphemizing its sexuality, reducing its obscene metaphors to the literal level of brute bodily referents. Thus Masetto's elaborate conceit of working the garden (3.1) is given concrete literal embodiment throughout the episode, and Pasolini explicitly weds tenor and vehicle in an imagistic juxtaposition that suggests the nuns' willing participation in the forthcoming sexual harvest. "Well, I have heard from all the women who have come here that nothing in the world is sweeter than what a woman does with a man"(29), says one nun to her companion. As she speaks, Pasolini photographs this nun in medium close-up with a huge cluster of grapes festooning the vine to her left. A cut to a subjective, low-angle shot of Masetto on a ladder gives visual prominence to his genitals and makes explicit their metaphoric link to the fruit of the vine. Pasolini literalizes an obscene metaphor by similar imagistic juxtaposition in the tale of Peronella (7.2). When the enterprising wife has her husband enter the jar to clean it from within, she has cleared the way for her lover Giannello to complete his exertions from without. With the words "Scrape, my husband, scrape, let's do things as we should! Uhm, higher, uhm, lower. That's right. . . . Come on, come on, scrape well. That's how I like it!"(36) Peronella engages in such successful double-talk that two mutually exclusive tasks are completed in obedience to one set of commands. The film enables us to see both the literal and figurative referents of her utterance and invites us to compare Peronella explicitly to the jar as a vessel to be entered by men and to be sold as a commodity. When Giannello promises to give Peronella's husband seven *denari*, the price includes an item that the seller had not bargained for: the sexual favors of his wife, enjoyed with impunity.

Because it is the profit motive that blinds Peronella's husband to his cuckoldry, the story well supports Pasolini's antibourgeois polemic. Much of Pasolini's adaptational strategy is dictated by this ideological requirement, such as the decision to juxtapose the tale of the nightingale (5.4) with that of the pot of basil (4.5), where the difference between comic and tragic outcomes in otherwise similar stories of forbidden young love hinges on the social status of the suitor.[15] Lisabetta's class-conscious brothers murder Lorenzo because his plebeian origins preclude marriage into the bourgeoisie, while Caterina's parents smile upon the union of their daughter with the well-born Ricciardo Manardi. To heighten the asperity of his social criticism, Pasolini relegates Boccaccio's Lorenzo from the Pisan working class to the Sicilian proletariat, adding regional bias to the victim's socioeconomic disadvantage.[16] The film's most scathing indictment of the bourgeoisie occurs in this episode, where Pasolini gives considerable dramatic development to the highly perfunctory textual murder. Boccaccio dispatches Lorenzo in two extremely compressed periods.

> The three brothers jested and chatted with Lorenzo in their usual manner, until one day they pretended they were all going off on a pleasure-trip to the country, and took Lorenzo with them. They bided their time, and on reaching a very remote and lonely spot, they took Lorenzo off his guard, murdered him, and buried his corpse.[17]

Pasolini's sequence, instead, is an agonizing exercise in homicidal foreplay, where the brothers amuse themselves with their victim and extract every possible ounce of psychological balm for their wounded middle-class male egos. The first grievance to redress is Lorenzo's slight to their masculine pride in his secret consorting with Lisabetta. In their fatherless family, the three unnamed and undifferentiated brothers serve as a collective paternal stand-in whose honor resides in their ability to protect Lisabetta's maidenhead and eventually to deliver her, intact, to the spouse of their choice. By violating their prerogative, Lorenzo has challenged their paternal authority and their very identity as males—an identity predicated on their exclusive control over Lisabetta's sexuality. Pasolini's fraternal threesome redresses this wound to its collective masculine pride in a ritual of communal urination. "Lorenzo, piss with us, it doesn't cost a thing. Come on, let's go," says the first brother with locker-room camaraderie. "But you, Lorenzo, don't think that we aren't men. . . . You thought wrong, you understand! We're men. We're men! Don't you see that we're men?" (53–54). This ominous flaunting of genitals foreshadows the climactic opportunity to vindicate their manhood which Lorenzo's murder affords them.

But Lorenzo's affront to the brothers is also socioeconomic, and they avenge their honor in a way that symbolically reasserts their class superiority. The entire sequence begins with a long shot of the hill that dominates the landscape and figures their proprietary hold on it, as well as furnishing Lisabetta with a topographical clue to Lorenzo's eventual burial site. What masquerades as a playful run through the woods has a twofold seriousness: it serves as a tour of the brothers' territorial wealth, and it anticipates the real predatory chase that is to follow. Pasolini's camera becomes an accomplice in this strategy, revealing the vastness of the property through long dolly shots that track the men as they race through the landscape at such speed that the horizontal lines of the terracing tend to break up this space into an abstract expanse of pure line, color, and movement. The effect is to denaturalize this nature as it becomes the arena for the enactment of man's most antisocial instincts. When the runners finally come to rest, the didacticism of their plot is made clear. This is "nostra compagna," one of the brothers observes. "Sit down, Lorenzo, because today there are no servants and masters" (54). This mock egalitarianism only heightens our awareness of the class gap and of the role it plays in motivating the conspiracy. To prove that this is indeed a day of fun and games, brother number two slathers the face of brother number one with grapes to the accompaniment of forced fraternal hilarity. Lorenzo plays along with what he takes to be innocent clowning, and reaction shots show him eating the proffered fruit, smiling, unaware that his will be the next face to be slathered—not with grape juice, but with the soil that Lisabetta will eventually clean off his features to ascertain the identity of the newly unearthed corpse. A cut to a low-angle shot reveals the brothers again in motion, now jumping over a pit that seems to mark the transition from benign foreplay to homicidal chase. Lorenzo hesitates on the brink of the pit, realizing that this leap will be irreversible.[18] A series of shots and reaction shots photographically recapituates this war of wills, whose concentration of numbers and power on the predators' side makes its outcome a foregone conclusion. In a medium close-up of the three brothers, Pasolini matches their cajoling facial expressions with their choral encouragements to jump: "*Forza*, let's go, come on. What's he doing? *Forza*. Join the race. Let's go, Lorenzo" (54).

A cut to Lorenzo shows the sudden seriousnesss of one who has belatedly caught on, who has seen the murderous underside of this jesting. After the camera singles out brothers number two and three in their enticements, Lorenzo's reaction shot is his most consequential, for it marks the delivery of his only word of dialogue in the entire sequence: "Why?" (55). This is a truly subversive question in that it challenges the social hierarchy of servants and the masters whose motivations are above employee scrutiny, and it disrupts the literal level of the brothers' murder plot by subjecting it to interpretation. When the third brother asks "What's wrong?" Lorenzo's seriousness gives way to a new kind of smile—no longer the smile of the innocent dupe, but the stoic acceptance of the victim who knows what awaits him on the other side. The tracking shots of the earlier part of the sequence resume, but the camera's movement is no longer horizontal as it follows Lorenzo up a slope, cutting back and forth from predators to prey until the sound of three rapiers being unsheathed confirms all our tragic presentiments. A jump cut to Lisabetta's window spares us the spectacle of the slaughter but intensifies its imaginative impact by forcing the viewers to complete the sequence with a murder of his or her own devising. Thus where Boccaccio's text dwells on Lisabetta's pathology of grief in decapitating her lover, planting the head in a basil pot, and worshipping its vegetal luxuriance until the brothers deprive her of even that consolation, Pasolini's emphasis is on the revenge itself and the way that the fraternal plot symbolically restores the proprietary and sexual power that Lorenzo had unwittingly usurped.

A similar antibourgeois stance dictates Pasolini's adaptive strategy in the Andreuccio tale (2.5). As the horse dealer who has come to Naples to buy wholesale in order to then sell the animals retail in Perugia, Andreuccio is the quintessential capitalist, the middleman who profits not by producing anything or performing a vital service, but by investing in a commodity and turning a profit by increasing its price without increasing its value. In making Andreuccio the pretext for antimercantile satire, Pasolini is following Boccaccio's lead where the tale's conclusion compresses into one period the intricate saga of capitalist trial and error. Advised to leave Naples immediately, Andreuccio "returned to Perugia, having invested, in a ring, the money with which he had set out to purchase horses" (McWilliam, 155). Part of the joke of this story is that Andreuccio thinks that he has come to Naples as a consumer—of horses, of wine, of women, and of food—and instead it is *he* who is consumed by a variety of con artists, from *la bella siciliana* to the two thieves who use him to rob the archbishop's tomb.

Pasolini takes Boccaccio's joke one step further. If Andreuccio is consumed by the city, he is also excreted from it in an analogy that explains an important omission from the text and a series of spatial and chromatic choices on Pasolini's part. In the *Decameron* story, Andreuccio experiences three infernal descents and three resurrections, a number whose theological ramifications are obvious and strategically used.[19] After the fall into the cesspool, Andreuccio is lowered into a well to be cleansed and is finally dropped into the tomb. Though Pasolini would hardly be averse to using trinitarian symbolism in a satiric way, he chooses to leave out the second descent, preferring to keep Andreuccio in his fecal state throughout the remainder of the episode.[20] Accordingly, the entire sequence is suffused with darkness and a chromatic predominance of browns and grays, and Naples is photographed as a series of dim, winding streets with distinctly intestinal overtones. Though it is never named in the film, Boccaccio explicitly labels the ill-famed neighborhood of Andreuccio's nocturnal wanderings "Malpertugio" or "evil opening" in an infernal allusion to the Dantesque Malebolge and in a revelation of the protagonist's obliviousness to the dangers of his setting. "The maid conveyed him to the lady's house, which was situated in a quarter called The Fleshpots [Evil Opening], the mere name of which shows how honest a district it was. But Andreuccio neither knew nor suspected anything of all this, being of the opinion that he was on his way to see a gentlewoman in a perfectly respectable part of the city" (McWilliam, 143). The long shot of Andreuccio's escape from the cesspool as he climbs out of a tiny opening in a sewage shaft, himself covered with feces, suggests that he is indeed the waste product of Malpertugio, of the intestinal system of the Neapolitan *mala vita* that consumes and excretes its victims when it has no more use for them. But the fact that Andreuccio succeeds in his business venture, recouping his original capital investment and actually turning a profit (the ruby ring was worth more than the 500 florins of his initial cash outlay), makes his fecal status at the end of the film's episode a telling retrospective commentary on the mercantile economy that underwrites his actions.

Other Pasolinian departures from Boccaccio's text have anticlerical logic. In the book, Masetto attributes his sudden restoration of speech to divine intervention—a fiction that the gullible abbess is only too happy to accept—while the film's Masetto confesses that his disability was a hoax, so that it befalls the mother superior to invent the fiction of the miracle. While Boccaccio's abbess is merely lecherous and gullible, Pasolini's is a deceiver—a conscious and self-interested abuser of her church's power to command belief. Similarly, in Pasolini's version of the Gemmata story (9.10), Don Gianni emerges as more villainous than Boccaccio's priest in his exploitation of the couple's abject poverty. Though Boccaccio describes Compar Pietro as "poverissimo" in the exposition to the tale, Pasolini makes explicit the causal link between poverty and the couple's sexual victimization by the priest in the dialogue preceding his consent to work his magic. "I beg you, for the love of God, Don Gianni, you see how poor we are. Perform this act of charity for us!" (60). The squalid domestic setting of the tale gives visual reinforcement to Pietro's plea for poverty relief through the priest's supernatural offices.

In the tale of Tingoccio and Meuccio, however, Boccaccio's own anticlericalism is put to other ideological uses. The *Decameron* story is a spoof on theological quibbling, on the scholastic mania for distinctions and degrees—a mania that finds legalistic expression in Dante's contrivance of the appropriate *contrappassi* for every possible subdivision of sin. Thus when Meuccio asks Tingoccio's ghost what punishment he suffers for sleeping with his *comare*, the sinner dismisses any theological hierarchy of "better" or "worse" adulteries. "Be off with you, you fool! There's nothing special down here about the mother of a godchild" (McWilliam, 582), Tingoccio had been told by a companion in the afterlife who was well versed in the nuances of divine justice. Though the film's Tingoccio makes the same profession of purgatorial indifference to *comari*, Pasolini's intent is less to spoof theological distinctions than to promote a generalized creed of free love.[21] When Meuccio races through the predawn streets of Naples to his own *comare*'s house and exuberantly mounts her, exclaiming "It's not a sin," the lasting message has nothing to do with godparentage and everything to do with generic sexual permissiveness. The referent of "It's not a sin" is what we see on the screen—two bodies copulating— not the pseudoscholastic quibble of Boccaccio's fabliau. It is appropriate that Pasolini's final episode gives retrospective justification to the film's corporeal semiotics, where naked bodies are seen as the only remaining vehicles of untainted expressivity in a technologically tainted world, "the last bulwark of reality," as he concluded in the "Abiura." Rereading the film in the light of Meuccio's proclamation, a series of episodes lines up behind the banner of guilt-free sexuality, beginning with the nun's insistence that copulation with Masetto "è un paradiso," where the metaphor retains its literal affiliation with the prelapsarian garden state. No story is more redolent of wholesome sexuality than that of Ricciardo and Caterina (5.4) whose lovemaking is neither prurient nor sentimentalized in the film. The predawn nuptials performed on the near-naked couple by Caterina's accommodating parents are an exercise in Edenic innocence, where for once the institutionalized powers of family and church see fit to sanction the course of natural passion.

Pasolini's politics of adaptation require him to make drastic changes in Boccaccio's figure of the artist as he is represented within the text. Though the medieval author internalizes himself within the *Decameron* as the isolated defender of the humanities against his philistine attackers in the introduction to the fourth day and again in the conclusion, it is in the ten frame-story youths that he most importantly incarnates the figure of the artist. Pasolini, instead, dispenses with the *brigata* of socially privileged storytellers who exemplify the courtly ideals of language and decorum so dear to the Italian elite and replaces these artist figures with the character of the fresco painter—Giotto's disciple—whose working-class affinities would make him more amenable to Pasolini's political strategy. The painter constitutes a rejection of all the middle-class behavioral ideals embodied in Boccaccio's *brigata*. The young people's attention to propriety in dress, meals, and diversion is utterly disregarded by the painter, who is at home in peasant's mantle, wolfs down his food, and obviously cares nothing for appearances. Though Pasolini's figure of the artist is clearly modeled on Giotto himself as he emerges from Boccaccio's fifth tale of the sixth day, the filmmaker has carefully edited out the opening lines of the *Decameron* story which reveal in Giotto a landowner returning from his property in the Mugello. In fact, Pasolini's Giotto has little in common either with Boccaccio's or with the somewhat business-minded Giotto we get from medieval archives.[22] Instead, Pasolini's painter is an anachronistic construct of a post-Romantic age: the genius rapt with inspiration who takes his models from life but must be motivated by some transcendent creative impulse. This new Giotto is thus not only a convenient vehicle for Pasolini's politics of art, he is a personal analogue to the filmmaker's idealized mode of creation.[23]

Nor is the Giotto figure alone in realizing his art. Pasolini goes to great lengths to document the teamwork on which his fresco painting depends, from the pigment grinding and chromatic mixing to the placement of scaffolding and the offering of brushes. Four of the fragments that intervene between tales in the film's second half involve Giotto's co-workers, whose interactions range from pranks and banter to serious, even inspired, cooperation. Though Giotto eats in the refectory with the friars while his apprentices dine less ceremoniously among themselves, the maestro shares sleeping quarters with them and seems to prefer their company. The workshop is a prime example of the Pasolinian utopias already explored in *Accattone* and *The Gospel According to St. Matthew* where a male community bonds in the service of a superhuman ideal, be it a spiritual or an aesthetic one. That this is a collective, working-class ethos, untainted by notions of property, family prestige, or personal honor, is proved by its opposition to the dystopia of Lisabetta's brothers, whose feigned egalitarianism and pseudocamaraderie had led to Lorenzo's fatal entrapment. Bound by their commitment to ownership and sexual control, the brothers formed a Pasolinian anticommunity whose governing assumptions revealed, by contrast, the positive values of the workshop's corporate identity.

The filmmaker's disposal of Boccaccio's frame story has momentous formal as well as political implications. True, Pasolini replaces Boccccio's *cornice* with a bipartite frame of his own when fragments of the Ser Ciappelletto story intervene between successive tales to glue together the first half of the film, while the Giotto figure gives rise to a framing figure for the second half.[24] But such a technique is fraught with ambiguities. When characters emerge from tales to become protagonists in a frame story that contains other tales, we are approaching the Chinese box structure that Pasolini will use to such advantage in *The Arabian Nights*. There, however, the ambiguity is authorized by the textual source, while here it is used to subvert the original by challenging its cherished assumptions about form. When a frame no longer serves to distinguish the work of art from that which is without, when container and contained coextend like the two edges of a Möbius strip, our deepest held convictions about aesthetic form are called into question. In the very narrations of his tales, Pasolini issues the same kind of formal challenge to his viewers. Because the transitions between episodes are so abrupt and unexpected that we often find ourselves well into the next story before we realize that the previous one is over, we miss any sense of narrative closure that would retrospectively order the tales.[25] Thus Pasolini denies us the formal satisfactions of complete stories with beginnings, middles, and ends just as he fails to give his film an expository introduction or a conclusion that would retroactively explain and organize the whole. In fact, the concluding frame-story fragment shows Giotto before the three panels of his fresco, but only two of them have been completed. The third panel remains empty, making the fresco cycle as imperfect (in the etymological sense of the term) as the film itself.[26]

By dispensing with Boccaccio's elegant and elaborate frame story, by playing havoc with the original sequence and thematic progression of the tales, by making personal and arbitrary the principle of order that had been so public and necessary in Boccaccio, Pasolini issues his most serious statement about the cultural and historical distance separating the medieval text from its cinematic imitation. Boccaccio's work, bearing witness to the decline in the scholastic worldview, nonetheless nostalgically holds onto its rigorous sense of structure, wherein the principles of order had to be explicit enough for the viewer "to re-experience the very processes of architectural composition," according to Erwin Panofsky.[27] By rejecting the *Decameron*'s meticulous structure, Pasolini is perhaps scolding Boccaccio for clinging to a vestige of scholastic order that was already obsolete—a hollow fiction at great variance with the realities of trecento Italian culture. But the criticism goes both ways, for Boccaccio's ordered cosmos points to the very impossibility of such ordering in the contemporary world. Pasolini thus endorses Frederic Jameson's argument that literary genres are predicated on the ideological possibilities offered by a culture at a given point in its development.[28] Boccaccio's culture offered (if somewhat nostalgically) the raw material for complete, coherent narrative forms, whereas Pasolini's obviously does not.

In the fresco painter, Pasolini combines a politically acceptable equivalent to the figure of the artist with a perfect medieval analogy to the filmmaker. Both the fresco cycle and the film require team efforts for their realization, both narrate through visual images, thus potentially reaching a much broader, more democratic audience than literature can, and both juxtapose a series of still frames to tell a story that unfolds in time and space. To further the analogy between the two media, Pasolini casts himself in the role of Giotto, and when the painter wanders in the marketplace outside the church to find models for his art, he literally constructs a frame with the fingers of both hands, placing two fingers vertically and crossing them with two fingers horizontally to form a square.[29] Thus, Giotto the painter sights his models the way Pasolini the filmmaker sets up his next shot. And not surprisingly, the figures that Giotto sights in the crowd are the protagonists in Pasolini's next episode.

This analogy between fresco painting and filmmaking lies at the heart of Pasolini's metafilm, for it is here that he can make explicit the

Pasolini himself plays Giotto, the internalized figure of the artist, who makes explicit the analogy between fresco painting and filmmaking.

mechanics of his medium and define the language appropriate to the cinema in opposition to the language of his literary source. In Boccaccio's *Decameron*, he has chosen a paragon of literariness against which to posit his own semiotics of corporeality. Again and again in his theoretical writings, Pasolini insists that the film lexicon, unlike the symbolic systems of verbal languages, has its source in reality. "If the cinema is thus no more than the written language of reality . . . it means that it is neither arbitrary nor symbolic; and therefore it represents reality through reality." [30] Though this source in reality does not deny film language the double articulation accorded all linguistic systems, it does give cinema a concreteness and an immediacy that distinguish it from purely symbolic codes. In the figure of Giotto, Pasolini is able to dramatize the genesis of film language in reality as the painter sights models from the "real-life" crowd in the marketplace outside the church. Indeed in these sequences Pasolini analyzes the constituents of his cinematic code, providing a visual gloss for his remarks in the essay "La lingua scritta della realtà." [31] As Giotto selects out the single elements to be included in his fresco panel, Pasolini implies the *cinémi*, or indivisible formal units that he equates to the phonemes of verbal languages. The completed fresco panel is the *inquadratura*, the smallest complete unit of meaning, or the cinematic equivalent of the linguists' moneme. In the juxtaposition of adjacent panels in the fresco cycle, Pasolini suggests the celluloid strip itself with its succession of still photographic compositions. Contiguity in the fresco cycle provides the linkage that montage accords cinematic stills. Pasolini's insistence on foregrounding the editing process is part of his anti-Hollywood polemic, his rejection of mainstream conventions that govern the "seamless" flow of images and render natural their succession, even while constantly shifting camera angles and shot distances. The Italian filmmaker instead employs a disjunctive editing style that flaunts the opacity of technique by being intrusive, by making us aware at every moment that our perspective is being manipulated. As Geoffrey Nowell-Smith so aptly observes, Pasolini displays "a wilful disregard of the constructive nature of the editing process . . . [and] a firm positive insistence on the single shot as the unit of reality." [32] Indeed, the format of the episode film makes more explicit than ever the disjunctions of montage, because the abrupt transitions between various tales are like so many jump cuts—seemingly arbitrary and unmotivated juxtapositions of discontinuous *inquadrature*. In a sustained fiction film, the logic of the narration may distract us from the crude fact of montage, whereas the episode film constantly reminds us of the mechanics of linkage.

Though his tendency to break up the surface of reality into fragments, along with his use of pastiche, suggest a postmodernist Pasolini, there are powerful counterarguments for such an alignment. Pasolini revels in the thickness and unity of meaning, in the proliferation
of semantic levels, that deny postmodernist disjunction and superficiality, for all his art ultimately tells the same Ur-story of humanity's
fall from a state of primal innocence and grace into the anti-Eden of
contemporary urban industrial existence. This makes his *Decameron* a
serious critical reading whose moments of surface jollity hardly suffice
to conceal its pervasive inner tension. Thus Pasolini polemically engages Boccaccio whenever the text departs from the filmmaker's ideological agenda, whenever Boccaccio's Middle Ages resist Pasolini's
need to idealize this archaic, subproletarian alternative to the contemporary status quo. Perhaps the most serious polemic revision of the
Decameron can be found in Pasolini's treatment of the tale of Ser Ciappelletto, whose structural position at the beginning of Boccaccio's text
signals its supreme importance for the medieval writer's own literary
program.

The first contrast to note is one of tone or atmosphere, an almost
ineffable difference in the aura of the two canonization scenes. Boccaccio, through the narrator Panfilo, describes the friar-confessor's sermon and its public consequences as follows:

> And in brief, with a torrent of words that the people of the town
> believed implicitly [alle quali era dalla gente della contrada data
> intera *fede*], he fixed Ser Ciappelletto so firmly in the minds and
> affections of all those present that when the service was over, ev-
> eryone thronged around the body to kiss his feet and his hands,
> all the clothes were torn from his back, and those who succeeded
> in grabbing so much as a tiny fragment felt they were in Paradise
> itself. (McWilliam, 80)

Immediately the term *fede* should put us on guard, for it is a vestige of
the con game that Ser Ciappelletto has been playing all along—as a
notary he has been selling his *fede* expensively, and the Burgundians
have been described as especially gullible, especially prone to believing any and all sworn oaths. Moving in a herd toward this body, ready
to tear off its shroud in their eagerness for physical tokens of transcendence, Boccaccio's Burgundians are little more than medieval group-
ies, brainless materialists incapable even of conceptualizing the beati-
tude to which they aspire through saintly contact. Panfilo's narrative
voice speaks from the superior perspective of class and demystified
reason, and he has nothing but contempt for Ciappelletto worship.

Pasolini's camera participates in the worshippers' reverence for the body of Ser Ciappelletto.

Pasolini's canonization scene is devoid of such condescension. His camera participates in the reverence of the suppliants who replace the violence and bestiality of Boccaccio's Burgundians with dignity, grace, and reserve. Shot in the Gothic vaulted crypt whose geometric center is occupied by the shrouded body on a tall black catafalque, the entire scene has a balanced, classical beauty heightened by the strains of Gregorian chant. The sequence ends with the poignant mise-en-scène of hands reaching from all sides to touch the corpse. Though the camera's perspective is that of a detached and physically elevated observer, it has none of the patronizing, demystified superiority of Panfilo's narrative voice, choosing instead to enter into the worshippers' own sense of awe at the spectacle of sanctity.

The reverential atmosphere of this canonization scene and several Pasolinian interpolations suggest that Ser Ciappelletto's confession may not have been mere showmanship after all. In the film's final tale, Pasolini has Tingoccio give Meuccio an apt reminder. "Oh, they say that at the moment of death whoever repents is saved!" (62). Significantly, the narrative of Tingoccio's death is interrupted by a dream vision that awakens the Giotto character—it is a vision of the Scro-

vegni Chapel Last Judgment in which the Christus Pantocrator is replaced by the Madonna and Child. By substituting the mother inter-
cessor for the judging Christ, Pasolini's film gives clemency priority
over punishment, mercy over divine retribution. This takes us back to
Ser Ciappelletto's deathbed confession and to the question of his soul's
fate in the afterlife. Despite some metaphysical hedging, Boccaccio finally damns Ciappelletto in Panfilo's epilogue to the tale:

> Nor would I wish to deny that perhaps God has blessed and ad-
> mitted him to His presence. For albeit he led a wicked, sinful life,
> it is possible that at the eleventh hour he was so sincerely repen-
> tant that God had mercy upon him and received him into His
> kingdom. But since this is hidden from us, I speak only with re-
> gard to the outward appearance, and I say that this fellow should
> rather be in Hell, in the hands of the devil, than in Paradise.
> (McWilliam, 81)

It is here that Pasolini's adaptation moves in the direction of ambiguity, for his oft-professed irrationalism, his mistrust for bourgeois
positivist thought, leads him to entertain the possibility of what Panfilo dismisses as "occulto" ("hidden").[33] Thus Pasolini engages in a
double adapative strategy—theologically elevating and stylistically reductive—in characterizing Ser Ciappelletto. The text's protagonist is a
subtle and ingenious con artist who runs rhetorical circles around the
somewhat simpleminded friar confessor. He bamboozles the holy man
through a variety of confessional tactics, including (1) telling half-
truths that leave out the damning second half—for example, that he is
a virgin (because his sexual preference is for men); (2) the confession
of trivial sins, such as his craving for lettuce while fasting; and (3) the
reversal of roles, such as his reprimand of the friar for spitting in
church and his insistence on the general need for greater spiritual
stringency. Pasolini's Ser Ciappelletto lacks such rhetorical inventiveness and, in fact, appears as simple as the friar in his verbal self-
presentation. The film's dialogue descends to the level of a vaudeville
routine in its comic tug-of-war when Ciappelletto offers to confess his
worst sin and then backs down out of feigned cowardice. "Tell it, and
we'll pray to God together," begs the friar confessor. "I can't," cries
Ciappelletto. "Come on, son, speak." "I can't, father." "But, son,
make this effort." "Nooo!" "In the name of God!" "No." "Yes." "No."
"Yes." "No." "Yes." "O.K. If you promise to pray for me, I'll tell you"
(42–43). The comic silliness of this exchange is only heightened by the
sobbing intensity of both men's delivery and the repetitive camera-
work of cross-cuts to close-ups of each speaker as he utters his re-

spective monosyllabic plea. At this point, the camera cuts to the two eavesdropping brothers who serve as the demystified public to the confession and confirm our sense that this is a virtuoso performance indeed. "The man is dying, but he's doing all this for us? Well, then, he really is a saint!" (43).

Clerical reassurances prompt Ser Ciappelletto's final outcry: "Oh what are you saying, father? My sweet mother, who carried me in her womb, day and night. For nine months she carried me in her womb" (43). It is crucial that, unlike Boccaccio's Ciappelletto, Pasolini's expires in the course of confessing and that his final sentence invokes his pregnant mother. Photographed in extreme close-up as he utters these last words, "For nine months she carried me in her womb," the protagonist dies with in utero thoughts. A cynical reader of this scene would ascribe Ciappelletto's new infancy to his final self-forgery, the delivery of a new baby fiction ready to start its life as the sanctified object of Burgundian gullibility. But recourse to medieval iconography would suggest otherwise. With Pasolini's training in art history and his love of figurative quotation, I cannot imagine that the Pisan "Triumph of Death" fresco, where the souls are imaged as newborns issuing from the mouths of corpses, was far from his mind when he conceived the dialogue and the mise-en-scène of Ciappelletto's last rites. Pasolini's focus on the dying man's mouth as he speaks of his prenatal past suggests that these final words have double reference—semantically to his first birth, iconographically to his second.

Death of old forms and rebirth into new ones is, of course, a way of talking about adaptations, especially transgressive adaptations that destroy as they create, challenging and subverting the authority of their textual models. If Ciappelletto's spirit leaves his flesh to find new life in the hereafter, Pasolini's resurrected *Decameron* does the opposite, giving flesh back to words, literalizing sexual euphemisms, replacing nightingales with genitals—in short, writing with bodies. Unfortunately, Pasolini's newfound corporeal expressivity was to be short-lived, as the "Abiura della *Trilogia dalla Vita*" so bitterly announces. "The 'reality' of innocent bodies has been violated, manipulated, tainted by consumer power: indeed, such violence on bodies has become the most macroscopic datum of the new human era."[34] In *Salò* (1975), Pasolini will continue to write with bodies, but these will no longer serve as the site for prefallen physiological expressivity. Now the naked flesh can express only allegorically—as the tablet on which Fascist history will write its most violent and obscene inscriptions on the Italian body politic.

7 · The Tavianis' *Padre padrone*

THE CRITICAL ACQUISITION OF CODES

The idea of filming Gavino Ledda's remarkable rise to a professorship in linguistics from the speechlessness of his roots in rural Sardinia came to the Tavianis as soon as they read its account in the national press.[1] They immediately set aside their planned documentary on Naples to pursue the new project, but a reading of Ledda's autobiography *Padre padrone: L'educazione di un pastore* had an immediate, sobering effect. They were daunted by the book's seeming perfection, by the total adequacy of Ledda's literary form to what he chronicles: his belated and triumphant entrance into language and his self-construction as a social being. "When we read the book," Vittorio Taviani told Jean Gili, "we had a double reaction, on the one hand a feeling of adhesion as readers, as literary readers (the book has its completion, and in that sense, it is one of the most beautiful books that we have read in these last years) on the other hand, a feeling of repulsion because the book, precisely because it was rather complete in its literary form, was concluded, and in a certain way, excluded us."[2] Enthusiasm as readers, repulsion as adapters: this ambivalence bespeaks the theoretical problem at the heart of the adaptive process. The closure and the self-sufficiency of the literary work suggest that its story and discourse are inseparable—that meaning is indistinguishable from its concrete artistic expression and that adaptation in another medium is categorically ruled out. It is as receivers of the text, then, that the Tavianis cannot imagine invading its closed world of signification and recoil at the idea of tampering with its expressive integrity.

But their relationship to the book soon enters a second phase where diffidence gives way to inventiveness as they evolve from consumers to creators of their own new text. "Having arrived at this point," Vittorio continues, "it was necessary to decompose the book into its constituent material . . . and make the material that came from the experience of Gavino Ledda, man and author of the book, confront our own material, and it was necessary to recompose all in a different work that has its own language, audio-visual language."[3] Such resignification is no simple matter, however, given the divergent practical requirements of cinematic discourse to begin with, and given this book's particular invitation to appropriate codes in critical ways. The very antiauthoritarian argument of Ledda's book requires an adaptation that interrogates textual authority and subjects the literary source to the relentless scrutiny of a rebellious son. Nor is the literary model the only target of the Tavianis' filial quarrel with authority, for neorealism has itself been the object of parricidal remarks by the filmmakers. "Our relationship with neorealism is a relationship of love-hate, of father-son. Born of a beloved and admired father, we denied it with the ungrateful violence of sons who realize themselves in the measure in which they destroy the father."[4] And since the very elements in neorealism that the Tavianis reject—its mimetic pretensions, its encouragment to uncritical identification with the protagonists, its formal transparency—are also characteristic of Ledda's autobiographical prose, the filmmakers' embrace of Brechtian, antinaturalistic, hyperbolic techniques may be seen as a simultaneous rebellion against both fathers: the textual authority and the cinematic precedent. Thus the stakes in adapting this book are indeed high for filmmakers who aspire to the very ideals of self-emancipation and self-definition that Gavino Ledda achieves in *Padre padrone*.[5]

The film contains a number of "allegories of adaptation" or "umbilical scenes" that describe the Tavianis' conflictive relationship to the text. The least obvious of such scenes, but the one that contains the rationale of the Tavianis' adaptive strategy, occurs during Gavino's military indoctrination. In the book, a captain reprimands one of Gavino's fellow Sardinian recruits for his stammering and incoherent response to the question "What is the flag?" and gives a tedious little sermon on patriotism. The film's equivalent scene includes a series of voice-over vocabulary lists suggested by the Italian word for flag, *bandiera*, and organized by phonetic similarities.[6] When the visual image of the flag gives way to the Sardinian landscape and the figure of the six-year-old Gavino hard at work, a new vocabulary list is recited whose sequence is ordered by semantics. These words are synonyms

for *boy*, followed by adjectives that narrow down the field to one particular kind of boy—one who is abused, brutalized, desperate, and
savage. This flashback recapitulates the entire first part of the film, and
in so doing, it shows how Gavino can relive his childhood therapeuti-
cally, through the insights afforded by language. The vocabulary list
continues with a group of pastoral synonyms that modulate, ironically, into terms associated with masturbation. It is a lesson on the
inadequacy of literature to represent Gavino's experience, and the
point is made by juxtaposing the conventional, urban stereotypes of
pastoral life with the reality of a solitude whose only pleasures are
onanistic.[7]

Now the voice-over turns angry as it moves to the pa—— words.
"Padre! patriarca, padrino [godfather], padrone [boss], padreterno
[eternal father], patrono [patron].[8] Unlike any of the earlier lists, this
one has etymological consistency, reverting to the Latin root and
simply varying suffixes. In no other case does language prove to be so
effective a tool for self-analysis, as if any variant at all on the root term
would give a name and an insight into some aspect of Gavino's subjugation. This final list reveals the way in which biological fatherhood
has provided the metaphoric justification for all wieldings of authority,
be they economic, political, or spiritual. It is this insight that leads
Gavino to his own form of militancy. Armed with language, he returns
to Siligo to confront his father and, in so doing, challenges the primal
biological authority on which all human injustice is based.

But Gavino is wary of escaping one form of authoritarian control
only to be subject to another. His acquisition of codes is thus selective
and critical. "For Gavino, the mastery of the code and of vocabulary is
not the mastery of an absolute given that one makes one's own and
gives you power," observes Vittorio Taviani. "At the first level of acculturation, that of words, at the same moment when Gavino pronounced certain words, he already saw them in a critical and ironic
way. . . . What interests us here is that the code is immediately acquired in a critical manner. . . . It is necessary to acquire culture and
transform it in relation to its practice."[9] Thus an important aspect of
Gavino's anti-authoritarian struggle is his refusal to accept codes passively, and his insistence on their critical appropriation.

Gavino's vocabulary lesson at the foot of the flag is an invention of
the Tavianis, and it serves as an alibi for an adaptive strategy that is
antiauthoritarian in its own right. By constructing a Gavino who is a
critical appropriator of codes, the Tavianis are justifying their own conflictual relationship with Ledda's textual authority. This leads us to the
Tavianis' most obvious "umbilical scene," where the film dramatizes

its literary filiation in its opening moments with the appearance of Gavino Ledda on-screen and a voice-over exposition identifying him as the author of the autobiography on which the film is based, "con libertà" (T., 39). The entire opening scene could be read as a gloss on this prepositional phrase, for it defines the imitative distance that so importantly separates the book from the film it inspired. A pan follows Ledda as he approaches the actor, Omero Antonutti, who will play the part of Efisio in the film. Antonutti has been standing in a meditative posture on the steps outside the schoolroom, as if awaiting his cue or marshaling his psychic energies for the task of becoming Efisio. Ledda hands him the branch that he has been whittling into a whip and explains, "My father also had this" (T., 39). Antonutti answers, "Oh yes, thanks," with a civility inconceivable for Efisio, and Ledda walks off-frame to the right.

This is an extremely complex piece of stagecraft whose ironies exceed the psychological fact that Gavino is handing his father the very instrument and symbol of his tyranny. By including the real Ledda in this prologue, the Tavianis pursue an ambiguous representational strategy, insisting on the one hand that this film has a referent in extra-aesthetic reality, and on the other hand that their film language is an autonomous sign system whose signified is indissolubly bound to its signifier. To accentuate the distance between cinematic sign and referent, the Tavianis cast in the role of Gavino the actor Severio Marconi, whose medium height and fair complexion contradict the stereotype of the short, dark Sardinian to which Ledda himself fully conforms.[10] As a way of further undercutting any documentary pretensions, the Tavianis have Ledda speak *their* lines, not the text of his own writings, so that he renounces his autonomy and becomes a representation of himself in cinematic terms.[11] Perhaps more important, the juxtaposition of documentary and fiction film calls attention to the artifice of what we are to see and immediately thwarts our suspension of disbelief, precluding any automatic identification between audience and protagonist.[12] This Brechtian technique of distancing and the consequent emphasis on the opacity of the medium, on its status as spectacle that refuses to masquerade as reality, reveals the Tavianis' critical appropriation of Ledda's text. For the autobiography presents itself as documentary truth and requires immediate, uncritical identification with its protagonist.[13] Thus by shattering the illusion of reality and precluding any unproblematic identification with the fictive Gavino, the Tavianis are immediately announcing their distance from the autobiographical source.[14]

Considerations of both an ideological and a practical sort dictate the

Tavianis' modification of the novel's temporality, which seeks to simulate the seamless flow of time between Gavino's sixth and his twenty-
fourth years. Both the film's two-hour time limitation and the Tavianis'
intent to break up Ledda's chronological continuum require a narrative
structure that is disjunctive, synthetic, and hyperbolic. Filled with cae-
suras and jump cuts, the film's strategy seems to involve subsuming
the developments of large blocks of time in a few representative incidents, whose elements may be invented or drawn from diverse textual
anecdotes.[15] The character of Cesare, for example, does not occur in
the novel. He is a composite of three army colleagues—Toti, the radio
specialist; Ottavio, the schoolteacher; and Rodolfo, the graduate of a
liberal arts high school in Florence—who become Gavino's mentors at
various phases of his military career. In another case of synthesis (and
also displacement), Gavino's many milk runs to Siligo on donkeyback
in weather conditions so bitter that he would weep and shout in agony
are subsumed in the fleeting appearance of a young boy named Matteo, whose thoughts are reported in subtitles as the sound track records his sobs. The scene of the famished servants who devour a caul-
dron full of the master's leftovers, though the five eaters are one spoon
short, is lifted from a visit to a wealthy shepherd in the book. In the
film, the pastoral overlord is replaced by the olive oil merchant whose
son's mystifying language bamboozles Efisio into selling at a loss.

Because the film does not have the luxury of the book's expanse to
detail the extreme conditions under which Gavino must struggle to
survive, its expressive economy must depend on hyperbole. Thus
Gavino's boyhood solitude in Baddevrustana seems unrelieved in the
film, while in the novel he makes frequent forays into Siligo and is
usually in the company (if you can call it that) of his father, who relo-
cates the entire family to the highlands in Gavino's eleventh year.
While the novel's Gavino scrimps and saves to buy the accordion
whose purchase is subsidized by a miraculous donation from his father, the film's protagonist buys the instrument on impulse, risking
paternal retaliation in his barter of two lambs for it. By sacrificing the
source of the family's livelihood, the Tavianis' Gavino dramatizes how
threatening this musical acquisition is to the economic status quo, and
by inviting paternal wrath, reveals his willingness to put himself on
the line in the interests of self-emancipation. In another hyperbolic
adaptation, the Tavianis' Gavino masters the accordion with no seeming effort, moving from his clumsy initial groping at the keyboard to
his serenade in the valley to his competent performance during the
lunch with the olive oil merchant and his son. In contrast, the autobiography traces Gavino's long journey to musical mastery, which in-

volves a series of lessons from his kindly Uncle Gellòn and arduous practice sessions in the wilds of Baddevrustana.

The speed of Gavino's ascent to literacy has a similar fairy-tale unreality. Where the novel's protagonist enters the army already equipped with an elementary school diploma (though obtained by less than rigorous means) and tediously makes his way through junior high proficiency with the sequential help of his three tutors, the film's Gavino starts from scratch in the army and is catapulted to high school equivalence through the agency of one composite mentor while still serving his military term. Gavino makes meteoric progress from dialectal stammerings to eloquence in Italian to expert appropriation of Virgilian verse within the span of several years, stretching the limits of our credibility for even this most motivated and talented of learners.

The film's chronology is thus highly disjunctive, with great temporal leaps that serve opposing purposes in the film's first and second halves. While in the adult portions of *Padre padrone* the jump cuts document linear progess toward enlightenment (musical mastery, the advent of literacy), the childhood ellipses imply that there is nothing new to report, that the omitted material was simply more of the same. In certainly the boldest of these jump cuts, the Tavianis compare Gavino's entire boyhood and adolescence in Baddevrustana to one long postorgasmic torpor. The jump cut occurs near the end of the critically acclaimed montage of choral lust, where coitions of every imaginable sort seem to move rural sexuality up the evolutionary scale. Thus little boys couple with chickens and adolescents with donkeys and sheep until graduation into adulthood entitles them to species-specific copulation. This sequence begins with Gavino's imitation of sexual behavior in the flock he is tending. A montage of other boys' experiments in "animal husbandry"[16] reveals that Gavino is not alone in his exertions and that indeed his sexuality is but one expression of the organic bonds that link humans to the animal world. When the montage sequence returns to Gavino, he is stretched out in a ditch, exhausted and drained from his consortings. This image dissolves to black and a subtitle appears on-screen to tell us that "Gavino has reached his twentieth year" (T., 51).

When the screen lightens to reveal a mature protagonist in the same position in the same pit as a ewe scrambles out of its depths, we realize that Gavino has experienced the entire past fourteen years as if in a postcoital stupor, and that rural temporality has been reduced to the rising and falling rhythms of sexual excitation. This is a powerful categorical indictment of the life to which Efisio consigns his son, where time is simply duration, the interval between orgasms, the *chronos* of

The site of his animal couplings, this pit represents the solitude and degradation of Gavino's pastoral state.

Frank Kermode's *Sense of the Ending,* whose only climaxes are sexual and whose progression keeps men bound to the cycles of nature, their bodies, and the daily struggle to survive.[17] Or, to use A. C. Charity's characterization of pre-Exodus time, the temporality of Gavino's rural existence is typified by repetition, ritual, certainty, stasis, the known quantity.[18] When Efisio tells the schoolteacher "Gavino won't be the first nor the last to get his elementary school degree at eighteen as I did" (T., 40), he is condemning his son to relive his own experience and that of his fathers by remaining in an inarticulate daze throughout the formative years, until it is too late to change and escape such genealogical bondage. The biblical language of the shepherds' self-portraiture during Gavino's serenade to the valley also testifies to the predominance of Genesis time in the rural community. "I am Gavino, son of Efisio the shepherd, who is son of Luca the shepherd. The cold of last night filled the sheepfold with fleas, I feel the most greedy ones under my armpits" (T., 54). These lyrics are conveyed in the subtitles that interpret the message encoded in Gavino's music. As if in echo, a flute responds from the other side of the valley, and the subtitles report this meaning: "I am Eligio, son of Giovanni the shepherd, who was son of Enrico the carabiniere. I ate cheese that was too fresh, if I breathe hard my tongue burns" (T., 55). Though this may seem a charming example of pastoral dialogue, there is a barely disguised indictment of this father-son genealogy that visits the privations of the shepherd's lot on subsequent generations whose socioeconomic identities, like their chromosomes, are genetically transmitted. Each two-sentence description is linked by a cause-and-effect logic that attributes the physical hardships (insect infestations, unripe cheese) to the necessity of reliving family history. ("I am ——, son of ——").

It is music that awakens Gavino from his refractory stupor, launching him on a linear course beyond the valley into history, uncertainty, personal risk, progress—the time of Exodus, as A. C. Charity defines it. But there is a false linearity in this second half of the film, characterized by Efisio's financial schemes for family advancement, and the Tavianis modify the book's home economics to play off such pseudo-progress against Gavino's authentic movement toward enlightenment. In the book, Abramo remains a shepherd and farmer until the end, when he sells all his animals, moves back to Siligo, and lends his capital at usurious rates. But throughout the film, Efisio traces the itinerary of incipient capitalism, moving systematically up the hierarchy from shepherd to landowner to loan shark, each step achieved through exploitative means. The book's olive grove, which Abramo had owned and cultivated from the very beginning, comes into Efisio's possession halfway into the film, marking a definite step up the economic ladder. His means of acquisition are also invented by the Tavianis, who create the character of Sebastiano, loosely derived from the book's accounts of Gavino's swashbuckling ancestor, Thiu Juanne, with significant changes.

The wealthy Sebastiano's violent death presents the narrative pretext for Efisio to acquire the olive grove by exploiting the young widow's distress. When the widow makes Efisio her agent, requesting that he sell her house, livestock, and olive grove, he insists on buying the latter at a reduced price as recompense for his services as middleman. "Do as you wish" (T., 57), she answers icily, too drained by grief to fight his ruthless opportunism. "I'm doing it for you all," Efisio claims. "Sebastiano is my witness" (T., 57). In explaining his motives, Efisio uses the standard familial justification for what is really his own impulse to self-aggrandizement: "For you, Gavino, I'm doing it. The olive grove will make you a real landowner" (T., 57). When the arctic frost destroys the grove, Efisio remains only temporarily nonplussed. No sooner does he catch his breath than he comes up with a new scheme: to sell all assets and bank them and to hire out his oldest daughter, Ignazia, for housework on the continent and his two middle sons for day labor—all the while pocketing their earnings. The bank revenues will be 10 percent, and he'll also lend out to relatives for a fee inversely proportional to the collateral that they can pledge. Some of the interest will go toward Ignazia's dowry, he benevolently offers, if the family's financial requirements so permit. "In sum, without being aware of it," explains Vittorio Taviani, "the father recapitulates— more in the film it seems, than in the book—the stages of a precise economic structure, the stages of capitalism" in his move from the working class, where he actively produces capital, through inheritance to bank investor, where he is the beneficiary of passive capital.[19]

Efisio's notions of progress have fallacious moral as well as economic bases, including his reaffirmation of the very injustice to which he had been subject as a member of the rural proletariat. The Tavianis satirize the kind of knowledge on which Efisio predicates his economic success in the multiplication tables that constitute his idea of mental gymnastics. "I have to keep my brain awake," Efisio resolves as he realizes that he's losing Gavino. "Seven times nine . . . sixty-three. Sixteen times sixteen . . . two hundred . . . fifty-six. Thirty-three times nineteen" (T., 55). And in the bank lobby scene awaiting the family's appointment with the vice-director, Efisio decides to bestow the gems of his wisdom on the ignorant Gavino. "I'll teach you. You're not stupid. Five times five" (T., 100). When Gavino answers, "Thirty," the pedagogue plants a resounding slap on his pupil's face. The Tavianis take their satire to ludicrous extremes by following Efisio and Gavino into the vice-director's office, where the father-teacher utilizes every second for the imparting of vital knowledge. "Five times five? Eight times three? Sixteen times four?" (T., 101) as if this multiplication exercise would make up for the decade or so of schooling and socialization that Efisio had denied his son.

But simple arithmetic hardly equips Efisio to solve the higher math of neocapitalism, where tariffs, quotas, and Common Market dealings are all thrown into the equation in mystifying ways by the technocratic son of the olive oil merchant who is about to fleece him. "He can't respond, first of all because he remains anchored in a strictly patriarchal, archaic economy, and he knows nothing about what is happening at the level of the Common Market, that is, at the level of general economic reality," the Tavianis explain.[20] Thus the code of five times

five embodies the strictly material, provincial and literal-minded economic notions of Efisio in the face of an economy governed by a cosmopolitan mathematics to which he has no conceptual access.

By portraying him as a failed acquirer of codes, the Tavianis perform
their most momentous adaptive changes on Ledda's text, for they represent Efisio as far more a victim of his society's semiotic limitations
than the autonomous perpetrator of evil that Abramo is.[21] Throughout
the book, fellow shepherds criticize Abramo's excesses, suggesting
that his abusiveness oversteps the limits of his culture and derives instead from some deep fund of personal malice. "But what are you
doing, taking Gavino to the hills at this age? Are you taking him up
there to wean him?" asks a passerby on the road to Baddevrustana.[22]
By using a metaphor of the trade (lambs were weaned by relocation in
a flock separate from their mothers') and one that reveals the unnaturalness of Gavino's conscription at such an early age, this critic conveys the unacceptability of Abramo's behavior according to the norms
of shepherd culture. And where the film portrayed as a certain Matteo
the wretched little boy, numb with cold, riding his donkey into town
with the day's milk, the book reveals this boy to be Gavino, whose
victimization by his father becomes the object of public disapproval.
When the kindly Tonni takes the frostbitten boy into his hut to thaw
out, his rhetorical question has all the power of a diatribe. "But really!
Couldn't your father take the milk to Siligo?" (G.L., 55). Popular censure reaches a fever pitch when Abramo decides to deport his entire
family from Siligo and settle them with him and Gavino in the highlands. Thus when Abramo pulls his other children out of school and
loads them onto the cart with their weeping mother, the townsfolk
express their condemnation in no uncertain terms. "People spat out
their last comments, blurting out and pontificating on some notorious
episodes of Papa's life" (G.L., 95).

Characteristically, Abramo's abuse of his son takes more dangerous
forms than Efisio's. The beating that knocks the film's Gavino unconscious comes close to blinding him in the book, where the doctor
threatens to turn Abramo in to the authorities for criminal child abuse.
And his neglect of Gavino's health results in a case of double pneu-
monia that brings the child to death's door when after a week of raging
fever and a persistent cough, Abramo finally deigns to seek a doctor's
assistance. And because the postcoital jump cut leaps over fourteen
years of Gavino's life, the film spares us the slave labor to which
Abramo consigns his son, who is sent out to farm other people's land
during the day, discharges his shepherd's duties in the evening, and

must awaken at 2 A.M. to tend the bulls who will power his plow the next day—all this on the smallest ration of sleep and the least nourishing of diets.

Most incriminating is the fact that Abramo is not himself the product of the brutality he visits upon Gavino. When son finally confronts father with his unconscionable child-rearing practices, the absence of violence in Abramo's own upbringing makes his abusiveness that much more arbitrary and blameworthy. "I know you were left an orphan when you were twelve," Gavino reminds Abramo. " Your brothers left you to yourself and your mother indulged you too. No one ever laid a hand on you" (G.L., 224–25). Thus the standard etiology for child abuse—the abuser's own history of victimization—has absolutely no relevance to Abramo's case and therefore offers no evidence to mitigate our judgment of him.

Though the horror of child beating is made palpable by its visualization on screen, the Tavianis do everything to deemphasize the idiosyncratic nature of Efisio's brutality. The battering that Gavino receives for leaving the flock untended to socialize with his neighbor Antonio is matched by the one administered to his playmate, suggesting that such violence is the universal punishment for filial disobedience. The Tavianis attempt to contextualize Efisio's behavior and to portray both father and son as victims of the same ethnographic predicament.[23] The moment most indicative of this attempt to "recuperate" Efisio comes in the aftermath of the beating, when the father cradles his unconscious son and gives vent to all the remorse and parental tenderness that his authoritarian role precludes.[24] "I won't move you, I won't move you" (T., 48), he promises, as the camera frames him in a close-up whose pietà resemblances suggest as much Efisio's parental grief as Gavino's personal Calvary.[25] Now Efisio opens his mouth to omit the sounds of a Sardinian *nenia* or dirge, and the song suddenly explodes into a polyphonic chant, as if folk tradition were singing through him, extending his pain through time and space to coincide with that of an entire people.[26] To visualize this extension, the camera pans from Efisio's face in close-up to include the whole valley of Baddevrustana in a synecdochal sweep that implies all of Sardinia.[27] When the camera pans back to Efisio holding the unconscious Gavino, this movement implicates father and son in a relationship with the land which dictates the pedagogy of punishment and regret. This is the "education of the shepherd" of Ledda's subtitle. It subjects all islanders to the implacable laws of the land and rewards only those who study in its school of survival.

Thus the Tavianis' Efisio is not the pathological monster of Ledda's

book, whose author vents his spleen in justified literary recrimina-
tions, but the product of a system that reproduces itself with each
generation.[28] "Like son, like father," we might say of the Tavianis' in-
tergenerational portrait, where Gavino's victimization is made to point
backward in time to an infinitely repeating genealogical pattern. Thus
the self-mutilating device by which Gavino cuts his lip in order to stave
off punishment (he does so to prevent Efisio's reprisals after buying
the accordion and later in the army to avoid classroom interrogation)
is repeated *by Efisio himself* during the climactic father-son confrontation, to reveal the commonality of their plight.[29]

Elsewhere, the Tavianis temper the virulence of Ledda's portrayal by
satirizing Efisio, not only in the "mathematical" scenes, where his
grandiose attempts to school his untutored son are reduced to five
times five, but in the scenes of violence, where Efisio's blustering and
prancing are shot from a variety of distances that alternately trivialize
and magnify his antics. In the snake-killing episode, this optical alter-
nation is used to striking effect, as a comparison with the textual
source suggests.

> My father had a huge cudgel and strode forward, master of every-
> thing. He would have consumed the stones themselves, to teach
> me this place was ours. . . . Like some unleashed natural force, he
> began to thrash bushes and up-turn stones checking every hole or
> crevice where he thought a snake might choose to lurk. He
> smelled them—he was like a hound. Immobilized but curious, I
> watched this pastoral drama unfold. The scene looked like the
> aftermath of a hurricane, bushes bent and windblown, stones roll-
> ing down toward the valley as if the whole hill had shrugged.
> (G.L., 16–17)

This is clearly the child's view, where a series of similes confer titanic
power on this master of the elements, making him Vulcan, Aeolus,
and Cerberus all at once. The film's sequence renders Efisio in both
heroic and ludicrous terms, appropriating now Gavino's view as a
child, now his view as a demystified and bemused adult. Having de-
posited the boy on a wall to watch his "pastoral drama" (G.L., 17),
Efisio descends into the snake pit and grabs a stick. The camera cuts
to a low-angle shot of Efisio's black-clad figure, motionless, poised for
attack in what is obviously the child's heroic image of the warrior-
father ready to do battle with his reptilian foe. A cut to Gavino as he
watches intently is followed by a high-angle shot of Efisio, who has
been galvanized into action. Leaping here and there, darting this way
and that and stopping just as suddenly, slashing bushes and overturn-

Gavino sits on a wall to watch the "pastoral drama" of his father's battle with the snake.

ing boulders, Efisio appears ridiculous, photographed at a distance that trivializes his pretentious exploits—hardly the hurricane unleashed of Ledda's account. With a return to close-range photography, Efisio regains his heroic stature, and when he whips Gavino with the dead snake, the film adds a note of paternal sadism missing in the book, where Abramo merely throws the bloody reptilian corpse on the boy's chest. But the film's juxtaposition of long shots and close-ups had essentially debunked the unalloyed heroism of the textual episode in which the encounter between man and beast assumed mythic proportions: Hercules against the Hydra, the Laocoon who wins.

A similar camera technique diminishes Efisio's stature in the film's worst scene of child abuse, where father beats son into unconsciousness. As Efisio prepares for the scourging, Gavino escapes, and the father follows him in a chase around the hut. Were the denouement of this scene not a battering but a comic reversal or a genuine escape, we would have read it as funny, with its fast-motion antics, its tricks and surprises, and the trivializing effect of long-shot photography. But as a prelude to the film's most tragic and poignant scene, the comic cinematography is disorienting and distancing, creating the ironic gap be-

tween protagonists and authorial perspective that the Tavianis always
seek when they feel too implicated in the drama and run the risk of
sentimental participation. "In our films irony is constant, especially in
the face of characters that we love the most," Vittorio Taviani told Aldo
Tassone. "It's a way of re-establishing proportions between man and
things, of cooling down a material that is too hot: living viscerally and
passionately your reality, you need detachment to be able to understand it."[30]

If cinematographic effects are used to distance us from the protagonist's predicament in the scenes of father-son conflict, they serve instead to immerse us in Gavino's consciousness in less contentious moments. In the early phases of his education as a shepherd, the boy's
acquisition of a mythopoetic vision is made cinematic by a series of
inspired devices that read almost like a theoretical justification for the
Tavianis' stylistic antinaturalism.[31] The entire first lesson of Gavino's
pastoral instruction unfolds in a fairy-tale atmosphere, as Efisio's voice
speaks in the singsong of a bedtime story while he recounts the wonders of Baddevrustana. We see neither father nor son on the donkey
ride that leads them to the highlands, but we view a long luminous
road reaching its vanishing point at the foot of the hill, and we hear
the donkey's hoofbeats, whose regularity has a hypnotic and sooth-
ing effect.

> I'll take you to where wild apples grow. I'll dig with my fingernails
> the underground chestnuts. If you're fast I'll teach you to catch a
> hare in a trap. Do you like hazel nuts? You'll gather them in
> bunches, and sometimes I'll take you to the rocks, to the young
> crows. You know that yesterday behind the hut I found a black-
> bird's nest with four eggs? (T., 42)

The magical aura of this monologue carries over to Baddevrustana,
but now it becomes more instructive, with imperatives and exhorta-
tions replacing the future verbs of discovery and delight. A strange
configuration of forms emerges in the dark which, once magically illuminated, turn out to be Efisio and Gavino in close-up, shot face-to-
face in profile, as the father continues to lecture his entranced son.
"Do you hear this rustling? You need to learn to recognize it. Lower
your eyes" (T., 42). The man and the boy both close their eyes and tilt
their heads down in concentration, but Gavino soon confesses his perceptual deficiencies. "I don't hear a thing" (T., 43). "Listen more
closely to the sound. It's the oak that marks our border. Turn your
head" (T., 43). The camera slowly pans from Gavino's rapt face, now
frontally photographed, to traverse a considerable distance in the

darkness before discovering an oak tree, shot from low angle and lit from below, as the rustling of its leaves grows in volume on the sound track. Like the pan in the pietà scene whose movements traveled a distance more metaphysical than real, this camera takes us into another order of experience—the mythopoetic vision of the child, or the animistic world-view of primitive folk belief which knows no boundaries between natural and human spheres.

The boy's gaze reverts to his father, who continues, "And this is the stream behind the woods. You saw it in passing" (T., 43). Another pan through the dark takes us to a torrent shot in full daylight, accompanied by the sounds of the waterfall in crescendo. "And this, listen, is Sebastiano who returns to town with his horse. He smokes with the lit end in his mouth so as not to be a target in the night. On his head ancient vendettas weigh" (T., 43). Sebastiano appears in medium shot on his horse, smoking his cigar in the prescribed manner—his personal trademark, to be reintroduced in the scene of foreplay with his young wife and in the prelude to the promised revenge. By including Sebastiano in this "vocabulary list" of shepherd pedagogy, the Tavianis achieve a twofold purpose, preparing us for the narrative of his murder, which is itself necessary to the film's socioeconomic argument (Efisio extorts the widow's olive grove for his dream of gentrification), while suggesting that blood feuds are part of the Sardinian landscape, as natural as oak trees and woodland streams. "Even for the dawn, you need to get used to hearing it with all its noises" (T., 43), concludes Efisio as sheep bells fill the sound track and the nocturnal scene gives way to an extreme long shot of the valley cloaked in its morning mist, dotted with flocks and the tiny figures of Gavino and Efisio at work. The mythopoetic lesson photographed in close-ups that magnified and fetishized its objects now yields to the quotidian reality of hard labor and solitude, revealed in a long shot that dwarfs father and son in the immensity of their natural setting.

It is sound that liberates Gavino from the solipsism and muteness of his shepherd's lot, as the music of Strauss's *Fledermaus* rescues him from the stultification of Baddevrustana, and as language finally equips him to communicate with others and to think critically about his plight. If we take the term *education* in its etymological sense as a "leading out," then sound becomes Gavino's true educator, enabling him to emerge from the cocoon of his solitude, which is itself given auditory expression in the death bell that fills the silence of the highlands. "And when one remains alone on the mountain and no one is around, absolutely no one—I know because they took me there," Gavino's mother tells him, "the silence is not silence, what do you think?

It's something forceful, that sounds like a death bell" (T., 41). That bell indeed tolls for Gavino when his father first leaves him alone at the sheepfold, and it is accompanied by the other device that the Tavianis use to externalize and dramatize the boy's desolation: his rocking motion—the self-stimulating, self-comforting gesture of the emotionally deprived child. In the spectacle of Gavino, photographed alone before the pointed, rock-encrusted hut, his own childish proportions accentuated by his big jacket and tiny legs clothed in short pants, as he sits rocking back and forth to the somber tolling of the death bell sounding within his mind, the Tavianis have created a composite visual-gestural-auditory image of a solitude bordering on the autistic.

Later in the film, the rocking and the bell will recur to signal Gavino's withdrawal into an earlier, solipsistic self when the force of his education—his "leading out"—becomes too threatening for his precarious psychic balance. Thus, in the army barracks, Gavino chooses to stay behind when the other recruits leave for a day on the town, and there on his bunk he seems to physically turn in on himself as the death bell tolls and he begins to rock in the atavistic gesture of self-consolation. The sound track carries over the echoes of the death bell into the next scene, set in the recruits' electronics class where Gavino's total incomprehension of the lecture plummets him into a desperation and a solitude that prompt his self-wounding and bring on the renewed tolling of the bell. Still vibrating with its echoes, the sound track of the next scene, in the Campo dei Miracoli of Pisa, blocks out all realistic set noises and keeps Gavino wrapped in its auditory cocoon as he rocks back and forth on his perch atop the leaning tower in an attempt to recapture the natural aloofness of Baddevrustana. At a certain point the rocking and the echoes stop, and we realize that Gavino has reached a turning point—the decision to break through the solitude signified by his inner world of sound and his gestural self-consolation—and now realistic noises enter the audio track, and a cut reveals Gavino at street level, talking animatedly with Cesare. Significantly, the final death bell tolls not for Gavino but for Efisio, who hears its somber tones the moment that he realizes he has lost Gavino and must face the moral and emotional vacuum left by his son's apostasy or confront him head-on with violence.

Gavino's entrance into language has thus been a manifold process involving the successive mastery of at least six codes: those of nature, of music, of communications technology, of written-spoken language, of literature, and of linguistic science. The code of nature can be further broken down into the mythopoetic language of animism, on the one hand, where sheep literally talk back, where streams and rustling leaves bespeak territorial borders and dawn announces its advent with characteristic sounds, and dialect, on the other, where speakers remain bound to the provincialism of a naturally determined world. When the strains of Strauss's *Fledermaus* rescue Gavino from his fourteen-year sequestration, it is the musical code, in its cosmopolitan, high-culture guise, which replaces the code of nature and allows the protagonist to participate in an "international, collective patrimony."[32] Music has telegraphic power for Gavino, who is on both the receiving and the sending end of this new instrument of communication.[33] When he broadcasts his ballad of the shepherd's woes across the valley with his accordion and receives another shepherd's musically encoded response, he has been able to transcend the material limits of his location in space and to share his plight with others.[34] It is not by accident that the radio he assembles in his army electronics class transmits this same Strauss waltz when the instructor tests it for Gavino's final exam. From the primitive musical projections of Baddevrustana to the radio, Gavino has made a quantum leap in communicative skills now that he has mastered the code of electronics. It is significant that the film's climactic father-son confrontation is triggered by a radio—reminder that Gavino has acquired the many codes that take him beyond Efisio's authoritarian reach.

Because sound is what frees Gavino from his predicament, it should come as no surprise that sound is also the Tavianis' primary means of cinematic liberation from realist codes. The film's auditory inventiveness has received much critical acclaim, and I would be remiss to slight its central part in the Tavianis' own antiauthoritarian campaign against the cinematic *padre padrone* of realist tradition. The Tavianis have specifically attributed the film's antirealism to the incongruities between its audio and visual elements, so that the sound track "often contradicts the image, discouraging the naturalistic identification with what happens on screen."[35] Thus where on-location shooting, authentic costumes and props, and the frequent use of nonprofessional actors ally the Tavianis' visual vocabulary with realism,[36] the use of a soundtrack that defies the conventions of verisimilitude complicates the film's stylistic identity. In most instances of such sound-image mismatching, the audio track reports the inner thoughts of the characters whose physical presence is recorded "objectively" on-screen. This is always the case when the death bell tolls, where the sound track records what amounts to an audio hallucination in a mind so lacking in stimuli that it conjures up its own sensory input.

The film's first example of sound-image disjunction also introduces the technique of polyphony which the Tavianis use to express the communal nature of the Sardinian experience.[37] Thus as Gavino is removed from his schoolroom and Efisio thunders at the children who dare hold his son up to ridicule, "Today was Gavino's turn. Tomorrow it will be yours" (T., 40), the camera singles out four faces in successive close-ups while the sound track reports each child's inner thoughts. The last interior monologue is followed by a cacophony of children's voices which then carries over into the beginning of the next scene, whose disparate setting and characters (Gavino and his mother in the kitchen) are at first totally inappropriate to the choral babbling that we still hear. A similar device is used near the film's end and solves a technical problem for the Tavianis: when Gavino returns to Siligo after his military service, the production notes called for several hundred extras to express the public scandal of his decision to forfeit a brilliant military career and come home against his father's wishes. But later, the Tavianis realized that the piazza should be empty to signal the desolation to which Gavino willingly returns after the hustle and bustle of the Pisan Campo dei Miracoli, for example. So the filmmakers resort to a compromise involving the customary sound-image disjunction, where the piazza is empty, but the audio track is full of censorious babble.[38]

Single-voiced thoughts join in a polyphonic crescendo in the scene where Sebastiano's corpse is being laid out for burial, and the consumerist desires of Gavino's entire family are triggered by the prospect of acquiring some of the dead man's patrimony. "Pardon me, I shouldn't do this, but I can't manage to think of anything but what I can have thanks to you," muses Gavino as he contemplates the corpse. "An accordion . . . a real one, all mother of pearl. I too will be a *padrone*" (T., 57). "I want to change my name," thinks Ignazia. "They gave me a man's name like my grandfather, Ignazio. I'll call myself Dina. Dina sounds like Mina. I'll be a singer like her. I'll sing on the continent . . . I'll sing" (T., 58). As if on cue, a song by Mina begins softly on the sound track, but the lyrics are soon obscured by the sound of the brother's voice-over. "I want . . . oh God, nothing comes to mind . . . absolutely nothing. . . . And yet, I know that I want so many things. I have to go in order. First . . ." (T., 58). Now his voice joins the babble of the family's rapacious thoughts to form a chorus as the Mina song builds to a crescendo. In the disparity between what we see (the corpse being laid out for burial) and what we hear (the ravenous desires of those who stand to benefit financially from this spectacle) lies the Tavianis' moral judgment on the consumerism of a society that allows a wish list to replace a funeral dirge.

Many instances of sound-image mismatching involve musical inappropriateness, as Mina's song, the Mozart clarinet concerto, and the regional anthem "Farewell Sacred Oaks of Sardinia" all ill-suit their respective scenes of funerary rites, father-son confrontation, and the insulting gestures of émigrés on the truck leading them to their port of embarkation. Though the Strauss waltz first occurs diegetically with the strolling accordionist's serenade, the Tavianis insist on its antinaturalistic presentation by playing a full-blown orchestration of it on the sound track of that scene. This is not so much a mimesis of Gavino's way of hearing the music as an interpretation of its importance to him. So momentous is the advent of this sound that nothing less than a symphony orchestra can convey its meaning for this fourteen-year victim of sequestration. And when Efisio himself hears the Strauss waltz after eavesdropping on Gavino's sleep talk of accordions and the festival of Muros, it is a sign of the father's realization that he is losing his son to the world outside Baddevrustana.

The Tavianis make fullest use of their musical techniques in the scene of the religious procession, where the generational clash is largely entrusted to the sound track. Led by a parade of village patriarchs, ten young men, all shepherds' hirelings, carry the statue of the village patron saint. Though a physical ordeal, the statue-bearing ritual gives these men, who are usually isolated from one another, the chance to unite and commiserate over their common predicament. The dialogue becomes a minieducation in class consciousness, beginning with a quarrel over who is shirking, continuing with a series of sexual put-downs, and concluding with an exchange about the dehumanization of their subaltern plight, which robs them even of a name. "To talk about you they say 'the servant of Thiu Pepe, the servant of Thiu Pepe'" (T., 63). "That doesn't apply to me," another chimes in. "My *padrone* calls me by name. He's my father" (T., 63). This comment acts with the force of revelation on Gavino, who finally learns to think of his struggle in social terms and is thus united in solidarity with the entire class that is allegorized by this statue-bearing collectivity. Now the dialogue takes a revolutionary turn. "I too will enroll on the list [of émigrés]" (T., 63). "Me, too." "Me, too." "Me, too." "Who else will enlist?" (T., 64). For the first time in the scene, Gavino speaks, adding his voice to a chorus that is about to slough off the weight of patriarchal culture figured by the patron saint and enter into a history of (at least attempted) self-determination. "Germany" (T., 64), proclaims one of the imminent émigrés. This serves as a battle cry, and when the youths resume the burden of the statue, they do so aggressively, with the energy of those about to take up a collective struggle. A solo voice is heard, softly at first, intoning the lyrics of a German beer-hall song,

"Trink, trink, Bruderlein trink, la la la la la la la la" (T., 64), where the brotherhood of resistance is cloaked in the companionship of alcoholic indulgence. Accelerating their pace, the ten statue-bearers march to a sound track now booming with the German song, which soon comes to overwhelm the Sardinian *miserere* chanted in momentary fugue. The Tavianis report that the configuration of this scene changed considerably in the editing room, revealing a last-minute decision to depend more on audio than visual elements to express the class struggle. "The sequence resolves itself in this conflict between the two sounds," the Tavianis explain, "and we also shot other frames, close-ups, reactions, however at the moment of editing, we realized that a single image, an extreme long shot, was sufficient, precisely in as much as the contrast took place at the level of sound. Therefore we eliminated in the editing phase anything that was a chopping up of images, of conflict of the two factions, to instead entrust it solely to the musical moment."[39]

Of course, the Tavianis' emphasis on sound is their medium-appropriate response to Ledda's emphasis on auditory codes as the key to self-emancipation. But there is an important aspect of Ledda's mastery of codes which the Tavianis choose to render through narrative, rather than auditory means. This is the aspect of linguistic thickness which will strike any reader of *Padre padrone*, whose Sardinian segments are filled with dialect phrases, written in italics and framed in parentheses, set in apposition to standard Italian locutions. These dialectal interventions serve a variety of purposes, reminding us that the author who writes them is a glottologist with a scientific interest in the dialect. But such a technique also suggests that dialect is perhaps the more authentic language for describing the Sardinian pastoral world, and that this book is therefore a translation *into Italian* of its dialect-specific narration. With each juxtaposition of Italian and dialect, Ledda implies a tension and a choice between rival modes of expression, each carrying its own considerable weight of political and cultural baggage. Finally, every juxtaposition serves as a replay of the entire linguistic itinerary that Ledda has traversed, from the muteness of his shepherd's state to the full eloquence of his current condition. Thus, each instance of dialectal paraphrasing defines the *then* and *now* of autobiography: how the protagonist who *was* became the author who *is* and gained the wherewithal to tell his story. In Dante's case, the wherewithal was *askesis* and conversion, the spiritual achievement of retrospective illumination, which allowed him to tell his story from the standpoint of revealed Christian truth. In Ledda's case, the wherewithal is first linguistic, with all the implications for personal and social enlightenment that such an acquisition necessarily entails. As with

Dante, Ledda's journey is cumulative and progressive, where each new phase subsumes all others, so that true linguistic expressivity means not leaving dialect behind but building it into the discourse, hearing its echo in every utterance, acknowledging the archaeology of each idiom, constantly retracing the itinerary from *then* to *now*.

It is in their narrative structuring of the film that the Tavianis adapt the linguistic thickness of Ledda's text. Where the autobiography ends with the protagonist's departure for Salerno after the violent encounter between father and son, the Tavianis insist on Gavino's return to Siligo, and his reasons for so doing are of great interest to the film's linguistic argument. "But perhaps it is only an egotistical calculation that keeps me here," admits the author, who appears on-screen at the conclusion to complete the film's documentary framework, "the fear that being far from my den, my people, my smells, I would revert to being mute as when I was in the sheepfold and in the livestock pens of Baddevrustana" (T., 114). Significantly, this last phrase is uttered first in Sardinian, then in Italian, revealing that for Ledda, linguistic deracination—the separation of language from its evolutionary roots—precludes full expressivity. And because we are beings *for* language, the achievement of true eloquence is also the achievement of true selfhood, so that Gavino's impulse to return is also a way of becoming whole, of recuperating the past by handing Efisio the stick that subjected him to patriarchal control and deliberately reliving that history.

When they bring Ledda back to Siligo at the film's end, the Tavianis blend the linearity of Gavino's progress with the circularity of his return to create a spiraling narrative structure where the protagonist constantly covers the same ground at higher cognitive levels. If we were to chart Gavino's itinerary, the map would read: Siligo—abortive embarcation for Germany—Siligo—military service on mainland—Siligo—university on mainland—Siligo.[40] The "linear circularity" of the spiral also dictates the logic of the film's conclusion, which is really three endings in one.[41] Severio Marconi the actor concludes his performance in the confrontation scene with Efisio as he resolves to leave Siligo and receives his father's parting gesture of ambivalence: a hand poised to caress, which then hardens into a fist clenched for beating. Now Ledda's voice-over initiates the second ending, which culminates in a replay of the film's opening schoolroom sequence, but with a slightly modified sound track. When Efisio thunders, "Today it's Gavino's turn. Tomorrow it will be yours," (T., 40), the camera singles out the same four children in close-up, but the sound no longer reports their inner thoughts. Instead, we hear the strains of the Strauss waltz that had heralded Gavino's Exodus from the Genesis of the pastoral

world. The music invites us to reinterpret Efisio's words, replacing
their dire prognostications in the first scene with this new promise for
revolutionary personal and cultural change. "Today, Gavino will begin
the struggle for self-emancipation" is the revised import of Efisio's earlier prophecy. "Tomorrow the chance will be yours." [42]

But the film is no naive revolutionary romance, for this would con-
demn it to the same kind of idealizing falsification that pastoral literature represents in the vocabulary list. The Tavianis make no bones
about the agonizing and pathogenic nature of Gavino's struggle,
which dictates the third and final ending of the film. As the Strauss
waltz dissipates from the sound track, the noise of wind takes its
place, and a comprehensive shot of the empty piazza presents a spectacle of unspeakable desolation. A lap dissolve reveals a long shot of
the author in Baddevrustana, seated on a rock as he so often had been
during his solitary childhood vigils. Another lap dissolve presents a
close-up of Ledda's back while he rocks in the habitual gesture of self-
consolation. As bitter as this image is—and it compares the injustice
of Gavino's need to struggle *alone* with the solitude that prompted this
childhood behavioral tick[43]—it is not without ambiguity. "In the last
frame we see that his shoulders stop [rocking]," the Tavianis explain,
"but we want to go beyond the pure image, as when in a previous
scene, on the bell tower of Pisa, exactly in the moment in which Gavino was photographed from the back, he had already decided to abandon his sense of anguish and to enter into contact with others. In the
last frame his shoulders stop, as if Gavino were ready for a new leap
forward." [44]

But the price of Gavino's rebellion has been exorbitant—almost too
much for any one psyche to bear. Nor do the Tavianis presume that
their own achievement of artistic independence from neorealist codes,
or even Ledda's textual authority, was bought at anything like the
price of Gavino's personal suffering. Though the filmmakers were at-
tracted to Ledda's story as an example of *utopia realizzata* after a film
career dedicated to the failure of individual activist attempts (*Un uomo
da bruciare, I sovversivi, San Michele aveva un gallo*) or collective utopian
fiascos (*Allonsanfan, Sotto il segno dello scorpione*), their conclusion is
hardly triumphalist.[45] Where there are three endings, there are really
no endings, and the withholding of closure on the narrative level has
important consequences for a political reading of *Padre padrone*, whose
cycle of waiting, anger, and corrective action is self-perpetuating, as
Gavino struggles like Sisyphus to make his personal victory a social
one.[46] For the material circumstances that victimized Gavino remain
unchanged by the film's end, and indeed the very terms of his solitary

triumph reveal how thoroughly he has been wronged. "We also think that if Gavino achieved a result," observes Vittorio Taviani, "the final injustice that is done to him by today's social structure is that he really had to attain this result all alone." [47] By retelling the author's story in a medium capable of reaching and moving a vast spectatorship, and by having Ledda return to Siligo to carry on the struggle, where the novel's action ended on the mainland, the Tavianis' adaptation does its part to make victorious Gavinos out of all the other schoolchildren in the classroom from which the six-year-old protagonist was so fatefully exiled.

8 · The Tavianis' *Kàos*

THE POETICS OF ADAPTATION

Any interpretation of the Tavianis' *Kàos* (1984) must begin with the end, with the epilogue, which teaches us retrospectively how to read the film we have just seen.[1] Itself based on Luigi Pirandello's "Colloqui con i personaggi, II," this epilogue introduces the figure of the writer as a character whose dream encounter with his long-dead mother frees up his imagination to write the five tales from the *Novelle per un anno* (1937) on which the Tavianis' adaptation is based. But the epilogue provides far more than the frame story, or narrative *antefatto*, to Pirandello's act of writing. It also stands as an "umbilical scene" or an "allegory of adaptation" in which the filmmakers dramatize their own filial relationship to the parent text and make explicit the principles that govern their adaptive approach. The epilogue thus gives retroactive signficance to a number of poetic and thematic motifs, from the film's title and epigraph to its framing device of the bell-ringing crow to the very logic of *amplificatio* which takes each Pirandellian story to the point where its central visual image undergoes a radical iconographic transformation. What the epilogue teaches us is that the Pirandellian struggle for artistic creation—a struggle played out with considerable urgency in *Six Characters in Search of an Author*, "Tragedia di un personaggio," and "Colloqui con i personaggi,"—finds its resolution in the Tavianis' faculty of memory conceived as a return to the geographic, ethnic, familial, and even cosmic origins of our imaginative life. And if the textual "Colloqui con i personaggi, II" is a plea for freedom—political freedom in a Risorgimento or World War I context, psychological freedom in a world of contingent, socially determined selves—then the Tavianis take this plea one step further by insisting on a third type of freedom toward which Pirandello's art strives. In *Kàos* the writer is also seen as struggling against the formal limits of his own medium, where the constraints of prose narrative keep him from soaring to the heights of imaginative expressivity. The Tavianis' Pirandello is therefore a poet manqué, an author whose art aspires to the condition of poetry and falls short of the expressive breakthrough that would free him from the restrictions of prose narrative form.

Thus construed, Pirandello offers the Tavianis a perfect pretext for self-definition, for the formulation of a poetics that distances their cinematic style from the realist representations of most postwar Italian filmmaking. In its transgression of naturalist codes, in its profoundly musical structure, and in its imagistic experimentation, the Tavianis' style provides a powerful response to Pasolini's call for a "cinema of poetry." The Tavianis' Pirandello therefore serves a double function, justifying an adaptive strategy that discovers the poetic latencies of the text, and showcasing their own achievement of an art that transcends the limits of conventional narrative filmmaking, or what Pasolini would call "the cinema of prose." [2]

Therefore the epilogue abounds with images of flight, images that slowly and mysteriously trigger some hidden creative mechanism in Pirandello's mind. Flight from the intolerable "pain of living" motivates the very action of the epilogue, which tells of Pirandello's sudden departure from Rome in response to a summons from his dead mother. As the character Luigi staggers off the train in Agrigento, drunk with sleep, he beholds a vision of a child, arms spread-eagle, who hurls himself down a sand pile. Later, in the carriage ride to his mother's villa, the driver stops to give his passenger a tourist's view of a Greek amphitheater; instead, Luigi envisions a young girl raising her arms for flight. Something is obviously stirring in the depths of Luigi's psyche, but it takes the encounter with his mother to make these impulses available to his art. "A hundred times you told me about that journey. A hundred times I've tried to write it—I never succeeded. There's something that escapes me. Tell me once more."

The anecdote that escapes Luigi, and that the Tavianis add to the literary original, subsumes all the earlier flight imagery of *Kàos* and explains how the filmmakers intend to free Pirandello from his own imaginative confines through cinematic adaptation. "What you probably don't remember is that in midjourney we stopped at an island, the Isola della Pomice," his mother begins. The scene in the villa then gives way to a flashback of surpassing lyricism, in which the mother as a thirteen-year-old girl embarks with her own mother and siblings

Luigi asks the ghost of his mother to recall the episode from her childhood that had always escaped him.

to join their father in Malta, where he has been exiled by the Bourbons for his part in the revolution of 1848. During a lull in the journey, the boat stops on an island rimmed with dunes from which the children plunge into the sea below. The rhythm of the children's leaps is perfectly synchronized with the rhythm of the sound track, music from the soprano aria "L'ho perduta me meschina" from Mozart's *Marriage of Figaro* that had begun as soon as Luigi recognized the ghost of his mother and that is thus intimately fused with her identity.[3] "We think that the cinema is the means of expression heir to music," the Tavianis told Aldo Tassone. "We two structure the films according to musical rhythms—never literary ones. In imagining, shooting, mounting the film, in its soundtracking, what leads us is the musical rhythmic progression."[4] This sequence thus illustrates their ideal of cinematic expressivity, where "musical rhythms" replace "literary ones." A lyric digression that does nothing to advance the plot, the anecdote is flagrantly non-narrative, occupying a mere pause in the action until the wind picks up and the voyagers can continue to Malta. But the Tavianis are not interested in the journey at all, in the *before* or *after* of this idyllic interlude—they care only to linger on this *meanwhile,* bliss-fully indifferent to its narrative uses. Perhaps this is why the episode had always eluded a Pirandello so wedded to narrative functionality and so intent upon the economy of style that any temptation to poetic indulgence had to be firmly resisted. By revising "Colloqui con i per-sonaggi, II" to include an episode that the original Pirandello would have been unwilling to countenance, the Tavianis trigger a conversion in the author which frees him from his imaginative limitations (as the filmmakers see them).

Though both the textual and filmed versions of "Colloqui con i per-sonaggi, II" are dramatized internal monologues in two voices, it is significant that Pirandello's is set in his Roman studio, where he is accustomed to interviewing "candidates" for his fiction between 8 A.M. and 1 P.M. every Sunday. As the setting indicates, Pirandello's fiction of artistic creation takes place under the sign of reason and order, where the passionate intensity of the Romantic artist is dis-placed onto the characters themselves, engaged in a titanic struggle to win their author's acceptance. This fiction leaves the artist cool and de-tached, the Olympian, if sometimes beleaguered, judge of which char-acters will be granted artistic life. One such visitor is Luigi's mother. "Is it possible, Mamma? You, here?" asks the textual Pirandello.

> She is seated, small, in her easy chair, not *here,* not in *this* my room, but still in *that* one in the *far away* house, where not even the others now see her seated any more and whence not even she now, *here* sees the things around her that she has left for always, the light of a warm sun, the sonorous and fragrant light of the sea, *here* the china cabinet that glitters with rich ornaments for the table, *there* the balcony that gives on to the wide road of the large marine town [emphases mine].[5]

The emphasis in this passage is less on the apparition of Luigi's dead mother than on the conjuring consciousnesss of the author, caught between the *qui,* the *questa* of this, his room, and the *là* and *quella* of the house by the sea. Though the synesthesia of visual, tactile, and aural elements in "the light of a warm sun, the sonorous and fragrant light of the sea" suggests a poetic sensibility lost in the undifferen-tiated stimuli of lyric experience, the constant interplay of demonstra-tive adjectives and adverbs, and the back and forth between them, calls our attention to the mechanics of the conjuring process and ab-stracts us from it.

In the film, it is significant that Luigi leaves his Roman studio and returns to his birthplace near Agrigento to meet the ghost of his mother. Far from the intellectual rigor of the textual Luigi's maternal interview, the Tavianis' unfolds in a state of dreamlike unreality. "I had slept the whole two-day journey," Luigi's voice-over tells us. "I wondered if I weren't still sleeping."[6] This question is never resolved, and it envelops the entire episode in an ambiguity that the oneiric visuals and the eerie music only reinforce. Luigi indeed seems to be sleepwalking throughout the episode, which is full of strange effects, including unsteady camera movements and flashes of children poised spread-eagle for flight.

In this dream state, Luigi encounters one of his own characters from "Mal di Luna," now hunched over and aged beyond recognition. His name is Saro, and he serves as Luigi's cab driver from the Agrigento train station to the writer's villa in Kàos. It is only when he deposits Luigi at his door and turns to leave that the writer finally recognizes Saro and calls him by name. Too far down the road for him to have heard with any verisimilitude, the cab driver turns around to look back, grateful and triumphant in his author's acknowledgement.[7] And when we notice that the Saro who turns back is the young and vibrant Saro of "Mal di luna," and that the music on the sound track is the folk song that gave voice to all his suppressed sensuality, we realize that this is the moment of creation, that by *remembering* Saro, Luigi has given him artistic life, and that the epilogue therefore antedates the composition of the stories that have just been represented on screen. In order for those stories to have been written, the epilogue's process of imaginative liberation and of triggered memory must have already taken place, making the "Colloqui con i personaggi, II" a doubly "originary" narrative—precondition not only to the Tavianis' adaptation, but to the writing of the literary source on which it is based.

This merging of beginnings and ends is, of course, the very theme of the epilogue, whose dead mother gives paradoxical birth to her already aged son by setting in motion his own creative impulses. Far from the generic nature of Pirandello's textual mother, whose teaching could be transmitted by any loved one who had died, the film's mother is exploited for her "motherness"—for her originary role as the giver of life. Luigi's journey to her, in his birthplace in Sicily, is atavistic in every possible way, as the film's epigraph reveals. "I therefore, am son of Kàos, and not allegorically, but in reality, because I was born in our countryside that is located near an intricate forest, called Càvusu by the inhabitants of Agrigento—a dialectal corruption of the genuine and ancient Greek word Kàos." Thus the return to the mother is paralleled by an etymological and historical return to Sicily's primeval past. The Italian phrase *intricato bosco* is the modern version of the

earlier folk idiom *Càvusu*, itself a corruption of the original Greek des-
ignation *Kàos*. The linguistic journey evokes of course a historical voyage back in time to the Greek colonization of Sicily whose architectural
traces are still visible in the temple of Segesta that serves as backdrop
to the film's opening credits. The philosophical implications of the title
are also used to great thematic advantage throughout the film. As the
confused, undifferentiated, unformed mass of primal matter that made
up the universe before the separation of elements and the creation of
light, *Kàos* also suggests the raw material of the artist who must endow
it with form. The chaos of primal matter lends itself specifically to one
side of Pirandello's dichotomous thought, which opposes life to art,
the unformed to the formed, the fluid to the fixed, the real to the true,
persona to *personaggio*.

The film's epilogue traces the difficulty and complexity of this passage from unformed matter to fully formed work of art, implying an
aesthetic journey through an *intricato bosco* like that of the writer's
birthplace. If this episode represents an umbilical scene or allegory
of adaptation, then nowhere is the relationship between parent text
and film thicker and more layered than in the adventure on the Isola
della Pomice. Here the lived experience passes into the memory of the
mother, who transmits it through conversation to her son in a dream,
who writes down the story, which gives rise to the cinematic adaptation. Thus the empirical event passes through the transforming filters
of memory, dream, and literature before arriving at its final filmic
destination.

Because the Tavianis' epilogue is far more interested in the return to
origins than is Pirandello's literary "Colloquio," and because it considers those origins to be psychological as well as familial, geographic,
and historical, Luigi's filmic encounter with his mother engages him at
far deeper psychic levels than does its textual counterpart. The "motherness" (as distinguished from "motherliness" or nurturance) of the
filmic interlocutor is thus emphasized in ways that take Luigi deep into
abysses of consciousness hitherto unplumbed by his art, so that his
journey back into a Sicilian past whose roots extend into Greek antiquity is also a journey into his own psychic chaos. If ontogeny recapitulates phylogeny, then Luigi's consciousness contains all the phases
of the civilization from which he springs. This makes the exchange
between mother and son far richer and more mysterious than the intellectual riddle that Pirandello's textual persona had posed and resolved with postmortem maternal help. When Luigi says, "I weep
because you can't think of *me* any more," he, like Pirandello's fiction-
alized author, is mourning the fact that he will no longer be the object
of his mother's conscious thought. But the Tavianis' emphasis on the

"motherness" of this interlocutor and on the writer's return to origins invite us to gloss this exchange with what we know about infant psychology, specifically the moment when the baby realizes that the mother returns his or her gaze and is therefore irrevocably "other." Such a revelation is a shock to the infant's developing psyche. It is the individual's first Fall from primal innocence, the first shattering of childhood's Edenic unity. The adult Luigi, whose identity is now predicated on such differentiation, grieves this second loss, the loss of the selfhood determined by the mother's gaze. But when she recommends that he "learn to see with the eyes of those who no longer see," she means that he must see through *her* eyes, appropriating *her* gaze. This reincorporation of the mother is the definitive return, for which the journey back to Sicily, to the motherland, had been but the geographical intimation.[8] Through this memory, Luigi is able to revert to a state of undifferentiated infantile consciousness, enjoyed now from the vantage point of the adult who can harness the vision in the service of art. The title *Kàos* has thus found its most consequential application in the primal mother-son bond which provides the very source of imaginative life.

"Learn to see with the eyes of those who no longer see," Luigi's mother had said. Indeed, all *Kàos* can be read as a lesson in seeing, in the healthy, open, chaotic vision of the authorial consciousness, and in the closed, fixed, pathological, *in malo* vision of the imaginatively impaired. The liberated optic of children bounding down the sand dune into an unknown sea finds its counterpart in the framing motif of the crow who soars above the Sicilian countryside between stories to unite them under the sign of its detached, aerial perspective.[9] Inspired by Pirandello's "Il corvo di Mízzaro," the Tavianis' frame story borrows from this tale only its proem, visualizing it in ways that emphasize its wit, its emotional contrasts, and its meta-artistic relevance. Though Pirandello does little to describe the shepherds who torment a male crow they find sitting on a nest of eggs, the Tavianis portray them as the primitively dressed highlanders who will later feature in the fourth full-fledged story, "Requiem." Combined with their outlandish costumes, the camera work and actions conspire to dehumanize these men, who first appear in extreme close-up peeking over a ledge in a strange disorienting mise-en-scène, and who act with a cruelty bordering on the bestial when they pelt the bird, suspended upside down, with his own eggs.[10] When the crow is rescued and freed by the kindest of the shepherds, who ties a bell around its neck with the announcement "Musica," its launch is made to coincide with the beginning of the film's own symphonic sound track. In so doing, the Tavianis' associate the bird's flight with their own creative process.

As the figure of the artist, the crow presides over the cinematic representation of four complete Pirandello tales—"L'altro figlio," "Mal di luna," "La giara," and "Requiem"—each of which undergoes a twofold adaptive change, including an imagistic intensification and a narrative *amplificatio*. Having identified the central image of the Pirandello story, the Tavianis push the plot beyond its original narrative logic in order to invest the image with a poetic, and often utopian, life of its own. Thus, in "Requiem," the coffin begins as a symbol of total defeat and ends, thanks to the Tavianis' elaboration, as a metonym for victory, a prop in the staging of "a good death," charged with positive values. The small casket of the opening scenes, carrying the remains of an infant child and signifying the double anguish of a father who must bury it in a distant cemetery, is replaced at the end by the coffin of the aged village patriarch, victorious in his campaign for local burial.

The jar also undergoes an imagistic transformation that reaffirms the utopian values of "Requiem." Perhaps because they were interested in the performative aspects of "La giara," the Tavianis relied as much on Pirandello's stage version of the story as on his original novella.[11] Unlike the film's other episodes, "La giara" is conceived theatrically, according to the canons of musical comedy where the action is structured melodically, the space is treated as a stage, and a chorus sings and dances, providing an internal, normative model for the spectator's own participation in the carnivalesque denouement.[12] By casting the well-known Sicilian comedy team of Ciccio Ingrassia and Franco Franchi in the leading roles, the Tavianis make explicit their vaudeville aspirations, and thus they assure the comic pleasure of their native audiences through familiarity and curiosity as to how the two comedians will square off against each other this time. The tall, angular Ingrassia and the short, squat Franchi also provide the perfect comic visual contrast between the story's two antagonists, Don Lollò Zirafa, owner of vast and fertile tracts of Sicilian olive country, and Zi' Dima Licasi, a mender of pottery possessing a miraculous glue whose secret he jealously guards. Whereas Pirandello's story is really a contest between two eccentric personalities, the Tavianis' episode becomes a contest between two civilizations, one based on individual property, oppression, and reason, the other on solidarity, freedom, and imagination. All the adaptive changes that the Tavianis bring to bear on Pirandello's text work to generalize this ideological clash so that by the time the final confrontation takes place on Don Lollò's threshing floor, it is two world orders, not just two individuals, whose fortunes are at stake.

Central to the Tavianis' adaptive strategy is their inclusion of a mistress in Pirandello's cast of characters.[13] Rigidly bound to Don Lollò's

Don Lollò treats his new jar with the pride and possessiveness of a jealous lover.

mythology of power, Sara sleeps in a tiny cot at the foot of her master's bed, reigns in her beauty publicly by wearing a hairstyle of the utmost severity, and feeds his egomania by calling him the new Charlemagne, making his agrobusiness the modern answer to medieval heroics, the *gesta francorum* of a postepic world. Indeed, keeping a mistress is less proof of Don Lollò's passionate yearning for intimacy than an extension of his proprietary domain, as the Tavianis reveal in his one sexual approach toward her. When a series of extreme close-ups shows us Don Lollò's hand crushing the olives so symbolic of his wealth, smearing the oil on Sara's face, and then licking it off—we realize that the master's lust is strictly territorial. The Sara figure is especially important because her defection from Don Lollò during the festivities of the story's climax amounts to a preference for one civilization over another, and so momentous is her choice that it literally transforms her into another person. If it were not for the editing, which shows a new woman among the revelers and cuts to a bewildered Don Lollò groping in bed for the hand of the Sara who is no longer there, we would be hard put to identify this smiling face, framed by black curls, with the astringent features and the severe chignon of the earlier mistress-slave. To heighten our awareness of her new sensuality, Sara receives from Zi' Dima a glance somewhere between shock and appreciation— a connoisseur's gaze that also registers the magnitude of her apostasy in joining his ranks.

The most consequential adaptive changes occur at the climax of the story where the Tavianis develop Pirandello's perfunctory descriptions into a full-fledged ideological confrontation. "As if on purpose, there was a moon that appeared as bright as daylight," writes Pirandello.

> At a certain hour, Don Lollò, having gone to sleep, was awakened by an infernal din. He went to a balcony of the farm and saw on the threshing floor, under the moon, so many devils: the drunken peasants that, having taken each other by the hand, were dancing around the jar. Zi' Dima, inside it, was singing at the top of his lungs. (2, 266)

As this passage represents Don Lollò's perspective (the nightmarish interruption of sleep, the revelation from the balcony, the glance from threshing floor to moon to the orgy in full swing), it is logical that he would see these peasants as infernal emissaries of a force bent on subverting his own. What damns this scene in Don Lollò's eyes is what recommends it for celebration in the Tavianis' film: the cosmic connectedness and the liberating powers of collective creativity. It is Zi' Dima's desire to see the moon that prompts the relocation of the jar from the margins of the threshing floor to its elevated center, so that its alignment with the lunar sphere makes this space a planetarium, obedient to the laws of its celestial models. And when Zi' Dima directs the movements of the dancers who orbit around him like so many satellites, the construction of his counter-cosmos is complete.

Now that Don Lollò has come crashing into this carnival scene from his luxurious bedroom, we can see how clearly the Tavianis have drawn the lines of battle between two diametrically opposed civilizations. Perhaps it all boils down to the contrast in their respective titles: *Don,* abbreviation for *dominus,* with its associations of overlordship and oppression, and *zio,* or uncle, implying the lateral bonds that unite equals and bind them in familial interdependence. In Don Lollò's final lamentation for "la mia giara, la mia povera giara," it is the first-person singular possessive adjective that prevails, whereas no sooner is Zi' Dima paid than he has the money spent on provisions for communal celebration. While Don Lollò is always figured in isolation (even in bed, for Sara is banished to a cot), Zi' Dima is always the center of a crowd, from the moment he walks into the farmyard to his climactic choreography of the dance. Not surprisingly, Don Lollò remains in utter solitude at the end, seated on the pedestal once occupied by the jar, while Zi' Dima is carried off in triumph on the shoulders of his admirers, out the same door that the cloud had entered to break the jar the previous night. While Don Lollò's is a civilization of litigation and double-entry bookkeeping, Zi' Dima's is a world of natural justice in which it is simply deemed wrong that the worker repay damages caused by the boss's wrongheadedness. Furthermore, where Don Lollò presides over a realm of drudgery and silence (he has to coerce a worker into singing for him), Zi' Dima's followers are spontaneous artists, singing and dancing as a natural expression of social concord.

Perhaps the most striking effect of Don Lollò's wealth is that it leaves him unsatisfied, obsessed with the mortality that will deprive him of his treasures. "God is unjust," he complains to Sara. "Look at that young boy. He has nothing. But he has sixty years of life before him. And I, who have all this stuff. What remains to me but fifteen, twenty years?" This bit of dialogue, which is the Tavianis' invention, serves a twofold purpose: it diagnoses the bankruptcy of Don Lollo's materialist civilization, and it prepares us for the climactic image of Zi' Dima's triumph. Where Pirandello's text simply says that "the jar went and shattered against an olive tree, and Zi' Dima won out" (2:266), the Tavianis' representation uses all the techniques of pantomime, iconography, and musical leitmotif to make this not the victory of one man, but that of his entire subculture. In the silence following the crash, a flute motif begins its trilling—the same motif heard when Zi' Dima had first fingered the edge of the jar early in the episode and had pronounced it fit for his glue. The melodic recurrence here is a hopeful sign, a reminder of the efficacy of this singular artisan. Now Zi' Dima begins to stir, rising unsteadily onto his feet, taking a few tentative lurching steps forward, brushing off his sleeves, adjusting his jacket and hat. Emerging from the shards, and trying out his limbs as if they were new, Zi' Dima bears a marked resemblance to a freshly hatched chick. In such an image of rebirth resides the triumph of the entire civilization figured in Zi' Dima, radiant with the new life denied Don Lollò by his bondage to the strictly material terms of his existence.

Now the medium-specific nature of the Tavianis' adaptation becomes clear, for the rebirth afforded by this jar-turned-egg requires a new visual style, a new way of imaging the physical world which challenges the old, fixed canons with their built-in hierarchies of importance.[14] It is the jar that gives the Tavianis this pretext by allowing them to dissolve the figural unity of the established gaze and enjoy the newly liberated opportunities for optical play. Visualizing the jar cracked in two, with one part toppled over and the other still standing, the Tavianis give to this last a humanoid form—the wayward spouse who leaves Don Lollò seduced and abandoned. But the most witty camera play is when Zi' Dima's head emerges from the top to create the composite image of the jar-man—an almost mythological hybrid, an Ovidian metamorphosis arrested in midchange. As jar-man Zi' Dima is able to capture the popular imagination, commanding eager obedience to his requests for food, roof, and relocation, and winning general appreciation for his role as master of ceremonies. In the guise of jar-man, Zi' Dima is perhaps best able to challenge Don Lollò's pseudoclaims to a manhood based on power and greed. Finally, as jar-man, Zi' Dima undergoes the gestation that will allow him to hatch into a new life of freedom for himself and his peers.

The moon that shines on the subversive world of the jar-man undergoes extensive elaboration in "Mal di luna." Pirandello's satellite is a duplex image whose two faces preside alternately over the action. When Batà first reveals the nature of his malaise, just as he is about to undergo its full force, Sidora turns to the moon and finds it "fiery, violet, enormous, newly arisen from the pale heights of Crocca" (1:1222). Later that same evening, after it has wreaked its damage on Batà, the moon climbs high into the sky, and Sidora can glimpse it through the grating of her window, "now limpid . . . all inundated by a placid whiteness" (1:1222). It is this second face that smiles over the denouement. As Saro prepares to leave the scene of the proposed adultery, he sees "from the grate of the high window, in the wall facing him, the moon which, if it was causing such pain for the husband over there, here it seemed to laugh, blessed and spiteful, at the wife's missed revenge" (1:1227). This second face is the face of the detached, witty, and ironic intelligence that manipulates earthly affairs from above, denying humans any control over their own affairs and punishing those with the arrogance to believe in human effectuality.

Although Pirandello's moon is seen as a strictly negative force, the Tavianis also put this image to positive poetic uses, as their adaptation of the infantile enchantment scene so powerfully suggests. Pirandello's Batà explains that

> the mother as a young woman, gathering corn, sleeping in the open farmyard, had kept him as a baby exposed to the moon all night; and all that night, he, poor innocent baby, with his little belly in the air, while his eyes wandered wildly, had played with the beautiful moon, flailing his little arms and legs about. And the moon had enchanted him. (1:1224–25)

The Tavianis make this scene an ecstatic moment of cosmic connectedness, joining child, nature, and the heavens in perfect concord. The scene far exceeds the illustrative needs of Batà's voice-over narration, which ends with the words "I played with the beautiful moon and the moon enchanted me" as the camera zooms in to the baby in his basket amid the tall ears of corn. At first we glimpse the moon only indirectly, through its reflection in a nearby pond. Now the mother enters into the frame, but she appears upside down in the mirror of the water's surface. Moving into our line of vision, she temporarily eclipses the moon as the symphonic sound track grows in volume. The camera pans to the mother, shown right side up, splashing herself in voluptuous abandon, and cuts to the moon's reflection in the water, marred by rippling. At last we return to the baby, whose face brightens into a smile and then turns serious, before the flashback ends with the image of the adult Batà in the glaring sunlight of the piazza.

In this rich and powerful scene of infantile enchantment the Tavianis embark on their dizzying strategy of symbolic proliferations.[15] Where Pirandello's image had been duplex, the filmmakers here announce the multiplicity and fluidity of their lunar associations, invoking the classical tradition of the triune goddess—Artemis, Hecate, Persephone—and folk cults of demonic influence. If the moon can be understood to signify the feminine principle (the menstrual cycle), romance (moonstruck), lunacy (the mental illness that waxes and wanes with lunar phases), instability, magic, and hence all that is passionate in human nature, all that escapes the control of the rational, solar world, then the Tavianis bring this totality of meanings to bear on the moment of Batà's enchantment. Most obvious is the traditional connection with female sexuality, as the mother's sensuous splashing in the moonlit pond and the juxtaposition of her face with the lunar sphere suggest. Rituals of bathing and purification also conjure up the mythological link with the moon goddess, with the implied analogy between Actaeon and the infant Batà who has witnessed something taboo and is metamorphosed into a beast for his transgression. The sexual hypothesis would also explain why Batà's malady would only surface in adulthood, and why it should be triggered, at least the second time we see it, by his glimpse of Sidora undressing for Saro.

Batà thus takes to pathological extremes the human linkage with natural forces that the Tavianis have represented with such enthusiasm elsewhere: in Efisio's lessons to Gavino about the music of nature (*Padre padrone*), in the synchrony of human desire with the meteorite showers of *Night of the Shooting Stars*, and in the primal connectedness of peasant culture as shown in the two stories "La giara" and "Requiem." Batà's childhood exposure was too much of a good thing— it had made him too good a reader of the moon's multiple significance, too receptive an admirer of her poetic powers. A literate, middle-class

Batà might have channeled his moon sickness into inspired verse, reaching the apex of Romantic expressivity in his primal communion with this natural object of so much human wonder. But the preliterate peasant Batà can only express his ravishment through his body, and the convulsions that wrack him reveal an intensity almost beyond mortal powers of endurance.

There is, of course, another element in the infantile enchantment scene which links it to the maternal theme of the epilogue, and to the primal chaos of the baby's undifferentiated perceptions. The mysterious mise-en-scène of reflected images, of the mother's face presented first upside down in the still waters of the pond, all suggest the mimesis of the infant's gaze, limited to the confines of the cradle or crib, prey to whatever figure chooses to loom, huge and arbitrary, above the baby's fixed horizon, unable to gain any sense of context which would establish a rational field of vision. When the mother's face temporarily eclipses the moon, we are supposed to view this from the mystified perspective of the baby who might well come to fuse the two spheres in his mind. If this is so, then the infant's perception of the mother as an extension of the self would apply, in Batà's case, to the moon, whose celestial movements would be incorporated into his own psyche by a kind of natural synchrony. Such a hypothesis seems borne out by the image of the baby's face which appears on screen immediately after the mother's apparition, where his infant's eyes sparkle with miniature lunar reflections, and a series of cross cuts between Batà and moon seems to consolidate this incorporation. Batà's moon sickness is thus an example of infantile chaos that never gives way to adult psychic differentiation, for while the mother's return gaze grants the baby the power to see himself as "other," the moon never releases Batà from her thrall. His monthly affliction is thus an infantile atavism, a return to a predifferentiated state that can only visit the formed, adult psyche as a terrible illness. Or as art.

All the amplifications that the Tavianis introduce in the story's crisis and denouement serve to increase our sympathy for the characters and to enrich the complexity of the lunar imagery. Nuncio Orto has masterfully shown how the preparations for the dinner party (there is no such party in Pirandello) reveal the decency of Batà and the ingenuousness of Sidora ("Just this once," she implores the Madonna, as if the Virgin were the patron saint of cuckoldry).[16] I would add that the dinner party, as a kind of adulterous foreplay, only increases the erotic investment of Saro in the proceedings, thus making his eventual renunciation of Sidora's embraces that much greater a sacrifice. Indeed, a comparison with the corresponding textual passage will reveal in the

Tavianis' Saro a self-denial of heroic proportions, contrasted to that of the sniveling lover manqué of Pirandello's tale.

> But Saro, usually so lively and spirited a "good timer," felt himself, on the other hand, languish bit by bit as the laughter dried up on his lips, and his tongue shriveled up. As if there were thorns on the little wall where he was seated, he flailed continually and swallowed with difficulty. And every now and then he cast a sidelong glance at that man there awaiting the siege of illness; he also extended his neck to see if behind the heights of Crocca the frightening face of the moon had appeared. (1:1226–27)

Pirandello's Saro is terrified even before Batà's attack, prey to a fear that he projects onto the sick man and onto the moon itself. This terror precludes sexual arousal, and if he condemns Sidora's seductive advances, it is because his own lust has been factored out of the equation, giving him a false claim to any superior position of moral self-righteousness.

Instead, the Tavianis' Saro is a full participant in Sidora's adulterous scenario, clearly aroused and himself halfway undressed when Batà's unearthly cries arrest his attention. "That's what he does?" asks Saro. "It's nothing," Sidora assures him. "You're afraid," she adds, hoping to shame him into proof of his manhood despite the werewolf's presence. But Saro is beyond such gamesmanship. "He's suffering," he answers, with a response that acknowledges his shared humanity with a Batà who is neither werewolf nor love rival. Like Pirandello's Saro, the Tavianis' suffers too, but his is a cosuffering, a compassion, which links two human beings in a synchrony of pain. And where the textual story ends with Saro's spiteful withdrawal from the adulterous plot, the film has him succor Batà, restraining the victim's self-destructive behaviors until Sidora herself emerges to take a custodial role. When Saro finally leaves with the repentant mother, the camera frames Sidora in the attitude of a pietà, cradling in her lap the bruised and battered head of her unconscious spouse.

Thus the Tavianis' adaptation becomes the story of multiple metamorphoses—of Batà from man to werewolf, of Saro from exploiter to friend, of Sidora from adulteress to wife. This strategy, of course, necessitates the most radical of imagistic changes in the moon itself, whose associations with female sexuality, instability, passion, and lunacy are totally reversed by the denouement. For it is the absence of the moon and the onset of rain that allows Batà to return home to see Sidora undressing for the tryst. When the moon suddenly reappears, it is unclear whether it is the lunar radiance or the revelation of his wife's infidelity that triggers Batà's final attack. In either case, the moon now presides over a very different event from those usually associated with its romantic or demonic powers. The conversion of two human beings from their worst to their best selves, the renunciation of *cupiditas* for *caritas*, the affirmation of the bonds of wifehood and friendship in the face of temptations to adulterous malfeasance—these are the operations of this most fickle and surprising of moons. Batà's infantile enchantment, which had so auspicious a start but bore such agonizing adult consequences, has resulted in a new kind of connectedness—the human solidarity born of compassion.

In contrast, the first complete story of the film, "L'altro figlio," presents an *in malo* version of the Tavianis' Utopia, where maternal instincts are twisted beyond recognition, mental activity is reduced to sterile repetition-compulsion, and vision has been blighted by a terrible imagistic interference. In the conclusion to the original novella, Maragrazia (so Pirandello calls her) immediately begins dictating the same letter that she always writes to her absent sons. There is no pause between the confession of her rape by one of her husband's murderers—a confession that is absolutely without therapeutic value—and the return to her obsessive behavior of before. But in the film, there occurs an interlude that reveals the key to the Tavianis' adaptive strategy and explains the way in which cinematic techniques can be applied to Pirandello's narrative to realize its poetic latencies and unleash the imagination that figuratively soars from the dune of the Isola della Pomice. In this amplification of "L'altro figlio" we encounter yet another example of the Tavianis' tendency to take the story to the point beyond which some central image exhausts its conventional meaning and transcends its narrative logic, taking on a poetic life of its own. The protagonist is about to recount to the doctor the discovery of her husband's decapitation. "Oh, what I saw!" recalls Pirandello's Maragrazia. The textual account continues:

> At this point, Maragrazia got up on her feet, overcome by horror, with her bloodshot eyes wide open, and extended a hand with her fingers clawed by revulsion. At first, she lacked the voice to continue. "In their hands . . ." she then said, "in their hands . . . those assassins . . ." She stopped again, as if suffocated, and gestured with that hand, almost as if she wanted to pitch something. "And so?" asked the doctor, riveted. "They were playing . . . there, in that courtyard . . . at bocce . . . but with the heads of men . . . black, full of dirt . . . they held them by the hair . . . and

one, that of my husband . . . he held it, Cola Camizzi . . . and he showed it to me." (1:871–72)

Maragrazia's delaying operation, whereby the decisive bit of information, the hideous epiphany of the decapitation, is withheld until the last possible moment, is a miniature version of Pirandello's rhetorical strategy throughout the story. "L'altro figlio" is a slow and systematic excavation of a deeply buried truth, aimed at finally identifying the mystery of its own title: who is this son, and why is he so emphatically "other?" Only with the revelation of the severed head does the full monstrosity of Maragrazia's unwilling motherhood become clear. The Pirandellian text is thus a series of interviews between the doctor and various interlocutors who keep on unlayering the truth that awaits Maragrazia's final exposé. Thus (1) an initial interview with Maragrazia brings to light Ninfarosa's epistolary bad faith, (2) an interview with Ninfarosa unearths the existence of an adoring "altro figlio," (3) an interview with that son reveals that his mother does not accept him as her own flesh and blood, and (4) the final interview with Maragrazia discloses the murder and rape for which she can never forgive the offspring of her shame.

The Tavianis' adaptive technique mimics Maragrazia's delayed and halting rhetorical strategy in recounting the incident. Just as the doctor of Pirandello's story must endure her ellipses, her hyperventilation, her gestures, and even her dilatory syntax, which places the greatest possible distance between subject and verb—"they were playing"— and the decisive prepositional phrase—"with the heads of men"— in an attempt to postpone the horror, so the Tavianis employ a variety of delaying tactics before revealing the identity of Camizzi's bocce balls. The Tavianis' scene opens with a high-angle establishing shot of a convent courtyard, filmed from the balcony where Maria Grazia (as she is called in the film) beholds the action of the game being played below. A thud on the sound track accompanies a close-up of Camizzi, author of the collective atrocities we are about to witness. Next we're shown a man squatting in close-up to observe the outcome of the pitch, before returning to Camizzi in close-up. Now a player in an alpinist's hat (emblem of the local Garibaldini) steps forward, but his turn is interrupted by a cut to a man languishing in a lateral archway, caressing an equally apathetic dog. The camera cuts to the pacing feet of the next bowler and to a low-angle shot of a man watching from the balcony before returning below to the completely bald head of the current player. A frizzy-haired nonparticipant is shown turning away in disgust, and then a high-angle shot from Maria Grazia's perspective on the balcony takes us down to a close-up of Trupia, Camizzi's second in command. It is only now that we are shown what the men are using for bocce balls as the camera follows, in close-up, the decapitated head of Maria Grazia's husband, which comes to a halt the moment that the horrified woman lets out her shriek of recognition. By juxtaposing the close-up of Trupia with the revelation of the severed head, the editing suggests Maria Grazia's own permanent linkage of the two in memory.

This atrocious epiphany gives retrospective organization to many of the visual, editorial, and aural idiosyncrasies of the scene. The shriek reveals, retroactively, how very silent the proceedings had been, devoid of musical commentary or dialogue—except for three words by Camizzi ("Subtract a point")—punctuated by the sound of footsteps and the thuds of the severed heads. Thinking back on the scene, we notice the macabre focus on the *living* heads of the bowlers, with their various hats and varying degrees of hairiness, from Camizzi's thick beard and mane to the bald pate of the second bowler. Nor had the camera ever shown a player at full length in medium shot—in its attempt to withhold the identity of the bocce balls, it had to shoot all figures in close-up or extreme close-up, thus dissecting and dismembering the brigands as they, in fact, had done to their victims.

Up to this point, the Tavianis have been closely following Pirandello's text, with their ingenious cinematographic expedients for rendering Maria Grazia's own rhetoric of delay. But now the film takes off on its own in a way that announces the new direction that this cinematic writing will take. Earlier in the film, the Tavianis had announced their quest for a film language that would be adequate to their adaptational needs—a writing that would not only do justice to Pirandello's own literary virtuosity, but that would unleash its own hidden expressive potential through the cinema's poetic powers. Such a quest had been made explicit when the camera showed us a close-up of the page on which Ninfarosa's phony letter is written, full of strange doodles and arabesques. The letter then dissolved into the image of a stone wall lining the road to emigration, with Maria Grazia's figure huddled against it, as if she too were one of its pieces. What this juxtaposition tells us is that like Ninfarosa, the Tavianis are *writing* in images, that they excel in metaphor, and that Maria Grazia's physical analogy with the stones lining the road to emigration will have important psychological and historical applications down the line.

It is to this same stone wall that the camera returns after Maria Grazia's flashback of atrocious epiphany. She is sitting against it as she pours out her history to the doctor, who gently takes her face in his hands, as if to undo the primal association of heads with horror and

Standing on the road to emigration, Maria Grazia looks in vain for someone to carry a letter to her two sons in America.

crime. "But he, your son, what is he guilty of?" asks the doctor. "Nothing, but he's the image of his father," she replies in a revelation of her inability to distinguish between the paternal cause of her outrage and the innocent filial result. The Tavianis reinforce this confusion by casting the same actor as father and son. While Maria Grazia's confession has no therapeutic value in the Pirandello text, it does seem to herald some turning point in the film's psychological case history. Maria Grazia does seem delivered of some horrible burden at the end of the flashback as the camera scans the stone walls and comes to rest on the son sitting behind one of them. A promising exchange of glances takes place, and Maria Grazia's position on the road, between the son who walks in one direction and the emigrant group departing the other way, spatializes her own inner dilemma: to continue in her longing for the two American sons, or to embrace this "altro figlio" and release her hold on the past. "They left without the letter," Maria Grazia remarks of the emigrant group, which has already set off on its journey. "Do you really still want to write that letter?" the doctor replies, convinced that she is ready to relent. A new, more fervent exchange of glances occurs between mother and son, and Maria Grazia's face indeed softens as she casts her gaze down, sobs, and looks up in what promises to be the longed-for emotional turning point that only confession can provide. This is where the Tavianis' imagistic writing takes over to align the film with Pirandello's own ending, but in a way that paradoxically announces its expressive freedom from the literary source. There are two head-sized squashes on the stone wall lining the road to the other son, and as the camera zooms in on them, we see Maria Grazia's face suddenly harden. She picks up one of the squashes to bowl it, making a loud, thudding sound reminiscent of the sounds in the brigands' courtyard, and we realize that Maria Grazia can some-how never get free from that space, that she is doomed to relive the primal outrage for the rest of her imaginative life. When the squash comes to rest just as her husband's head had in that diabolical game, her son correctly interprets his mother's code for rejection and resign-edly walks away—the breakthrough forever denied him. Maria Grazia huddles against the stone wall to dictate word for word the letter that she had recited to Ninfarosa at the episode's start, showing that she has made no linear progress toward enlightenment or emotional thaw-ing, that the interlude between beginning and end had been of no psychological consequence.[17]

By including a medical doctor in the lineup of characters and by having him conduct an investigation, the Pirandello text presents "L'altro figlio" as a *caso*, a strange case reminiscent of the pathology so dear to the literature of naturalism. But in keeping with the scientific pretensions of naturalism, Pirandello's viewpoint remains that of an objective observer, one who stays outside and who seeks truth in a factual, observable, and reportable way. As a psychological cipher, and as a foreigner (i.e., a non-Sicilian) with no vested interest in the incidents he observes, the doctor offers the perfect entrée into this world of women left behind. Abandonment occasions three distinct responses in these women: the industrious solidarity of the female chorus that populates the town of Farnia, the carpe-diem attitude of the beautiful Ninfarosa, and the abject self-pity and passivity of the nearly catatonic Maragrazia. And since Maragrazia's extreme response to abandonment has its own unique causes, this explication remains the work of patient, scientific investigation from without.

The Tavianis, instead, are interested in presenting her pathology from within, and they do so by appropriating her gaze, by approxi-mating the mental slippage that makes squashes into severed heads and human beings into stone. That the episode is filmed from Maria Grazia's perspective is announced in the opening shot, which is

framed by a set of doorposts and which establishes our own photo-
optic on the forthcoming narrative events. In Maria Grazia's flashback,
these same doorposts are revealed to be those of her house, providing
a metaphor for her own threshold of vision. Later in the flashback, a
window frame through which Maria Grazia views the events in the
courtyard calls our attention to issues of perspective and reminds us
that we are inside the observing consciousness of the protagonist. By
casting the same actor as father and son, the camera replicates Maria
Grazia's own confusion of cause and effect and reveals that we are
seeing the story through her eyes. Finally, Maria Grazia herself calls
attention to vision in her letter to her sons, where she promises that
"from his eyes I'll choose the bearer [of this letter], because it is by the
eyes that we can know the hearts of men." And though the *topos* of
"the windows of the soul" makes these eyes into passive organs, it can
also imply the moral value of visual style—that our *way of seeing things*
reveals who we are and how we function in the world. It is to this
latter aspect of the gaze that the Tavianis have turned their attention
in filming "L'altro figlio" from such a perverse, maternal point of view.

Mothers are also motherlands, as we learned in the epilogue, where
Pirandello's return to the maternal ghost was a rediscovery of his Sicilian roots and the primal chaos of origins. As *in bono* and *in malo* personifications of the motherland, Luigi's parent and Maria Grazia represent diametrically opposed attitudes to the founding of the modern
Italian state. In fact, the Risorgimento features importantly in the "Colloqui con i personaggi, II" as a heroic occasion for adventure, personal
sacrifice, and risk taking in the name of a better future.[18] Maria Grazia's
relationship to the Risorgimento reveals the other side of such political
idealism in the introversion and defeatism that characterize so much
of Sicily's response to a history superimposed from above. Significantly, the Tavianis' Maria Grazia reacts with some ambivalence to the
Risorgimento at first, but that ambivalence solidifies into categorical
condemnation as the story unfolds. In both versions of "L'altro figlio,"
Maria Grazia calls Garibaldi "Canebardo," Sicilianizing his name as
she will personalize his meaning for her life, but in the film, she is
initially more positive about his revolutionary project, as a comparison
of text and adaptation will reveal. "Have you ever heard of a certain
Canebardo?" Pirandello's Maragrazia asks. "Garibaldi!" answers the
doctor. "Yes sir, the one who came to our area and made countryside
and city rebel against every law of man and God?" (1:870). The Tavianis' Maria Grazia describes him as "Canebardo, Canebardo, he said
that he would bring freedom and . . . he came to our area and made
countryside and city rebel against the unjust laws," while her flash-

back shows the Red Shirts distributing grain to a hungry populace.[19] Bringer of freedom and economic equity and inciter of justified insurrection, the film's Garibaldi is thus both history's revolutionary and Maria Grazia's criminal first cause.

The protagonist's ambivalence toward the Risorgimento is expressed cinematically in the opening of her flashback, which is set in a theatrical space dominated alternately by a Garibaldi idealized according to official iconography, and by a villanous Cola Camizzi, the fiercest of all the newly liberated brigands, sitting atop a black bull that constitutes the evil imagistic counterpart of the general's white horse. This is folk myth made visible.[20] By ending the scene on the foregrounded figure of the malevolent Camizzi, immobile and clearly in charge, the Tavianis suggest that the image of Garibaldi that had occupied a far deeper plane and had passed out of frame uneventfully has been completely upstaged by the criminal beneficiaries of his amnesty.[21] Linguistically, Maria Grazia's ambivalence is resolved by her refusal correctly to pronounce the general's name. Even after the doctor had pointed out her mispronunciation, the woman persists in calling him "Canebardo," just as she insists on Sicilianizing and personalizing his meaning. Like the emotional turning point of the story where Maria Grazia could opt for maternal tenderness by forgetting her savage past or could choose to relive her victimization, Garibaldi offered Sicily a revolutionary promise, an opportunity to open out to history and embrace progressive social change. But instead, Sicily chose to turn in on itself, to nurse its ancient wounds—those of colonialism, of brigandage, of millenial rape and plunder at the hands of foreigners and outlaws.

The pathology of the motherland embodied in Maria Grazia generates its dialectical opposite in the America of the emigrant's dreams. "Dear sons," Maria Grazia begins all her letters, "it is your mother who writes to you in your beautiful land of gold from this our land of tears." Politically, economically, and imaginatively, it is the "terra d'oro" that feeds and perpetuates the "terra di pianto," providing that alternative that then defines Sicily as its reactionary polar opposite. By siphoning off its progressive, working-class element, emigration leaves Sicily's fields untended, her political system unreformed, and her collective fantasy alone to nurse its wounds. The "terra di pianto" and "terra d'oro" live in symbiosis, determining not only how the Sicilians envision their land but how those newly settled in America must sustain their half of the myth. "They never tell of the misery they find over there," says one grieving father about to lose his son to emigration. The road on which the episode is set may be a one-way street to America, but the symbiotic myth is surely a two-way thoroughfare of meanings.

Sicily, as the unnatural mother who cannot hold onto her sons, generates several possible, antithetical roles for her American rival. At a certain point, the promised land is figured as the good mother, or in one man's parting monologue to his son, as the *chioccia* or brood hen who summons her baby chicks with the cry *pio, pio, pio*. The bird image returns us to the framing motif of the crow that had earned the initial opprobrium of a group of shepherds because it had been found sitting on a nest of eggs. Juxtaposed with the narrative of "L'altro figlio," this maternal male only heightens our awareness of the unnaturalness of Maria Grazia's refusal to accept her good son, while insisting on venerating the two delinquents who had abandoned her, in an abandonment made allegorically necessary by Sicily's inability to mother.

Elsewhere, America is figured as the loving mistress whom one enjoys and perhaps exploits but never leads into lawful wedlock (that privilege belongs only to daughters of the motherland). "Play the man with women," one father advises his son, "but don't marry a foreigner." The self-appointed language instructor of the emigrating group sees fit to teach only three words—women, kiss, and love—to the men whose unnatural motherland has thrown them into the arms of the seductress across the sea. It is this same self-styled expert on America who unwittingly makes the most ferocious commentary on the future status of Italian emigrants to the land of gold. In demonstrating to a fellow traveler the latest song and dance from the States, this Americanist inadvertently makes the young man into a black minstrel by teaching him a "Jim Crow" routine, revealing the underclass to which the New World will soon consign him. In this fleeting digression, the Tavianis manage to explode the entire illusion of the land of gold on which emigrant mythology is based.

"Look at things with the eyes of those who no longer see," Pirandello's mother had said, but Maria Grazia sees only with the eyes of the past, with the eyes of one whose history has such a stranglehold on her imagination that she remains forever fixed in time, unable to move, change, or open herself out to a future of emotional progress. Like Maria Grazia, Sicily turned inward and refused history, choosing instead to nurse its millenial wounds. Now, the most general use of the Tavianis' metaphoric writing becomes clear in the double articulation of the stones that are both the material building blocks of Sicily and key to Maria Grazia's petrified mode of thought. As she closes in on herself throughout the episode, the woman huddles against this backdrop of stone, merging with it, and as Pauline Kael aptly observes, the actress's "unlined, broad, childlike face has something stony about it," a quality that reflects not only the emotional numbness that prompts her to reject her adoring other son, but her petrification in the Petrarchan sense of obsessive return to a primeval hurt. Where Pirandello called the other son Rocco Trupia, it is significant that the Tavianis give this name to the brigand father and leave the son nameless, the innocent and anonymous victim of an original sin that petrifies. As Kael rightly concludes, "Sicily seems to spawn people who leave or turn to stone."[22]

Thus, where severed heads became bocce balls in the Pirandello story, the Tavianis add other links to the metaphoric or paradigmatic axis, so that squashes become heads that become bocce balls that turn people into stone. Why? Because the filmmakers have found an imagistic equivalent for the primal violence of murder, decapitation, and demonic gamesmanship in linguistic transgression, in the overlapping of the paradigmatic onto the syntagmatic axis in a way that Roland Barthes calls "teratological," "scandalous," "perverted," "abnormal," and for all that, aesthetically energizing![23] The hyperimage of the severed head, which the Tavianis' virtuoso editing had created through its techniques of delaying and dissective montage, has such a hold on Maria Grazia's imagination that it hovers over her consciousness, ready to slip as a metaphor into any available slot in the syntagmatic chain of images to halt their progression and force her to go back in time. Thus, as the crisis approaches and Maria Grazia nears the point where she could escape her obsessional trap and embark on a linear course of sentimental growth, a gratuitous natural detail triggers imagistic associations that propel her along the paradigmatic axis and block the narrative flow. The interference of the paradigmatic on the syntagmatic is indeed teratological as Barthes claims, for the very transgressive nature of the linguistic operation matches the severing of heads from bodies, and the monstrous usage of them, in turn, as metaphoric substitutes for bocce balls. The linguistic violence thus matches the violence done to the human body, and by extension, to the corporate body of the family, which is decapitated by the loss of its paternal "head." The rape that engenders the "altro figlio" is just one more example of monstrous substitution, where Trupia, the murderer, takes his slain victim's place as the sire of sons.

While putting such linguistic transgression to powerful poetic uses in exploring the pathology of Maria Grazia, the Tavianis also use it meta-artistically to reveal the way in which their adaptation aspires to the condition of poetry as it seeks freedom from the constraints of

prose narration. When paradigmatic fields spill over onto syntagmatic
ones, the hyperimage of the head comes to determine the narrative
outcome, defying naturalistic conventions of cause and effect and the
melodramatic logic of the emotions. Thus Maria Grazia's story of enslavement to an involuntary memory paradoxically reveals the techniques that free the Tavianis from the textual memory of Pirandello.
"It is probably around this transgression [of paradigmatic onto syntag-
matic]," said Barthes, "that a great number of creative phenomena are
situated, as if there were a junction between the field of aesthetics and
the defections from the semantic system."[24] Or, to extend Barthes's
hypothesis, it is as if the Tavianis were constantly making paradigmatic intrusions into the syntagmatic progression of Pirandello's text.
And if those paradigmatic intrusions involved specifically cinematic
techniques (lap dissolves from epistolary scribbles to stone walls,
squashes that roll like bocce balls to a sound track of ominous thuds),
it is at the intersection of these two axes that the artistry of adaptation
takes place. Here chaos reigns—the healthy, open chaos of unformed
matter that invites artistic creation, and the pathological chaos of the
mind that closes in on itself. It is no accident that the custodians of
this chaos are mothers: Maria Grazia and the Pirandellian parent of
the epilogue. And although Maria Grazia represents the antimother,
unable to entertain the true filial love of her other son because of the
primordial chaos that blocks her, she finds redemption in the mother
of Pirandello, chaotic in the best sense, inspirer of his art. In the crow
of Mìzzaro, protagonist of the film's frame story and anomalous figure of transsexual maternity, we see a Pirandello suspended between
masculine and feminine, earth and sky, literary prose and cinematic
poetry. And when the crow is transformed into the flying young girl
of the epilogue, the liberation of Pirandello is complete.

9 · Fellini's *Casanova*

ADAPTATION BY SELF-PROJECTION

One of Fellini's greatest strengths in filming the story of Casanova is paradoxically what has made him most vulnerable to critical attack: his insistence on treating the *Memoirs* as a literary construct and on answering that text with a text of his own.[1] "Who knows who Casanova was? We are judging a character in a book. And the character becomes detached—a reference point onto which people project themselves."[2] In treating Casanova as a fictional character who invites the work of literary interpretation, Fellini resists the trap into which most Casanova critics fall—that of mistaking the text for the man, of talking about the *Memoirs* as an objective document of historical and autobiographical authenticity without considering any of the complex literary questions implicit in the genre of the confession. With the exception of Georges Poulet, whose masterful essay on Casanova addresses the literary problems involved in the act of recording one's life story, other critics have discussed Casanova the man as he emerges from the *Memoirs*, assuming that the identity of author and subject entitles them to ignore the ironic distance between creator and creature, the retrospective imposition of order on the scattered fragments of life experience, and so on.[3] This critical (or uncritical) bias leads to absolute pronouncements about Casanova as an individual and as a product of his age, using the *Memoirs* as unconditional evidence for such claims. The perfect referentiality of the text is never doubted; hence the work of Casanova criticism has remained an attempt to recuperate the man and the century to which the *Memoirs* unequivocally point. Fellini, however, has dared to call into question the absolute referentiality of the text, to admit that we can know Casanova only as a literary construct, and to answer that fiction with another one: *Fellini's Casanova*. If we were to apply to *Casanova's* case, with slight modification, the story/ discourse distinction discussed in my introductory chapter, then *story* would be replaced by *life story* ("situations" or "facts," as Fellini will call them), and *discourse* would divide into the *Memoirs* as the literary embodiment of those situations (with all the license to fictional play built into the writing process itself) and the film as their cinematic "rewriting." Fellini himself gives voice to the story/discourse distinction in a statement that warrants lengthy quoting for its considerable interest to the study at hand.

> A work of art is its own unique expression. Those transpositions from one art form to another I find monstrous, ridiculous, off the mark. My preferences are for original subjects written for the cinema. I believe the cinema doesn't need literature, needs only film writers, that is, people who express themselves according to the rhythms and the cadences of film. Each work of art thrives in the dimension which conceived it and through which it is expressed. What can one get from a book? Plot [*le situazioni* in the Italian original]. But plot itself has no significance. It is the feeling which is expressed that matters, the imagination, atmosphere, illuminations, in sum, the interpretation. Literary interpretation of events [*fatti* or "facts" in the Italian original] has nothing to do with cinematic interpretation of those same events. They are two completely different methods of expression.[4]

If the film is an interpretation of events or facts, it follows that such interpretations will be as numerous as the individuals who choose to make them. "To be sure," Fellini claims, "at least 400 films could be made on Casanova, each one different from the others."[5]

If we were to entertain, for heuristic purposes, the adaptive triangle discussed in my introductory chapter, where the literary and cinematographic interpretations occupy two points mediated by the hypothetical preliterary idea (what Fellini calls events or facts), then the work of invention begins in the very *intuition* of those events or facts. Although Fellini's gospel of cinematic purity has led him rigorously to oppose literary adaptations in favor of original screenplays, his practice has led him time and again to adapt classical works—*Toby Dammit* in 1967, based on Edgar Allan Poe's "Never Bet the Devil Your Head"; *Satyricon* in 1968–69, derived from the Petronian model; and *La voce della luna* in 1989, adapted from Ermanno Cavazzoni's *Poema dei lunatici*. In adapting literary works, what inspires him are the loopholes and breaches in the text, the vacuums that invite the work of Fellinian "in-fill." "Confronting the huge gaps in the classical text, Fellini would be forced to rely on his personal fantasy to bridge and even enlarge them, or the operation would fail completely," Peter Bondanella convincingly argues with respect to *Satyricon*, whose challenge to the filmmaker's inventiveness helped him to overcome a severe crisis of confidence.[6]

With Casanova, too, it is the void that attracts Fellini, the textual vacuum that demands to be filled by a director whose *horror vacui* is well known. What emerges from Fellini's many published comments on the *Memoirs* is that despite the 4,545 pages of reminiscences, dense with personal adventure and intrigue, Casanova is curiously absent from the text. For Fellini, the *Memoirs* read like "a species of telephone directory," and Casanova emerges as a "vacuum . . . a completely exterior person . . . whose adventures failed to touch him. . . . He roamed the whole world. . . . and it is as if he never moved from his bed."[7]

Consequently, the descriptive in *Fellini's Casanova* is more than just an indication that the auteur theory of filmmaking is at work here. It is Fellini's declaration of independence from any received notions of who Casanova was and what his life meant. By casting Donald Sutherland in the title role of the film, Fellini further reveals his interpretive autonomy. "The true motive of my choice is precisely the 'lunar' face of Sutherland, totally estranged from the conventional image that people have of Casanova: the Italian with dark, magnetic eyes, raven hair, swarthy complexion, the classic type of the Latin lover, in short, his archetype. And therefore the operation that I want to perform with Casanova, of estrangement, or overturning the traditional model, is precisely this." Fellini could not be more explicit about his polemic intent in making a film that takes issue with so cherished a cultural icon. "Casanova must be completely reinvented," he once said, acknowledging in the verb *reinventare* the fact that the man had been invented to begin with and that we can only know Casanova inductively, from the literary discourse of the *Memoirs*, subject to the manipulations and fictional play that all such writing entails.[8] And yet viewers have taken Fellini to task for assuming this interpretive position, flaying him for daring to deviate from stereotyped conceptions of Casanova and his age as if these were inviolate truths only to be questioned at great critical and commercial risk. "There isn't a moment of genuine eroticism," laments one critic of the film, and another complains that "Casanova does not move against the rich backdrop the historical period offered but drifts through the bizarre mists of

Fellini's imagination."[9] Andrew Sarris's comments perhaps best exemplify the general criticism that Fellini's adaptation fails to live up to
its source. "There is no particular insight into—nor even much information about—either Casanova or the eighteenth century. There is no
eroticism or sensuality and no good conversation."[10] Here, an objective view of Casanova is held up as the standard against which Fellini's
interpretation is measured, and when he disappoints the expectations
so generated, the critics are loathe to forgive. Because this stereotype
is obviously of such importance to the film's reception, and because
Fellini is waging an outright war against it when he proclaims his
policy of "estrangement," we would do well to examine the received
wisdom on Casanova with some care.

What becomes immediately obvious is that Casanova is not an easy
man to pin down. Right away the tradition divides into two strains,
one concerning his cultural stature, and the other deriving from the
folklore surrounding his prodigious sexuality, which provides the
most evident and infamous of the Casanova stereotypes. Such is his
hold over the popular imagination that the name has become a virtual
synonym for male promiscuity, and thus we find in the *Grande dizionario della lingua italiana* entries not only for *Casanova* ("gran seduttore
di donne, persona dedita alle avventure amorose") but also for *casa-
novismo* ("propensione per le avventure erotiche, per le conquiste fem-
minili").[11] Accordingly, Casanova becomes the sexual superstar of
unlimited capacities whose reputation earned Fellini's film early and
predictable coverage by *Playboy*, and whisperings from Cinecittà about
"some of the wildest sex scenes ever filmed."[12] In discussing Casanova's erotic myth, another legend is often invoked—that of Don
Juan—and inevitably comparisons are made in favor of the Venetian
who enjoys women but does not destroy them in the manner of his
Spanish counterpart.[13] Thus he is seen as the benign seducer whose
pleasure is predicated on reciprocity, and whose aim is the possession of bodies, not souls. "Casanova loved many women but broke
few hearts," writes Havelock Ellis, and Owen Holloway declares,
"There was no victimizer and no victim, otherwise there would be no
pleasure."[14]

If there is a popular consensus on the erotic dimension of Casanova's myth, the other aspects of it call forth a far less unanimous response. That Casanova was an important cultural figure, however,
there can be no doubt. His considerable literary activities, his dallyings
with the upper echelons of eighteenth-century European society, his
political and economic intrigues all conspire to make him an object of
considerable scholarly interest.[15] Yet the history of reactions to the cul-

tural Casanova has been anything but homogeneous. Responses have varied, not surprisingly, with the eras and individuals who have studied the *Memoirs*, making the fortune of Casanova an index to the norms of the various ages and societies that have looked upon him. His own age, as Roberto Gervaso points out, was divided with regard to its illustrious son, so that Chiari (a confessed enemy) found him not only a pedantic boor but a man whose values changed with the prevailing political breezes, while the Prince of Ligne ranked him with Louis XV, Frederick the Great, D'Alembert, and Hume in cultural importance. The nineteenth century in its prim intolerance was naturally hard on Casanova, Gervaso reports, and post-Risorgimento Italy made Casanova a foil for its nationalistic concerns, so that Molmenti condemned him for his absence of political loyalties and Jonard for prostituting himself to the Inquisition.[16] The basis of Edmund Wilson's judgment of Casanova is likewise political. Speculating on the sparse critical attention accorded Casanova in the English-speaking world, Wilson suggests that Casanova's unhesitating acceptance of a corrupt social order makes him a disagreeable study. The critic combines political censure with puritanical squeamishness when he argues, "What is good in Casanova makes serious readers too uneasy and what is inferior disgusts them too much for him to become an accepted classic."[17] Diametrically opposed to Wilson is Owen Holloway, who sees in Casanova's adaptability to whatever norms suit his immediate purposes proof of the freedom and individuality that is the best issue of the Enlightenment.[18] Roberto Gervaso concurs in this judgment, gainsaying his compatriots who scorn Casanova in their post-Risorgimento zeal. Thus Casanova "was only a free man in a country where liberty was not indigenous, nor could it be, where the most Tartuffesque servility and the most reactionary conformity reigned."[19]

Perhaps the best example of how Casanova criticism reveals more about the critic than the subject is Havelock Ellis's celebration of Casanova as "natural man *in excelsis*." For Ellis, Casanova is wonderfully anomalous in his ability to behave according to the dictates of nature in that most unnatural of worlds—eighteenth-century society: "He was only abnormal because so natural a person within the gates of civilization is necessarily abnormal and at war with his environment." It soon becomes clear that Ellis, like Rousseau, makes this noble savage a measure of all his own discontents with the contemporary social order. Casanova shows by contrast all that is wrong with our own lives, conditioned as they are by the work ethic and dedicated to the denial of pleasure. "Casanova chose to *live*. A crude and barbarous choice it seems to us, in our hereditary instinct to spend our lives in wasting

the reasons for living," Ellis complains, bearing out Fellini's own interpretation of Casanova as "a myth onto which one projects his own
repressed thirst for life, a void that each of us can fill."[20]

Considering the history of Casanova criticism from the eighteenth
century to the present, we come to realize that the protagonist's fortune has hardly been consistent and that the referent of the *Memoirs* is
anything but univocal.[21] Nor is the editorial history of the *Memoirs* innocent of its polymorphous reception. Because the complete twelve-
volume version was only released by the Brockhaus publishing firm in
1962–63, the public up until that time had to content itself with highly
abridged editions that lent themselves to unscrupulous editorial manipulations. By exaggerating "in the most indecent way, the spicy,
scabrous parts of the work, falsifying even its language . . . this image
of Casanova as a pornographic, whoring writer was born," Gervaso
explains.[22] Thus when film critics are scandalized by Fellini's infidelity
to the real Casanova and his age, they are privileging only part of a
complex and often contradictory tradition. Fellini has seen the *Memoirs* for what they are—a literary text—and has chosen to respond to
them with his own admittedly idiosyncratic interpretation in another
discursive mode. As such his film is simply a discourse among discourses, not a heretical rejection of some absolute, preliterary truth to
which the *Memoirs* unconditionally point.

Fellini, of course, is not the first to "reinvent" Casanova. Arthur
Schnitzler did so in his scathing novella, *Casanova's Homecoming*, which
shows us what the *Memoirs* would be like stripped of the author's carefully contrived self-presentation. This imagined episode of seduction
and fraud on the eve of Casanova's return to Venice as a spy for the
Inquisition is a sordid tale devoid of the kind of witty self-deprecation
that would have made it palatable in the *Memoirs*. The opening line of
the book, "Casanova was in his fifty-third year," articulates the theme
of decline that will govern the entire text.[23] Casanova is here presented
as a vain and querulous old man whose intelligence allows him to
rationalize away his foul deceit of a young woman and the murder of
her lover. In many ways, this revisionist Casanova anticipates Fellini's
own treatment of a man in the downswing of his career and suggests
that the filmmaker is not alone in questioning the received wisdom on
his protagonist.

Having established what Fellini is reacting against in his *Casanova*,
we may move to a consideration of how he has "reinvented" his character and to what purpose. At this point we should follow the lead of
several critics who have turned to good use one of the commonplaces
of Fellini criticism: that all of his films are, to some extent, autobio-

graphical.[24] This is most obviously true of *I vitelloni, La dolce vita, 8½, The Clowns, Roma,* and *Amarcord,* while the trilogy *La strada, Nights of Cabiria,* and *Juliet of the Spirits,* featuring his wife, Giulietta Masina, allows us to see in her roles the female counterpart of his own autobiographical concerns. The filmmaker once said that he would be autobiographical even if he were telling the life story of a sole (unfortunately the pun does not obtain in Italian),[25] and there is no reason to think that this personalizing tendency would be absent from *Casanova.* But the autobiographical element in this film is not to be found so much in its commentary on eros and human relationships as in its commentary on the artist as performer and his anxieties about the nature of that performance. Fellini indeed reinvents Casanova in his own image, making his story into a meditation on the problems of aesthetic creation. The film thus becomes a meta-artistic statement in the well-established tradition of *8½.*[26]

What entitles us to see Casanova as the figure of the artist is his flair for performance—a penchant that Fellini makes explicit when he claims "Casanova is Venetian, a contemporary of Goldoni; he has the theater in him, he recites."[27] Casanova does in fact recite. He recites Ariosto before an irreverent public toward the end of his days at the Castle of Dux. He recites Tasso as he is about to jump to his death in the River Thames. He recites Petrarch as a prelude to the seduction of the mechanical doll, Rosalba. Often he is pictured self-consciously seeking the proper pose for the creation of a desired theatrical effect, such as his entrance into his mother's box in the opera house of Dresden. And it is by no means coincidental that the one woman he professes truly to love, Henriette, is herself a performer—a cellist of some talent. Jack Kroll comments that this lady is in many ways the feminine equivalent of Casanova, and I would add to this observation that she reflects him most momentously *as* performer.[28] Her unexpected display of virtuosity on the stage at Du Bois's is what seals Casanova's undying passion for his mysterious companion.

Of course, the theme of performance is most relevant with regard to Casanova's sexuality. He is the erotic exhibitionist *per eccellenza,* performing prodigies before the admiring audience of the coital contest at the Lord Talou's, and before the more onanistically involved audience of the orgy with Astrodi, the hunchback, and others in Dresden. It is not by chance that this bacchanal is celebrated with the members of a theatrical troupe in a bedroom that trembles with Casanova's every thrust and becomes a kind of stage to the much-aroused public of onlookers. A sexual performance of a hardly less subtle sort takes place on the stage of the hunchback Du Bois, who acts the part of the

Casanova and Maddalena win the admiration of their unseen voyeur De Bernis through this acrobatic exercise in lovemaking.

female praying mantis consuming the vital fluids of her insect partner in the consummation of a murderous lust. Sex becomes a performance of a pseudomystical kind for the benefit of the aged and superstitious Marchioness D'Urfé, who is to be the recipient of Casanova's regenerative sperm. This performance is to climax the *grand'opera* of impregnation that will allow the soul of the lady to pass into the body of the son she will conceive with Casanova's help. The real audience of this spectacle, however, is Marcolina, the young woman observer whose timely exposure of her bottom helps elevate Casanova to the task at hand. It is her erotic complicity that reveals the true nature of Casanova's sexual success, for she as spectator is able to arouse him, suggesting the aphrodisiac function of the audience in general.

This theme has already been enunciated in the first sexual encounter of the film, as the critic Stephen Farber so aptly points out.[29] Casanova has been summoned to a rendezvous with a beautiful and mysterious nun. When told that this session will be witnessed by the nun's lover, the French ambassador De Bernis, who will watch through an aperture

in the wall, Casanova is hardly daunted: "O, this is wonderful, really!
It will add a different flavor" (90).[30] In fact, the presence of the ambassador seems to act as a stimulant to the couple, whose Olympic exertions win the approval of their distinguished observer. "Where is this
gentleman with such bizarre tastes hiding?" (91), Casanova inquires as
a prelude to their imminent performance. Maddalena answers with a
question. "Have you seen there on the wall those two big fish?" The
camera now cuts to an alcove decorated with a painting of two large
piscine images in profile, whose eye sockets serve as peepholes for the
voyeuristic ambassador from France. As the lovemaking progresses,
we realize that the mise-en-scène of the film's first amorous tryst establishes both the terms of spectatorship and a metaphorics of sexuality
that will make all that follows mere variations on a theme. Significantly, the sexual arena proves to be a round room, walled with mul-
tifaceted mirrors that break up images and create a diffuse, aqueous
play of light. A tunnel-like corridor leads from a seaside entrance into
the sexual arena, whose circumference makes a half circle before it is
met by the opening to the alcove containing the fish mural and a bed.
Thus a gaze in either direction along this axis reveals maritime imagery—the movement of waves at one end, piscine representations at
the other—reducing the entire space to a submarine world, a fish bowl
whose occupants engage in a coupling of the most subhuman sort. If
this aqueous scenery suggests a multitude of readings—the uterine
associations of Freud, the watery Venetian setting of Casanova's early
years—it is also an objective correlative for Fellini's own response to
the *Memoirs*. "It is non-life," Fellini told Aldo Tassone, "with its empty
forms which are composed and decomposed, the charm of an aquar-
ium, an absent-mindedness of sealike profundity, where everything is
completely hidden and unknown because there is no human penetration or intimacy."[31]

   Throughout the film's first scene of lovemaking, Fellini returns to
the voyeuristic eye of Ambassador De Bernis, either by showing us the
painted fish in close-up, or by showing us what the voyeur himself
sees from his fishy perspective. That Casanova and Maddalena are
consciously performing for an audience is obvious. "Your lover shall
be cuckolded. And we will dedicate ourselves to this goal all night"
(92), Casanova announces loudly enough for De Bernis to hear. To
signal that the show has begun, Casanova turns on the music box of
his mechanical bird, devoted mascot of all his amorous exploits, making this machine the maestro whose rhythms will choreograph their
sexual ballet. The lovers position themselves strategically in De Bernis's line of vision as they disrobe, so that when the camera is not in

the mirror room, filming them in close-up, it is either peering at them from the alcove, catching tantalizing glimpses of their cavortings, or peering at them in a view that includes alcove and mural at the other end. At one point, early in the lovemaking, a cut to the fish's socket reveals De Bernis's eye fluttering excitedly within. Once the foreplay is over, the transition to coitus is signaled by a scenographic shift—with Maddalena's legs wrapped around her lover's waist and her arms walking the floor, the couple wheelbarrows into the alcove where Casanova looks up to reassure himself of the ambassadorial witness.

From the voyeur's perspective, we behold more acrobatic prodigies on the bed, punctuated by frontal views of the painted fish from close-up and long shot, foregrounded by tumbling bodies that remind us how much their sexual exuberance depends on this watchful eye.[32] Just as Casanova's coitus lacks inventiveness ("In the horizontal position, you were wanting in fantasy, let's say," in De Bernis's own words), here Fellini's camera work becomes quite pedestrian, focusing alternately on Maddalena's expressions of orgasmic ecstasy and Casanova's intense and sweaty brow. To complete the nonconnectedness of this lovemaking, Casanova immediately distances himself from Maddalena after his climax, and their postcoital lassitude is filmed in a distinctly morguelike way. Now the fish eye begins to talk, as the ambassador pronounces his verdict. "Good, very good, my dear boy. I would say that you have rendered an excellent service" (93), and despite his one reservation, De Bernis is generally encomiastic.

But the denouement of this scene brings a complicating dimension to the figure of Casanova as performing artist, and because this detail constitutes an addition to the episode in the *Memoirs*, it invites our attention as a clue to Fellini's interpretive strategy.[33] Having received the praises of the ambassador, Casanova takes this occasion to press another kind of suit: "Your approval is a motive of great pride for me. Nonetheless, with your permission, I would like to make clear that my capacities transcend those to which you have borne witness. I have studied engineering, literature, and I am skilled in the art of politics and the science of economy" (94). Casanova embellishes this list with mention of his discoveries in alchemy, the cabala, and statecraft and asks the ambassador kindly to commend him to the king of France. As he speaks, Casanova is shot from the fish-eye perspective, but he withdraws ever further through the arch separating alcove from mirror room during the course of his entreaty. An extreme close-up of the empty socket confirms our worst suspicions—the voyeuristic eye that rivets itself on Casanova's erotic performance is blind to the protagonist's "higher" gifts of intellect and taste. We, as participants in the

Casanova is carried in triumph after winning the coital contest in the household of Lord Talou.

fish-eye view, are there both when De Bernis is present and when he is not. We are both the full and vacant eye socket, privy to the disparity between Casanova's grandiose self-image and his image in the eyes of the world.[34]

This establishes the theme of cognitive dissonance which will characterize the protagonist's actions and reactions throughout the film and will make *Fellini's Casanova* such a rich commentary on the psychology of self-delusion. Casanova thus attributes his fame to cultural factors, imagining, for example, the hero's welcome he will get in the Elysian Fields upon committing suicide: "I will meet Horace, Dante, I will converse with Petrarch, Ariosto" (147). Similarly, he congratulates himself on being invited to the salon of the Marchioness D'Urfé, "the most prestigious and coveted prize of every personality of art and culture" (111). But Casanova's real reputation is based on animal appeal alone, as the Prince Del Brando slyly suggests. "I know you—by reputation, Signor Casanova, I am a great admirer of yours" (162). Casanova tries to construe this compliment in a higher sense by acknowledging the aristocratic status of its source. "I thank you. The admiration of a gentleman like yourself makes me undoubtedly proud" (163). But the prince will not let his remark be flatteringly mis-construed, and so he makes explicit its lowly intent. "Oh! Your merits have been compared to those of a stallion . . . and sometimes to those of an animal a bit less noble" (163). It is not enough for the prince merely to degrade Casanova to the level of beast; he must relegate him to an inferior rung on the animal hierarchy.[35] Casanova's social pre-tensions could not be more savagely undone. At this point, however, the host of the evening's festivities, Lord Talou, defends Casanova's higher calling: "Shh! This gentleman from Venice is a poet, philoso-pher, mathematician, learned in who knows how many things!" (163). But the events to follow immediately confirm Casanova's other repu-tation—that of the stallion ready to service all mares—when he wins the copulation contest against Righetto, Del Brando's coachman. Casa-nova's self-delusional powers are such, however, that he is able to turn this proof of his animal magnetism into its very opposite by insisting that amatory skills are a function of the brain's higher powers. "Only a body sustained by ingenuity, intelligence, and culture reaches such heights . . . and I speak to you with knowledge of the cause. It requires a considerable moral maturity, not to mention fantasy and above all the knowledge of that which is the movement of fluids, stellar and planetary influences" (164). Though this logic seems to convince Lord Talou, who pronounces the contest between Casanova and Righetto one of "brute force against intelligence" (165), the conduct of their exertions gives the lie to Casanova's theoretical claims. He and Rig-hetto assume the same posture and perform the same calisthenics, and though Casanova's partner is the more subdued and dignified, the vio-lence done to her seems all the greater for it. Nor does Casanova's self-proclaimed refinement make him the least bit sensitive to the tears of shame shed by La Romana, his consort in this sexual marathon.[36] One is therefore hard put to explain what distinguishes Casanova's perfor-mance from Righetto's on the moral and intellectual grounds to which he claims title.

Casanova's worthy aspirations are contrasted with the squalid re-ality of his performance in a scene set appropriately enough in a the-ater. It is the day after his orgy with the acting troupe, and Casanova is among the audience of their stage presentation—a sacred drama of a proto-Wagnerian sort. As the final applause dies down, the audience does an about-face and bows to the august personages occupying the royal box. Casanova remains longer than the others, transfixed by this image of inaccessible glamor. It becomes clear that such a royal spec-tacle is the ultimate performance—the one that expresses the society's highest ideals of conduct and taste. Thus the stage troupe on one side of the theater and the royal family on the other suggest the polar extremes of Casanova's own performing career. The acting company, with whom he had cavorted the night before, represents the true nature of his own talents, while the nobility suggests the ideal to which he aspires in promoting his superior gifts of intellect before so many unlistening courts. It is his aged mother who reveals the wanton untruth of his pretensions as she sneers down at him from her balcony seat in the same theater, playing audience to the unsuccessful performance of his courtier's role. "And you, what are you doing here?" (184). Casanova answers with the usual self-aggrandizing fictions. "I am here on business . . . for an excellent project, I can say it, Mother. An excellent occasion. Yes" (184). The mother, however, has obviously heard this recitation before and recognizes it as just more self-persuasion. "I get it. The usual stories. The usual lies" (184).

Casanova's sexual reputation precedes him wherever he goes, assuring him a certain kind of welcome on the many stops that punctuate his travels throughout eighteenth-century Europe, as the Prince Del Brando's comments have already suggested. Similarly in Berne, when Casanova describes himself to the entomologist's daughter Isabella as a creature of air and water, she adds, "And also fire. I have heard this said of you" (174). Though convinced that his popular appeal transcends his sexuality, Casanova does not hesitate to use that sexuality as a way of drawing attention to himself and to his "higher" attributes. And as long as he is able to live up to his own myth of sexual superstar, he can delude himself into believing that his attraction is due as much to his upper organs as to his lower ones. But once he loses his potency, the painful truth of his appeal becomes clear. Casanova is no longer a sought-after man of court and is reduced to the level of a dignified beggar, pleading the cause of his intelligence before the most indifferent audiences. Thus in the debauched court of Würtemberg, Casanova implores a feeble-minded and somnambulant duke to (1) appoint him ambassador to the court of Saxony, (2) entertain his plans for fortifying his city based on the principles of Democritus and Leucippus, and (3) accept some seeds that contain the secret of eternal youth. This speech is all but ignored by the otherwise engaged audience, and Casanova is left to act out a love scene as solipsistic and ineffectual as his plea to the duke had been. The "seduction" of the mannequin Rosalba consequently becomes the erotic equivalent of the narcissistic ravings to an unlistening audience which immediately preceded it.[37]

Failure and despair are the inevitable ends of a career based on the ephemeral power to please audiences. Accusations of impotence by the Charpillon women lead Casanova to the brink of suicide, while his loss of the arm-wrestling contest to the giantess, who is the very apotheosis of Woman in her physical grandeur, suggests the loss of his power over females and the attendant loss of his overall popular appeal. In the face of this decline, Casanova must retreat further and further into his delusional system, convincing himself that his success is still and always has been predicated on intellect alone. The final scenes of the film, set in the gloomy castle at Dux, show Casanova in his dotage clinging to this fiction despite the ever more disparate evidence of public opinion. Thus the sadistic castle guards hold him up to merciless ridicule while unknown latrine artists paint his portrait in excrement—a display that sends Casanova into a frantic defense of his unappreciated genius. "I am a celebrated Italian writer. Certainly you will recognize my name . . . Giacomo Casanova, of Venice, man of letters, philosopher" (201). So insulated is he from the reality of his public image that he actually attributes his fame to an obscure novel, *Icosameron*. "I believe that, after my death, I will be spoken of for many years in the future as the author of that work" (201). In this pitifully self-deceived statement, Casanova reveals himself at two removes from the reality of his reputation. If he will be remembered by posterity, it will be for his sexual career and for the *Memoirs* that are its written record, not for a fictional work preposterously entitled *Icosameron*.

Paradoxically, the only public that appreciates Casanova's nonsexual attributes is the Inquisition itself, which condemns him for just those cultural pursuits that he continuously promotes so unsuccessfully before other courts. The Inquisition indeed considers him to be the writer, scientist, and philosopher that he always claims to be, for it is precisely his dabbling in black magic and his writing of heretical tracts that earn him the disfavor of this judiciary body. Thus the one time Casanova's cherished self-image is honored, the consequences are nothing less than disastrous.

Though Fellini carries this theme of self-deception to its cruelest extremes at the end of the film, his tone undergoes a subtle but distinctive change. No longer the highly judgmental observer of the disparity between Casanova's self-image and his image in the eyes of the world, the camera eye becomes sympathetic to Casanova's plight and begins to judge the insensitivity of his public. When the aged protagonist slowly descends the stairs dressed in ruffles and lace to recite Ariosto before a young and irreverent audience, Fellini is able to be compassionate without being patronizing. "Who knows," Fellini told Aldo Tassone in a 1975 interview, "perhaps as an old man when the servants of the Count of Waldenstein mocked him and played atrocious jokes on him, and he—bedecked with plumes and powdered like an old clown—continued to act as he had before the French Revolution without realizing that the times had changed, that his muddled, completely bombastic life had been reduced to a tottering and sick carcass, there, then, he might perhaps have aroused a little bit of sympathy, of empathy—who knows." [38]

Set in a salon of severe, Nordic elegance, the scene begins with a pan of a gathering of young people who chat and sip tea as one long-haired male guest looks straight into the camera in a Fellinian trademark shot that calls attention to issues of spectatorship, optical positioning, and the psychological alignments of the gaze. A cut to the profile of the young count of Waldenstein, alert with anticipation, signals that something of consequence is about to happen. Now Casanova appears, photographed at considerable distance, slowly descending a monumental staircase. Immediately the count arises to announce, "I'd like to have you meet Giacomo Casanova" (203). As the camera pans left to an inattentive listenership, the count's voice continues offscreen. "An adventurer who has been much talked about. Now he's here as my librarian" (203). Miscellaneous comments spoken in German, and probably inaccessible to most of the film's Italian- and English-speaking public (though available by interlinear translation to readers of the screenplay), reveal bits and pieces of the Casanova myth already circulating in his lifetime, and very much at odds with his own scholarly self-image. "'Casanova, the one who escaped from the Leads?' 'It seems he was a womanizer' . . . 'He invented the lottery' . . . 'What an apparition. Look! To be applauded!' . . . 'I thought he was dead.' 'Is it true that he's mad?' 'He must be an amusing man. How old is he? Oh, but he's ancient!'" (203). "Giacomo, come, we're waiting for you! My guests want to listen to you" (204), the count finally calls out. Furnished with a body of preconceptions and eager to measure the real man against his myth, this young audience is a figure for the film public itself in its reception of Fellini's demystified Casanova. Thus we initially identify with this group of young spectators and entertain the same curiosity they do about the man who slowly descends the staircase.

Walking stiffly, dressed in extravagant white knee-high pants and tights, with a blue ruffled shirt and a white powdered wig, obeying the count's offscreen commands to "recite something for us" (204), this aged Casanova seems no more than a marionette of himself, manipulated by invisible strings. After making a deep bow to his audience, Casanova advances into medium close-up, where a glaring white light gives his powdered face a ghostly luminescence. A cut to the crowd and a tittering sound track reveal Casanova's uneasy view of the proceedings—a view with which we increasingly come to identify. Now the camera returns to Casanova, shot in full figure as he declaims the required verses from Ariosto. The passage from *Orlando Furioso* only heightens the pathos of this act, where the reference to Roland's "immense vigor" reminds us of Casanova's own sadly diminished physical prowess.[39] There follows a long-held, fixed shot of Casanova's performance which takes radical exception to Fellini's characteristically mobile camera technique. In the filming of this segment, according to Paul Schwartzman's report from the set, Fellini was at his improvisational best, capitalizing on the cast's genuine awe at Sutherland's impassioned delivery of Ariosto to dramatically realign our sympathies.[40] Indeed the scene is handled so deftly that it succeeds in winning our affection for this objectively clownish presence, and we are held in a kind of suspense lest the audience show him the slightest disrespect. When the inevitable giggle interrupts Casanova's performance, we too feel diminished by this blow to his dignity. A cut to a medium closeup of a laughing threesome finalizes our divorce from the crowd's perspective. When the camera returns to Casanova, his arms are still raised in their declamatory pose, but now his head has turned cameraward, his expression a mixture of surprise, fury, and hurt. As he lowers his arms, his gaze remains riveted on the audience in protracted disbelief and rage. Incredibly, the titters persist, and a cut back to the crowd reaffirms its impudence. When the camera returns to Casanova, his face remains frozen, but now he bows to take his leave, never abandoning his adherence to the strictest standards of courtly etiquette. As he remounts the monumental staircase, a female voice offscreen offers its apology, and a cut to the guards shows two of them nodding complicitously while one turns to follow Casanova up the stairs with his eyes. In his slow and silent ascent, Casanova takes us with him, distancing us irrevocably from the censorious world that judges him from below.

What accounts for this dramatic shift of perspectives? Why should Fellini suddenly abandon the harsh moralism with which he has judged his protagonist throughout the film? The answer, I believe, lies in Fellini's own identification with this protagonist in his moment of supreme vulnerability. It is here that Casanova becomes the perfect vehicle for the artist's anxieties about the loss of his own creative powers, addressing the problem that he has not hesitated to confront elsewhere, most notably, of course, in *8½*. "In fact, *Casanova* expresses well my fears, with its insistence on decadence, on ruin, on ice, on moving oneself like a robot," Fellini confessed in an interview with Dante Martelli.[41] Indeed, Casanova's fate prefigures that of the artist who has lost the power to please his public—a power whose evanescence is analogous to that of sexual potency itself. This is the most obvious personal anxiety that Fellini would find embodied in his hero, but there is also the more subtle problem of cognitive dissonance which the artist and protagonist may share. Casanova has constantly attributed his popularity to his "higher" gifts of learning and wit, while we have been shown the true brute force that underwrites this appeal. A similar danger faces the filmmaker, whose pretensions may be of the noblest sort, but who must also appeal to the crowds to financially realize his art.[42] What, asks Fellini, if this mass appeal so compromised the higher intent of the work that it became the only source of its attraction? The filmmaker would then be as self-deluded as poor Casanova, who must continually protest, "But I have a mind too!" Such a fear might legitimately beset a filmmaker whose reputation for scandal has stayed with him since *La dolce vita* and whose recourse to freaks, caricatures, and bathroom humor has made such critics as John Simon wince more than once.[43]

In the figure of Casanova, Fellini is able to address these fears, and herein may reside the explanation for Fellini's curiously unerotic treatment of this wildest of libertines. By rejecting the sensationalism of his subject, Fellini is doing precisely what Casanova cannot—the filmmaker resists seducing his public in the false hope of then communicating some higher message. Instead he shows the failure of such a strategy in Casanova, whose higher message is never heard. Fellini is intent on being heard, but this intention does not reduce the film to a sterile didacticism, for there is enough ambivalence in his treatment of Casanova, as seen from the perspective of the sympathetic ending, to give the film a highly personal tinge.[44] Once Fellini shifts points of view in the final scenes and admits his identification with the declining Casanova, the lyric moments throughout the film retrospectively organize themselves into an elegy for lost powers and for the spectacles they once so generously provided. We realize, having reached the film's end and met the aging protagonist, that all has been told with *this particular* Casanova in mind, and the narration becomes an extended lament in the *laudatio temporis acti* tradition. Nostalgia thus determines the mood of the film, but it is not the false kind that paints all as sweetness and light. It is a nostalgia that acknowledges the bad with the good and only laments the protagonist's inability to bring about either one.

The overall structure of the film must therefore be considered in light of the elegiac mood of the final scenes which retrospectively informs the entire work, making it a series of nostalgic moments governed by the logic of memory. Unlike the original *Memoirs*, which follow a strict chronology, the film wanders back and forth in time, moving according to the poetic associations of juxtaposed images. Consequently, thoughts of suicide upon his abandonment by Henriette cause Casanova to leap ahead in time and space to London, many years later, when impotence and despair tempt him to suicide once again. Memories occur within memories as the aged Casanova reminisces about a conversation with Marcolina in which he remembers to her the tale of Henriette. Image pairs punctuate the film, giving form and pattern to reminiscence. Insects recur as metaphors of predatory, homicidal love in the praying-mantis dance of the hunchback Du Bois and the near-fatal disease suffered by Casanova at the hands of the entomologist's lovely daughters in Berne. Doll-like women whom Casanova must "bring to life" include the bloodless Annamaria and the literally mechanical Rosalba. Huge, primitive earth-mother images like La Saraghina of *8½,* Oenotea of *Satyricon,* and the tobacconist of *Amarcord* usher in two of the film's most intense visionary moments. The first is the opening scene of the film, which, like the annual witch-burning ceremony at the beginning of *Amarcord,* features a communal rite of some antiquity. *Fellini's Casanova* begins at carnival time with the revelation of an enormous female head, reminiscent of a long line of Fellini heads, from the *Testone* of *I vitelloni* to those of Constantine in *Satyricon* and Mussolini in *Amarcord.* The female head of *Casanova* represents a principle of panfemininity, as the watching crowd chants: "Coquette and embroiler, who is given to us by lot as bride and mother, mother-in-law and stepmother, sister and grandmother, daughter and Madonna, we order you with sweat and with work to flourish for him who knows how to seize you" (87). Later in the film another colossal figure is again All Women—the giantess, whose apparition saves Casanova from suicide and whose presence subsumes many of the earlier lyrical moments of the film. Her poignant lullaby "Pin pinin/Valentin" echoes that of the dressmaker's girls as they witness Casanova's courtship of the doll-like Annamaria. This last is herself recalled, along with the marionette, Rosalba, in the several dolls that the giantess sings to sleep with her song.

A nostalgic motif elevated to the level of a thematic concern is that of the eroticized city. Venice is figured as a love object in the opening scene of the film, invoked by chanting crowds as "true figure, true nature, unloosed in rays like dawn, that makes one and all fall in love with her" (85). The subsequent wordplay *Venessia-Venusia* substanti-

ates this marriage of sexual and political themes.[45] More explicit yet is
Casanova's choice of La Romana as his partner in the coital contest
held in the Roman palace of Lord Talou. When the crowd hails the
hero's triumph with cries of "Rome is yours! Well done! Rome is
yours!" (171), it becomes clear that Casanova has figuratively con-
quered the city in the person of La Romana. Sexual politics makes an
appearance at the dinner party of Du Bois in Parma when Casanova
likens the divided loyalties of that city-state to the uncertain erotic in-
clinations of Du Bois himself. "We were invited to a concert in the
house of the hunchback Du Bois, an eccentric gentleman of uncertain
amorous confines, as uncertain as the confines of the Duchy of Parma
divided between the Spanish and the French" (132). Thus Parma's
double domination by France and Spain is likened to bisexuality—a
phenomenon whose perversity is then imaged in the dance of praying
mantis and victim. Though this performance is an ostensible indictment of heterosexual love, the fact that it is enacted by two men who
take such obvious pleasure in it serves to implicate the double sexual
appetite. Thus the erotic and political themes are both degraded by
their conjunction in the Parmesan household of Du Bois and in the
Roman one of Lord Talou. Yet the negative treatment of this theme is
only one small aspect of the cumulative poetic force it is to gain from
the association Venice-Venus throughout the film. Casanova's exile
from his beloved city, like the loss of his only beloved, Henriette, will
be the richest source of the nostalgia that so typifies the film's poetic
mood. Thus when Casanova makes his dramatic escape from prison,
climbing up the slippery tiles of its roof to behold the cupolas of San
Marco in the moonlight, he bursts into tears. These are not the tears
of relief that Casanova sheds in the *Memoirs*,[46] they are tears of nostalgia, spilled in the knowledge that he may never again see this city that
has been so cruel and yet so seductive, like the mistress who oscillates
between rewarding her lover and abusing him.

   The poetic mood of nostalgia is perhaps most succinctly caught in a
single image toward the film's end which is anything but gratuitous,
despite the inexplicable objections of one critic.[47] It is the aftermath of
the opera in Dresden, and Casanova stands alone on the floor of the
empty theater to see the massive candelabra lowered and extinguished
one by one. For the janitors of the theater, this is a purely mechanical
act as they call out the numbers of each fixture to be snuffed out. But
for Casanova, and for us, it is a supremely significant moment, anticipating the extinction of his own powers and the end of the spectacle
of life at its prime.[48]

   Critics have wrongly, I think, interpreted this elegiac tone in a moral sense, reading it as a sermon on the vanity of worldly pleasures.[49] Such viewers see in the final sequence of the film—Casanova's dream vision of a return to Venice—a commentary on his life of cold, narcissistic exhibitionism.[50] But this interpretation flies in the face of the actual emotions elicited by the scene, whose beauty is hardly condemnatory. Coming in the wake of Casanova's debacle at the court of Waldenstein, the dream vision is as much consolation as self-explication. The reverie begins with the line, "The other night I had a dream" (205), and, as if on cue, the scene shifts to Venice, to the Grand Canal of the film's opening carnival celebration. But now the lagoon is iced over and Casanova is alone in a silence broken only by the desolate sound of the wind. As he kneels down to peer into the ice, the shot dissolves to darkness from which two staring eyes emerge—the eyes of the great Venessia-Venusia head that had been dredged out of the lagoon in the opening scene, only to break the supporting cables with its inordinate weight and to sink back down into oblivion. If *Casanova* is about the quest for the unattainable, as Joseph Markulin has convincingly argued, then the sea goddess's head absorbs all the meanings of that quest, and its reappearance in the dream summarizes all that has eluded the protagonist's grasp during his life's aimless wanderings.[51]

Next a live figure enters the frame, shown only from the waist down and therefore devoid of identity. When Casanova turns around and whispers, "Isabelle," we realize that this partially revealed figure is the film's incarnation of unattainable love. In perverse response to his call, a gorgeously costumed woman scurries away. Now four shadowy figures come down the steps of the church, and mysteriously vanish in middescent. Fellini cuts back to Casanova, walking obliquely toward the camera in pursuit of another elaborately costumed woman, discernible only by her flounces as they recede from the lower right-hand corner of the frame. Another cut, this time to the icy expanse before the Rialto bridge, shows a bevy of lavishly attired ladies, likewise running away. Now a splendid carriage fills the screen in profile, the vehicle of transport into fairy-tale worlds. Its door slowly opens, and at its window appear the pope and Casanova's mother—twin withholders of favors sought but never attained. The pope then points to something downscreen which we cannot see and shakes his hand at Casanova in a gesture of affectionate reproach. A cut to the bridge shows Rosalba in silhouette, and when Casanova enters the frame, the silence finally yields to the wistful music of the glass harmonica. Rosalba turns to him and offers her hands—touching, the dancers rotate together; then she twirls alone and he follows after.

Fellini cuts to the dreamer's present, to an extreme close-up of ancient eyes staring under a tensely knit brow. This jump cut is of signal importance, not only because it reinscribes us in the consciousness of the aged Casanova, but because it completes the film's commentary on spectatorship. This new set of eyes replaces the earlier ones that have witnessed Casanova's life performance and pronounced it wanting: De Bernis's voyeuristic eyes and the irreverent, uncomprehending eyes of the Waldenstein court. Now Casanova has taken control of all such gazes in a retrospective glance that contains all earlier ones and puts them to the service of his own autobiographical art. This final act of viewership is therefore an act of self-appropriation—it means that Casanova has at last closed the gap between his cherished self-image and his image in the eyes of his detractors and voyeurs. What counts, he comes to realize, is not the witness of the De Bernises and the Waldensteins of this world, but the self's view of the self, which includes these earlier gazes and transcends them by means of memory, dream work, and art.

A shadow descends over Casanova's ancient eyes, which fade back to the Casanova and Rosalba of the reverie, her glazed head resting on his shoulder as they rotate together on the axis of some unseen base, the mechanical figurines on a music box. Though desperate and chill, this final image is far too lyrical for the condemnation that critics have found in it. If the dream is about unattainability and a narcissistic self-involvement that precludes any relationships of consequence, it is also about the imaginative act that, like the ice, can freeze this dance and hold it before the mind's eye. It is this imaginative act (suggesting the writing of the *Memoirs*) that so dignifies Casanova in the final scenes of the film and makes him the figure of the artist onto whom Fellini cannot help but project all the anxieties and hopes of his creative calling.

10 · Fellini's *La voce della luna*

RESISTING POSTMODERNISM

In the publicity announcements that surrounded the release of *La voce della luna*, Fellini constantly understated the influence of Ermanno Cavazzoni's novel *Il poema dei lunatici* on the final form that his adaptation would take.[1] The novel lent to the film only "a certain vibration, a certain transparency," serving as a triggering device for Fellini's own autonomous creativity.[2] Before he had even read *Il poema dei lunatici*, the Frankfurt book fair ad for this "saga di ilare follia padana" ("saga of hilarious Po River Valley madness") had been enough to arouse a curiosity indicative of the freedom with which Fellini would eventually adapt Cavazzoni's novel to the screen. "I think that those three lines awakened sleeping intentions, ghosts of unmade films and images of the countryside under the mountain of San Marino."[3]

Though the novel ultimately disappointed the hopes aroused by the Frankfurt ad ("I immediately sought and read the book, which was very different from what I had imagined"), it is perhaps in the gap between those expectations and the reading experience that Felini's film took shape.[4] The novel awakened "old atmospheres, hints, whims, intentions, characters, situations of films that I never made, and that have lain there for a number of years, buried in certain depths from which they continue to radiate, to make themselves known."[5] This is the same language that Fellini used to describe his reaction to the ad, and it suggests that the commercial reduction of the novel to "una saga di ilare follia padana" alone would have sufficed to inspire *La voce della luna* by a kind of hyperbolic exercise of *amplificatio*. But despite these disclaimers, I would argue that Cavazzoni's book played a much greater part in the film's elaboration, ultimately providing the impetus for Fellini's argument against postmodernism, and for the indignation that puts this film in the epoch-defining category of *La dolce vita, Roma,* and *Ginger and Fred.*

As the title suggests, *Il poema dei lunatici* is less a novel than an extended literary experiment in which the first-person narrator, known only as Savini, recounts the events of a month-long odyssey through the landscape of the Po River valley. A good natured, wonderstruck young man whose ingenuousness borders on the imbecilic, this persona enables Cavazzoni to dispense with any of the conventions of realist literature—historical or geographic specificity, psychological verisimilitude, narrative causality, reader identification, formal closure—because Savini is characterized precisely by his indifference to such normal concerns. "I have yet to understand the things that have happened to me" begins the narrator,

> and I think about them constantly. For myself, I am not sure how I would define the things that I have done and the things that I have said in the situations in which I found myself. It is for this reason that I have decided to bring them to the attention of people who might understand them better than I. We shall see. Having said this, I feel more at ease, and I have nothing further to add, except to describe the things that happened, as they appeared to me.[6]

In some ways a conventional heralding of the confessional genre—the need to make public a series of private revelations, the cathartic effect of such publicizing, the impulse toward intelligibility—this preface puts the burden of realist signification on the reader, "who might understand [the things that have happened to me] better than I." Though such a flattering appeal to reader intelligence resembles the traditional *captatio benevolentiae,* here it is an assertion of the gap between a realist public and a narrator who refuses to impose logical structures and causal explanations on his experiences. Savini, then, is a literary resister, if only inadvertently.

His story begins as a quest for bottles containing messages allegedly located in the bottoms of wells. Wandering about the countryside, the protagonist is mistaken for a drainage inspector and is given the name Savini. The rest of the novel's several hundred pages consists of encounters between Savini and groups or individuals who either tell stories or engage in conversational flights of fantasy with him that verge on the surreal. Savini's most memorable and enduring encounter is

Gonnella (left) acquaints Ivo with the intricate workings of his paranoid fantasy.

with Gonnella, a former prefect who has been forced to retire and who entertains intricate paranoid fantasies about the conspirators who await him in ambush. Much of the reader's pleasure in Savini's partnership with Gonnella comes from the juxtaposition of their two transformatory perspectives: the one given to finding the fantastic in the most ordinary occurrences, the other convinced that malevolent forces lurk behind the facades of social pretense. Gonnella has never accepted his forced retirement and reads it as a sign that he has simply been promoted to a prefecture of a higher order, so he appoints Savini his deputy and asks him to report on the populations inhabiting the far-flung confines of his new jurisdiction. Savini's extravagant anthropologizing (there are populations that attach themselves to thoughts, others composed of Harpylike Madonnas, still others that say only "perdinci") is matched by the prefect's rewritings of heroic history, from the Aztecs to Alexander the Great to the Mongols. The final section of the book alternates between episodes of increasing prefectorial aggression—Gonnella seems to pick fights with everyone—and revisionist histories of Christianity and of nineteenth-century Europe. Garibaldi is portrayed as a victim of advanced Alzheimer's disease at the moment of the landing in Marsala, the Battle of Waterloo is told from the perspective of a local inhabitant whose garden is trampled, and Judas is seen as ultimately betrayed by Christ.

Though Savini's mind wanders through an imaginative cosmos unbounded by temporal or physical constraints, his body traverses the most ordinary of landscapes, with stops in cafés, pizzerias, and barbershops along the way. This incongruity is only experienced by Savini and Gonnella as a stimulus to ever more fantastic elaborations: a typical Emilian townscape becomes a fairy-tale Turkish kingdom, a bar-pizzeria becomes a site for tense prefectorial surveillance. It is worth noting that the fantasies are never posited as already fabricated faits accomplis. We witness them *in progress*, and we trace their development from some tiny domestic perception to their full-blown paranoid or mythopoetic realization. Thus, what begins as a Savinian daydream about dripping faucets evolves into a fantasy about populations of miniature men who inhabit pipes and sewers, and whose activities culminate in political rallies and naval battles of apocalyptic proportions. But Savini had only started this imaginative ball rolling—it had been carried along by a chorus of receptive listeners who had, one by one, added to the fantasy until it received its climactic, Swiftian formulation by Pigafetta, the undertaker, expert on things subterranean. Because this is a cumulative, collective fabrication, the emphasis is on *process*, on the *production* of a fantasy that seems open-ended and potentially infinite, defying the closure that the pronouncements of an undertaker would lead us to expect. All this makes *Il poema dei lunatici* a metafantasy, that is, a book that foregrounds the workings of the imagination and celebrates the operations of a metamorphic vision, able to transform the banalities of daily life, or official history, into the stuff of triumphant daydreams.

It is as metafantasy that Cavazzoni's book lends its considerable power to Fellini's own polemic against postmodernism—a polemic begun at least as early as *Ginger and Fred* with its indictment of a media culture headed toward exhaustion and terminal self-quotation. If postmodernism heralds the death of the subject and the end of personal style, as Frederic Jameson argues in his landmark essay, and hence the end of auteurist cinema, then Fellini has a great stake in rejecting the postmodernist moment, or in looking for ways out.[7] *La voce della luna* is his quest for just such a way out, and Cavazzoni's metafantastic novel provides an example of the transformatory vision needed to disprove the postmodern argument that "there is nothing new to say."

Following Jameson's example, I will be using postmodernism as an umbrella term to cover "postindustrial society . . . consumer society, media society, information society, electronic society or high tech and the like," and I will employ it to designate an era that defines itself as coming *after* another moment of creative plenitude, and whose defining activities are therefore one remove from the production of primary value.[8]

The sound track of the film's opening credits announces that there is indeed something new to say, but it is indistinct and preverbal, consisting of bird noises and the tolling of bells.[9] Finally, a hushed and echoing human voice is heard chanting the name "Salvini."[10] Following the film's opening titles we see a non-naturalistic nocturnal space, with an old country well placed in left center amid swirls of fog. On the sound track we hear a voice distinctly call, "Ivo Salvini," and the film cuts to a longer shot, centered on the well, with the image of a man some distance before it. The sudden human apparition on-screen after the calling of a name makes this opening scene an invocation: Ivo is literally called into being by the voices, which will renew their appeal to the protagonist throughout the course of the film. The magical connection between the man, the moon, and the well is established in the next shot, a close-up of the well's two chains, one vertical and one slightly angled, forming a strange abstract pattern with the lunar sphere to the left of both, as if this satellite, in some off-kilter way, were authorizing the creation of Ivo. The camera cuts to a position behind the well, framing Ivo from the waist up as he turns to us to ask: "Did you hear too? They're calling me. They called me" (6), breaking all rules of realist propriety by looking directly into the camera and addressing us as the audience of spectacle.

This opening scene, then, is the film's generative allegory. It tells the story of its own invocation by some external force that we might well be tempted to identify with Cavazzoni's text. But this invocation does not exhaust itself with Ivo, for he in turn invokes us as a public, creating us as a community through our participation in a shared paranormal receptivity. This originary scene, shot in a style that foregrounds its own artifice, thus serves to showcase the process of artistic creation, specifically the tranformatory means by which voices beget men and spectacles beget audiences.

It is significant that the one scene in Fellini's film taken directly from Cavazzoni's book is perhaps the novel's most explicit demonstration of the workings of the transfiguring imagination. This is the account of Nestore's marriage to Irene, whose gargantuan sexual appetites lead him to a state of collapse.

I remember she used to say: 'My little Nestorino,' and she would let out a sort of hissing noise that she saved specially for these moments, and a sort of chuffing noise that was all her own, which was like the noise of a steam engine.

I no longer knew who she was at times like these; she was a kind of steam boiler, with superhuman strength. I'm of the opinion that she probably worked like a steam engine, because she would get all hot, and the pressure would build up, and then I would be like a poor piston in her hands. I think that she was probably coming to the boil a bit inside, and needed to let off steam. (C. 40)

The image begins as a simple simile, comparing an attribute of his wife during sexual excitation to the steam of a locomotive. Irene herself, by metonymy, becomes the locomotive, and Nestore ceases to call her by any other name than La vaporiera (the steam engine) throughout the rest of his narration. In I. A. Richard's terms, the sexual energy of this "tenor" drives the "vehicle" to dilate and proliferate into a series of ancillary images: the steam heater, the piston, the processes of pressurization and temperature elevation. Nestore continues to elaborate his conceit at great length, pausing only once to interpret his own metaphorizing procedure. "And perhaps I still loved her a bit, since I was her husband. But at the same time I used to say to myself: 'It's amazing how people can change'" (C., 42). If a woman's super-abundant sexuality turns her into a machine, Nestore performs the opposite rhetorical operation on his dishwasher, endowing the appliance with all the tender sentiments so lacking in his wife-locomotive. "So gradually, she [the dishwasher] came to fall in love with me, and dreamed of being alone with me; and, to be honest, this was my great hope too" (C., 58). Nestore's habit of metaphoric thought, his tendency to abstract himself from physical particularity and to experience his domestic life as a series of metaphysical conceits, finds its behavioral analogue in his predilection for rooftops. As a child, Nestore tells Savini, he had spent a great deal of time wandering about the roofs of half the city, in love with the omniscience and the invisibility that such a vantage point accorded him. "When you live on rooftops, you don't have a lot to say, you're just happy, and you try to get even higher, and disappear" (C., 45).

The film's corresponding scene is bracketed by devices that call attention to Nestore's powers of imaginative transcendence. His marriage with Marisa (the film's Irene) has just broken up, and as she vacates the apartment, her new lover, Zardetto, prepares to carry her off on his enormous Harley-Davidson. "Come here, my little filly," Zardetto calls, "you're like my motorcycle . . . pure dynamite, and this is your bomber, tailor-made for you. . . . Come on, aren't we two an atomic couple?" (53). Significantly, Salvini responds not to the content of Zardetto's sexual self-advertising but to its rhetorical form, objecting to his wanton use of metaphor. "Excuse me, but how can you call a woman a filly, dynamite, motorcycle? Really, I can't imagine" (53). The seeming irrelevance of Salvini's response primes us for Nestore's own story, which will tell us precisely how women become metaphysical conceits, how sexual drive converts tenors into literal vehicles of mechanized energy, transforming their lovers into equally mechanized metaphoric accomplices (pistons, bombers, etc.). Despite the debacle of Nestore's marital insufficiency, the film's version of the story is reso-lutely positive in its substitution of imaginative for sexual prowess. Importantly, the setting for this part of the story is Nestore's rooftop, and it is prefaced with a vague, appreciative reference to his imminent apotheosis. "I owe a lot to Marisa, I owe her everything" (67). At the end of Nestore's reminiscence he reiterates his debt to Marisa in more precise terms. "I owe it to her and to her way of making love if that day, from the train tracks I felt myself fly into the sky, beyond the electric wires, beyond the tree tops. I was flying, I was flying . . . to live suspended in the air has always been my vocation, and now I know how to do it" (72). In the novel, it is not Nestore but Gonnella who flies off in Savini's imagination, liberated from the material con-straints of his earthly plight after an Armageddon-like battle with his imagined pursuers. By rewarding Nestore rather than Gonnella in the film, Fellini privileges the mind's metaphorizing constructions over its paranoid ones, seeing in them the key to imaginative transcendence.

It should come as no surprise that Fellini would accept the challenge to engage Cavazzoni's text in its most technically poetic moment. The inferiority of cinematic to literary expression has traditionally been ar-gued on the grounds of metaphor—film's basis in the real makes it a necessarily literal-minded medium, according to its detractors, inca-pable of metaphoric associations. Virginia Woolf's denial of film's figu-rative expressivity is typical of such high cultural condemnations.

Obviously the images of a poet are not to be cast in bronze, or traced by pencil. They are compact of a thousand suggestions of which the visual is only the most obvious or the uppermost. Even the simplest image: "my luve's like a red, red rose, that's newly sprung in June," presents us with impressions of moisture and warmth and the glow of crimson and the softness of petals inex-

tricably mixed and strung upon the lilt of a rhythm which is itself
the voice of the passion and hesitation of the lover. . . . All this,
which is accessible to words, and to words alone, the cinema must
avoid.[11]

In filming Nestore's story, then, Fellini is meeting a double challenge:
that of literature's historical claim to expressive superiority on the
grounds of metaphor, and that of this specific novel's high degree of
poetic abstraction—something that Cavazzoni himself had foreseen as
a serious obstacle to adaptation ("I thought it would be impossible to
develop a script from such an abstract book").[12]

Far from daunting Fellini, it was the very difficulty of rendering Nestore's metaphysical conceit in terms of pure cinematic physicality that
spurred the filmmaker's inventiveness. In his resolve to make a medium-specific adaptation of Cavazzoni's passage, Fellini scrupulously
avoided recourse to verbal solutions. The film therefore excludes all
verbal references to Marisa's transformation, even omitting any allusion to her nickname, La vaporiera. Instead, the metamorphosis takes
place audiovisually, with a series of sounds, camera movements, angles, and cuts, which convinces us that this woman has indeed become
a train.[13]

The scene begins with a zoom onto the fateful sofa where Nestore
and Marisa will end their sexual journey. Surrounding the sofa are a
series of romantic and erotic objects that are systematically deprived
of all associations with conventional lovemaking. The mirror above the
couch, standard decor for pornographic doubling and lovers' self-
spectatorship, here becomes simply a hyperbolic multiplier of Marisa's
frenzy. The moon out the window, which Marisa invokes as a romantic aphrodisiac ("Look what a moon, Nestore" [70]), becomes instead
a signifier of lunacy and imbalance, of the superabundance of natural
forces that can turn a woman into a locomotive. A highly mobile camera, changing angles constantly, moving along the couch as if it too
were on rails, seems to participate alternately in Marisa's sexual excitation and in Nestore's growing bewilderment. A mirror shot now affords us an unusual high-angle, skewed perspective on the lovemaking which decomposes the bodies into a miscellany of flailing limbs,
with an emphasis on Marisa's churning legs. These legs then recur as
shadows when the camera follows them in a pan along the walls. At
one point, Nestore looks up and for a split second beholds a framed
photograph of a locomotive. It is this image that gives retroactive logic
to the surreal effects we have seen so far—the churning legs, the white
smoke issuing from Marisa's head, the chugging sounds emitted from

some unidentified source (Marisa? the couch?). With the insertion of the photograph of the locomotive, Fellini has made explicit the terms of Cavazzoni's conceit, and he has done so in a way that is justified by the scene's physical context—it is part of the interior decor of Nestore's apartment, no less strange than the feathery frame surrounding the mirror on the wall or the sofa cushion with a wheel embroidered on its front.

Triggered by the photograph, Nestore's own metaphoric associations multiply, and now we are shown large puffs of steam against a skyline of electric poles, moving by at great speed, and later in the lovemaking, the camera cuts to fast-moving tracks. Fellini has indeed met the adaptive challenge of Cavazzoni's metaphor by bringing all the virtuoso techniques of his filmmaking to the fore: a variety of camera angles, special effects, fast cutting, and inventive sound. And just as the result of his physically exhausting, debilitating, failed marriage on Nestore is paradoxically liberating, so is Fellini's massive technical response to Cavazzoni's ethereal metaphorizing. When Nestore exults that "I owe it to her and to her way of lovemaking if that day from the railroad I felt myself rise up into the sky, above the electric wires, above the tree tops" (72), the camera cuts to those very images of foliage and electric poles that had flashed by during the scene of intercourse with Marisa. But now the camera goes higher still, into the clouds, leaving tracks and wires far below in a celebration of film's own powers of imaginative transfiguration.

If the film is about the triumph of fantasy and the transforming power of the imagination, it is also about the considerable cultural forces that work against such inventiveness. Those forces can be grouped under the rubric of *postmodernism*—a term whose use Fellini himself authorizes in his description of the film's set and whose generalization to the world of contemporary media culture will go far toward explaining the filmmaker's own authorial dilemma. "I believe that I made not a town, but *the town*," Fellini observes, "an Italian super-town with the piazza on which there are, massed together, the Gothic church, the Renaissance fortress, the little nineteenth-century apartment building, the rationalist Fascist building, and the postmodern church made of transparent plastic. An assemblage of obvious facades, an invisible town" (viii).

In this busy, generic main square, Fellini is of course revisiting all the provincial townscapes of his film career, from the site of Il Matto's high-wire apotheosis in *La strada* to its most elaborate representation in *Amarcord*, whose original title was to have been "Il borgo." [14] *La voce della luna* is thus an explicit update of the generic Italian town, provid-

ing a measure of Italian progress, or devolution, from "the archaic
Italy of the eternal, sacred family; provincial, backward, uncouth,"
as Goffredo Fofi notes, "to [the Italy] at the avant-garde of too many
things, the only country perhaps in Europe and in the world to mix in
such an extreme way advances and sluggishness, and to exalt with
such insistence its own collective superficiality." [15] More than a simple
addition to the eclectic, palimpsestual nature of most Italian city-
scapes, the new church made of transparent plastic embodies a postmodernism that wipes out the historicity and cultural thickness of all
the surrounding styles. The many shiny plastic subdivisions of this
facade are both reflective and refractive, breaking up the surrounding
spaces and volumes into so many decontextualized images. It is this
church that both brings Fellini's piazza up-to-date and consumes it
through a postmodern operation of endless imagistic replication, making the film's "assemblage of obvious facades, an invisible town." It is
no accident that the first figures to enter this church are the workmen
who bring in one of the many mass-produced Madonnas being delivered in a truck. And when the parish priest, Don Antonio, claims, "It
is the most beautiful of them all" (41), such insistence only heightens
our awareness of the sameness of these religious icons, and of their
mechanical reproducibility. The kind of worship inspired by this im-
personal, postmodern goddess is typified by the plea of an elderly
suppliant. "Madonna, bestow grace on my grandson, let him be paid
for the Vespa he sold, poor thing" (42).

Fellini's set suggests both the internationalization and the ongoing
parochialism of the postmodern condition. Prominent on the piazza is
the Gran Caffè Europa, heralding the abolition of national borders in
1992,[16] yet nothing in the film suggests movement toward such cosmopolitanism except Gonnella's imagined performance of the Strauss
waltz, whose status as a wish-fulfillment fantasy proves the very lack
of Europeanism at the high cultural level. Off to one side of the piazza is the Bank of Reggiolo and of Tucson, suggesting the intrusion
of multinational capital into the confines of small-town life. But the
choice of the sister city suggests the coming together of two provin-
cialisms, rather than any glamorous opening out to the world as a
whole. The piazza is also filled with topical references that serve to
define the contemporary Italian scene, from camera-toting Japanese
tourists to African street vendors (*Vu Comprà*) to a series of former
mental patients released when the CIM (Centers of Mental Hygiene)
were closed in Italy in 1978. Of course, the distinction between sanity
and psychopathology is called into question throughout the film, as is

The king and queen of the *gnocchi* festival embody the excesses of an advanced consumer society.

the presumption of the three psychiatrists, Dr. Brambilla, Dr. Falzoni, and Il dottorino, to preside over the mental health of the polis.

La voce della luna is organized around three mass celebrations that reveal how far Italy has traveled from the naive, traditional collectivity of *Amarcord*. Where the earlier film opened with the witch-burning ceremony that ushers in spring, this seasonal rite of nature is replaced in the later film by the Gnoccata or gnocchi festival—a consumerist orgy of conspicuous bad taste. The king and queen of the festivities, both chosen for their obesity, are rendered even more grotesque by their costumes: huge carapaces that represent a compromise between the human torso and the *gnocco*. In this costuming, then, Fellini dramatizes the metamorphosis of consumers into their objects of consumption, suggesting the kind of collapse of distinctions which typifies postmodern space.

The Miss Farina contest presents another index of Italy's slippage into rampant consumerism, through a series of cinematic recalls, beginning with Giuseppe De Santis's Miss Mondina contest in *Bitter Rice* (1948). Exemplifying the aspiration of a postwar subsistence culture to the glamor of its American model, the Miss Mondina contest suggested a world of dehumanizing labor (the *mondina* was a female field worker whose backbreaking job it was to weed the rice paddies) and a deeply destructive wish-fulfillment fantasy. It is after being crowned Miss Mondina that Silvana in *Bitter Rice* makes her suicide leap. Fellini did his own parody of the American beauty contest in *I vitelloni*, where Sandra Rubini is crowned Miss Sirena (mermaid) in a campaign to publicize an Italian seaside resort. Far from Silvana's suicide leap, Sandra's coronation ends in a mere swoon—she is pregnant by her boyfriend, Fausto, and has been keeping the secret until now. If Miss Mondina reflects the confusion and devastation of the immediate postwar condition, and Miss Sirena marks the fatuous prosperity of *Il Boom*, then Miss Farina exemplifies the satiety and self-satisfaction of an advanced consumer society. Now the worker (*mondina*) and the mermaid (*sirena*) are replaced by flour (*farina*)—the product neither of human work nor of the imagination, but of industrialized refinement. And when a rain of flour pours down on Aldina after her coronation, she seems more dirtied than glorified by this poor substitute for confetti. The consumerist excesses of the Gnoccata climax in Aldina's victory dance with Dr. Brambilla, who lewdly licks all the ragu sauce off his partner's fingers one by one, reducing Miss Farina to the level of the very commodities that her crowning is designed to promote.

Youth culture is satirized in the film's next great collective episode, where the newly deputized Ivo and his boss, Gonnella, enter a huge farm building that allegedly houses their enemies. "They've discovered us!" Gonnella exclaims. "They're coming toward us! Do you see them? Don't move, we'll wait for them here" (107). What the prefect mistakes for the approaching enemy is really his own reflection, along with that of Ivo, in two large mirrored panels that move apart to reveal a cavernous discotheque, filled with masses of churning bodies and the overamplified music of Michael Jackson. If not enemy territory, this space is certainly presented as alien: dark, smoke-filled, loud, it is populated by young men and women in extravagant punk attire who are clearly enjoying an environment that by most standards would be considered infernal. To underscore its alterity, Fellini positions giant traveling amplifiers "in the complicated shapes of space ships" (107) throughout the dance hall and figures the disc jockeys as faceless, hooded, violently assertive choreographers more in the tradition of Darth Vader than of Patrick Swayze or John Travolta. In their anti-

The protagonists' encounter with youth culture takes place in this space-age discotheque.

quated quests for truth, both Ivo and Gonnella reveal the postmodern heterocosm for what it is. Nothing could be more inhospitable to Ivo's search for his fairy-tale princess than this discotheque, whose female occupants are so depersonalized by their environment that they can all claim to fit into Cinderella's tiny glass slipper, though Ivo must unlace the most difficult punk footgear to try it on.

Gonnella's protest, however, offers the more obvious indictment of postmodernism in its failure to acknowledge a hierarchy of culture. "What can you know of it?" he mutters to the young revelers. "Have you ever heard the sound of a violin? . . . No, because if you had listened to the voices of violins as we heard them, now you would be standing in silence and you wouldn't have the impudence to believe that you are dancing. Dance is . . . an embroidery, it is a flight, it is a glimpse of the harmony of the stars, it is a declaration of love. . . . Dance is a hymn to life" (111). Implicit in Gonnella's diatribe is a Romantic notion of art as the expression of an individual's privileged relation to experience. The ensuing daydream of Gonnella's waltz with his lady exemplifies those pronouncements and diametrically opposes the mass culture of the surrounding discotheque. As the crowded dance floor clears to make room for the waltzing couple, we see the postmodern moment give way to its Romantic antithesis. Up to this point, the sequence had been filmed in the MTV style of music videos, with fast takes and quick cuts that piqued the spectator's visual curiosity without ever satisfying it. But when Fellini films the waltz interlude, his technique becomes more traditional as the camera pans the crowd to settle on the Duchess of Alba, singled out by a spotlight amid the smoky anonymity of the dance floor.

With her advent on-screen, the disco music stops, and the camera cuts to a close-up of Gonnella, who bows his head slightly and holds out his hand to her. A cut back to the duchess signals her acceptance of the invitation to dance, and isolated notes on the harp indicate the build-up of the melody that will eventuate in the full orchestral version of the Blue Danube. Now a long shot locates Gonnella and the duchess in the center of a circle of young onlookers as the music reaches a crescendo in a volume-appropriate response to the waltzers' growing self-confidence. Unlike disco dancing, which is not coupled or governed by rules, Gonnella's waltz with the duchess is intensely relational, embodying a sentimental as well as a cultural wish-fulfillment fantasy. After a series of alternating close-ups and long shots, the dancers reach their finale with a romantic twirl to the cheers of the bystanders. But now Gonnella's daydream dissipates into nothingness as the young dancers leap up and visually obscure the waltzers, while Strauss is overwhelmed by the beat of Michael Jackson.

The film's final collective rite—the episode of the capture of the moon—retrospectively defines Fellini's entire quarrel with postmodernism as a quarrel with a video culture that instantly reduces all experience to the level of mass communicability. Reporters are ubiquitous in the film, providing access to diegetic information much as the drunken journalist Orlando did in *E la nave va*. But Fellini's message in *La voce della luna* is that postmodern culture values experience only in that it can be instantly recorded and transmitted for public consumption, preferring what Jean Baudrillard terms "simulacra" to any originary experience that would precede its representation in images.[17] Not surprisingly, the Gnoccata coincides with a media event of equal, if not greater, historical importance in the opening of a private television station that will broadcast local news to an international public. "We will have our station like the biggest capital cities of Europe" (89), gloats a television reporter in his interview with the business magnate Cochi who owns the network. What raises this provincial *cittadina* to the level of a great European capital is not cultural achievement but simply the technological capacity to transmit signals and to appropriate the screen of the world for their proliferation.

Thus the harvest festival of a ritualized agrarian past has not only turned into the consumer orgy of a postboom economy but has lost all vestiges of its original regional identity when it is reduced to a broadcast beam for global projection. Far from a rite of rural self-celebration, the *sagra* becomes yet one more element in a megasystem of televised messages to consume. Even when the head chef speaks of his art, his language is necessarily that of advertising jingles: "If you want to enjoy life not as a fool (*sciocco*), you must taste the *gnocco*. And if you want to always be hard (*dritto*), you must try the gnocco fried (*fritto*)" (96), in a merging of sexuality and gastronomy which typified many of Fellini's advertising spoofs in *Ginger and Fred*. When Cochi's wife expresses disappointment that her husband has financed a television network rather than investing in livestock ("He could have bought a thousand cattle, you know" [89]), she reveals the connection that Jameson makes between the image culture and late capitalism, the phase that postdates simple market or even monopoly economies and corresponds instead to the financial space of multinationalism.

Even when actual broadcasting is not taking place, television remains an intrusive presence throughout the film. As Nestore and Ivo climb onto the rooftop of his building and survey the skyline from this perspective, the sense of liberation is only partial—antennas bristle from every surface. "I crowned the town with a forest of T.V. antennas," Fellini explains, "to say something: T.V. is a possession, and there exists no authoritative exorcist who can succeed in distancing the intoxicating invasion of millions of images, its antennas are lightning rods that discharge into our homes armies of chatterboxes . . . an incessant kaleidoscope of lights and sounds that estranges us, confuses us, distracts us, and sometimes, fortunately, puts us to sleep."[18] Later, when the film's protagonists escape the brawl at the Gnoccata and sit alone in a field while Ivo tells Gonnella of the mysterious empty room that beckoned him with its secrets when he was a child, the background is filled with a large billboard whose only contents are the two letters, *T.V.* Another refuge from contemporary media culture, Adele's traditional small-town household, is also prey to video pollution. Presided over by the portrait of their grandmother, this simple, ordered domestic space promises a return to the family idyll of prevideo bourgeois society. Instead, the television in the living room provides a constant din to which Adele's two young daughters, improbably named Kuriele and Malimba, respond with violent, high-tech enthusiasm.

"Sdeng, sdeng! Ta ta ta! Out with the laser ray . . . ultrasonic ray . . . pam . . . pam . . . pam" (115). When not reciting lines from science fiction movies, the girls make demands of their mother in the form of advertising jingles. "Mamma, we want gelatin, tin. . . . We want the gelatin that the television says, the gelatin, tin, tin" (116).

As extensions of television advertising, and as its precursors, billboards and signs fill the piazza with imagistic enticements to buy, using slogans in English and Arabic as well as Italian to flaunt the cosmopolitanism of multinational capital.[19] Sandrùn pork products advertise in English that "with us nothing goes wasted," a car is advertised as Katorch 3 (*catorcio* is Roman dialect for "jalopy"), an elephant emits shaving cream from his trunk, Leonardo Da Vinci's aged self-portrait is used to sell insurance, a nude couple embraces under a condom, accompanied by the English slogan "Together your guardian angel."[20] This mixture of incongruous cultural registers, and the recruitment of every available physical surface in the piazza to proliferate images and verbal injunctions to buy, creates a dense, claustrophobic atmosphere that contracts the expanse of the movie screen to the confines of a television set. Thus Tullio Masoni claims that "the crowd pressed into the frame, the exasperated collision of the colors, the crush of the scenographic material against the surface of the screen as if it really were the glass of a monitor" reveal Fellini's uneasy surrender to the vulgarity of video culture.[21]

But the filmmaker saves his most scathing attack on television for the final sequence of the capture of the moon, which becomes a media event of the most reductive sort. In his attempt to express the enormity of this occurrence, it is the reporter who inadvertently implicates the communications industry in this crime against nature. "The fact, then, that it is indeed our station to transmit to the world with its first direct broadcast an event destined to make history adds another charge of emotion to the excitement that has overcome us" (123). Such is the public's hunger for televised mediation of experience that the local populace prefers to watch the captured moon on a huge screen in the piazza rather than travel several kilometers to see it in person. Fellini's camera plays the accomplice by never directly filming the captured moon, but by showing it instead at two removes: from the perspective of the crowd watching its televised image on the screen within the screen.[22]

Thus, what degrades this moon is not so much its seizure and detention in the farm building as its flattening into a two-dimensional image and its reduction to the familiar confines of a television monitor.[23] And it is precisely in this flattening that postmodernism performs its most consequential operations, denying the "depth models" that organized high modernist space, according to Jameson's formulation.[24] If we accept Frank Burke's overview of Fellini's career as a progression from realism to representation to signification, where the referential value of the sign is progressively weakened and the link between signifier and signified within the sign is strained to such an extent that meaning can be said to inhere only in the relationship between signifiers, then the scene of the captured moon marks the end of this signifying itinerary.[25] Much of the time, the crowd in the piazza simply watches itself on the huge television screens mounted at the sides of the square, suggesting a feedback loop that equates senders with receivers and makes the whole system "a gigantic simulacrum," in Baudrillard's words, "never again exchanging for what is real, but exchanging in itself, in an uninterrupted circuit without reference or circumference."[26] What Fellini is exposing is the closed circuitry of communications systems: the self-signifying tendencies of a medium that must decode and recode in its own terms all that is alien to its technology.[27] Thus, lunar distance, depth, and mobility are reduced to proximity, flatness, and stasis as the moon becomes yet one more datum in a global information culture.

This hermetically sealed world denies not only an "outside," but an "after." When invited to ask a question of the moon, a high church official insists that no news can enter this closed-circuit system. "But what can one ask it? The moon has nothing to reveal. For us, everything has already been revealed" (128). If we were to postmodernize the Christian theological referent of the prelate's remark, we would arrive at Edoardo Bruno's concept of an *afterhistory* that precludes novelty of any sort and limits all human actions to sterile self-repetition.[28]

Not everyone accepts the hermetic enclosure of the media culture, however. There is Onelio, the audience member who takes seriously the reporter's invitation to ask questions of the moon. Like Leopardi's shepherd in "Canto notturno di un pastore errante dell'Asia," Onelio asks probing, destabilizing questions that defy the media's powers of instant recodification it its own consumable terms.[29] "Whose fault is it? . . . What is expected of us? . . . What were we born for? . . . If we're engaged [in life], I want to know the conditions of the agreement. They must tell me what we're doing here" (128–30). In brute form, these questions reveal a nostalgia for what Jean-François Lyotard calls "the grand narratives of legitimation" which postmodern culture has rendered obsolete.[30] When the gathered dignitaries simply patronize the questioner, refusing to entertain his challenge to the epistemology of a video age, he goes on a rampage that eventually frees the moon.

Infuriated by their condescension, Onelio shoots a hole through the moon's televised image, and in the ensuing melee, the television crews stop filming. A calm descends over the empty piazza as the screens go blank, and the moon is restored to its customary place in the heavens.

Though Gonnella's paranoia is hardly liberating, it too represents a way out of the postmodern condition. He refuses to stop at the surface of experience, interpreting all appearances as mere fictions that conceal conspiracies against him. "They train each one of them to play his part," Gonnella explains to Ivo. "Did you see the doctor? Did you see his clothes? The typical clothes of a doctor. Truer than this it is not possible. Instead it's all fake, completely fake" (82). Fellini's Gonnella, like his counterpart in Cavazzoni's novel, is an allegorist, a reader of experience who shuns literal-mindedness and insists on a world of dire meanings concealed beneath the surface of the obvious. What attracts Gonnella to Ivo is the latter's own allegorical bent, his simpleton's failure to accept the forms of social pretense and to ask with destabilizing candor what stands behind the exterior of things. "I read in your eyes," says Gonnella, "that you don't play along. Congratulations!" (81).

Though his partner in allegory, Ivo's interpretive style is diametrically opposed to that of Gonnella, who comes to experience with a fixed set of paranoid presuppositions about how the world works. Ivo, instead, sees hidden truth with no preconceived notion of what he will find but only a compulsion to look for it. In Ivo's childish wonder at the world, and in his link to the countryside and his grandmother's farm, Fellini has incorporated an autobiographical recall, an echo of "an age, a season of life in which perhaps one experienced mysterious, ineffable perceptions" such as those underlying the ASA NISI MASA scene of *8½*.[31] Like Gelsomina in *La strada* or the protagonist in *Juliet of the Spirits*, Ivo has privileged access to hidden messages that exceed human powers of sensation.[32] But in his quest for breakthrough experiences and revelations of a higher order, Ivo, like Giulietta, seems far more desperate and driven than did Gelsomina, who had only to strive against the limits of the verisimilar. Where Fellini used his protagonist's paranormal gifts as an argument against the confines of the realist mode in *La strada*, Ivo's talents serve an analogous function in the filmmaker's push against the self-enclosed universe of postmodern signification. Ivo gives voice to the urgency of his quest in an exchange with the psychiatrist (il dottorino) who had treated him during his hospitalization. "The fact is that I can't take it any more . . . in this suspense, always waiting, as if on a threshold. . . . I must know, you must succeed in making me understand" (46). As Fellini's proxy in his quest for an "outside" beyond the limits of media culture, Ivo expresses the desperate impulse to escape its suffocation and claustrophobia, its indifference to those truths that are not technologically reproducible. The film's tension derives from the constant clash between a culture that lowers all experience to the common denominator of mass communicability, and a protagonist who resists that process by considering a series of literary, cinematic, spatial, and perceptual alternatives to what Jameson calls the postmodern "cultural dominant."

Ivo himself is the successor to a long and rich theatrical tradition, dating back to the *Commedia dell'arte* and the various wily servants who populated its stages. He has been compared to Arlecchino, Brighella, and Stenterello, and Fellini has even called Ivo a "lunar Pierrot," thus explaining Benigni's white powdered face and his perennial lovesickness.[33] Other cultural progenitors include Ivo's "nineteenth-century godfathers," as Fellini calls them—Pinocchio and Leopardi. "They seem the most congenial guardian angels of this puppetlike rascal and romantic, nocturnal vagabond who sighs under the windows of the Blue Fairy."[34] When Adele ushers Ivo into his childhood bedroom, the set proclaims this double ancestry with a portrait of the young Leopardi on the wall and a life-size wooden effigy of Pinocchio seated beside it. These twin icons serve retrospectively to organize the nineteenth-century allusions that had punctuated the entire film, from his grandmother's nicknaming him Pinocchino to Ivo's own pastiche of Leopardi citations as he contemplates the sleeping Aldina. "Che fai tu luna in ciel; dimmi che fai, silenziosa luna" ("Canto notturno di un pastore errante dell'Asia," ll. 1–2), "Travagliosa è la mia vita: ed è, né cangia stile, o mia diletta luna" ("Alla luna," ll. 8–10) (32). Ivo also has an explicitly cinematic genealogy. Like Gelsomina, he has a pantomimic expressivity that links him to an entire comedic tradition of film performers, from Buster Keaton to Charlie Chaplin to Stan Laurel. The silent film tradition also offered Fellini a model for the anthropomorphized moon in Méliès's *Voyage dans la lune* (1902), where the satellite becomes a face and gets shot in the eye. By quoting Méliès, Fellini stakes his claim to a cinematic heritage of illusionism and triumphant spectacle, thus thickening and historicizing his own film's poetic discourse.

Just as Ivo represents a series of influences from cultural and cinematic worlds far removed from the postmodern moment, he also represents an alternative, nonconsumerist point of view. The voyeuristic country men who visually devour the striptease of the aunt of one of them, and who appropriately pay money for the spectacle, cannot convince Ivo to join such spectatorship. (The presence of a television set in the aunt's living room, blatantly positioned between herself and her admirers, suggests that the model for her visual exhibitionism is television itself, with such late-night fare as "Colpo Grosso").[35] Ivo's response to the stripper's breasts is anything but prurient, as he seeks to distract the money-collecting nephew with the following narration:

> Juno, the wife of Jupiter, must have had beautiful breasts, big as that lady's. You know the story of the time that she fell asleep under a tree with her beautiful naked breasts, and there was the baby Hercules near and he saw those big boobs and he threw himself to suck and suck until . . . Juno woke up all of the sudden and the milk squirted and spread in the sky and thus the Milky Way was born." (9)

This mythopoetic reaction to the sight of the stripper's breasts is diametrically opposed to the lewd, consumeristic perspective of the other viewers. Ivo's storytelling suggests abundance, spectacle, and fertility, rather than the degradation and exploitation of the country men's gaze. Furthermore, the tale that he tells is a cosmogony, signifying the birth of a new universe of experience based on perceptual codes of a different order.[36]

Ivo's pursuit of alternative perspectives motivates him to go underneath, above, or through the confines of daily life.[37] He climbs down a well to better hear its voices, scales Nestore's roof to learn about imaginative transcendence, gets under his grandmother's bed to discover "a world of things" (26), climbs a ladder in her farmhouse to approximate the experience of becoming a poplar tree, tries to descend into the city's sewer system with Guanin to explore its depths, watches the crowning of Miss Farina from under the platform, and climbs a ladder in the mausoleum to seek "a place in the world where there is an opening, a hole that gives on to the other side" (25). It is this quest for an other side which propels Ivo's odyssey throughout *La voce della luna* and inspires his speculations about what happens to the sparks that go up the chimney, and to the musical notes when they dissipate in the air. His desire for an opening that will provide access to an outside, and privileged knowledge beyond the surface of contemporary media culture, finds its most elaborate spatial analogue in Ivo's fantasy of the empty room. "Everything began in that room," he tells Gonnella, "when there was a suspended silence like this. It is in a silence like this that screeching of those birds, those whistles, those bell chimes arrive, and I hear some words that I seem to understand, but I don't . . . they are so fast, pressing. I grasp only some syllables, *perciò* [therefore], for example, or *comunque* [however]. Once they said very clearly *quindi, quindi, quindi* [therefore]" (99). For Ivo, the break-through moments occur in spatial and auditory voids, when the pollution of the contemporary media subsides enough to allow the perception of other signals.

A musical interval is seen as providing equally powerful access to an outside, as the oboist explains to the town's three psychiatric superintendents: "Composing certain chords shouldn't be allowed! . . . It is precisely from those pauses, those intervals that ghosts, darkness, and cold enter and at that point, music does what it wants with you. How can you defend yourself from something that promises, promises, and never maintains it, ever?" When one of the doctors inquires about the content of this promise, the oboist specifies: "What it promises to everyone: joy, serenity, oblivion, and that we will all be happy, all accepted, and me too, and instead it's not true, no, no!" (19). What the oboist's anguish suggests are the very utopian possibilities of the "other side," and the tragedy of its elusiveness.

Ivo's own closest contact with the other side occurs soon after his dialogue with Gonnella about the empty room, as if the mere memory of it were enough to trigger his compulsion to break out. When the prefect launches into a tedious discussion of his family tree, Ivo disappears, only to be found shortly afterwards emerging from a well. "It's always they who alert me," explains Ivo.

> They had a different frenzy. "Run Salvini, run Salvini, now or nevermore," they were saying to me. I found the well immediately. But when I went down the rope of the bucket, there was a clanging, a confusion of voices, a hurricane of sounds that drowned my mind and at the same time I had the impression of being on the point of understanding. Everything would have been clear to me. Can you imagine? To live finally free, free in your heart. It is so simple, something that has always belonged to us. I want to cry when I see that instead everything is so dark, so far away. . . . Must things continue this way? Always? Without ever being able to believe in a friendly voice? Nothing firm, secure. (101)

Like the oboist who glimpsed a utopian promise in a musical interval, Ivo is on the brink of a breakthrough to the other side, but he never succeeds in penetrating its space and deciphering its cryptic truth. His desperate plea to Terzio Micheluzzi, his rescuer from the well, is a plea to understand. "I must succeed in understanding, I must understand, Terzio" (101). But instead all he fathoms are the *perciòs*, *comunque*s and *quindi*s of the voices in the empty room—conjunctions with nothing to conjoin, fragments, discontinuities, and gaps. The moon, which finally does address Ivo with the playful mocking voice of Aldina in the film's closing moments, makes explicit his superior powers of receptivity but denies him any privileged understanding. "But it's a great gift, it's luck, so-called Salvini," the moon states. "What do they want from me?" Ivo replies. "They make fun of me, I can't understand them. What are they telling me?" "You mustn't understand," answers the moon. "Woe to understanding. And what would you do then? You must only listen, only hear them, those voices, and hope that they never get tired of calling you" (136). If to understand is to penetrate the other side, then Ivo is doomed to remain on the brink, on the threshold, unable to cross over but unable to step back and dismiss the utopian promise.[38] Ivo's vocation is to bear witness to the call of other voices, despite the impossibility of ever embracing their truth. What obstructs their message is the static and white noise of the media culture, the interference of rival signals, of competing, mutually exclusive uses of the air waves, so that even the moon's dialogue with Ivo is preempted by them. "Oh God," the moon exclaims, "you made me forget the most important thing! Excuse me a moment." It is at this point that the moon takes on a likeness to Aldina, now in the guise of a television anchorperson, who announces with great fanfare the commercial break ("Pubblicitàaa . . . aaa . . . aaa" [136]).[39] As the film ends, Ivo continues his vigil on the threshold, insisting on the search for the impossible outside, testifying to its call. "And yet," Ivo pleads, "I think that, if there were a little more silence, if we all created a little more silence, maybe we'd be able to understand something" (37).

This, then, is the condition of the artist, trapped in the postmodernist "universal inside," unable to get out of the web of signifiers of which he is both producer and product, doomed to push against a threshold which will never fully open onto that other side.[40] It is this awareness that tinges Fellini's indictment of postmodernism with an uneasy undercurrent of ambivalence, for no matter how much the filmmaker regrets the tyranny of the media culture, he is so implicated in it that there is no outside from which he can possibly sit in judgment.[41] Thus Fellini's denunciation is never unequivocal. Like his spoof of television commercials in *Ginger and Fred*, whose carnivalesque exuberance exposed the director's own ill-concealed complicity (he has himself filmed various commercials over the years), *La voce della luna* has a series of ecstatic moments that allow Fellini to indulge his love of spectacle. The scene of the discotheque is a prime example of Fellinian showmanship at its most flamboyant, and Ivo's obvious

Ivo returns to the well, determined to fathom the hidden truth of the voices that call him from its depths.

delight in the event must temper any categorical condemnation that we might attribute to the filmmaker's perspective. As the French critic Thierry Jousse observed, "It is the intolerable contradiction between the two [attitudes] that nourish the avidity, the Fellinian bulimia." [42]

If there is no way out of the universal postmodern inside, can there be a cinema of resistance? Fellini's answer is a modest yes, if only in his commitment to dramatize that struggle, to foreground the process of artistic inspiration, and to watch that process play itself out on the threshold of an impossible revelation. It is here that Cavazzoni's novel serves Fellini so well, providing that model of metafantasy, or a writing that privileges its own visionary process, to arm him for combat against the imagination-deadening forces of the contemporary media. But I hesitate to equate Ivo's voices exclusively with the inspirational appeal of Cavazzoni's novel. To give those voices too precise a label—be it the literary source, or death, or psychopathology, or mystical transcendence—would be to circumscribe the mystery of the other side. Worse, it would enable the postmodern cultural dominant to appropriate it as discourse, to colonize it and relegate it to the level of electronic reproduceability.

As the film comes full circle in the final scene and Ivo returns to his initial position beside the well, bent over to hear its voices, we realize that he has made no progress toward understanding their meaning. In the two-hour odyssey through a postmodern landscape, we have only learned what those voices are not: decipherable, codifiable, consumable. Unable to cross over, but unwilling to suppress the longing for an outside, the contemporary artist is consigned to the threshold, where he can only represent the postmodern dilemma in all its urgency and hope, as the moon says to Ivo, that the voices "never get tired of calling you."

■ ■

Appendix: Film Synopses and Credits

La terra trema (1948)

La terra trema tells the story of 'Ntoni Valastro's dissatisfaction with
the economic status quo, and of his resolve to get a better price from
the fish wholesalers by having the younger men bargain with them,
rather than the elderly, who are more accepting of injustice. When
the wholesalers refuse to budge on their prices, 'Ntoni leads a wharfside rebellion against them and ends up in jail, along with his co-
insurgents. But the wholesalers are stymied without their suppliers
and parley for the fishermen's release from prison. With his newfound
sense of power, 'Ntoni decides to try to circumvent the wholesalers by
going into business for himself. This entails mortgaging the family
house to purchase the means for preserving the fish and transporting
them to market. An abundant catch of anchovies and a jubilant collective rite of salting them marks the high point of the film's economic plot, which has its sentimental analogue in 'Ntoni's courtship
of Nedda (this is the film's equivalent of the book's Barbara Zuppida),
and Mara's (the film's Mena) courtship by the bricklayer Nicola. The
wheel of fortune begins its downward turn when a storm at sea destroys the family boat. Nedda abandons 'Ntoni and a police officer,
Don Salvatore, begins to woo Lucia (the film's Lia) with the promise of
necklaces and scarves. Reduced to selling their anchovies at a loss to
the vindictive wholesalers, the Valastros at first refuse but are finally
forced to concede. After 'Ntoni's brother Cola joins a smuggling ring
and leaves Aci Trezza, Padron 'Ntoni takes sick and must be removed

to a hospice in Catania. Lucia's seduction by Don Salvatore forces her into exile, and 'Ntoni turns to drink. As the Valastros are evicted from the house by the medlar tree, Mara tells Nicola that she is no longer fit for marriage. The family's fortunes reach their lowest ebb when 'Ntoni, with his two remaining little brothers, must swallow his pride and suffer the boss's insults as they hire themselves out for day work on other men's boats.

DIRECTION	Luchino Visconti
SUBJECT	Based on *I Malavoglia* (1881) by Giovanni Verga
SCREENPLAY	Luchino Visconti
PHOTOGRAPHY	G. R. Aldo
MUSIC	Selected and coordinated by Luchino Visconti and Willy Ferrero
EDITING	Mario Serandrei
PRODUCTION	Salvo D'Angelo for Universalia

CAST
'Ntoni	Antonio Arcidiacono
Cola	Giuseppe Arcidiacono
The Grandfather	Giovanni Greco
Mara	Nelluccia Giammona
Lucia	Agnese Giammona
Nicola	Nicola Castorina
Don Salvatore	Rosario Galvagno
Lorenzo	Lorenzo Valastro
Nedda	Rosa Costanzo

The Leopard (1963)

The film begins in May 1860 when Risorgimento history forcefully intrudes upon the closed world of the Sicilian Prince Fabrizio Corbera di Salina. Convinced by his nephew Fabrizio Falconeri that his class interests are best served by collaborating with the forces for change, Fabrizio accepts Garibaldi's landing in Marsala with relative calm. As if no momentous upheavals were taking place, the prince moves his household from the suburbs of Palermo to his fiefdom in Donnafugata for the annual summer vacation, votes for a united Italy under the Savoy monarchy in the October 22 plebescite, contracts a marriage between Tancredi and Angelica, the daughter of the rapacious mayor of Donnafugata, Don Calogero Sedara, and attends a ball where aristocratic Palermo celebrates its apparent survival of the revolution. The final political event of the novel is reflected in the ball scene when the unctuous Colonel Pallavicino boasts of his success in stopping Garibaldi at the Battle of Aspromonte (August 1862), thus quelling the Risorgimento's revolutionary impulse.

TITLE IN ITALIAN	*Il Gattopardo*
DIRECTION	Luchino Visconti
SUBJECT	Based on the eponymous novel by Giuseppe Tomasi di Lampedusa (1958)
SCREENPLAY	Suso Cecchi d'Amico, Pasquale Festa Campanile, Enrico Medioli, Massimo Franciosa, Luchino Visconti
PHOTOGRAPHY	Giuseppe Rotunno
SETS	Mario Garbuglia
COSTUMES	Piero Tosi
MUSIC	Nino Rota and unpublished waltz by Verdi
EDITING	Mario Serandrei
PRODUCTION	Goffredo Lombardo for Titanus

CAST	
Fabrizio	Burt Lancaster
Tancredi	Alain Delon
Angelica	Claudia Cardinale
Don Calogero	Paolo Stoppa
Stella	Rina Morelli
Don Ciccio Tumeo	Serge Reggiani
Father Pirrone	Romolo Valli
Chevalley	Leslie French
Colonel Pallavicino	Ivo Garrani
Cavriaghi	Mario Girotti
Francesco Paolo	Pierre Clementi
Concetta	Lucilla Morlacchi

Two Women (1960)

Two Women tells the story of the young widow, Cesira, and her daughter, Rosetta, during the Nazi occupation and Allied liberation of the region. Fearful of famine, bombardment, and military depredation, the women decide to flee Rome and seek refuge in the mountains of Ciociaria, a rugged region between Rome and Naples where Cesira had been born and raised. Before leaving Rome, however, Cesira has a momentary fling with Giovanni, friend of her deceased husband and custodian of the family property in her absence. The women's escape from Rome has as its first stop the squalid farmhouse of a mercenary and untrustworthy family led by its matriarch, Concetta. After a harrowing flight from their predatory hosts, Cesira and Rosetta join other evacuees to form a colony at Sant'Eufemia among the peasants who permanently inhabit the village. Contact with Michele Festa, an anti-Fascist intellectual, opens Cesira's eyes to the larger political and moral questions posed by the war. In an episode central to the novel's didacticism, Michele tries to convert the residents of Sant'Eufemia to his brand of Christian-Marxism by reading from the Gospels, but audience inattentiveness thwarts his efforts. After a grueling winter of discomfort and shortage, the Allied advance brings deceptive security, for it is now that the tragedies begin: Michele is killed by a band of retreating Germans, and Rosetta and Cesira are gang-raped by a brigade of Moroccan "liberators." In the aftermath of her trauma, the young woman turns to promiscuity and flaunts her sexual experience before her mother's eyes. But when Cesira informs her of Michele's death, Rosetta gives vent to a grief that restores her humanity and reunites her with her mother.

TITLE IN ITALIAN	La Ciociara
DIRECTION	Vittorio De Sica
SUBJECT	Based on the eponymous novel by Alberto Moravia (1957)
SCREENPLAY	Cesare Zavattini
PHOTOGRAPHY	Gabor Pogany
SETS	Gastone Medin
MUSIC	Armando Trovajoli
EDITING	Adriana Novelli
PRODUCTION	Carlo Ponti for Champion
CAST	
Cesira	Sophia Loren
Rosetta	Eleanora Brown
Michele	Jean-Paul Belmondo
Giovanni	Raf Vallone
Florindo	Renato Salvatori

The Garden of the Finzi-Continis (1970)

The action takes place in Ferrara and spans roughly the years 1938–43. The protagonist is Giorgio (though he remains unnamed in the novel), a young man from a bourgeois Jewish family who becomes infatuated with the lovely, aristocratic Micòl Finzi-Contini. Giorgio's contact with the elusive Finzi-Contini family, recounted in flashbacks, includes sporadic childhood glimpses of them in synagogue, at school when Micòl and her brother Alberto come to take state-administered exams for private students, and once in June 1929 when the thirteen-year-old girl invites him to scale the garden walls—an invitation that is thwarted by the arrival of the servant Perotti. It takes Giorgio nine years to be invited back into the garden, whose gates have been finally opened to admit the Jews expelled from the local tennis club in compliance with Mussolini's racial policy. The year is 1938, the narrator is twenty-one, and his infatuation with Micòl, who takes him on guided tours of the garden, becomes increasingly intense. The protagonist's visits to the Barchetto del Duca become a regular feature of this luminous Indian summer, whose meteorological and sentimental delights end when a rainstorm forces the young couple to seek shelter in the Finzi-Continis' carriage. Paralyzed by sexual inhibitions, Giorgio is unable to accept Micòl's fleeting invitation to intimacy. Her sudden departure for Venice mystifies the protagonist who continues nonetheless to frequent the Finzi-Continis' estate, availing himself of Professor Ermanno's study to research his thesis, now that he has been expelled from the public library. Micòl's return at Passover prompts a series of futile attempts to win her affections, culminating in a disastrous, failed embrace in her bedroom. A journey to visit his brother Ernesto who is studying in Grenoble exposes Giorgio to news of Nazi persecution but does nothing to cool his ardor for Micòl upon his return. What shatters Giorgio's amorous fantasy is a nocturnal trip into the garden where he beholds the postcoital spectacle of Micòl and Malnate in the cabin, or Hütte, by the tennis court. A rapprochement with his father takes place in which the older man admits to his own failed "love affair" with Fascism. A series of disastrous occurrences propel the film to its tragic conclusion: Alberto dies, Malnate is killed on the Russian front, and the Finzi-Continis are rounded up by Fascist police to share the fate of the rest of Ferrara's Jewish population. Giorgio, however, has managed to escape.

TITLE IN ITALIAN	Il Giardino dei Finzi-Contini
DIRECTION	Vittorio De Sica
SUBJECT	Based on the eponymous novel by Giorgio Bassani (1962)
SCREENPLAY	Ugo Pirro, Vittorio Bonicelli
PHOTOGRAPHY	Ennio Guarnieri

SETS   Giancarlo Bartolini Salimbeni

COSTUMES   Antonio Randaccio

MUSIC   Manuel De Sica

EDITING   Adriana Novelli

PRODUCTION   Gianni Hecht Lucari, Arthur Cohn for Documento Film

CAST
Micòl   Dominique Sanda
Giorgio   Lino Capolicchio
Alberto   Helmut Berger
Malnate   Fabio Testi
Giorgio's father Romolo Valli

The Gospel According to St. Matthew (1964)

In the film's opening scene, Joseph casts a disapproving eye on his
pregnant bride-to-be but is soon reassured by an angel that Mary's
imminent motherhood is divinely ordained. The three Magi, informed
by a star, arrive in Jerusalem in search of the newborn king of the Jews.
They are ushered before Herod, who feigns approval of their quest
and asks only that they inform him of the infant's whereabouts. There
follows a wordless enactment of the adoration scene in which the Magi
bestow their gifts upon the child. Later, an angel awakens the holy
family from sleep to warn them to flee into Egypt, thus sparing the
baby Jesus the fate of the other infants of Bethlehem, murdered by
Herod's troops in the Massacre of the Innocents. Once Herod himself
is dead, the holy family in Egypt is informed by an angel that it is safe
for them to return home.

A jump cut of many years takes us to the River Jordan, where John
the Baptist predicts the coming of the Messiah. When Christ appears
on camera, an intense exchange of glances reveals to John that his
prophecy has reached its fulfillment. The newly baptized Christ withdraws to the desert for fasting and prayer, where he is confronted by
Satan who tempts him, in vain, with promises of wordly dominion.
Now Christ begins to recruit an apostolic following and to give proof
of his powers to heal and work miracles: he brings calm to the residents of a madhouse, cures a leper, multiplies fishes and loaves of
bread to feed a hungry crowd, and walks on water to reach his disciples afloat. The central portion of the film is punctuated with examples of Christ's charismatic ministry, culminating in "the stupendous, interminable Sermon on the Mount" (these are the filmmaker's
own words). So severe is Christ's discipline that it precludes even fa-

milial attachments, prompting him to refuse an audience with his mother and brothers, and to pass by his mother's house without deigning to stop. But as Christ's cult grows, he is subjected to intermittent harassment by the Pharisees, Israeli religious authorities, who accuse him of violating Jewish law.

The story of John the Baptist reaches its climax in the scene of Salome's dance—a performance that brings such pleasure to Herod II that he grants her wish to have the saint beheaded. Soon, Christ will reveal his own sacrificial destiny to his disciples in one of the many scenes of group wandering about the Holy Land. In such scenes, pedagogical moments abound: among his fellow Nazarenes, Christ remarks that prophets are never appreciated at home; amidst a group of children, he exhorts his followers to be childlike in the eyes of God; and he tells a rich man in search of spiritual enlightenment to first renounce his wealth.

Now the events of the Passion begin to take their course. Christ makes his triumphal entry into Jerusalem on a donkey, drives the merchants and moneylenders out of the Temple, and stands up authoritatively to the high priests, who interrogate him on the fine points of Jewish law. The threat that Jesus poses to the religious establishment becomes palpable in the ever-increasing crowds that come to hear his ministry and in the soldiers sent to monitor any revolutionary outbursts. At the house of Mary of Bethany, Christ's hair is anointed with precious unguents, but Judas is critical of such wastefulness. After Christ justifies Mary's action as a preparation for his burial, Judas goes to Caiaphas, the high priest of Jerusalem, and reports his willingness to betray his master for thirty silver coins. At the Last Supper, Jesus announces the eucharistic function of the bread and wine and intimates that betrayal will come from within the apostolic ranks. On the Mount of Olives, Christ predicts that Peter will deny him three times before the cock crows, and he then withdraws with James, John, and Peter to pray. While his companions sleep, Christ undergoes the Agony in the Garden—an anguished admission of his reluctance to suffer—followed by a surrender to the will of God. Now come the troops for his arrest, led by Judas, who kisses Christ and thus identifies him for the authorities. After the trial and condemnation by Caiaphas's court, Peter thrice denies any association with the accused. Judas, wracked with guilt, returns the "blood money" to Caiaphas and withdraws to a wilderness to hang himself. At the trial before Pontius Pilate, the Roman governor, the crowd overrides the judge's willingness to pardon Christ.

Crucifixion events now unfold in quick succession. Christ is taken to Golgotha, nailed to the cross, and left to die before the anguished witness of his mother, John, Joseph of Aramathea, Mary of Bethany, and Mary Magdalen. At the moment of death, a violent earthquake occurs. When calm is restored, Christ's body is brought down from the cross, laid in its shroud, and taken for burial. Later, when a small band of followers comes to mourn at the tomb, they find an angel before the open door who reports that the body is no longer there, that Christ has arisen from the dead. Ecstatic with the news, the followers race off in search of their Savior, who appears to them in Galilee and greets them with the words "Behold, I am with you always, until the end of the world."

DIRECTION	Pier Paolo Pasolini
SUBJECT	Based on the scriptural text
SCREENPLAY	Pier Paolo Pasolini
PHOTOGRAPHY	Tonino Delli Colli
SETS	Luigi Scaccianoce
COSTUMES	Danilo Donati
MUSIC	J. S. Bach, W. A. Mozart, A. Webern, S. Prokofiev, Negro spirituals, Russian revolutionary songs
MUSIC COORDINATORS	Carlo Rustichelli, Luis Bacalov
EDITING	Nino Baragli
PRODUCTION	Alfredo Bini for Arco Film
CAST	
Christ	Enrique Irazoqui
The young Mary	Margherita Caruso
The old Mary	Susanna Pasolini
Joseph	Marcello Morante
John the Baptist	Mario Socrate
Peter	Settimio Di Porto
Judas	Otello Sestili
Matthew	Ferruccio Nuzzo
John	Giacomo Morante
Andrew	Alfonso Gatto
Simon	Enzo Siciliano
Philip	Giorgio Agamben
Bartholomew	Guido Cerretani
James, son of Alphaeus	Luigi Barbini
James, son of Zebedee	Marcello Galdini
Thaddeus	Elio Spaziani
Thomas	Rosario Migale
Caiphas	Rodolfo Wilcock
Pontius Pilate	Alessandro Clerici
Herod I	Amerigo Bevilacqua
Herod II	Francesco Leonetti
Salome	Paola Tedesco

Angel	Rossana di Rocco
Joseph of Aramathea	Eliseo Boschi
Mary of Bethany	Natalia Ginzburg

The Decameron (1971)

Framing fragment—a character whom we later come to identify as Ser Ciappelletto bludgeons someone to death, throws the corpse over a precipice and spits into the void.

Pasolini's First Tale (Boccaccio's Day 2, Tale 5)—Andreuccio of Perugia comes to Naples to buy horses. While bargaining in a marketplace, he is spotted by a prostitute, *la bella siciliana*, who invites him to her bed-chamber, claiming to be his long-lost sister, the natural daughter of his father and a Sicilian noblewoman. After telling Andreuccio an intricately wrought saga of her fictional peregrinations, *la bella siciliana* detains him with food and drink. While visiting the outhouse, Andreuccio falls through a sawed-off plank and ends up in a sewer, while his hostess pilfers his wallet and locks him out of her house. Two thieves who have smelled his stench discover Andreuccio and invite him to rob the archbishop's tomb, where he hands over all the ecclesiastical vestments but the ruby ring that he was sent in for. The two thieves seal him in the sarcophagus, but Andreuccio is saved by the next band of grave robbers, whose leader gets his leg bitten by the enterprising Perugian and runs away in terror. Andreuccio emerges from the tomb and dances out into the morning light, the proud owner of a well-earned ruby ring.

Framing fragment—a street-corner entertainer tells a *Decameron* story while Ser Ciappelletto works the crowd, picking the pocket of one unsuspecting bystander and using the proceeds to proposition a young boy.

Pasolini's Second Tale (Boccaccio's Day 9, Tale 2)—Narrated by the street-corner entertainer, this story is about a young nun who is discovered in flagrante with a priest in her cell. When the abbess is told the news, she hastily gets dressed in the dark and mistakenly dons the breeches of her own lover in place of her wimple. The accused nun remarks on this strange headwear, forcing the abbess to acknowledge her hypocrisy. She does so by shifting rhetorical gears in midvituperation and announcing her newfound tolerance for lapses in monastic chastity.

Pasolini's Third Tale (Boccaccio's Day 3, Tale 1)—Masetto feigns muteness in order to be hired for garden work in a convent. First two, then all eight of the nuns come to avail themselves of his more intimate services. When the abbess joins his clientele, demand begins to exceed supply, and Masetto finally breaks his silence. His restored speech is attributed to divine intervention, and Masetto's employment conditions are improved so that the requirements of propriety, worker equity, and monastic appetites are fulfilled to the great satisfaction of all parties.

Pasolini's Fourth Tale (Boccaccio's Day 7, Tale 2)—Peronella's husband comes home unexpectedly as she and her lover, Giannello, are otherwise engaged. With the husband is a prospective buyer of the large jar in which Peronella has hidden her lover. Giannello's pretext for being there, according to Peronella, is to buy the jar, which desperately needs an interior cleaning job. The husband obligingly enters to perform the task, while Giannello completes the coitus interruptus of the opening action.

Pasolini's Fifth Tale (Boccaccio's Day 1, Tale 1)—Messer Musciatto sends the iniquitous Ser Ciappelletto to the north country to collect revenues. After a nightmarish journey past a series of memento mori, Ser Ciappelletto arrives at the home of his hosts—two brothers who practice the art of usury—only to fall desperately ill at the dinner table while singing Neapolitan songs. Rather than embarrass his hosts by dying unrepentant in their home, Ser Ciappelletto agrees to the administration of Last Rites, and he produces a deathbed self-portrait of such virtue that his friar confessor has him canonized in short order.

Pasolini's Sixth Tale (Boccaccio's Day 6, Tale 5)—Giotto and Messer Forese are traveling to Naples when a cloudburst forces them to seek shelter with a peasant who lends both men cloaks to protect them from the elements. Thus arrayed, Forese cannot resist poking fun at his fellow traveler. "Master, do you think that if a stranger came upon us who didn't know you and saw you in such a get-up, could he ever think that you're one of the best painters of the day?"

Framing fragment—Giotto arrives at the church of Santa Chiara to the great pomp and circumstance of the town worthies. The scaffolding is put in place, the workers are poised for action, as Giotto climbs up and begins to sketch. Later, he circulates in the marketplace looking for ideas and returns to his work, having sighted the models for the next story.

Pasolini's Seventh Tale (Boccaccio's Day 5, Tale 4)—At a garden party, Ricciardo and Caterina arrange to rendezvous on her balcony that night. Caterina convinces her mother that she has heat-induced insomnia that can only be alleviated by sleeping outdoors to the song of the nightingale. When the solicitous parents ascend to the balcony the next morning to see how their daughter has slept, they find that the nightingale is a metaphor and that its literal referent has been sleeping with Caterina all night. Disaster is averted when Lizio realizes that the well-born Ricciardo is indeed a good catch, and he presides over a wedding ceremony of the most impromptu sort.

Framing fragment—While eating in the refectory, Giotto is siezed by so powerful a creative impulse that he unceremoniously gobbles down his food, takes his leave of the monastic company, summons his workers from their post-prandial repose, and hurries to resume his painting.

Pasolini's Eighth Tale (Boccaccio's Day 4, Tale 5)—Lisabetta is not so lucky in her love. The fate of this nubile, fatherless girl of a wealthy family is in the hands of three proprietary brothers who become infuriated when they learn of her affair with the working-class Lorenzo. On the pretext of a country outing, the brothers lure Lorenzo into their murderous trap and bury him in a solitary place. In response to Lisabetta's incessant weeping and wailing, the ghost of Lorenzo appears to her in a dream to reveal her brothers' treachery and the whereabouts of his grave. Once permission is granted for Lisabetta to leave the premises, she verifies the ghostly information by unearthing the corpse. Determined to keep some relic of Lorenzo, Lisabetta severs the head and plants it in a basil pot in her bedroom where it will serve as the object of loving contemplation and grief.

Framing fragment—Giotto is surveying the marketplace for models when his gaze alights upon a country priest and his peasant friend who is fondling the horse that he cannot afford to buy.

Pasolini's Ninth Tale (Boccaccio's Day 9, Tale 10)—The two characters sighted by Giotto in the market, Don Gianni and Pietro, set out for the latter's native town of Barletta where he hopes to lodge the priest for the night. His wife, Gemmata, had made plans to sleep at the house of her neighbor, Zita Carapresa, to make room for their guest in the couple's only bed. When Pietro arrives home with his friend, Gemmata breaks the news that they cannot host Don Gianni as planned because Zita Carapresa is to be wed that night. To relieve his hosts' embarrassment, the priest claims that he would rather sleep in the stall with his horse, which he magically transforms into a beautiful wench each night. This gimmick inspires Gemmata with an idea for alleviating their poverty: Don Gianni can teach Pietro the spell for turning her into a horse during the day and restoring her to womanhood each night. Lust easily overcomes friendship as the priest agrees to work his magic spell, but when Pietro realizes what it means to attach the tail, he puts an end to the proceedings.

Frame fragment—The apprentices whistle at work as Giotto continues to paint.

Pasolini's Tenth Tale (Boccaccio's Day 7, Tale 10)—Two members of Giotto's workshop, Tingoccio and Meuccio, cruise the marketplace in pursuit of their *comari*. Discussing mortal sin and divine justice, the two cronies vow that whoever dies first will return to describe the afterlife to his friend. Tingoccio's enthusiastic couplings with his *comare* seem to bring on an early death, but true to his word, he returns as a ghost to inform Meuccio that copulation with *comari* does not worsen Purgatorial pains. Thus reassured, Meuccio races over to his own *comare's* house exclaiming, "It's not a sin," as he mounts her.

Framing fragment—Giotto and his workers celebrate the completion of his fresco with toasts, jingles, and the authorial question: "Why realize a work of art when it's so beautiful just to dream of it?"

DIRECTION	Pier Paolo Pasolini
SUBJECT	Based on the eponymous collection by Giovanni Boccaccio (1350)
SCREENPLAY	Pier Paolo Pasolini
PHOTOGRAPHY	Tonino Delli Colli
SETS	Dante Ferretti
COSTUMES	Danilo Donati
MUSIC	Coordinated by Pasolini and Ennio Morricone
EDITING	Nino Baragli, Tatiana Casini Morigi
PRODUCTION	Franco Rossellini for PEA

CAST
Ser Ciappelletto	Franco Citti
Friar confessor	Giuseppe Zigaina
Andreuccio	Ninetto Davoli
Peronella	Angela Luce
Giotto	Pier Paolo Pasolini
Virgin Mary	Silvana Mangano

Padre Padrone (1977)

As a six-year-old resident of Siligo, a small town in the province of
Sassari, Gavino has no sooner started school than his father Efisio
(called Abramo in the text) swoops into the classroom and carries him
off to the highlands of Baddevrustana where he is to tend the family
sheepfold. There, in the sole company of his father, who often leaves
him alone for milk runs into town, Gavino receives the pastoral education of the book's subtitle: protecting the herd from its human and
animal predators, milking sheep so that they don't defecate into the
pail, killing serpents, clearing rocks from pasture land, and so on. His
solitude and his inability to communicate in anything but the most
provincial of dialects are somewhat alleviated by the eventual acquisition of an accordion, which he learns to play with remarkable skill.
When a rich neighbor, Sebastiano, is killed in a feud, Efisio coerces the
widow into selling him the olive grove for a pittance in exchange for
his help in the sale of the estate. Efisio's dreams of familial evolution
beyond the shepherds' subsistence economy are all contingent on the
yield of this grove, which is decimated one night by a winter frost.

Mass emigration of Siligo's young male population fuels Gavino's
desire to escape, but he is prevented from embarking for Germany
(Holland in the text) by his father's failure to have signed the requisite
permission forms. Gavino's determination to leave finds eventual fulfillment in his father's vision of a military career for his first-born son.
Adjustment to army life poses special problems: worse than the shock
of military regimentation, however, is Gavino's verbal incompetence—
he can neither understand nor speak Italian. By sheer force of will,
he overcomes the homesickness that blocks any intellectual or emotional growth and seeks out a mentor, Cesare, (in the book there
are three) to oversee his educational progress. In training as a radio
technician, Gavino's great moment of triumph comes during his final
exam when the instructor switches on the machine he has assembled
and music seems to flow through its various wires and tubes. Determined to leave the military and return to Siligo to further his academic
career, Gavino is opposed by his father who sees the life of the mind
as unproductive and therefore parasitic. Gavino rebels against his father's murderous work demands and the two come to blows, forcing
the young man to leave and pursue his academic ambitions on the
mainland.

DIRECTION	Paolo and Vittorio Taviani
SUBJECT	Based on the eponymous book by Gavino Ledda (1975)

SCREENPLAY	Paolo and Vittorio Taviani
PHOTOGRAPHY	Mario Masini
SETS	Giovanni Sbarra
COSTUMES	Lina Nerli Taviani
MUSIC	Egisto Macchi
EDITING	Roberto Perpignani
PRODUCTION	Giuliani G. De Negri for RAI
CAST	
Efisio	Omero Antonutti
Gavino as a child	Fabrizio Forte
The adult Gavino	Severio Marconi
The mother	Marcella Michelangeli
Sebastiano	Stanko Molnar
Cesare	Nanni Moretti

Kàos (1984)

"L'altro Figlio"

Maria Grazia is dictating yet another letter to her two sons in America who have failed over the last fourteen years to respond to any of her many epistolary entreaties. Her dictation to the scribe, Ninfarosa, has some urgency about it—she wants to entrust the letter to one of the new batch of emigrants scheduled to leave for America on the following day. This time, Maria Grazia finds out that the letter is covered with meaningless scribbles: Ninfarosa had been deceiving her all along. The old woman experiences paradoxical pleasure from this news, for it justifies her sons' fourteen-year silence. A young doctor who has taken an interest in Maria Grazia's case kindly offers to transcribe a real letter for her, but first he seeks an explanation for the existence of a third son, the victim of lifelong rejection by his mother: "l'altro figlio" of the title. In an extended flashback, we learn that Maria Grazia's husband had been beheaded by brigands, one of whom had kidnapped and raped her, engendering this bastard son. In the aftermath of her confession, Maria Grazia has a moment of hesitation when it seems that she might finally accept this "altro figlio" as her own, but then she reverts to her old hatred and ends by dictating yet another letter to her two wayward sons in America.

"Mal di luna"

It is the twentieth day of married life for the young Sidora and her considerably senior husband Batà who has taken her to live in his solitary farm, located miles from the nearest town. When the full moon sends Batà into paroxysms of destructive and self-destructive rage, his bestial metamorphosis is but the fitting fulfillment of a hostile, inhuman environment that offers no shelter from exposure to the intensity of natural forces. Beside herself with fear, Sidora flees to her mother in town the next morning, where Batà eventually follows after awakening from his postconvulsion torpor. There in the piazza he gives a public account of the moon sickness that afflicts him every month for the duration of one night. To win back his wife he proposes that Sidora spend those werewolf nights in the company of her mother—terms to which the bride agrees when assured that Saro, the man she loves but whose feckless character had made him unsuitable for marriage, will be included among her monthly protectors. Sure enough, with the next full moon, mother and potential lover arrive at the farm, but when the old woman obligingly repairs to a back room to clear the stage for love, Saro's pity for the werewolf takes precedence over his desire for Sidora, and he renounces his adulterous quest.

"La giara"

A gigantic new jar (accompanied by great symphonic fanfare) is being delivered to the farm of Don Lollò Zirafa, who needs it to contain the abundant oil yield of this year's olive harvest. In the film, Don Lollò insists on displaying the jar, as fat and majestic as an abbess, with a sound as clear and resonant as a cathedral bell, in the center of his threshing floor, elevated on a pedestal. That night, a mysterious cloud passes over the jar and leaves it broken in two, punishing the owner for his overweening pride. When Don Lollò awakens to the spectacle of his cloven jar, he is grief stricken, and when he is assured that Zi' Dima Licasi can repair the damage with his magic glue, the bereaved owner insists on the ulterior application of stitches, much to the chagrin of the pottery mender. There follows a comic war of wills in which Zi' Dima attempts twice to walk out on the project when Don Lollò stops him with the threat of violence to his hump back. With the help of a young boy, he sands down the broken edges, bores holes in preparation for the stitches, applies the glue, and enters the jar while his assistant fits together the two pieces. Once the stitches have been sewn, Zi' Dima tries to exit from the jar, but finds the neck too small to accommodate his hump. Don Lollò refuses to let Zi' Dima break the vessel, insisting on a consultation with his lawyer to ascertain his proprietary rights. Zi' Dima must indeed reimburse Don Lollò for the jar, advises the lawyer, but the object's value must be appraised in its damaged state. Zi' Dima rejects even this compromise, and refuses to

budge from his terra cotta lodgings, ordering the assembled peasants
to buy food and drink for a banquet, solicitous of the fact that they
had remained late at the farm for his sake. An infuriated Don Lollò,
awakened from his sleep by the revelry, hurls himself at the jar and
sends it crashing to pieces. And Zi' Dima emerges victorious.

"Requiem"
  The episode begins with a Tavianian invention—the agonizing journey of a young father as he transports the coffin of his newborn son
through a series of hostile landscapes to the graveyard of the nearest
town. The length and difficulty of the journey reveal all the Tavianis'
sympathy for a group of highlanders who are struggling for permission to bury their dead in their mountain village of Margari, rather
than make the harrowing descent to the city cemetery far below. The
founder of the mountain village is about to die, and he insists on local
burial, but the municipal authorities deny him permission and send a
brigade of carabinieri to enforce the law against interment outside
sanctified grounds. They arrive at Margari to find the old man seated
before the open grave, surrounded by his community, calmly awaiting
death. Though the film's highlanders leave the graveside as they're
told, they soon come back, pretending that their founder has just died
and feigning such intense grief and fury that the carabinieri flee in
their wake, leaving the old man to resume his customary seat by the
open grave. The coffin, topped with the skull cap and the perfectly
polished shoes that will adorn the body in death, gives an air of luxury
and peace to the scene, which closes with a long shot, classically balanced, centered on the old man surrounded by his community, against
the background of a bell tower and a lush, welcoming landscape—the
utopian dream made visual.

DIRECTION	Paolo and Vittorio Taviani
SUBJECT	Based on *Novelle per un anno* (1939) of Luigi Pirandello
SCREENPLAY	Paolo and Vittorio Taviani, Tonino Guerra
PHOTOGRAPHY	Giuseppe Lanci
AERIAL SHOTS	Folco Quilici
SETS	Francesco Bronzi
COSTUMES	Lina Nerli Taviani
MUSIC	Nicola Piovani
EDITING	Roberto Perpignani
PRODUCTION	Giuliani G. De Negri for RAI/Filmtre

CAST
"L'altro figlio"
  Maria Grazia   Margherita Lozano
"Mal di luna"
  Batà   Claudio Bigagli
  Sidora   Enrica Maria Modugno
  Saro   Massimo Bonetti
  Sidora's mother   Anna Malvica
"La giara"
  Don Lollò   Ciccio Ingrassia
  Zi' Dima   Franco Franchi
"Requiem"
  Salvatore   Biagio Barone
  The old patriarch   Salvatore Rossi
  Father Sarso   Franco Scaldati
  The baron   Pasquale Spadola
"Colloquio con la madre"
  Luigi Pirandello   Omero Antonutti
  Pirandello's mother   Regina Bianchi

Fellini's Casanova (1976)

The Carnival celebration in Venice provides the setting for the film's opening scene. A huge head of the goddess Miuna is dredged out of the Grand Canal, only to sink back down into the waters when the support cables break under its excessive weight. Casanova, masquerading as Pierrot, receives a message that he is to meet Maddalena, the mistress of the French ambassador De Bernis, for a tryst. There follows a love scene whose exuberant acrobatics are meant for the voyeuristic eye of the ambassador himself, who applauds the performance but remains deaf to Casanova's plea for patronage. Upon his return from the rendezvous, Casanova is arrested, tried, and convicted by the court of the Inquistion. Incarcerated in I Piombi (the Leads prison) adjoining the ducal palace, Casanova takes solace in the memory of seductions past, particularly in that of the anemic Annamaria whose malaise is cured by her lover's virile attentions. The film makes only perfunctory reference to Casanova's escape from prison—the best known and most frequently anthologized episode of the *Memoirs*—before shifting to the Parisian salon of the Marquise D'Urfé. There Casanova obliges this eccentric lady in her quest for immortality through a cult ritual that requires his regenerative sperm. He is assisted in this ceremony by Marcolina, the erstwhile mistress of his brother, who exposes her naked bottom and elevates Casanova to the task of inseminating the aged Marquise. In the next episode, Casanova returns to Italy, where he meets the woman destined to become his one true love. Henriette, dressed in military attire, mysteriously traveling with a Hungarian captain, soon becomes Casanova's mistress. At a dinner party in Parma, in the home of the hunchback Du Bois, Henriette reveals her talents as an accomplished cellist, and Casanova is ravished by her charm. The next morning, she disappears from his life, as mysteriously as she had entered it a short time before.

Many years later, in London, Casanova is excoriated by the Charpillon women, a mother and daughter, who accuse him of embezzlement and impotence. At this low point in his fortunes, Casanova considers suicide but is diverted by the appearance of a giantess who lures him from the waters of the Thames into a phantasmagoric amusement park. His quest for the giantess ends with the vision of her bathing in the company of two dwarfs. The film now shifts to Rome, to the household of the English ambassador Lord Talou. Here Casanova wins a coital contest against Righetto, the coachman of Prince Del Brando, in a competition speciously billed as one between brute force and intellectual prowess. In Switzerland, Casanova is bewitched by Isabella, the daughter of an entymologist, whose experiments with insects have a voodoo effect on her human admirer. Isabella agrees to a rendezvous in a hotel in Dresden, but when she fails to appear, Casanova takes solace in the sexual attentions of an entire theater troupe led by an old acquaintance of his, the actress Astrodi. An orgy of epic proportions take place, followed by the scene of the troupe's onstage performance of Norse epic in the theater of Dresden the next day. As the theater empties out, Casanova lingers, only to be recognized and reproached for filial neglect by his aged, arthritic mother. Unable to exit from her box alone, his mother is carried to her coach by Casanova, who responds to her reprimands with the usual reformatory promises.

The next episode finds Casanova in Würtemberg, seeking an audience with the feebleminded duke, who is more interested in listening to a sea shell than to Casanova's pleas for patronage. It is here that Casanova encounters the mechanical doll Rosalba and performs with her the most impassioned love scene in the film. Casanova ends his life's odyssey at Dux, in the castle of Waldenstein, where he is relegated to eating in the kitchen and becomes the brunt of universal ridicule, from verbal put-downs to latrine art. When he is finally called upon to exhibit his learning for the count, Casanova is met with snickering disrespect by the young courtiers. This humiliation leads him to his final revery, where he conjures up a youthful self on the frozen waters of the Grand Canal, beset with images of loves and favors lost.

DIRECTION	Federico Fellini
SUBJECT	Based on the *Memoirs* of Giacomo Casanova
SCREENPLAY	Federico Fellini, Bernardino Zapponi
PHOTOGRAPHY	Giuseppe Rotunno
SETS AND COSTUMES	Danilo Donati
MUSIC	Nino Rota
EDITING	Ruggero Mastroianni
PRODUCTION	Alberto Grimaldi for Universal-Fox-Gaumont-Titanus

CAST

Casanova	Donald Sutherland
Madame d'Urfé	Cecily Brown
Henriette	Tina Aumont
Maddalena	Margareth Clementi
Isabella	Olimpia Carlisi
Dubois	Daniel Emilfork
The giantess	Sandy Allen
Marcolina	Claretta Algrandi
Annamaria	Clarissa Roll
Astrodi	Marika Rivera
Casanova's mother	Marie Marquet
The Duke of Würtemberg	Dudley Sutton
Mechanical doll	Adele Angela Lojodice

La voce della luna (1989)

At the opening of *La voce della luna,* Ivo Salvini (played by the Tuscan comic Roberto Benigni) is listening to voices from a well when an uncouth group of country men overtakes him on their way to a striptease performed by the aunt of one of them. Ivo is forced to join their voyeuristic venture but is unable to pay his share. Only the arrival of the elderly Pigafetta, the undertaker, saves him from a beating; Pigafetta invites the young man to join him on his nightly rounds. At the cemetery, a journalist interviews a musician who has chosen to live in his mausoleum niche rather than be haunted by a melody whose chromatic intervals threatened to drive him insane. A storm breaks out and reminds Ivo of a childhood episode of rescue by his grandmother who called him "Pinocchino." The storm triggers another memory—this time, of a nocturnal attempt to break into the house of his beloved Aldina. Aided by his sweetheart's sister, Susy, Ivo gains entrance to the house and is able to gaze rapt at Aldina's sleeping face, which reminds him of the moon and inspires him to quote Leopardi. Aldina awakens in fright and throws a silver shoe at Ivo, who catches it and treasures it throughout the remainder of the film: Cinderella's glass slipper, as one of the town psychiatrists will later call it. Another nocturnal wanderer is Gonnella, a retired prefect (played by the celebrated film comic Paolo Villaggio), who returns home to his dreary rooming house to the feigned solicitude of his geriatric neighbors—projections of his own paranoid fear of aging and death.

Daylight brings us to a crowded and boisterous town square, crammed with hucksters selling women's clothes, Japanese tourists photographing everything in sight, and trucks filled with mass-produced Madonnas making a delivery at the local church. Here Ivo encounters the construction firm of the Micheluzzi brothers, Terzio, Vito, and Giuanin. Giuanin is at work on the city's sewer system, and he invites Ivo down to explore its depths—a descent that the managerial brother, Vito, vehemently forbids. It is here that the Nestore episode occurs, and it ends with the rescue of Ivo from the roof by the third Micheluzzi brother, Terzio. Restored to ground level, Ivo joins the town's evening promenade where he meets and befriends Gonnella, as preparations for the yearly *gnoccata*, or gnocchi festival, are under way. Climaxing the *gnoccata* is the crowning of Miss Farina 1989, a contest won by Aldina, who performs her victory dance with the elderly and lecherous Dr. Brambilla, leader of the town's mental health triumvirate. Aldina's obvious enjoyment of Brambilla's advances prompts Ivo to act. He orders a generous helping of gnocchi and empties it on Brambilla's head.

In the subsequent mayhem, Ivo and Gonnella escape to the countryside, and while the prefect boasts about his family tree, his companion disappears down a well. Terzio Micheluzzi comes to the rescue once more, and Ivo rejoins Gonnella to explore the confines of the latter's prefecture. The two men arrive outside a forbidding stone farm building, which they enter with trepidation to find that it houses an enormous discotheque. Ivo delights in the crowds of young women who eagerly try on his Cinderella slipper and promise to reveal to him the secret of their femininity. Gonnella, in contrast, wishes the disco music away and replaces it with an imagined performance of the Blue Danube waltz, which he dances with his sometimes companion the Duchess of Alba. As the festivities break up, Ivo is rescued by his sister Adele and is driven home to a family dinner and bed. But Nestore magically awaits him in the next room with the news that the moon has been captured and is being held prisoner nearby.

In town, a massive round-table conference has been convened, and images of the captured moon are projected on giant screens flanking the main square. When a member of the audience directs a series of existential questions to the assembled dignitaries and is met with official silence, or condescension, he goes berserk and literally shoots the television screens, causing everyone to flee in terror. In the emptied piazza, Ivo looks up at the sky to find the moon restored to its accustomed place. With Aldina's voice, the satellite speaks to Ivo of his privileged access to paranormal experience but interrupts herself to announce a commercial break. In the final scene of *La voce della luna*, Ivo is back in the countryside, next to the well of the opening sequence, straining to hear its voices.

DIRECTION	Federico Fellini
SUBJECT	Based on *Il poema dei lunatici* (1987) by Ermanno Cavazzoni
SCREENPLAY	Federico Fellini, Tullio Pinelli, Ermanno Cavazzoni
PHOTOGRAPHY	Tonino Delli Colli
SETS	Dante Ferretti
COSTUMES	Maurizio Millenotti
MUSIC	Nicola Piovani
EDITING	Nino Baragli
PRODUCTION	Mario and Vittorio Cecchi-Gori for Penta Film

CAST

Ivo Salvini	Roberto Benigni
Gonnella	Paolo Villaggio
Aldina	Nadia Ottaviani
Marisa	Marisa Tomasi
Nestore	Angelo Orlando
Oboist	Sim
Susy	Susy Blady
The Reporter	Dario Ghirardi
Terzio Micheluzzi	Dominique Chevalier
Giuanin	Nigel Harris
Vito Micheluzzi	Vito

■■■■■■■■■■■■■■■■■■■■■■■■■
Notes

Introduction: Literature and Film

1. Alberto Farassino, "Libri da Schermo," *La Repubblica,* July 29, 1989, p. 10. This and all subsequent translations, unless otherwise noted, are my own.
2. Ibid.
3. The story of film's impact on contemporary fiction has been the object of great critical interest. See, for example, Keith Cohen, *Film and Fiction: The Dynamics of Exchange* (New Haven, Conn.: Yale University Press, 1976), especially part 2, "Cinematic Form in the Novel"; Antonio Costa, "Palomar e l'effetto *rebound,*" *Annali d'Italianistica* 6 (1988), 252–60. On the film novel, see Gavriel Moses, "Film Theory as Literary Genre in Pirandello and the Film Novel," 38–68, and John Welle's introduction, pp. 9ff., both in the same volume of *Annali d'Italianistica;* Emilio Garroni, "Che cosa, a che cosa, e da che cosa," *Cinema nuovo,* August–October 1968; Alain Robbe-Grillet, "A Future for the Novel," in *For a New Novel,* trans. Richard Howard (Freeport, N.Y.: Books for Libraries, 1970), pp. 15–24; Alan Spiegel, *Fiction and the Camera Eye: Visual Consciousness in Film and in the Modern Novel* (Charlottesville: University Press of Virginia, 1976).
4. See Stefania Parigi, "Aggiornamento bibliografico," in *Annali d'Italianistica* 6 (1988), 262; Gian Piero Brunetta, "Letteratura e cinema: Da un rapporto di subalternità ad uno di prevalenza," in *Cinema e letteratura in Italia: Attualità di un dialogo* (Lugano: Cenobio, 1983), p. 28.
5. This last is Roman Jakobson's definition of *literariness*—language that calls attention to "the form of the utterance rather than to its referential capacity." See Robert Scholes, *Semiotics and Interpretation* (New Haven, Conn.: Yale University Press, 1982), p. 58.
6. Brunetta, "Letteratura e cinema," p. 28.
7. Lino Micciché, *La ragione e lo sguardo: Saggi e note sul cinema* (Cosenza: Lerici, 1979), p. 147.
8. See Alberto Asor Rosa, "Il neorealismo o il trionfo del narrativo," in

Cinema e letteratura del neorealismo, ed. Giorgio Tinazzi and Marina Zancan (Vicenza: Marsilio, 1983), p. 83.

9. Dudley Andrew, *Concepts in Film Theory* (New York: Oxford University Press, 1984), p. 104.

10. On film's civilizing mission, see Joy Gould Boyum, *Double Exposure: Fiction into Film* (New York: Universe Books, 1985), p. 4. On the cinema's origins in folk art, see Erwin Panofsky's classic essay, "Style and Medium in the Motion Pictures," in *Film: An Anthology,* ed. Daniel Talbot (Berkeley: University of California Press, 1972), pp. 15–32. See also Cohen, *Film and Fiction,* p. 45; and Jurij Lotman, *Semiotics of Cinema,* trans. Mark Suino (Ann Arbor: University of Michigan, Department of Slavic Languages and Literatures, 1976), p. 12.

11. Gian Piero Brunetta, "La migrazione dei generi dalla biblioteca alla filmoteca dell'italiano," *Italian Quarterly* 21 (Summer 1980), 83, 86.

12. Ibid., p. 88. For his influential formulation of the way in which social institutions become ideological conduits, see Louis Althusser, "Ideology and Ideological State Apparatuses," *Lenin and Philosophy and Other Essays,* trans. Ben Brewster (New York: Monthly Review, 1971), pp. 127–86.

13. The degree of D'Annunzio's participation in the making of *Cabiria* is controversial, and critics have come full circle on the question. Although earlier scholars had believed the publicity about D'Annunzio's authorship of the screenplay (cf. Vernon Jarratt, *The Italian Cinema* [New York: Macmillan, 1951], p. 17), it was later believed that he merely penned the intertitles. Recent scholarship, exemplified by Brunetta in "La conquista dell'impero dei sogni: D'Annunzio e Pirandello" (*Annali d'Italianistica* 6 [1988], 26), is returning to the original hypothesis of a fuller authorial intervention.

14. On the crisis of the novel, see the introduction to *Letteratura e cinema,* ed. Gian Piero Brunetta (Bologna: Zanichelli, 1976), p. 2. Christian Metz discusses the way in which film replaces the social functions of the nineteenth-century novel in "The Fiction Film and Its Spectator: A Metapsychological Study," trans. Alfred Guzzetti, in *The Imaginary Signifier: Psychoanalysis and the Cinema* (Bloomington: Indiana University Press, 1982), p. 110.

15. Brunetta, "Letteratura e cinema" in *Cinema e letteratura in Italia,* p. 31.

16. Ibid., p. 32.

17. Ibid., pp. 32–33.

18. Cesare Zavattini, "Alcune idee sul cinema," published as an introduction to the screenplay of *Umberto D* (Milan: Fratelli Bocca, 1954), p. 5. For an English translation of this important essay, see "Some Ideas on the Cinema," trans. Pier Luigi Lanza, in *Film: A Montage of Theories,* ed. Richard Dyer MacCann (New York: Dutton, 1966), pp. 216–28 (subsequent page references to the Italian version of this essay are included in the text).

19. The figure of the asymptote is applied suggestively by André Bazin in *What Is Cinema? 2,* trans. Hugh Gray (Berkeley: University of California Press, 1972), p. 82.

20. Carlo Lizzani, "Eravamo eclettici," in *Cinema e letteratura,* ed. Tinazzi and Zancan, p. 103.

21. Ibid.
22. Guiseppe De Santis and Mario Alicata, "Verità e poesia: Verga e il cinema italiano," *Cinema*, October 10, 1941, p. 217.
23. Fausto Montesanti, "Della ispirazione cinematografica," *Cinema*, November 10, 1941, p. 281.
24. Ibid.
25. Giuseppe De Santis and Mario Alicata, "Ancora di Verga e del cinema italiano," *Cinema*, November 25, 1941, pp. 314–15.
26. Asor Rosa, "Il neorealismo," p. 86.
27. Lizzani, "Eravamo eclettici," p. 104.
28. Visconti, "Tradizione e invenzione (1941)," in *Visconti: Il cinema*, ed. Adelio Ferrero (Modena: Comune di Modena, 1977), p. 30.
29. See Luigi Chiarini, "Tradisce il neorealismo," pp. 882–88, Cesare Zavattini, "Una grossa botta in testa al neorealismo," pp. 888–92, and Guido Aristarco, "Dal neorealismo al realismo," pp. 859–61, and "È realismo," pp. 892–99, all in *Antologia di 'Cinema nuovo' 1952–1958*, ed. Guido Aristarco (Florence: Guaraldi, 1975). For a fuller elaboration of Aristarco's important theoretical pronouncements, see "Esperienza culturale ed esperienza originale in Luchino Visconti," published as an introduction to the screenplay for *Rocco e i suoi fratelli*, ed. G. Aristarco and G. Carancini (Bologna: Cappelli, 1960), pp. 13–47.
30. For his notion of the "typical" see Georg Lukács, *Realism in Our Time: Literature and the Class Struggle*, trans. John Mander and Necke Mander (New York: Harper & Row, 1964), p. 122. For his concept of the "necessary anachronism" see Georg Lukács, *The Historical Novel*, trans. Hannah Mitchell and Stanley Mitchell (London: Merlin, 1962), p. 64.
31. See Brunetta, "Letteratura e cinema," in *Cinema e letteratura in Italia*, p. 35; Lizzani, "Eravamo eclettici," p. 108.
32. Brunetta, "Letteratura e cinema," in *Cinema e letteratura in Italia*, pp. 35–36.
33. On the simultaneity of cinematic and literary embodiments of the same idea, see Pasolini's remarks quoted in Pio Baldelli, *Film e opera letteraria* (Padua: Marsilio 1964), p. 346.
34. See Angelo Moscariello, *Cinema e/o letteratura* (Bologna: Pitagora, 1981), p. 98.
35. Ibid., pp. 98–99.
36. The "well-narrated" film is Farassino's phrase. See "Libri da schermo," p. 10.
37. Ibid. On the literature-film matchmaking agency, see Massimo Moscati, *Manuale di sceneggiatura* (Milan: Mondadori, 1989), p. 226.
38. The following observations on contemporary adaptive practices are based on Farassino, "Libri da schermo," p. 10.
39. See the introduction to *Modern European Filmmakers and the Art of Adaptation*, ed. Andrew Horton and Joan Magretta (New York: Ungar, 1981), p. 3.
40. Quoted in Griffith, Mrs. D. W. *When the Movies Were Young* (New York: Benjamin Blom, 1968), p. 66.
41. Jean Mitry, "Remarks on the Problem of Cinematic Adaptation," trans. Richard Dyer, *Bulletin of Midwest Modern Language Association* (1971), p. 1.

42. A. J. Greimas, quoted in Michel Mathieu-Colas, "Frontières de la narrato-logie," *Poétique* 65 (February 1986), 97.
43. *Resymbolization* is Boyum's term, *Double Exposure*, p. 50.
44. See V. I. Pudovkin, "The Plastic Material" in *Film: A Montage of Theories*, pp. 23–33.
45. For the Tavianis' remarks, see Jean Gili, *Le cinéma italien* (Paris: Union Générale d'Editions, 1978), p. 381. For Micciché's formulation, see his *Visconti e il neorealismo* (Venice: Marsilio, 1990), p. 153.
46. I am indebted to Dudley Andrew for this idea. Such a concept of cinematic writing allowed even a purist like Truffaut to countenance literary models for the cinema. See Andrew's "On Certain Tendencies of the French Cinema," in *A New History of French Literature*, ed. Denis Hollier (Cambridge, Mass.: Harvard University Press, 1989), pp. 994ff. For an extended meditation on cinema as writing in a poststructuralist sense, see chapter 3 of Peter Brunette and David Wills, *Screen/Play: Derrida and Film Theory* (Princeton, N.J.: Princeton University Press, 1989). Especially useful is the suggestion that cinema's relationship to "the real" is best described as *anagrammatic* rather than *analogic* (p. 88), since the latter term is associated with more traditional concepts of realism, whereas the former term helps us to locate cinema within the all-inclusive Derridean category of writing as a "structure of differential repetition" (p. 77).
47. On the challenge that literature poses to cinematic expressivity, see Charles Eidsvik, "Toward a 'Politique des Adaptations,' " in *Literature/Film Quarterly* 3 (Summer 1975), 260; Boyum, *Double Exposure*, p. 18; Alberto Abruzzese, "Scrittura, cinema, territorio," in *Cinema e letteratura*, ed. Tinazzi and Zancan, p. 128.
48. Moscariello, *Cinema e/o letteratura*, pp. 11, 6.
49. John Ellis, "The Literary Adaptation: An Introduction," *Screen* 23 (May/June 1982), 3–4.
50. Jean Mitry, *Esthétique et psychologie du cinéma*, II, (Paris: Éditions universitaires, 1965), p. 347.
51. Robert Richardson, *Literature and Film* (Bloomington: Indiana University Press, 1969), p. 68.
52. On the deferred and immediate syntheses of literature and film, see Jean Ricardou, *Problèmes du nouveau roman* (Paris: Éditions du seuil, 1967), pp. 70–72; Umberto Eco, *La struttura assente: Introduzione alla recerca semiologica* (Milan: Bompiani, 1986), pp. 158–59; and Seymour Chatman, *Story and Discourse: Narrative Structure in Fiction and Film* (Ithaca, N.Y.: Cornell University Press, 1983), p. 119.
53. Wolfgang Iser, *The Implied Reader: Patterns of Communication in Prose Fiction from Bunyan to Beckett* (Baltimore: Johns Hopkins University Press, 1974), p. 283.
54. Metz, "Fiction Film and Its Spectator," p. 104 (subsequent page references are included in the text).
55. Quoted in Ernesto Guidorizzi, *La narrativa italiana e il cinema* (Florence: San-

soni, 1973), p. 25; see also Edgar Morin, *Il cinema o dell'immaginario* (Milan: Silva, 1962), p. 137.

56. This is Galvano della Volpe's very useful term. See *Il verosimile filmico e altri saggi* (Roma: Samonà e Savelli, 1971), pp. 105–10.

57. See, for example, Joy Boyum, *Double Exposure*, pp. 24ff.; Dudley Andrew, "Metz and the Semiology of the Cinema," in *The Major Film Theories* (New York: Oxford University Press, 1976), pp. 212–41; Eco's chapter 4 in *La struttura assente*, pp. 149ff; Christian Metz, "Oltre l'analogia: l'immagine," in *Letteratura e cinema*, ed. Brunetta, pp. 143–49.

58. See Bazin, *What Is Cinema?* 1 and 2, trans. Hugh Gray (Berkeley: University of California Press, 1967–71); Siegfried Kracauer, *Theory of Film: The Redemption of Physical Reality* (New York: Oxford University Press, 1960); Zavattini, "Alcune idee sul cinema"; Pier Paolo Pasolini, "La lingua scritta della realtà," in *Empirismo eretico* (Milan: Garzanti, 1972), pp. 198–226. This theme runs throughout Pasolini's theoretical writings on film. For an English translation of the collection, see *Heretical Empiricism*, ed. Louise K. Barnett, trans. Ben Lawton and Louise K. Barnett (Bloomington: Indiana University Press, 1988).

59. See Giorgio Tinazzi, "Un rapporto complesso" in *Cinema e letteratura*, ed. Tinazzi and Zancan, p. 23.

60. *Cosmophany* is Metz's witty term, cited in Andrew, *Major Film Theories*, p. 224. On the intrusiveness of perceptual codes, see Teresa de Lauretis, *Alice Doesn't: Feminism, Semiotics, Cinema* (Bloomington: Indiana University Press, 1984), p. 46.

61. See Eco, *La struttura assente*, pp. 152, 154. On the way in which Metz's semiotics of the cinema opposes Bazin's cinematic ontology, see the chapter on "The Semiology of the Cinema" in Peter Wollen's *Signs and Meaning in the Cinema* (London: Indiana University Press, 1972), pp. 116ff.

62. Panofsky, "Style and Medium," p. 32.

63. On the articulations of film language, see Gerald Mast, "Literature and Film," in *Interrelations of Literature*, ed. Jean-Pierre Barricelli and Joseph Gibaldi (New York: MLA, 1982), p. 298; Cohen, *Film and Fiction*, p. 89; and Lotman, *Semiotics of Cinema*, p. 35.

64. Mast, "Literature and Film," pp. 300–301.

65. See Eco, *La struttura assente*, p. 152.

66. See Chatman, *Story and Discourse*, p. 72.

67. Mast, "Literature and Film," p. 300.

68. Andrew, "Metz and the Semiology," pp. 225–26.

69. Cohen, *Film and Fiction*, p. 3.

70. Mathieu-Colas, "Frontières de la narratologie," pp. 103–4.

71. Christopher Orr, "The Discourse on Adaptation," *Wide Angle* 2 (1984), 72.

72. André Lefevre, "Literary Theory and Translated Literature," *Dispositio* 7, nos. 19–21 (1982), 17. For a similar notion, see Gianfranco Bettetini's idea of "retestualizzazione" in *La conversazione audiovisiva* (Milan: Bompiani, 1984), p. 35.

73. See, for example, Cohen, *Film and Fiction*, p. 1; Susan Sontag, "A Note on

Novels and Films," in *Against Interpretation* (New York: Farrar, Straus & Giroux, 1966), p. 245; Boyum, *Double Exposure*, p. 16; Franco Ferrarotti, "Riflessioni preliminari su 'Cinema, letteratura e contesto sociale' " in *Cinema e letteratura in Italia*, ed. Brunetta, p. 18.

74. Mario Verdone, "Futurismo: Film e letteratura," *Annali d'Italianistica* (1988), p. 73.

75. Concerning the popular origins of the novel, see Claude-Edmonde Magny, *The Age of the American Novel*, trans. Eleanor Hochman (New York: Ungar, 1972), p. 4.

76. On the novel's aspirations to complete visualization, see Alberto Abruzzese, "Scrittura, cinema, territorio" in *Cinema e letteratura del neorealismo*, eds. Giorgio Tinazzi and Marina Zancan (Venice: Marsilio, 1983), p. 124. In more grandiose fashion, Garroni argues that film fulfills an impulse existing not only in literature and theater but "nel nostro modo di avere esperienze, nel mondo di senso in-cui-siamo-sempre essenzialmente" ("in our way of experiencing, in a world of sense in-which-we-are-always, essentially"). See "Che cosa," p. 10. Vasco Pratolini is equally grandiose in his effusions about film as the culmination of humankind's legendary and epic strivings for self-mirroring in art. See Marina Zancan, "Tra vero e bello, documento e arte," in *Cinema letteratura del neorealismo*, p. 70. Sergei Eisenstein celebrates the continuity of literary and cinematic creation by claiming as film's precursors the Greeks, Shakespeare, and of course, Dickens. See "Dickens, Griffith and the Film Today" in *Film Form: Essays in Film Theory*, trans. Jay Leyda (New York: Harcourt Brace & World, 1949), pp. 232–33.

77. Pasolini, "La sceneggiatura come 'struttura' che vuol essere altra struttura," in *Empirismo eretico*, p. 188. For the English translation, see *Heretical Empiricism*, p. 187.

78. Luigi Chiarini, *Il film nella battaglia delle idee* (Milan: Fratelli Bocca, 1954), pp. 54–55, 57.

79. Moscati, *Manuale di sceneggiatura*, pp. 38, 39.

80. See Micciché, *La ragione e lo sguardo*, p. 174; Pasolini, "La sceneggiatura," pp. 188ff.

81. See, for example, Rebecca West, "Tonino Guerra and the Space of the Screenwriter," *Annali d'Italianistica* 6 (1988), 162–78. This was also one of the leitmotifs of the University of Texas symposium "Word, Script, Image: The Art of Screenwriting," Austin, Texas, October 23, 1989. See also Budd Schulberg, "The Auteur Syndrome," *New York Times*, December 4, 1989, 27.

82. Pasolini, "La sceneggiatura," p. 190.

83. Ibid., p. 195.

84. Abruzzese, "Scrittura, cinema, territorio," p. 122.

85. Giuliana Muscio, quoted in Moscati, *Manuale di sceneggiatura*, p. 41.

86. Micciché sees in the movement from treatment to script a form of adaptation. See *La ragione e lo sguardo*, p. 175.

87. Abruzzese, "Scrittura, cinema, territorio," p. 123.

88. Andrew, *Concepts in Film Theory*, p. 106.

1 • Visconti's *La terra trema*

1. For a synopsis of the film and for its credits, see the Appendix.
2. On Verga's appropriation by the Left, see Adelio Ferrero, "La parabola di Visconti," in *Visconti: Il cinema*, ed. Ferrero (Modena: Comune di Modena, 1977), p. 21, and Vitilio Masiello, *Verga tra ideologia e realtà* (Bari: De Donato, 1970), p. 13ff.
3. Giuseppe De Santis and Mario Alicata, "Verità e poesia: Verga e il cinema italiano," *Cinema*, October 10, 1941, p. 217.
4. Visconti, "Tradizione e invenzione (1941)," in Ferrero, *Visconti: Il cinema*, p. 38 (Further page references are included in the text).
5. Quoted in Micciché, *Visconti e il neorealismo*, (Venice: Marsilio, 1990), p. 78.
6. Giuseppe Ferrara, *Luchino Visconti* (Paris: Seghers, 1963), pp. 99–100. In fact, *La terra trema* has been hailed as the masterpiece of neorealism by such critics as Pierre Leprohon, *The Italian Cinema* (New York: Praeger, 1972), p. 112, and Luigi Chiarini, *Film nella battaglia delle idee* (Milan: Fratelli Bocca, 1954), p. 130. Ferrara argues that with *La terra trema* neorealism reached self-consciousness. (see p. 30).
7. Giovanni Verga, *Tutte le novelle I* (Verona: Mondadori, 1967), p. 168 (Page references are included in the text).
8. For a moving example of this improvisational technique, see Roy Armes, *Patterns of Realism* (London: Tantivy, 1971), p. 124.
9. For an analysis of how antirealist this voice-over narration is, see Geoffrey Nowell-Smith, *Luchino Visconti* (New York: Viking, 1973), pp. 50–51. Lino Micciché, however, provides a powerful defense of the voice-over technique, arguing that it represents Visconti's "auto-exegesis" (*Visconti e il neorealismo*, p. 169), that it supports the film's realism by overtly formulating its ideological *presa di posizione* (p. 175), and that it reveals the unbridgeable glass gap between the world of the Sicilian fisherfolk and its bourgeois audience, as well as its auteur (p. 179ff.).
10. For the text of Visconti's treatment, see "*La terra trema*—Appunti per un film documentario sulla Sicilia (1948)," in Ferrero, *Visconti: Il cinema*, pp. 35–42.
11. Ibid., pp. 35–36.
12. See Pio Baldelli, *Luchino Visconti* (Milan: Gabriele Mazzotta, 1982), p. 92.
13. The transformation of Verga's unfocused 'Ntoni into Visconti's politically enlightened protagonist has received considerable critical notice. See, for example, Fernaldo Di Giammatteo, "Il primo Visconti—La storia e gli 'eroi del male,'" in *Bianco e nero 37* (*La controversia Visconti*) (September–December 1976), 21; Luciano De Giusti, *I film di Luchino Visconti* (Rome: Gremese, 1985), p. 48. On 'Ntoni Valastro's "senso storico della ribellione," see Giuseppe Ferrara, "*La terra trema*: il centro del neorealismo," included in Ernesto Guidorizzi, *La narrativa italiana e il cinema* (Florence: Sansoni, 1973), pp. 102–3.
14. The influence of Resistance ideals in the shaping of Visconti's conception of *La terra trema* is a critical commonplace. See Baldelli, *Visconti*, p. 61; and

Di Giammatteo, "Il primo Visconti," p. 26. On the specifically Marxist content of 'Ntoni's elevated political consciousness, see De Giusti, *I film di Luchino Visconti*, p. 48.

15. That *La terra trema* updates and completes *I Malavoglia* without negating or artificially adding to it, see De Giusti, *I film di Luchino Visconti*, p. 48; and Vito Attolini, *Dal romanzo al set: Cinema italiano dalle origini ad oggi* (Bari: Dedalo, 1988), p. 112.

16. Masiello, *Verga tra ideolgia e realtà*, pp. 21–22 (subsequent page references are included in the text).

17. On the alternative literary expressions of European unease, see ibid., p. 23. Luigi Russo alludes to the Vichian ideal in *Giovanni Verga* (Bari: Laterza, 1959), p. 140, and Pio Baldelli to "noble savages" in *Film e opera letteraria* (Padua: Marsilio, 1964), p. 144.

18. Di Giammatteo, "Il primo Visconti," p. 18, also sees Verga as a satirist.

19. Giovanni Verga, *I Malavoglia* (Verona: Mondadori, 1968), p. 61. Subsequent allusions to the novel are to this edition, and page references are included in the text.

20. As Lino Micciché puts it, Padron 'Ntoni's initiative constitutes a "negative infraction" in the novel, while 'Ntoni's is a "positive infraction" in the film. See *Visconti e il neorealismo*, pp. 164, 166.

21. All quotes from the voice-over narration come from my translated transcriptions of the Italian-language version. The English-subtitled version lacks the voice-overs, so they are not included in the screenplay published in *Visconti: Two Screenplays*, trans. Judith Green (New York: Orion, 1970). All my references to the dialogue are to this edition, and page numbers are included in the text.

22. Louis Althusser, "Ideology and Ideological State Apparatuses," in *Lenin and Philosophy and Other Essays*, trans. Ben Brewster (New York: Monthly Review, 1971), p. 162.

23. It is a critical commonplace that Visconti's aestheticism works against his socially progressive themes. See, for example, Luigi Chiarini, *Il Film nella battaglia delle idee* (Milan: Fratelli Bocca, 1954), p. 131; Baldelli, *Visconti*, p. 72; André Bazin, *What Is Cinema? 2*, trans. Hugh Gray (Berkeley: University of California Press, 1972), p. 45; and Glauco Viazzi, cited in De Giusti, *I film di Luchino Visconti*, p. 49. For a summation of such criticism, see Ferrara, *Luchino Visconti*, pp. 32–33.

24. For an example of such criticism, see Baldelli, *Visconti*, p. 79. For a defense of the *sciara* scene, see Ferrara, "*La terra trema*," pp. 103–4.

25. Similarly, Lino Micciché, in his attentive reading of this scene, sees in it "a transfiguration of the real toward a tragic absoluteness, a sort of ancestral suspension of time that fixes and dilates that human suffering according to archetypal dimensions." See *Visconti e il neorealismo*, p. 114; also see p. 145.

26. Passage cited earlier from Visconti, "Tradizione e invenzione (1941)," p. 31.

27. By alluding to Bellini's *Sonnambola*, Visconti is paying homage to Catania's

celebrated opera composer and to his own passion for melodrama. Geoffrey Nowell-Smith argues that opera informs the entire mode of *La terra trema*. See his *Visconti*, pp. 51ff.

28. For criticism of Visconti's use of dialect, see Baldelli, *Visconti*, p. 91. For a defense of dialect in the film, see Ferrara, "*La terra trema*," p. 101.

29. Flaherty's influence on Visconti has received much critical notice. See, for example, Ferrara, *Luchino Visconti*, p. 33; and Nowell-Smith, *Luchino Visconti*, p. 41.

30. On Eisenstein's influence, see Nowell-Smith, *Luchino Visconti*, p. 41.

31. According to De Giusti, the three scenes include those of the wharfside revolt, the salting of the anchovies, and the wait of the women (discussed earlier). See *I film di Luchino Visconti*, p. 45.

32. On Visconti's preference for mise-en-scène over constructive montage, and his systematic use of deep-focus photography, see Bazin, *What Is Cinema?* 2, pp. 42–43.

33. Gianfranco Contini discusses Verga's multilayered technique in his introduction to the Mondadori edition of *I Malavoglia*, pp. 15–16.

2 · Visconti's *Leopard*

1. For a synopsis of the film and for its credits, see the Appendix.

2. Quoted in Roy Armes, *Patterns of Realism*, (London: Tantivy, 1971) p. 120.

3. Mentioned in the Introduction. For the term, see Galvano della Volpe, *Il verosimile e altri saggi* (Rome: Samonà e Savelli, 1971), pp. 107–8.

4. Quoted in Vito Attolini, *Dal romanzo al set: Cinema italiano dalle origini ad oggi*, (Bari: Dedalo, 1988), p. 183.

5. So violent were the polemics that they polarized critics into two camps, "gattopardisti" and "antigattopardisti." See Giancarlo Buzzi, *Invito alla lettura di Giuseppe Tomasi di Lampedusa* (Milan: Mursia, 1972), p. 146.

6. James Hay, in "Visconti's *Leopard:* Remaking a National Popular History," *Forum Italicum* 21 (Spring 1987), 36–48, adds another factor to our consideration of the adaptive process. The film also participates in "the general production of . . a popular memory" (36) and, as such, is a response to an entire cinematic tradition of historical films in prewar and postwar Italy.

7. On this tension between aesthetics and ideology in Visconti, and how he sees his own contradiction reflected in Lampedusa, see Luciano De Giusti, *I Film di Luchino Visconti* (Rome: Gremese, 1985), p. 91; Giuseppe Ferrara, *Luchino Visconti*, (Paris: Seghers, 1963), p. 73, and Lino Micciché, *Cinema italiano degli anni '60*, (Padua: Marsilio, 1975), p. 223.

8. Quoted in Gaia Servadio, *Luchino Visconti, A Biography* (New York: Franklin Watts, 1983), p. 177.

9. Geoffrey Nowell-Smith, in *Luchino Visconti*, (New York: Viking, 1973), pp. 116–17, sees this as Fabrizio's final act of detachment from the historical compromise of his class.

10. On their disparate reactions to Pallavicino, and its implications for their own relationship, see De Giusti, *I Film di Luchino Visconti*, p. 98.
11. Quoted in ibid.
12. For the shooting script, see Luchino Visconti, *Il film "Il Gattopardo,"* ed. Suso Cecchi d'Amico (Bologna: Capelli, 1963). In quoting from the film's dialogue, however, I have preferred to use my own transcriptions of the film's soundtrack, as there are major discrepancies between it and the published screenplay.
13. Quoted in Servadio, *Luchino Visconti*, p. 179. On the overall politicizing and historicizing dimension of Visconti's adaptive strategy, see Attolini, *Dal romanzo al set*, p. 184.
14. On the postwar recurrence of *trasformismo* appropos *Senso*, see Nowell-Smith, *Visconti*, p. 90.
15. Buzzi, *Invito alla lettura*, p. 154.
16. Ibid., p. 160.
17. On Aristarco's objections, see De Giusti, *I Film di Luchino Visconti*, p. 100. Other critics have seen this as proof of the pessimistic distance separating *Senso* from *The Leopard*. See, for example, Ferrara, *Luchino Visconti*, p. 74; Pio Baldelli, *Luchino Visconti* (Milan: Gabriele Mazzotta, 1982), pp. 242–43. Attolini, in *Dal romanzo al set*, p. 184, and Miccichè in *Cinema italiano degli anni '60*, p. 222, reverse the direction of such criticism by seeing in Fabrizio an awareness superior to that of the decadent, aristocratic, and nihilistic protagonist of *Senso*, Franz Mahler. For discussions of the continuities in Visconti's Risorgimento critique as expressed in the two films, see Peter Bondanella, *Italian Cinema from Neorealism to the Present* (New York: Continuum, 1991), p. 200; Carlo Lizzani, *Il Cinema italiano, 1895–1979*, 2 vols. (Rome: Editori Riuniti, 1979), p. 280, and Nowell-Smith, *Visconti*, pp. 106, 112–16. For Visconti's own comments on such continuities, see Servadio, *Luchino Visconti*, p. 177. For a Gramscian reading of *Senso*, see my *Italian Film in the Light of Neorealism* (Princeton, N.J.: Princeton University Press, 1986), pp. 166ff.
18. Antonio Gramsci, *Il Risorgimento*, ed. Maria Corti (Turin: Einaudi, 1952), p. xiii.
19. Giuseppe Tomasi di Lampedusa, *The Leopard*, trans. Archibald Colquhoun (New York: Pantheon, 1960), p. 40. Unless otherwise noted, all quotes from the novel will be to this translation, and page references are included in the text.
20. For these insights on the circularity of the historical process and its astral exemplars, I am indebted to the guest lectures given by Gian-Paolo Biasin at the University of Texas at Austin, 1975.
21. Gramsci, *Il Risorgimento*, p. 44.
22. In fact, the narrator maintains a critical distance from his protagonist, despite his immersion in Fabrizio's consciousness—and this distance widens as the novel progresses. See Gregory Lucente, *Beautiful Fables: Self-consciousness in Italian Narrative from Manzoni to Calvino* (Baltimore: Johns Hopkins University Press, 1986), p. 204. Olga Ragusa discusses the French

critic Louis Aragon's insight into the distinction between authorial intent and the protagonist's overt judgments in "Stendhal, Tomasi di Lampedusa, and the Novel," *Comparative Literature Studies* 10 (1973), 196.

23. Gramsci, *Il Risorgimento*, p. 63. On the contemporary applications of Visconti's Risorgimento critique, see Baldelli, *Visconti*, pp. 227–28.
24. See, for example, Alicata's comments in Buzzi, *Invito alla lettura*, p. 155.
25. Georg Lukács, *The Historical Novel*, trans. Hannah and Stanley Mitchell (London: Merlin, 1962), p. 42.
26. Ibid., p. 63.
27. The novel's much-criticized nostalgia is justified by its historicizing consciousness, according to Alessandro Bencivenni, *Luchino Visconti* (Florence: La Nuova Italia, 1983), p. 53.
28. The narrator's own propensity for flashforwards that comment ironically or pathetically on the narrative action only accentuates Fabrizio's prospective nostalgia. See Carl Rubino's analysis of these temporal leaps in "A Bomb Manufactured in Pittsburgh, Pa.: Past, Present, and Future in *The Leopard*," *Forum Italicum* 21 (Spring 1987), 16–25.
29. According to Lucente, the novel also has such a political double focus. See *Beautiful Fables*, pp. 220–21.
30. Lukács, *Historical Novel*, p. 76.
31. On the "class and sexual bases" of Tancredi's desire for Angelica, see Nowell-Smith, *Visconti*, pp. 107–8.
32. See Vitilio Masiello, *Verga tra ideologia e realtà* (Bari: De Donato, 1970), p. 72.
33. On "world-historical" and "maintaining" characters, see Lukács, *Historical Novel*, p. 43. For the concept of the "typical," see Lukács, *Realism in Our Time: Literature and the Class Struggle*, trans. John Mander and Necke Mander (New York: Harper & Row, 1964), p. 122.
34. Nowell-Smith, *Visconti*, p. 108. Critics who marvel at such physicality include David Ehrenstein, "Leopard Redux," *Film Comment* 19 (September/October 1983), 17, and Pauline Kael in her review of the film in the *New Yorker*, September 19, 1983, p. 126.
35. Fox offered Visconti the options of Spencer Tracy, Anthony Quinn, or Lancaster for the role. It is hard to know whether applause or a sigh of relief should be the appropriate response to Visconti's decision.
36. Miccichè, *Cinema italiano degli anni '60*, p. 223.
37. Hay, "Visconti's *Leopard*," p. 46.
38. Fox released *The Leopard* in a mutilated version in the United States and Britain, cutting its original 185 minutes to 161, dubbing the voices with considerable ineptitude, and altering the film's original color technology in unfortunate ways.
39. See the interview in Alain Sanzio and Paul-Louis Thirard, *Luchino Visconti, cinéaste* (Paris: Persona, 1984), p. 95.
40. Ibid., p. 96.
41. For a list of American epigones, see Ehrenstein, "Leopard Redux," p. 18.
42. As my students Michael Schreyach and Kimmy Barrio astutely pointed out, the painting that Visconti included in the film is not "Death of the Just

Man" (as specified in the novel) but "Return of the Prodigal Son" (sometimes referred to as "The Son Punished"). This painting does indeed represent a dying patriarch surrounded by grieving family members.

43. Bondanella points out the mortuary implications of the Salinas' portrayal in this scene in *Italian Cinema*, pp. 200–201, as does Baldelli, *Visconti*, p. 240.

44. On the consonance between Visconti's style and the immobility of his subject matter, see De Giusti, *I Film di Luchino Visconti*, p. 93, and Genêt, "Letter from Paris," *New Yorker* 39 (July 13, 1963), 72. On the static, tableau quality of the film, see Jonathan Miller's review in the *New Yorker* 39 (August 17, 1963), 56.

3 • De Sica's *Two Women*

1. For a synopsis of the film and for its credits, see the Appendix.

2. *Two Women* was made in 1960, after five years of directorial inactivity by De Sica, and it was hailed as a spectacular comeback, constituting one of the top four box-office successes of the year. See Brunetta, *Storia del cinema italiano dal 1945 agli anni ottanta* (Rome: Editori Riuniti 1982), pp. 525, 750. According to Brunetta, Loren was the only Italian diva able to compete with her Hollywood counterparts. See ibid, p. 751. Her performance earned her the Oscar, the Nastro d'argento, and the Cannes awards for best actress of the year. On the film's softening of the novel's ideological sting, see Micciché, *Cinema italiano degli anni '60* (Padua: Marsilio, 1975), p. 36.

3. On Moravia's depredation by filmmakers, see Ernesto Guidorizzi, *La narrativa italiana e il cinema* (Florence: Sansoni, 1973), p. 67. For Attolini's discussion, see *Dal romanzo al set: Cinema italiano dalle origini ad oggi* (Bari: Dedalo, 1988), p. 213. For Moravia's own account of why his novels are so conducive to adaptation, see his interview in Angelo Moscariello, *Cinema e/o letteratura*, (Bologna: Pitagora, 1981), p. 158.

4. Alberto Moravia, "Il romanzo-saggio: perchè la prima persona," in *Il punto su: Moravia*, ed. Cristina Benussi (Bari: Laterza, 1987), 106.

5. Alberto Moravia, "L'intreccio ideologico," in ibid., p. 102.

6. Alberto Moravia, *Two Women*, trans. Angus Davidson (New York: Farrar, Straus & Cudahy, 1958), p. 136. All quotations will be from this edition, and page references are included in the text.

7. Cesira's straightforward style accords with Moravia's overall aspiration to a "popular" narrative technique that refuses to divide the public into a specialized elite of "readers" vs. "mass consumers" but seeks to address a general constituency. See Mario Ricciardi, "Lo stile di Moravia" in *Alberto Moravia: il narratore e i suoi testi* (Rome: La Nuova Italia Scientifica, 1987), pp. 37ff.

8. The novel has an autobiographical basis in Moravia's own exile from Rome during the Nazi occupation. Between September 1943 and June 1944 he and Elsa Morante hid in the home of the lawyer Mosillo in the Ciociaria

town of Fondi. See Giancarlo Pandini, *Invito alla lettura di Alberto Moravia* (Milan: Mursia, 1973), p. 87.

9. Michele speaks for Moravia's communist intellectualism, which reached its fullest realization and its termination in *La ciociara*. See Moravia's remarks in ibid., p. 86. See also Carlo Salinari, "La normalità nella storia: *La ciociara*," in Benussi, *Il punto su*, pp. 144–45.

10. On the narrative's "diachronic and limited omniscient perspective," see Gian-Paolo Biasin, "Lucia secondo Moravia," *Verri*, 5th ser., no. 1 (1975), 58.

11. See Jan Kozma-Southall, "Omen and Image: Presage and Sacrifice in Moravia's *La ciociara*," *Italica* 61 (Fall 1984), 207–19. I am indebted to this article for much of my discussion of animal imagery.

12. See ibid., pp. 209ff., and Biasin, "Lucia secondo Moravia," p. 60.

13. The association of Rosetta's violation with Italy's violation by war is made explicit in Kozma-Southall, "Omen and Image," p. 209, and Pandini, *Invito alla lettura*, p. 87.

14. For a more elaborate political reading of the bordello in *Love and Anarchy*, see my *Italian Film in the Light of Neorealism*, (Princeton, N.J.: Princeton University Press, 1986), chap. 14.

15. For the connection between a ravished body and a text, see Stephanie H. Jed, *Chaste Thinking: The Rape of Lucretia and the Birth of Humanism*, (Bloomington: Indiana University Press, 1989), pp. 44–45.

16. Arguing in favor of Nietzschean "genealogy" as demystified historical writing vs. conventional history as an idealized, transcendent process, Foucault figures the body as a text, as an "inscribed surface of events . . . totally imprinted by history." See "Nietzsche, Genealogy, History," in *The Foucault Reader*, ed. Paul Rabinow (New York: Pantheon, 1984), p. 83. Also see Jed, *Chaste Thinking*, p. 68.

17. Laura Mulvey, "Visual Pleasure and Narrative Cinema," *Screen* 16 (1975), 6–18. On the tendency in Western visual arts to fetishize the image of the female body and present these bodies for the consumption of the male spectator, see John Berger's classic study, *Ways of Seeing* (New York: Viking, 1977), especially chap. 3. On voyeurism and fetishism as two modes of pleasure in looking and on their function in mainstream cinema, see Janet Bergstrom, "Sexuality at a Loss: The Films of F. W. Murnau," in *The Female Body in Western Culture*, ed. Susan Suleiman (Cambridge, Mass.: Harvard University Press, 1986), p. 257; and Mary Ann Doane, "Film and the Masquerade: Theorizing the Female Spectator," *Screen* 23 (September/October, 1982), 76. As is the case with all provocative, ground-breaking work, Mulvey's essay has been controversial. Her "writing out" of the female spectator has been addressed and opposed by such scholars as Doane, in the above article, and Tania Modleski in *Women Who Knew Too Much* (New York: Methuen, 1988).

18. For a fuller treatment of the optical alignments in *Bicycle Thief*, see my *Italian Film*, chap. 2.

19. For a vivid and amusing account of his battles to contain Loren's *divismo*,

see De Sica's *Lettere dal set*, ed. Emi De Sica and Giancarlo Governi (Milan: Sugar Edizioni, 1987), pp. 56ff.

20. Brunetta notes that De Sica loses the "mobility of his gaze and capacity to penetrate deeply . . . as if his gaze were hypnotized by the power of his actress." See *Storia del cinema italiano*, p. 751.

21. For a provocative, feminist reading of Mariology as the idealization not of the mother, but of the "relationship between her and us"—a relationship that bears a plurality of often surprising meanings, see Julia Kristeva, "Stabat Mater," in Suleiman, *Female Body in Western Culture*, pp. 99–118.

22. On the predominance of this image, see Ruth Prigozy, "A Modern *Pietà*: De Sica's *Two Women*," in *Modern European Filmmakers and the Art of Adaptation* ed. Andrew Horton and Joan Magretta (New York: Ungar, 1981), p. 84.

23. Franco Pecori sees this as a particularly important moment in the establishment of Loren's "divistic" function in the film. See *Vittorio De Sica* (Florence: La Nuova Italia, 1980), p. 79.

24. In the absence of a published screenplay, I have transcribed and translated the film's dialogue here and will do so throughout this chapter.

25. Mary Ann Doane gives a feminist reading of this cliché with respect to Bette Davis's role in *Now Voyager*. See "Film and the Masquerade," pp. 82–84.

26. On Michele's ideology, see Bruna Baldini Mezzalana, *Alberto Moravia e l'alienazione* (Milan: Ceschina, 1971), pp. 142ff.

27. Prigozy regrets the film's edulcoration of Michele's ideology in "A Modern *Pietà*," p. 86.

28. On the use of deep focus in the mountain scenes, see ibid., p. 85.

29. For a vivid and instructive account of his shooting strategy in this scene, see De Sica's *Lettere dal set*, pp. 70–72. Prigozy analyzes the technique in "A Modern *Pietà*," p. 87.

30. The identity of the rapists as Moroccans is deeply problematic for the contemporary reader and film viewer. Whether Moravia's choice (and De Sica's faithfulness to it) is dictated by unconscious racism is impossible to determine, but the Moroccan attribution did provide an easy out for novelist and filmmaker. To make the rapists German would be to upset the ideological balance of the story and its irony. If the story's argument is antiwar in general, then there can be no absolute good guys and bad guys—the Germans had already done their dirty work in murdering Michele, so to balance the scales, and to create the irony that the liberation does not usher in the kingdom of God on earth, the rape had to be done by the Allies. But European or American rapists are much too commercially unpalatable. If the rapists had to be Allies, at least make them exotic and "other," nonwhite and therefore capable of committing any bestiality that the racist mind thinks them capable of. Whatever Moravia's and De Sica's inner motivations, the historical record and popular stereotyping does provide ample testimony to pillaging and rape by the Moroccan

troops. See Susan Brownmiller, *Against Our Will: Men, Women, and Rape* (New York: Simon & Schuster, 1975), p. 75.

4 • De Sica's *Garden of the Finzi-Continis*

1. For a synopsis of the film and for its credits, see the Appendix.
2. Giorgio Bassani, *The Garden of the Finzi-Continis*, trans. William Weaver (New York: Harcourt, Brace, Jovanovich, 1977), p. 11. All quotes will be from this edition and page numbers will be included in the text.
3. On the garden's impenetrability, see Guisi Oddo De Stefanis, *Bassani entro il cerchio delle sue mura* (Ravenna: Longo, 1981), p. 131.
4. For Micòl's status as "knower," see Marilyn Schneider, *Vengeance of the Victim: History and Symbol in Giorgio Bassani's Fiction* (Minneapolis: University of Minnesota Press, 1986), p. 123; and Adriano Bon, *Come leggere "Il Giardino dei Finzi-Contini"* (Milan: Mursia, 1979), p. 37.
5. Sue Walrond-Skinner, *A Dictionary of Psychotherapy* (New York: Routledge & Kegan Paul, 1986), p. 92.
6. Ibid., p. 324.
7. In the absence of a published screenplay, I have transcribed and translated the film's sound track here and throughout this chapter.
8. On the novel's dual perspective, see Anna Dolfi, *Le forme del sentimento* (Padua: Liviana, 1981), p. 44.
9. See Bon, *Come leggere*, p. 58.
10. De Stefanis sees the novel as a "foscoliano sepolcro." See *Bassani entro il cerchio*, p. 95. Schneider argues for the "urgency of funerary ritual" where "death—or better, the burial of the dead—preserves the memory of life" throughout Bassani's fiction. See *Vengeance of the Victim*, p. 3. On the temporal distance, see De Stefanis, *Bassani entro il cerchio*, p. 95.
11. On the politicized critical reception of Bassani, see Schneider, *Vengeance of the Victim*, p. 7, and Bon's helpful anthology in *Come leggere*, pp. 85ff.
12. Schneider, in *Vengeance of the Victim*, pp. 125ff., argues that Micòl's distance is a precondition to the novel's writing. On her function as muse, as Stilnovistic Beatrice or Montalian Dora Markus, see De Stefanis, *Bassani entro il cerchio*, p. 98.
13. Gian Carlo Ferretti sees in Bassani the coming together of two contradictory tendencies—that of "prosa d'arte" and that of anti-Fascist, politically committed writing: "Bassani lives lucidly the conflict to the breaking-point, becoming in this sense the most emblematic writer of his generation." Quoted in Bon, *Come leggere*, p. 94.
14. For the ground-breaking study of Edenic prototypes to these Renaissance literary gardens, see A. Bartlett Giamatti, *The Earthly Paradise and the Renaissance Epic* (Princeton, N.J.: Princeton University Press, 1966), especially his chapters on Tasso and Ariosto.
15. Stanley Kauffmann, for example, complains that the plot is divorced from

its political theme. See his review in the *New Republic* 166 (January 19, 1972), 33. Colin Westerbeck, Jr., on the other hand, cites the parallel between Jewish political disappointments and Giorgio's romantic ones. See "Deportation from Paradise," *Commonweal* 95 (March 3, 1972), 525.

16. Garbo's precedent is invoked by Arthur Cooper in "Viva De Sica," *Newsweek* 79 (January 10, 1972), 58; and Pauline Kael in "The Fall and Rise of Vittorio De Sica," *Deeper into Movies* (New York: Bantam, 1974), p. 459.

17. Douglas Radcliff-Umstead notes the importance of this return gaze in *The Exile into Eternity: A Study of the Narrative Writings of Giorgio Bassani* (Cranbury, N.J.: Associated University Presses, 1987), p. 164, n. 17.

18. See Laura Mulvey, "Visual Pleasure and Narrative Cinema," *Screen* 16 (1975), 6–18.

19. Mary Ann Doane, "Film and the Masquerade: Theorizing the Female Spectator," *Screen* 23 (September/October, 1982), 83, 84.

20. Indeed, Manuel De Sica's music sets the tone for the nostalgia that suffuses the garden scenes, as proved by the fact that the director would listen to his son's score to prime himself for the filming. See Franco Pecori, *Vittorio De Sica*, (Florence: La Nuova Italia, 1980), p. 102.

21. On the temptation to make a film that indulges exclusively in such pathos, see Vito Attolini, *Dal romanzo al set: Cinema italiano dalle origini ad oggi* (Bari: Dedalo, 1988), p. 225.

22. I argue this extensively in the introduction to *Italian Film in the Light of Neorealism* (Princeton, N.J.: Princeton University Press, 1986).

23. Charles Thomas Samuels, *Encountering Directors* (New York: Putnam, 1972), p. 159. De Sica's own satisfaction was generally shared by the critical world, which accorded the film the Golden Bear prize at the festival of Berlin in 1971 and the Oscar for the best foreign film in 1972.

24. Bassani's famous refutation of the film, revealingly entitled "Il giardino tradito," is reprinted in Bassani, *Di là dal cuore* (Milan: Mondadori, 1984), pp. 311–21. In 1970, he had collaborated with Vittorio Bonicelli in drafting a screenplay that was later submitted to Ugo Pirro for modifications. The resulting script so compromised the integrity of the Bassani-Bonicelli version that the novelist dissociated his name from the production.

25. For an excellent comparative discussion of the narrative structure in novel and film, see Stanley G. Eskin, "The Garden of the Finzi-Continis," *Literature/Film Quarterly* 1 (Spring 1973), 171–75.

26. Samuels, *Encountering Directors*, p. 162. Many critics concur with De Sica's sense that *The Garden* is a return to an earlier, better time in his filmmaking career. See Cooper's *Newsweek* review, "Viva De Sica," p. 58; Kael's "Fall and Rise," p. 457; Attolini, *Dal romanzo al set*, p. 225; Hollis Alpert, "Lovely Ladies," *Saturday Review* 55 (January 8, 1972), 19; and Jay Cocks, "Requiem," *Time* 99 (January 17, 1972), 54. Pecori, in *De Sica*, p. 103, observes that the film presents a "moving glance backward" and is "lucidly self-critical."

27. This passage exemplifies the ambivalence that Pasolini sees at the center of Bassani's realism: "the numerical and mental narrowness of the Jewish

bourgeoisie of Ferrara" vs. "the grandeur that is conferred by the 'diaspora' and by the tragedy of persecution." *Descrizioni di descrizioni* (Turin: Einaudi, 1979), p. 265. Bon notes that in this passage, Bassani abandons his customary ironic detachment and adopts a tone that is "essential, definitive, hallucinated." See *Come leggere*, p. 43.

28. Andrea Gurwitt, *Selective Focus: Film Adaptations of "The Conformist" and "The Garden of the Finzi-Continis,"* honors thesis, Wesleyan University, 1988, p. 56.

29. Gurwitt further notes that this seder is photographed with a predominance of close-ups, emphasizing the isolation and individuality of its celebrants, while Giorgio's seder guests were photographed in groups to emphasize their collective identity. Ibid., p. 62.

5 · Pasolini's *Gospel According to St. Matthew*

1. For a synopsis of the film and for its credits, see the Appendix.

2. "It is so far from being merely a story that we cannot deal with it in literary terms . . . our difficulty is enormously increased when we try to pass judgment on the story itself once it has been turned into a screenplay," observed Brendan Gill in "Seeking After a Sign," *New Yorker* 42 (March 5, 1966), 157.

3. *Pier Paolo Pasolini: Materiali critici,* ed. Alfredo Luzi and Luigi Martellini (Urbino: Argalìa, 1973), pp. 314–15 (hereafter referred to as *Materiali critici.*

4. Enzo Siciliano, *Pasolini: A Biography,* trans. John Shepley (New York: Random House, 1982), p. 275.

5. Lino Micciché argues that the film is neither a Christian nor a Marxist reading in *Cinema italiano degli anni '60* (Padua: Marsilio, 1975), p. 164.

6. Erich Auerbach, *Mimesis: The Representation of Reality in Western Literature,* trans. Willard R. Trask (Princeton, N.J.: Princeton University Press, 1971), p. 17. On the absence of conventional narrative structuring devices, see M. E. M., "The First Gospel on Film," *Christian Century* 81 (December 23, 1964), 1599. For an elaboration on *Teorema*'s interpretive pattern, see my chapter on the film in *Italian Cinema in the Light of Neorealism,* (Princeton, N.J.: Princeton University Press, 1986) pp. 245–62.

7. See "Il cinema di poesia," in Pier Paolo Pasolini, *Empirismo eretico* (Milan: Garzanti, 1981), pp. 167–87. For its translation, see *Heretical Empiricism,* ed. Louise K. Barnett, trans. Ben Lawton and Louise K. Barnett (Bloomington: Indiana University Press, 1988). Pasolini's semiotics of the cinema has been highly controversial, prompting a great deal of critical debate. See, for example, Christian Metz, *Film Language,* trans. Michael Taylor (New York: Oxford University Press, 1974), pp. 205ff.; Ronald Abramson, "Structure and Meaning in the Cinema," in *Movies and Methods,* ed. Bill Nichols (Berkeley: University of California Press, 1976), pp. 558–68; Antonio Costa, "The Semiological Heresy of Pier Paolo Pasolini," in *Pier Paolo Pasolini,* ed. Paul Willemen (London: British Film Institute, 1977), pp. 32–42.

For a comprehensive criticism of Pasolini's film theory, see Teresa de Lauretis, "Language, Representation, Practice: Re-reading Pasolini's Essays on
Cinema," *Italian Quarterly* 21–22 (Fall 1980–Winter 1981), 159–66.

8. Roman Jakobson's influential theory of language can be found in "Two
   Aspects of Language and Two Types of Aphasic Disturbance," *Fundamen-
   tals of Language* (The Hague: Mouton, 1956), pp. 55–82. Pasolini's editing
   technique reinforces such verticality. For a superb analysis of his approach
   to editing, see Geoffrey Nowell-Smith, "Pasolini's Originality," in *Pier
   Paolo Pasolini*, ed. Willemen, p. 10.

9. *Materiali critici*, p. 313.

10. While Adelio Ferrero finds the film "grounded in a concrete-sensuous, ma-
    terialized landscape" in *Il cinema di Pier Paolo Pasolini* (Padua: Marsilio,
    1977), p. 58, Marc Gervais argues that the film lacks the neorealists' ven-
    eration for temporal and spatial anchoring. See his *Pier Paolo Pasolini* (Paris:
    Seghers, 1973), p. 45. Pasolini makes revealing comparisons between his
    style in *The Gospel* and that of Rossellini in *Francesco, giullare di Dio*, which
    he characterizes as "naturalistic" and poetic in a "sentimental lyrical" way,
    while his own style is less "photographic and more figurative" and his
    poetics "less lyric and more epic." See *Con Pier Paolo Pasolini*, ed. Enrico
    Magrelli (Rome: Bulzoni, 1977), p. 66.

11. Pasolini actually made a fifty-minute documentary about his Palestine trip,
    entitled *Sopraluoghi in Palestina* (1964). On his disappointment with what
    he found there, see *Materiali critici*, pp. 321–23.

12. Oswald Stack, *Pasolini on Pasolini: Interviews with Oswald Stack* (Blooming-
    ton: Indiana University Press, 1969), p. 82. On Pasolini's reinvention of
    Palestine in southern Italy, see Fabien Gérard, *Pasolini, ou le Mythe de la
    Barbarie* (Brussels: Éditions de l'Université de Bruxelles, 1981), p. 70.

13. *Materiali critici*, p. 349.

14. Ibid., p. 313.

15. On Pasolini's casting, see Gunnar D. Kumlien, "A Marxist's Christ," *Com-
    monweal* 82 (July 2, 1965), 472; Stack, *Pasolini on Pasolini*, p. 79; and Andrew
    Greeley, "St. Matthew without Passion," *Reporter* 34 (June 30, 1966), 39.

16. These hats, which appear in Piero's *Baptism of Christ* (1440s) were appar-
    ently inspired by the haberdashery of Greek Orthodox emissaries to the
    Council of Florence in 1439. See Peter Murray and Linda Murray, *The Art
    of the Renaissance* (London: Thames and Hudson, 1985), p. 125.

17. Stack, *Pasolini on Pasolini*, p. 83.

18. Ibid., p. 91.

19. *Materiali critici*, p. 312.

20. Gervais, *Pasolini*, p. 52.

21. Quoted in Giuseppe Zigaina, *Pasolini e la morte: Mito, alchimia e semantica
    del 'nulla lucente'* (Venice: Marsilio, 1987), p. 24. Zigaina points out Pasoli-
    ni's admiration for Gadda's linguistic pluralism (p. 23) and examines its
    implications for the filmmaker's style.

22. For "magma of techniques," see *Pier Paolo Pasolini nel dibattito culturale con-
    temporaneo* (Pavia: Amministrazione provinciale di Pavia, 1977), p. 118.

23. Quoted in ibid., p. 117. On the music in *Accattone*, see Pasolini's remarks in "An Epical-Religious View of the World," *Film Quarterly* 18 (Summer 1965), 40.
24. Ibid.
25. Ibid., p. 118. On the expressive liberation that Pasolini experienced in filming *The Gospel*, see Gérard, *Pasolini*, p. 69.
26. See Frederick Hartt, *History of Italian Renaissance Art* (Englewood Cliffs, N.J.: Prentice-Hall, 1979), pp. 309–10.
27. In an otherwise admiring review, Stanley Kauffmann points out the inappropriateness of the song's lyrics. See "Pasolini's Passion," *New Republic* 154 (March 26, 1966), 33.
28. *Materiali critici*, p. 352.
29. Ibid., pp. 351–52.
30. Moira Walsh, "The Gospel According to St. Matthew," *America* 114 (February 26, 1966), 307, sees Pasolini's work as an expression of disdain for film portrayals of the Gospels. Other critics who cite Pasolini's antispectacular restraint are J. Robert Nelson, "Pasolini's Miracle," *Christian Century* 83 (March 16, 1966), 335, Dwight MacDonald, "Il Vangelo secondo Matteo," *Esquire* 62 (December 1964), 76–78 +; Hollis Alpert in *Saturday Review* 49 (March 26, 1966), 46; Richard Schickel, "A Stark, Astonishing Life of Christ," *Life* 60 (March 11, 1966), 10; and Robert Hatch, who faults the film's austerity, in *Nation* 202 (March 7, 1966), 280.
31. Sandro Petraglia, *Pier Paolo Pasolini* (Florence: La Nuova Italia, 1974), p. 59.
32. Stack, *Pasolini on Pasolini*, p. 87.
33. Quoted in *Pasolini nel dibattito culturale contemporaneo*, p. 108. For a similar statement by Pasolini, see *Materiali critici*, pp. 313, 319. The fanaticism and severity of this Christ have occasioned a great deal of critical comment. See, for example, Gérard, *Pasolini*, p. 69; Gervais, *Pasolini*, pp. 47ff.; Philip Hartung, "Pasolini's Matthew," *Commonweal* 83 (March 4, 1966), 642; Pia Friedrich, *Pier Paolo Pasolini* (Boston: Hall, 1982), p. 21; Micciché, *Cinema italiano degli anni '60*, p. 163; and Alpert's review in *Saturday Review*, p. 46.
34. Christ's aloofness from the people, so powerfully visualized in this scene, has been seen as problematic by many critics. For an incisive formulation of the criticism that Christ fails to perform the Gramscian function of the "organic intellectual," never forging a link with the masses, see Naomi Greene, *Pier Paolo Pasolini: Cinema as Heresy* (Princeton, N.J.: Princeton University Press, 1990), pp. 78–79.
35. On the film's indifference to historical inquiry, see Micciché, *Cinema italiano degli anni '60*, p. 164.
36. See Gérard, *Pasolini*, p. 68; and Siciliano, *Pasolini*, p. 271. On the filmmaker's profound desire to promote such a dialogue, see Greene, *Pier Paolo Pasolini*, pp. 70–81.
37. Stack, *Pasolini on Pasolini*, p. 97. Kumlein in "Marxist's Christ" argues that Pasolini's film has indeed "swept away most objections to the dialogue" (472).
38. On Spanish refugees and the Slavic babies, see *Pasolini nel dibattito culturale*

contemporaneo, p. 109; for the Holocaust analogy, see the directions in the screenplay, Pier Paolo Pasolini, *Il Vangelo secondo Matteo,* ed. Giacomo Gambetti (Milan: Garzanti, 1964), p. 54; on the police and *squadristi,* see Bondanella, *Italian Cinema: From Neorealism to the Present* (New York: Continuum, 1990), p. 182.

39. *Pasolini nel dibattito culturale contemporaneo,* p. 109.
40. On the Pharisees and Sadducees, see Ferrero, *Il cinema di Pasolini,* p. 59; on colonial cruelty, see the directions in the screenplay, p. 246.
41. Quoted in *Materiali critici,* p. 313.
42. In *Pier Paolo Pasolini,* p. 79, Greene argues that the absence of reaction shots is one more visual proof of Christ's isolation and aloofness from the masses.
43. Pasolini calls Matthew's Christ the most revolutionary of all the Gospels' portrayals, in Stack, *Pasolini on Pasolini,* p. 95. For critical comments, see Siciliano, *Pasolini,* p. 266; Alpert, *Saturday Review,* p. 46; Gervais, *Pasolini,* p. 47.
44. On Pasolini's intense personal investment see Brunetta, *Storia del cinema italiano dal 1945 agli anni ottanta* (Rome: Editori Riuniti, 1982), p. 659; and *Materiali critici,* p. 307. On the film's autobiographical dimension, see Friedrich, *Pasolini,* p. 21; Siciliano, *Pasolini,* p. 270; and Petraglia, *Pasolini,* p. 58.
45. Ferrero sees the film's Christ as an especially Pasolinian figure. See *Il cinema di Pasolini,* p. 58.
46. Siciliano, *Pasolini,* p. 270.
47. The essay can be found in *Empirismo eretico,* pp. 269–76. For the English translation, see Barnett, *Heretical Empiricism,* pp. 267–75.
48. For Pasolini's anticlericalism, see Gervais, *Pasolini,* p. 51.
49. Stack, *Pasolini on Pasolini,* p. 77. For similar Pasolinian descriptions of this visceral religiosity, see ibid., p. 14, and Pasolini, "An Epical-Religious View," p. 32. See also *Materiali critici,* pp. 343–44; and William Van Watson, *Pier Paolo Pasolini and the Theater of the Word,* (Ann Arbor, Mich.: UMI Research Press, 1989), p. 9.
50. Admiration without adoration is Sandro Petraglia's interpretation. See his *Pasolini,* p. 58. Pasolini himself states that while Christ is not the son of God, "I believe that Christ is divine . . . that is, that in him humanity is so lofty, strict, and ideal as to exceed the common terms of humanity." Quoted in Siciliano, *Pasolini,* p. 270.
51. Nelson, "Pasolini's Miracle," p. 335; Walsh, "Gospel According to Matthew," p. 308; for the OCIC, see Siciliano, *Pasolini,* p. 58.
52. The quoted term is Petraglia's. See his *Pasolini,* p. 58.
53. Quoted in Magrelli, *Con Pier Paolo Pasolini,* pp. 67–68.
54. Several critics have noted the coexistence of two very different camera styles in the film. See Ferrero, *Il cinema di Pasolini,* pp. 58–59; and Bondanella, *Italian Cinema,* p. 184. However, Naomi Greene in *Pier Paolo Pasolini,* p. 74, is not convinced by the two-points-of-view argument.
55. Stack, *Pasolini on Pasolini,* p. 89.

56. *Materiali critici*, p. 312.
57. *New Catholic Encyclopedia*, 1967 ed., S. V. "Matthew, Gospel According to St.," 9:499.
58. On Matthew's apostolic emphasis, see ibid., 9:497, 501.
59. See "Cinema di poesia," in *Empirismo eretico*, pp. 175ff.
60. Ibid., pp. 179ff.
61. Pasolini claimed that this pronouncement was the key to his film. See *Pasolini nel dibattito culturale contemporaneo*, p. 108.
62. Quoted in Stack, *Pasolini on Pasolini*, p. 84. On his use of documentary techniques in these scenes, see Magrelli, *Con Pier Paolo Pasolini*, pp. 72–73; and Gervais, *Pasolini*, p. 46.

6 ▪ Pasolini's *Decameron*

1. This is a revised and expanded version of an earlier article entitled "The *Decameron*: Pasolini as a Reader of Boccaccio," *Italian Quarterly* 21 (Fall 1980–Winter 1981), 175–80. For an outline of Pasolini's narrative sequence, synopses of the individual tales, and the film's credits, see the Appendix.
2. On the new phase in Pasolini's production, see Peter Bondanella, *Italian Cinema from Neorealism to the Present* (New York: Continuum, 1991), p. 287; and Adelio Ferrero, *Il Cinema di Pier Paolo Pasolini* (Padua: Marsilio, 1977), p. 118.
3. On this "sequel mania," see Bondanella, *Italian Cinema*, p. 291; and Mario Quaragnolo, *Dove va il cinema italiano?* (Milan: Pan, 1972), p. 165.
4. Gideon Bachmann, "Pasolini Today," *Take One* 4 (1973), 21.
5. Interview published in *Pier Paolo Pasolini*, ed. Paul Willemen (London: British Film Institute, 1977), p. 71.
6. Sergio Arecco, *Pier Paolo Pasolini* (Rome: Partisan, 1972), pp. 74–75. See also Fabien Gérard, *Pasolini, ou le Mythe de la Barbarie* (Brussels: Éditions de l'Université de Bruxelles, 1981), p. 84.
7. Bachmann, "Pasolini Today," p. 21.
8. "Abiura dalla *Trilogia della vita*" is included in the volume of screenplays by Pasolini, *Trilogia della vita: Il Decameron, I racconti di Canterbury, Il fiore delle mille e una notte*, ed. Giorgio Gattei (Milan: Mondadori, 1987), p. 7. See also Fulvio Panzeri, *Guida alla lettura di Pasolini* (Milan: Mondadori, 1988), pp. 140–41.
9. Sandro Petraglia, *Pier Paolo Pasolini* (Florence: La Nuova Italia, 1974), p. 108.
10. On the *eros-thanatos* connection, see Vito Attolini, *Dal romanzo al set: Cinema italiano dalle origini ad oggi* (Bari: Dedalo, 1988), p. 176; and Ferrero, *Il cinema di Pasolini*, p. 121. *Vitalism* is Ferrero's term.
11. On the deglamorizing of the medieval image in the media, see the review by Colin Westerbeck, Jr., in *Commonweal* 95 (November 12, 1971), 158.
12. The essay is published in *Empirismo eretico* (Milan: Garzanti, 1981), pp. 5–24. For the English translation, see Louise K. Barnett, ed., *Heretical Empiri-*

cism, trans. Louise K. Barnett and Ben Lawton (Bloomington: Indiana University Press, 1988), pp. 3–20.

13. Pasolini, *Trilogia della vita*, p. 26. All quotes from the film's dialogue come from this edition of the screenplay. The translations are mine, and subsequent page references are included in the text.

14. On Pasolini's reversal of Boccaccio's gentrifying operation, see David Bevan's superb insights in "Pasolini and Boccaccio," *Literature/Film Quarterly* 5 (1977), 26ff.; and Ferrero's elegant commentary in *Il cinema di Pasolini*, p. 119. Several critics have read this scene as an explicit formulation of Pasolini's adaptive mode. See Bondanella, *Italian Cinema*, p. 287; Bevan, "Pasolini and Boccaccio," 27; and Ben Lawton, "Theory and Praxis in Pasolini's *Trilogy della vita*," *Quarterly Review of Film Studies* 2 (November 1977), 400. The reader is referred to Lawton's learned and thorough study, whose explication of Pasolini's thematic patterns and art historical allusions, especially to the work of Giotto and Breughel, are invaluable interpretive contributions, and ones to which my own reading is deeply indebted.

15. Several critics have seen this juxtaposition as ideologically motivated. See Bondanella, *Italian Cinema*, p. 288; and Lawton, "Theory and Praxis," p. 404.

16. Bondanella, *Italian Cinema*, p. 288.

17. Giovanni Boccaccio, *The Decameron*, trans. G. H. McWilliam (Middlesex, England: Penguin, 1981), p. 367. Henceforth, page references will be included in the body of the text with the notation "McWilliam."

18. In "Pasolini and Boccaccio," p. 28, Bevan aptly observes: "The brothers . . . feel the need to play with their victim until the moment when he finally understands that he is about to be killed."

19. For a fine study of Boccaccio's satire of the sacraments in this tale, see Greg Lucente, "The Fortunate Fall of Andreuccio da Perugia," *Forum Italicum* 10 (1976), 323–44.

20. Angelo Moscariello has another explanation for Pasolini's omission of the well episode, suggesting that the filmmaker wanted to avoid the "aspetto avventuroso" of the original. See *Cinema e/o letteratura* (Bologna: Pitagora, 1981), p. 148.

21. On the film's categorical endorsement of guilt-free sexuality, see Bondanella, *Italian Cinema*, p. 289.

22. John Larner, *Culture and Society in Italy, 1290–1420* (New York: Scribner, 1971), p. 274.

23. Naomi Greene sees an analogy between the fresco painter's delight in the physical aspects of his art (pigments, cartoons, etc.) and Pasolini's lifelong impulse to "'seize' reality in a tangible way." See *Pier Paolo Pasolini: Cinema as Heresy* (Princeton, N.J.: Princeton University Press, 1990), p. 186. In contrast, several critics read this figure of the artist as self-satire, as a putdown of artistic pretensions. See, for example, Westerbeck's review in *Commonweal* 95, p. 158.

24. On this twofold frame, see Greene, *Pier Paolo Pasolini*, p. 188.

25. According to Philip Strick in his review for *Sight and Sound* 41 (Spring 1972), 110, this technique is detrimental to the humorous effect of the punchline.

26. For his extremely thought-provoking speculations on this third panel, see Lawton, "Theory and Praxis," p. 409.

27. Erwin Panofsky, *Gothic Architecture and Scholasticism* (New York: Meridian Books, 1968), p. 59.

28. Frederic Jameson, "Metacommentary," *PMLA* 86 (1971), 9–18.

29. On fresco painting as a form of medieval didactic filmmaking, see Lawton, "Theory and Praxis," pp. 406–7. On the collaborative nature of fresco painting and filmmaking, see Roger T. Witcomb, *The New Italian Cinema* (New York: Oxford University Press, 1982), p. 128. On the epistemological implications of Pasolini's inclusion of himself as *subject* in *The Trilogy*, see Gian Piero Brunetta, "La visione di Pasolini," *Italian Quarterly* 82–83 (Fall 1980–Winter, 1981), 152ff. For Pasolini's comments on his performance of the Giotto role, see Petraglia, *Pasolini*, p. 107.

30. Pasolini, "Battute sul cinema," in *Empirismo eretico*, p. 229. For the English translation, see Barnett, *Heretical Empiricism*, p. 225.

31. This essay is published in *Empirismo eretico*, pp. 198–226. For the English translation, see Barnett, *Heretical Empiricism*, pp. 197–222.

32. Geoffrey Nowell-Smith, "Pasolini's Originality," in Willemen, *Pier Paolo Pasolini*, p. 10. On Pasolini's tendency to "decompose to the maximum the narrative unity," see Gian Piero Brunetta, *Storia del cinema italiano dal 1945 agli anni ottanta* (Rome: Editori Riuniti, 1982), p. 662.

33. On Pasolini's irrationalism, see his comments in *Pier Paolo Pasolini nel dibattito culturale contemporaneo* (Pavia: Amministrazione provinciale di Pavia, 1977), pp. 92ff.

34. Pasolini, "Abiura," p. 8. On Pasolini's progressive disenchantment with liberated sexuality, see Ben Lawton, "The Evolving Rejection of Homosexuality, Sub-Proletariat, and the Third World in Pasolini's Films," *Italian Quarterly* 82–83 (Fall 1980–Winter 1981), 170.

7 · The Tavianis' *Padre padrone*

1. For a synopsis of the film and its credits, see the Appendix. On the film's genesis, see the Tavianis' statements in Franca Faldini and Goffredo Fofi, *Il cinema italiano d'oggi* (Milan: Mondadori, 1984), p. 538. In this and the following chapter dedicated to the adaptations of Vittorio and Paolo Taviani, I will consider the brothers as a single filmmaking unit, because their collaboration is so complete that it is impossible to factor out either one's individual contribution. Even in conversation, their ideas appear to be interchangeable, and many published interviews fail to specify which brother is speaking, lumping the interlocutors into one fraternal voice. For an account of this remarkable collaboration, see Marco De Poli, *Paolo e Vittorio Taviani* (Milan: Moizzi, 1977), pp. 9–10.

2. See Jean Gili, *Le cinéma italien* (Paris: Union Générale d'Éditions, 1978), p. 381.

3. Ibid.

4. Quoted in Fulvio Accialini and Lucia Coluccelli, *Paolo e Vittorio Taviani* (Florence: La Nuova Italia, 1979), p. 10. This is not to suggest, however, a total rupture from neorealist tradition, which informs the Tavianis' emphasis on the Sardinianness of the story, on the "sense of place as crucial for the identity of the protagonist," as Marcia Landy aptly argues in "Neorealism, Politics, and Language in the Films of the Tavianis," *Annali d'Italianistica* 6 (1988), 248. On the incorporation and supercession of neorealist norms, see David Ansen, "Father and Son," *Newsweek* 91 (Jan. 16, 1978), 81. Tony Mitchell in "Towards Utopia, By Way of Research, Detachment, and Involvement," *Sight and Sound* 48 (Summer 1979), 178, and Ben Lawton in "Italian Neorealism: A Mirror Construction of Reality," *Film Criticism* 3 (Winter 1979), 20, both apply the story's oedipal theme to the Tavianis' stylistic struggle. On the vast distance separating neorealism from the "almost expressionist" mode of *Padre padrone*, see Robert Kolker, *The Altering Eye: Contemporary International Cinema* (Oxford: Oxford University Press, 1983), pp. 114ff.

5. It is thus wonderful and ironic that the father of neorealism, Roberto Rossellini, presided over the Cannes juries that awarded *Padre padrone* both the Golden Palm and the International Critics' awards in a sweep that no film to date had ever achieved. For an account of the political intrigues behind the prizes, which were awarded to the Tavianis over strenuous mainstream objections, see Mino Argentieri's "Una tragedia ottimista," published as the introduction to the screenplay, *Padre padrone di Paolo e Vittorio Taviani*, ed. Mino Argentieri (Bologna: Cappelli, 1977), p. 22. See also Pier Marco De Santi, *I film di Paolo e Vittorio Taviani* (Rome: Gremese, 1988), p. 99.

6. Both Mark Graham in his superb article *"Padre padrone* and the Dialectics of Sound," *Film Criticism* 6 (Fall 1981), 26, and Nuccio Orto in *La notte dei desideri: Il cinema dei fratelli Taviani* (Palermo: Sellerio, 1987), p. 40, offer incisive analyses of the phonetic and semantic principles that govern these lists.

7. See Vittorio's remarks on how city dwellers idealize and sanitize the rural condition in Gili, *Le cinéma italien*, p. 391. See also the Tavianis' comments in Christian Biegalski and Christian Depuyper, "Paolo et Vittorio Taviani," *Cinéma*, no. 224–25 (August/September 1977), 20, about how Gavino's lexicon demystifies the pastoral.

8. See the screenplay, Paolo and Vittorio Taviani, *Padre Padrone* (Bologna: Cappelli, 1977), p. 105. Subsequent page references are in the text, preceded by "T." All translations of the screenplay are mine.

9. Quoted in Gili, *Le cinéma italien*, p. 391. For a similar affirmation, see Vincenzo Camerino and Antonio Tarsi, *Dialettica dell'Utopia* (Manduria: Lacaita, 1978), pp. 111–12.

10. See Accialini and Coluccelli, *Paolo e Vittorio Taviani*, p. 106.

11. "But already in this moment the two authors subtly deceive the spectator: the words of Ledda belong to the Tavianis," write Accialini and Coluccelli, ibid., p. 99.

12. On the Tavianis' inclusion of the historical Ledda to thwart audience identification, see their comments in Biegalski and Depuyper, "Paolo et Vittorio Taviani," p. 22. For an extended discussion of this scene's self-conscious commentary on the conventions of spectacle, see Kolker, *Altering Eye,* pp. 114–16; and Argentieri, "Una tragedia ottimista," p. 22.

13. For the book's self-presentation as "*testimonianza*" or objective truth, see Accialini and Coluccelli, *Paolo e Vittorio Taviani,* p. 105.

14. See Nuccio Orto, *La notte dei desideri,* p. 24.

15. For the Tavianis' own comments on the difference between the novel's temporality and that of the film, see Biegalski and Depuyper, "Paolo et Vittorio Taviani," p. 14. On the Tavianis' disruption of the novel's temporal continuum, see Lino Micciché, *Cinema italiano degli anni '70* (Padua: Marsilio, 1980), p. 280. Pauline Kael sees the film as a series of epiphanies or a progression of slides in "The Sacred Oak," *New Yorker* 53 (October 3, 1977), 127.

16. This is Tom Lehrer's euphemism, quoted in Graham, "Dialectics of Sound," p. 25.

17. For Frank Kermode's magisterial study of fictions of temporality, see *The Sense of an Ending* (New York: Oxford University Press, 1975).

18. See A.C. Charity, *Events and their Afterlife: The Dialectics of Christian Typology in the Bible and Dante* (Cambridge: Cambridge University Press, 1966), especially chaps. 1—3.

19. Quoted in Gili, *Le cinéma italien,* p. 389.

20. Quoted in Biegalski and Depuyper, "Paolo et Vittorio Taviani," p. 17.

21. The Tavianis make explicit their desire to render Efisio less malignant than Abramo, more victim than monster. See Camerino and Tarsi, *Dialettica dell'Utopia,* p. 110. See also Landy, "Neorealism," p. 243; and Argentieri, "Una tragedia ottimista," p. 30.

22. Gavino Ledda, *Padre padrone,* trans. George Salmanazar (New York: Urizen Books, 1979), p. 7. Subsequent page references to the autobiography are included in the text, prefaced by "G.L."

23. Hence their insistence on seeing the father-son conflict as an example of a sociological condition, rather than of individual psychopathology. See Biegalski and Depuyper, "Paolo et Vittorio Taviani," p. 18; De Poli, *Paolo e Vittorio Taviani,* p. 53; De Santi, *Film di Paolo e Vittorio,* p. 107; Graham, "Dialectics of Sound," pp. 21ff; Orto, *La notte dei desideri,* p. 45; and Gaston Haustrate, "Les sentiers de l'Utopie," *Cinéma,* no. 226 (October 1977), 77, 79. On the "pedagogical" nature of Efisio's violence, see Micciché, *Cinema italiano degli anni '70,* p. 280.

24. See the Tavianis' comments in Gili, *Le cinéma italien,* p. 382.

25. Robert Kolker sees the pietà allusion as ironic, precipitating a break in the viewer's identification with the characters' suffering. See *Altering Eye,* p. 117. See also De Santi, *Film di Paolo e Vittorio Taviani,* p. 107.

26. See Ermanno Comuzio, "Musica e suoni protagonisti nel cinema dei fratelli Taviani," *Bianco e nero*, no. 5–6 (September/December, 1977), 117–18.

27. Mario Aste observes that Ledda's experience is an allegory for the historical plight of Sardinia as a whole. See *"Padre Padrone* and the 'Sardinian Question': From Ledda's Novel to the Tavianis' Film," *Romance Languages Annual* I (1989), 27.

28. Marcel Martin notes that father and son are victims of the same systemic exploitation in *"Padre padrone," Écran* 62 (October 15, 1977), 45. See also Orto, *La notte dei desideri*, p. 26.

29. Graham sees this transfer of roles as an example of "the dialectic turning of the tables." See "Dialectics of Sound," p. 27.

30. Quoted in Aldo Tassone, *Parla il cinema italiano* (Milan: Il Formichiere, 1980), 2:372. Such ironic distancing seemed to irritate some American reviewers, who found the performances and the narrative unengaging See, for example, Frank Rich, "Wild Child," *Time* no. 111 (January 16, 1978), 82; and the review by Robert Hatch in *Nation*, no. 226 (January 14, 1978), 30.

31. "Almost as in a dream, to the child everything presents itself under the effects of a deforming lens that annuls depth and consequentiality, negating a way of understanding space and time according to laws of the principle of reality." Quoted in Accialini and Coluccelli, *Paolo e Vittorio Taviani*, p. 98. Pauline Kael sees the film as animistic rather than naturalistic. See "The Sacred Oak," p. 127. On the use of sound to represent Gavino's animistic sensibility, see Graham, "Dialectics of Sound," p. 25.

32. Gili, *Le cinéma italien*, p. 396.

33. See ibid., p. 397; and Comuzio, "Musica e suoni protagonisti," p. 119.

34. Orto, *La notte dei desideri*, p. 34.

35. Quoted in Biegalski and Depuyper, "Paolo et Vittorio Taviani," p. 22. See also De Santi, *Film di Paolo e Vittorio*, p. 103.

36. On the Tavianis' quest for ethnographic authenticity, see De Poli, *Paolo e Vittorio Taviani*, pp. 49–50.

37. See Graham, "Dialectics of Sound," p. 22.

38. For an account of this editorial decision, see the Tavianis' comments in Biegalski and Depuyper, "Paolo et Vittorio Taviani," p. 26.

39. Quoted in Camerino and Tarsi, *Dialettica dell'Utopia*, p. 109.

40. On the cyclicity of Gavino's journey, see Accialini and Coluccelli, *Paolo e Vittorio Taviani*, p. 101.

41. The Tavianis discuss their threefold conclusion in Gili, *Le cinéma italien*, p. 386.

42. Gavino's acculturation and his resolve to return to Sardinia as an activist committed to bringing about a heightened mass consciousness through education make him an "organic intellectual" in Gramscian terms, according to Marcia Landy in "Neorealism," p. 243. See also Aste, *"Padre Padrone,"* p. 28.

43. See Gili, *Le cinéma italien*, p. 387.

44. Quoted in Camerino and Tarsi, *Dialettica dell'Utopia*, pp. 112–13. On the provisional nature of this ending, see Orto, *La notte dei desideri*, p. 47.

45. See Marcel Martin, "*Padre padrone*," p. 45; and Biegalski and Depuyper, "Paolo et Vittorio Taviani," pp. 13, 24.
46. Accialini and Coluccelli identify this cycle as the film's central dynamic in *Paolo e Vittorio Taviani*, p. 102.
47. Quoted in Gili, *Le cinéma italien*, p. 387.

8 • The Tavianis' *Kàos*

1. With the exception of the Epilogue ("Colloquio con la madre"), which is summarized amply in this chapter, the film's other episodes are condensed in the Appendix, where the credits can also be found.
2. Pier Marco De Santi suggests the aptness of Pasolini's "cinema di poesia" for the Tavianis' filmmaking. See *I Film di Paolo e Vittorio Taviani* (Rome: Gremese, 1988), p. 7. The Tavianis have often spoken of their father-son relationship with neorealism—a relationship based on an admiration which prompts them to question, challenge, and finally transcend their model. On their antinaturalist, nonmimetic style, see their statements in Jean Gili, *Le cinéma italien* (Paris: Union Générale d'Éditions, 1978), pp. 378, 394; Fulvio Accialini and Lucia Coluccelli, *Paolo e Vittorio Taviani* (Florence: Nuova Italia, 1979), p. 10. See also Vito Attolini, *Dal romanzo al set: Cinema italiano dalle origini ad oggi* (Bari: Dedalo, 1988), p. 189; Marcia Landy, "Neorealism, Politics, and Language in the Films of the Tavianis," *Annali d'Italianistica* 6 (1988), 236ff.; Marco De Poli, *Paolo e Vittorio Taviani*, (Milan: Moizzi, 1977), p. 68; and David Denby, "Poets and Peasants," *New York* 19 (February 24, 1986), 62.
3. For the Mozart identification, see De Santi, *Film di Paolo e Vittorio*.
4. Quoted in Aldo Tassone, *Parla il cinema italiano* (Milan: Il Formichiere, 1980), 2:359. For other discussions of their films' musical structure, see Gili, *Le cinéma italien*, p. 359; De Poli, *Paolo e Vittorio Taviani*, p. 66; Accialini and Coluccelli, *Paolo e Vittorio Taviani*, p. 5; and De Santi, *Film di Paolo e Vittorio*, pp. 18, 23.
5. Luigi Pirandello, *Novelle per un anno* (Milan: Mondadori, 1939), 2:1105. All quotes will be from this edition. Henceforth, volume and page numbers are included in the text. All translations are mine.
6. In the absence of a published screenplay, I have transcribed and translated the film's dialogue.
7. Richard Corliss notes that Saro is a character of Luigi's imagination in "Folk Artistry," *Time*, no. 127 (January 27, 1986), 64.
8. Marcia Landy notes that Luigi's imagined exchange with his mother reenacts the process of mourning—of incorporating the dead parent in order then to be able to let go. See "Neorealism," p. 250.
9. Hence Pier Marco De Santi in *Film di Paolo e Vittorio* sees the bird as a unifying motif (p. 126) and as a figure of the artist-storyteller (p. 129).
10. On the Tavianis' intensification of the textual torment, see Nuccio Orto, *La notte dei desideri: Il cinema dei fratelli Taviani* (Palermo: Sellerio, 1987), p. 85.
11. Both "La giara" and "L'altro figlio" have stage versions. While the Tavianis took nothing from the play of "L'altro figlio," adapting only its short-story

version, they did borrow some of Pirandello's own theatrical additions to the original of "La giara."

12. For Vittorio Taviani's comments on the American genre of the musical comedy, see Tassone, *Parla il cinema italiano* 2:375. On the carnivalesque dimension of the climactic scene, see Landy, "Neorealism," p. 249; and Orto, *La notte dei desideri,* p. 103.

13. On this addition to the dramatis personae, see ibid., p. 99.

14. The Tavianis explicitly state the need for a new visual canon in Accialini and Coluccelli, *Paolo e Vittorio Taviani,* p. 3.

15. On the polyvalence of the Tavianis' moon, see Orto, *La notte dei desideri,* p. 103.

16. See ibid., pp. 90ff.

17. See ibid., p. 94. On the failure of the confession to liberate Maria Grazia, see Landy, "Neorealism," p. 248.

18. The mother's reminiscences are set in the "'heroic' period of our Risorgimento history—that of conspiracies and of armed insurrection," writes Orto in *La notte dei desideri,* p. 118.

19. Ibid., p. 113.

20. On Garibaldi's representation in the film, see De Santi, *Film di Paolo e Vittorio,* p. 126; and Orto, *La notte dei desideri,* p. 111. For a Gramscian reading of Garibaldi's revolutionary failure as figured in Maria Grazia's plight, see Orto, *La notte dei desideri,* pp. 110ff.

21. Orto, *La notte dei desideri,* p. 114.

22. See Pauline Kael's review in the *New Yorker* 62 (March 10, 1986), 119, 120.

23. See Roland Barthes, *Writing Degree Zero and Elements of Semiology,* trans. Annette Lavers and Colin Smith (Boston: Beacon, 1968), p. 86.

24. Ibid.

9 · Fellini's *Casanova*

1. This chapter is a revised and expanded version of an article that appeared under the title "Fellini's *Casanova:* Portrait of the Artist" in the *Quarterly Review of Film Studies* 5 (Winter 1980), 19–34. For a synopsis of the film and for its credits, see the Appendix.

2. *Il Casanova di Federico Fellini,* ed. Gianfranco Angelucci and Liliana Betti (Bologna: Cappelli, 1977), p. 49.

3. See Georges Poulet, *Mesure de l'instant: Études sur le temps humain* (Paris, 1968), 4:105–39.

4. Federico Fellini, *Comments on Film,* ed. Giovanni Grazzini, trans. Joseph Henry (Fresno: California State University Press, 1988), p. 28.

5. Quoted in Dario Zanelli, *Nel mondo di Federico Fellini* (Turin: Nuova ERI Edizioni RAI, 1987), p. 85.

6. See Peter Bondanella, "Literature as Therapy: Fellini and Petronius," *Annali d'Italianistica* 6 (1988), 183.

7. For this montage of Fellinian quotes, see Antonio Chemasi, "Fellini's *Casanova:* The Final Nights," *American Film* 1 (September 1976), 10.

8. Quotes from Angelucci and Betti, *Il Casanova di Fellini*, pp. 36, 32. For a similar statement of his desire to portray a new and unfamiliar Casanova, see Pier Marco De Santi, "Da Casanova a Fellini," in *Saggi e documenti sopra 'Il Casanova' di Federico Fellini*, ed. Pier Marco De Santi and Raffaele Monti (Pisa: Quaderni dell'Istituto di Storia dell'Arte dell'Università di Pisa, 1978), p. 9. Other possible Casanovas included Marlon Brando, Al Pacino, Robert Redford, Michael Caine, Jack Nicholson, and in Italy, Gian Maria Volonté and even Alberto Sordi. On this superstar lineup, see Tullio Kezich, *Fellini* (Milan: Rizzoli, 1988), p. 447.

9. Stephen Farber, "Casanova: Love's Labors Lost," *New West* 2, January 31, 1977, p. 74; Christopher Porterfield, "Waxwork Narcissus," *Time* 109, February 21, 1977, p. 70.

10. Andrew Sarris, "*Fellini's Casanova:* A Failure in Communications," *Village Voice* 22, February 28, 1977, p. 39.

11. *Grande dizionario della lingua italiana*, ed. Salvatore Battaglia (Turin, 1962), 2:827.

12. Leo Janos, "The New Fellini: Venice on Ice," *Time* 107, May 17, 1976, pp. 76–77.

13. Roberto Gervaso, "La fama di Casanova," *Nuova Antologia*, no. 522 (October 1974), 257.

14. Havelock Ellis, *Affirmations* (Boston and New York: Houghton Mifflin Co., 1922), p. 99; Owen Holloway, "Casanova: The Perfect Adventurer," *Listener*, 43 (1960), 881.

15. For a summary of Casanova's literary activities, see Norman V. Carlson, "Casanova: The *Memoirs* and the Man," *Quarterly Newsletter*, 32 (Winter 1966), 4.

16. See Gervaso, "La fama di Casanova," pp. 254–59.

17. Edmund Wilson, *The Triple Thinkers and The Wound and the Bow* (Boston: Northeastern University Press, 1984), p. 156.

18. Holloway, "Casanova," p. 881.

19. Gervaso, "La fama di Casanova," p. 259.

20. Ellis, *Affirmations*, pp. 94–96; Angelucci and Betti, *Il Casanova di Fellini*, p. 32.

21. For a supplemental survey of scholarly and professional perspectives on Casanova, see Fausto Pauluzzi, "Materials on Fellini's *Casanova:* An Update," *Italian Culture* 7 (1986–89), especially pp. 125–35.

22. Quoted in *Casanova rendez-vous con Federico Fellini*, ed. Gianfranco Angelucci and Liliana Betti (Milan: Bompiani, 1975), p. 115.

23. Arthur Schnitzler, *Casanova's Homecoming*, trans. Eden Paul and Cedar Paul (New York: Simon and Schuster, 1930), p. 1.

24. Jack Kroll, "A Sterile Casanova," *Newsweek*, 89, January 24, 1977, p. 61; and Paul Schwartzman, "Fellini's Unlovable Casanova," *New York Times Magazine*, February 6, 1977, p. 35.

25. Penelope Gilliat, "Of Dreaming and Mayhem," *New Yorker*, 50 September 23, 1974, p. 95.

26. On *Casanova* as an "auto-caricature" or "self-portrait," see Kezich, *Fellini*, pp. 449, 459, and the psychologist Renzo Canestrari's comments in Ange-

lucci and Betti, *Casanova rendez-vous*, p. 90. On Fellini's identification with Casanova, see De Santi, "Da Casanova a Fellini," pp. 10, 40.

27. Angelucci and Betti, *Il Casanova di Fellini*, p. 22. On Casanova's biographical connections with the theater, see the interview with Casanova-expert Piero Chiara in Angelucci and Betti, *Casanova rendez-vous*, p. 89.

28. Kroll, "A Sterile Casanova," p. 61.

29. Farber, "Casanova," pp. 74–75.

30. Because the screenplay was not available in English, I am translating from the Italian version found in Angelucci and Betti, *Il Casanova di Fellini*. The page numbers of the Italian passages from which I have translated are included in the text.

31. *Federico Fellini, Essays in Criticism*, ed. Peter Bondanella (New York: Oxford University Press, 1978), p. 28.

32. De Bernis's invisible witness is so authoritative, according to Elio Benevelli, that it makes the ambassador the virtual scriptwriter of this amorous mise-en-scène. See *Analisi di una messa in scena* (Bari: Dedalo, 1979), p. 18.

33. For this episode in the *Memoirs*, see vol. 4, chaps. 3–11.

34. Marie Jean Lederman notes this disparity in "Art, Artifacts, and *Fellini's Casanova*," *Film Criticism* 2 (Fall 1977), 45, as does Don Willis in "Two Views on *Fellini's Casanova*," *Film Quarterly* 30 (Summer 1977), 26.

35. Joseph Markulin discusses the "dehumanization of man in the direction of the animalistic" in "Plot and Character in *Fellini's Casanova*: Beyond *Satyricon*," *Italian Quarterly* 23 (Winter 1982), 67. Markulin also notes the failure of Casanova's claims to higher talents (p. 69), and the disparity between self-image and popular stereotype (p. 70).

36. See Benevelli, *Analisi*, p. 72.

37. For a Freudian reading of this episode, where Rosalba is seen as a projection of Casanova's own unfulfillable desire for phallic presence, see ibid., pp. 81–82.

38. Bondanella, *Federico Fellini*, p. 31. To add to the pathos of this aged Casanova, Fellini takes great pains to reveal his sartorial obsolescence by clothing him according to the codes of prerevolutionary fashion, while the youthful listening public is dressed in severe, neoclassical simplicity. See De Santi, "Da Casanova a Fellini," pp. 38–39. On Casanova's failure to apprehend this new, postrevolutionary reality, see Raffaele Monti, "Totale artificiale" in De Santi and Monti, *Saggi e documenti*, p. 91.

39. See Benevelli, *Analisi*, p. 85.

40. Schwartzman, "Fellini's Unlovable Casanova," p. 35.

41. Originally published in *La Repubblica*, August 24, 1978. Reprinted in *Il cinema italiano d'oggi, 1970–84*, ed. Franca Faldini and Goffredo Fofi (Milan: Mondadori, 1984), p. 257.

42. Marie Jean Lederman also considers Fellini's projection of artistic anxieties onto Casanova. While she suggests that cinema itself may be a degraded art form in the eyes of the filmmaker and that Fellini might have preferred to create in the less mutable media of "stone or paint or words" (p. 45), I feel that Fellini's anxieties concern a failure to live up to specifically *cine-*

matic ideals—that is, the ideals of *cinema d'arte.* For Lederman's comments, see "Art, Artifacts," pp. 43–45.

43. See John Simon, "*Casanova:* Dead Film in a Dead Language," *New York* 10, February 21, 1977, pp. 57–58; "The Tragic Deterioration of Fellini's Genius," *New York Times,* November 24, 1974, D-17; and "Films," *Esquire* 82, December 1974, pp. 20–23. As Don Willis put it, "Fellini the Thinker, the Serious Artist, [is] forever undermined by Fellini the Showman, seduced by pageantry, movement, and sheer size." See "Two Views," 25.

44. In an otherwise negative review of the film, Lino Miccichè finds in this ending a welcome clarification of "the Fellinian discourse" and a much needed infusion of dramatic tension. See *Il cinema italiano degli anni '70* (Venice: Marsilio Editori, 1980), p. 271.

45. For the Venerial associations of Casanova's birthplace and an intriguing Freudian reading of the film's opening scene, see Peter Bondanella's *Cinema of Federico Fellini* (Princeton, N.J.: Princeton University Press, 1992), pp. 310–11.

46. See *Memoirs,* vol. 4, chap. 16.

47. Porterfield, "Waxwork Narcissus," p. 70.

48. Appreciative critics of this episode include both Don Willis (p. 27) and Albert Johnson (p. 31) in "Two Views." The former sees the candle snuffing as the culmination and denouement of all the film's imagery of fire, as does Benevelli in *Analisi,* p. 78.

49. See, for example, Farber, "Casanova," p. 76.

50. Thus, Fellini's assistant director Gerard Morin comments: "So this is what Fellini thinks it all comes down to—a vacuous man dancing with a mechanical doll. Only a middle-aged man growing cynical could make such a statement." Quoted by Janos, "The New Fellini," p. 77. Likewise Schwartzman sees in this scene "a symbol of death synonymous with Casanova's icy incapacity to love, despite his numerous lovers" in "Fellini's Unlovable Casanova," p. 35.

51. See Markulin, "Plot and Character," p. 72.

10 · Fellini's *La voca della luna*

1. For a synopsis of the film and for its credits, see the Appendix. *Il poema dei lunatici* (Turin: Bollati Boringhieri, 1987) is Cavazzoni's first novel. He is professor of philosophy at the University of Bologna.

2. Quoted in Tullio Masoni, "La voce della luna," *Cineforum* 30 (March 1990), 83. For an account of how the book functioned as a mere stimulus for the filmmaker's inventive faculties, see Cavazzoni's entertaining description of his working relationship with Fellini in "Federico sulla luna," *Panorama,* August 20, 1989, p. 86.

3. Quoted in Lietta Tornabuoni, *La voce della luna* (Florence: La Nuova Italia, 1990), p. 17.

4. Ibid.

5. From "Premessa dell'autore," Federico Fellini, *La voce della luna* (Turin: Ei-

naudi, 1990), p. vi. This is the published screenplay, which will be the source of any quotes of the film's dialogue. The English translations are mine, and page references to the Italian original are included in the text.

6. Ermanno Cavazzoni, *The Voice of the Moon*, trans. Ed Emery (London: Serpent's Tail, 1990), p. 7. Future references are included in the text, preceded by "C."

7. Frederic Jameson's, "Postmodernism or the Cultural Logic of Late Capitalism," *New Left Review*, no. 146 (July/August 1984), 53–92, was recently published as the first chapter of a book for which it provided the title. Future references to this essay will be to its book version (Durham, N.C.: Duke University Press, 1991), pp. 1–54.

8. Ibid., p. 3.

9. On the intricacy of Fellini's sound track, see Gianfranco Angelucci's "Nota," to the screenplay, pp. xi–xii.

10. This slight alteration of the spelling of Cavazzoni's protagonist's last name—Savini—is Fellini's first transformatory move.

11. Virginia Woolf, "The Movies and Reality," *New Republic* August 4, 1929, p. 309.

12. Quoted in Giovanna Grassi, "I segreti del poema di Fellini," *Corriere della sera*, July 23, 1988, p. 3.

13. The primacy of "plastic" over verbal expressivity in Fellini's filmmaking is a recurrent theme in Peter Bondanella's *Cinema of Federico Fellini* (Princeton, N.J.: Princeton University Press, 1992). See also Fellini's own statements that "the plasticity of the whole, the light, colors, can suddenly suggest to you that perhaps that sentence isn't necessary; it can be expressed with a gesture or with an object. Cinema for me has become more and more a pictorial expression, a suggestion by the light that recounts images." Tornabuoni, *La voce della luna*, p. 25.

14. In fact, the film is full of self-citations, as Gian Luigi Rondi points out in "La voce della luna di Federico Fellini," *Rivista del cinematografo* 60 (1990), 7.

15. *L'Unità*, February 9, 1990, p. 1. For other critical comments on Fellini's latest vision of Italian provincial life, see Bruno Roberti, "Lo strapaese impazzito," *Filmcritica* 41 (March 1990), 98; and Masoni, "La voce della luna," p. 83.

16. This is Masoni's observation in "La voce della luna," p. 83.

17. Jean Baudrillard, *Simulations*, trans. Paul Foss, Paul Patton, and Philip Beitchman (New York: Semiotext, 1983), p. 146. See, also Susan Sontag's incisive comments on our need "to have reality confirmed . . . by photographs," which is "an aesthetic consumerism to which everyone is addicted" (p. 24)—an addiction that is caused by, and in turn aggravates, the sense of a depleted reality (pp. 160–61) in *On Photography* (New York: Delta, 1973).

18. Tornabuoni, *La voce della luna*, p. 20.

19. On the invasiveness of advertising and the way it organizes our living

space, see Jean Baudrillard, "The Ecstasy of Communication," in *The Anti-aesthetic: Essays on Postmodern Culture*, ed. Hal Foster (Seattle: Bay, 1983), pp. 129–30.

20. Tornabuoni, *La voce della luna*, pp. 11–12. On the ubiquity of advertising in the film, see Marcello Garofalo, "La voce della luna," *Segnocinema* 10 (March 1990), 48.

21. Masoni, "La voce della luna," p. 83.

22. On the demand for technological mediation of experience, see Michelangelo Buffa, "Fellini l'ultimo," *Filmcritica* 41 (March 1990), 95.

23. See Thierry Joussè, "La fé e életricité," *Cahiers du cinéma*, no. 431/432 (May 1990), 21.

24. Jameson, *Postmodernism*, p. 12.

25. For Frank Burke's elegant scheme, see "Federico Fellini: From Representation to Signification," *Romance Languages Annual* 1 (1989), 34.

26. Baudrillard, *Simulations*, pp. 10–11.

27. It is Serge Toubiana who applies the figure of the closed circuit to Fellini's climactic scene in "Chut! Une Image," *Cahiers du cinéma*, no. 431/432 (May 1990), 17. Similarly, as Frank Burke says of television in *Ginger and Fred*, "It can only signify its will to ceaselessly signify." See "Federico Fellini," p. 39.

28. Edoardo Bruno, "Dialogo con i morti," *Filmcritica* 41 (March 1990), 92.

29. Bondanella notes the Leopardian echo in this question in his *Cinema of Federico Fellini*. His chapter on *La voce della luna* includes an extended meditation on the Leopardian elements throughout the film, pp. 329–30.

30. See Jean-Francois Lyotard, *The Postmodern Condition: A Report on Knowledge*, trans. Geoff Bennington and Brian Massumi (Minneapolis: University of Minnesota Press, 1984).

31. The quote is from Tornabuoni, *La voce della luna*, p. 17.

32. Bondanella points out the link between Gelsomina and Ivo in his *Cinema of Federico Fellini*, pp. 328, 333.

33. Quoted in Rondi, "La voce della luna," p. 7. See also "La voce della luna," *Immagine e pubblico* 8 (January/March 1990), 17. Benigni himself invokes Arlecchino and Brighella in discussing his and Villaggio's roles in the film. See "Entretien avec Roberto Benigni," *Cahiers du cinéma*, no. 431/432 (May 1990), 24.

34. Quoted in Tornabuoni, *La voce della luna*, p. 34.

35. Masoni, "La voce della luna," p. 83.

36. Thierry Jousse observes that the film's opening scenes evoke the beginning of the world in "La fé e életricité," p. 21.

37. On Ivo's impulse to flee the oppression of the contemporary world, see Gianfranco Angelucci, "La voce della luna e altre fellinità," *Cineteca* 6 (April/May 1990), 10. Luca Norcen points out Ivo's need to see *altro* in "La voce della luna," *Cinema nuovo* 37 (January/February 1990), 43.

38. On Ivo's threshold position, see Garofalo, "La voce della luna," p. 48.

39. The barbarity of commercial interruptions of television programming is the recurrent theme of Fellini's antitelevision diatribe. For the latest in his cam-

paign to have his films broadcast without commercial breaks, see Leonetta
Bentivoglio, "Federico Fellini: Vade retro spot," in *Il Venerdì della Repubblica*, July 26, 1991, p. 19.

40. Ivo's status as an artist surrogate is made explicit in Fellini's comments on
paranormal receptivity. "It is the privilege, an election that certain sensitive creatures have, the *chiamati* (called ones), and the type of psychology
to which the artist belongs." Quoted in Tornabuoni, *La voce della luna*,
p. 37.

41. On the abolition of critical distance in postmodernist space, see Jameson,
Postmodernism, p. 46.

42. Jousse, "La fé e électricité, p. 22.

Index